ENGAGING
the Written Word
of GOD

ENGAGING
the Written Word
of GOD

J. I. PACKER

HENDRICKSON PUBLISHERS

Paternoster:
thinking faith

Engaging the Written Word of God
Hendrickson Publishers Marketing, LLC
P.O. Box 3473
Peabody, Massachusetts 01961-3473

ISBN 978-1-59856-961-2

First published in 1999 by Paternoster Press
Paternoster Press is an imprint of Authentic Media, 52 Presley Way, Crownhill, Milton
Keynes, MK8 0ES, UK www.authenticmedia.com

Printed in the United States of America

First Printing — October 2012

Library of Congress Cataloging-in-Publication Data

Packer, J. I. (James Innell)
     Engaging the written Word of God / J. I. Packer.
          p. cm.
     Includes bibliographical references (p.   ).
     ISBN 978-1-59856-961-2 (alk. paper)
          1. Bible—Evidences, authority, etc. 2. Bible—Hermeneutics. 3. Bible—Criticism,
     interpretation, etc. I. Title.
     BS480.P235 2012
     220.6—dc23
                              2012026060

Contents

Foreword

When Martin Luther wrote the Preface to the first collected edition of his many and various writings, he went to town explaining in detail that theology, which should always be based on the Scriptures, should be done according to the pattern modelled in Psalm 119. There, Luther declared, we see that three forms of activity and experience make the theologian. The first is prayer for light and understanding. The second is reflective thought (*meditatio*), meaning sustained study of the substance, thrust, and flow of the biblical text. The third is standing firm under pressure of various kinds (external opposition, inward conflict, and whatever else Satan can muster): pressures, that is, to abandon, suppress, recant, or otherwise decide not to live by, the truth God has shown from his Word. Luther expounded his point as one who knew what he was talking about, and his affirmation that sustained prayer, thought, and fidelity to truth whatever the cost, become the path along which theological wisdom is found is surely one of the profoundest utterances that the Christian world has yet heard.

In introducing this mass of fugitive pieces I would only say that behind each of them lies a conscious attempt over more than forty years to hew to Luther's line, in hope that by adhering to his theological wisdom I might arrive at substantive wisdom in and through the grace of our Lord Jesus Christ. How far I have attained my goal is something that readers must judge for themselves. In retrospect, writing this material does not seem to have been time wasted, and it is my prayer that no one who explores it will feel that their time has been wasted either.

I thank Jim Lyster, Isobel Stevenson, Tony Graham and the rest of the staff at Paternoster for all their hard work in putting this collection together.

PART ONE

GOD'S INERRANT WORD

CHAPTER 1

Encountering Present-Day Views of Scripture

Three general observations will make clear the standpoint from which I write.

Theology and Religion

First, *when you encounter a present-day view of Holy Scripture, you encounter more than a view of Scripture*. What you meet is a total view of God and the world, that is, a total theology, which is both an ontology, declaring what there is, and an epistemology, stating how we know what there is. This is necessarily so, for a theology is a seamless robe, a circle within which everything links up with everything else through its common grounding in God. Every view of Scripture, in particular, proves on analysis to be bound up with an overall view of God and man. Nowadays, awareness of this fact seems to be fairly general, due to the intense and self-conscious preoccupation with questions of method that has marked theology, along with most other fields of study, during the past half-century. We all now know (don't we?) that your method and presuppositions—in other words, the things you take for granted—will always have a decisive influence on your conclusions. So there should certainly be no difficulty in getting agreement on the point that you do not encounter any view of Holy Scripture, or of any other doctrinal matter, at proper depth till you see it as part of a larger intellectual whole and understand how it relates to and 'works' within the unity of that larger unit. Indeed, to take the full measure of a view of Scripture, you must go wider than that and explore its implications for religion. For each set of theological convictions (of which the view taken of Scripture will form an integral part) belongs to a total view of religion, that is, of right behaviour and relationships toward God, as well as of right beliefs and reasonings in one's own mind. No theology can be properly evaluated except in the light of the religion which it prescribes, explains, and justifies.

Calvin saw this, hence he composed his theological textbook under the title *Institutio Religionis Christianae* (Instruction in Christian Religion), writing into it a treatment of the basic realities of Christian living and making it breathe a spirit of devotion and doxology throughout. Puritans and seventeenth-century continental Reformed theologians saw the point too and hence defined theology in ways that highlighted its practical and religious thrust; thus, Perkins called it 'the science of living blessedly for ever,'[1] and Turretin described it as '*theoretico-practica . . .* more practical than speculative.'[2] More recently, the Anglican Austin Farrer showed himself aware of the same point when he said somewhere that something must be wrong with Tillich's theology because it could not be prayed. (Nor can it; Tillich himself later in life made the sad admission that he had given up prayer for meditation.) The evaluative relevance of the practical implications of a position is surely too plain for anyone to deny.

But for all that, the link between theology and religion is something that Protestant theologians today, as for the past hundred years, repeatedly ignore. They talk and write as if they see theology as just an intellectual exercise of forming and analysing notions; they treat the practical bearing of these notions as someone else's concern rather than theirs; they isolate topics artificially for speculative treatment, thus losing sight of the very nature of theology; and they fail to draw out the wide-ranging implications of each notion for Christian obedience. The trouble no doubt is that these theologians have been too busy keeping up with the philosophical Joneses in the secularized university circles, where so much of their work is done and discussed, and have been too little concerned to sustain their churchly identity and role. On this, Eric Mascall speaks the word in season:

> What I hold as essential for the theologian is that his theologizing should be an aspect of his life as a member of the Body of Christ; he needs to be under not only an academic but also a spiritual ascesis, as indeed all the Church's greatest theologians have been . . . the theologian needs insight and he needs conversion, neither of which are simply the routine application of rules.[3]

Agreed! But meanwhile we have to cope with the effects of a century of failure at this point, and the effects are that, on the one hand, theology has been made to look like an intellectual game divorced from life and, on the other hand, theological notions are not usually evaluated by the test that is most decisive, namely whether they further or impede the practice of biblical religion. Thus, for example, Clark Pinnock, in his helpful chapter in *Biblical Authority*, 'Three Views of the Bible in Contemporary Theology,' observes the convention and lacks the element of practical and religious evaluation that his avowed concern for spiritual renewal might have been thought to require.[4] In this essay I try to write pastorally and practically, as a would-be church theologian, rather than in the manner of a secularized academic.

Evangelicalism and Scripture

Second, *when you encounter the Evangelical view of Holy Scripture, you are encountering the source, criterion, and control of all Evangelical theology and religion.*

Collingworth's open-textured dictum that the Bible alone is the religion of Protestants can mean several things, not all of them acceptable, but it fits Evangelicalism most precisely. Methodologically, Evangelical theology stands apart from other positions by its insistence on the clarity and sufficiency of the canonical Scriptures, and Evangelical religion is distinctive by reason of the theology and the method of application that determines it. Let me spell this out.

Roman Catholicism, Anglo-Catholicism, and Orthodoxy characteristically say that though the God-given Scriptures are a sufficient guide for faith and practice in themselves, they are at key points unclear and can rightly be understood only by the light of the church's God-taught tradition. By contrast, Protestantism's many blends of rationalism, mysticism, and existentialism (unstable compounds, all of them) characteristically say that while it is fairly clear what beliefs and behaviour patterns the Bible writers want their readers to adopt, the books vary so much from each other, and Scripture as a whole stands at such a distance from the modern world, that the Bible cannot be a sufficient guide for today till what it says is sieved, edited, and recast in the light of all that our age takes for granted. Let it be said that both positions invoke the Holy Spirit, the former as author of both Scripture and tradition, the latter as illuminating mind and conscience to enable each individual to formulate his personal understanding of Christianity. Let it also be said that both types of position are held with learning and integrity and admit of a great deal of internal debate and adjustment (a factor that tends to prolong the life of scholarly options), and there is no sign of their imminent decease. Not, of course, that their vitality implies that either is wholly right.

Against both, Evangelicalism characteristically says that Scripture is both clear and sufficient; that the God-given Scriptures are the self-interpreting, self-contained rule of Christian faith and life in every age; that, though the canonical books were composed over a period of more than a thousand years, during which significant cultural shifts become apparent in the records themselves, they do in fact present within the framework of progressive declaration and fulfilment of God's saving purpose in Christ a consistent view of how God deals with men; that, since God does not change nor, deep down, does man, this view remains true, timely, and final; and that the central covenanted ministry of the Holy Spirit is to lead us to the Scriptures that he inspired, to open the Scriptures to us, and so to induce both conceptual and relational knowledge of the Father and the Son to whom the Scriptures introduce us. It is further characteristic of Evangelicalism to insist that both the church and the individual Christian must live by the Bible (that is, by appropriate contemporary application of biblical principles); that the proper task of the teaching and preaching office that God has set in the church is to explain and apply the Scriptures; and that all beliefs, disbeliefs, hopes, fears, prayers, praises, and actions of churches and Christians must be controlled, checked, and where necessary reshaped—*reformed,* to use the good old word—in the light of what God is heard saying as the Spirit brings biblical principles to bear.

Evangelicals see this methodology as entailed in acknowledging the divine authority of the teaching of Christ's apostles, whose message we have firsthand in the New Testament letters, and of their Lord, to whose mind, as all sober criticism allows, the Gospels give ample access. For the teaching of Christ and the apostles includes, on the one hand, a use of Old Testament Scripture, taken in conjunction with their own message, which assumes that God's definitive instruction comes in both, and, on the other hand, a diagnosis of the fallen and unaided human mind as dark, perverse, insensitive, incapable, and untrustworthy in spiritual matters, needing to be enlightened and taught by God at every point. Though all men have an inescapable awareness of God that comes by way of his creation (Rom. 1:19–21, 28, 32), there can be no natural theology of traditional Thomist type: only through Scripture are these inklings of our Maker brought into true focus, by being integrated with the revelation of the living God that Scripture contains.[5] Scripture here means the Old Testament that Christ and his apostles attest, plus the New Testament, which their own inspiration produced, and for true knowledge of the true God we are shut up to Scripture absolutely. So, at any rate, Evangelicals see the matter.

Scripture shows us Jesus Christ, and it is happily true that Christians of many schools of thought—Roman Catholic, Orthodox, neo-orthodox and 'liberal evangelical' Protestants, and charismatics of all sorts—speak from time to time of the ministry of the Christ who is Saviour, Lord, and God and of communion with him through the Spirit, just as Evangelicals do. Sometimes it is urged that those who speak so should be seen as all Evangelicals together, sharing a common faith in Christ and proclaiming a common message about him. For the measure of truth in this estimate we should thank God. Yet the deeper and, for our present purposes, the more relevant truth is that the rigorous biblical methodology described above sets the Evangelical position apart as something distinctive and unique. My own standpoint in this present essay is that of a would-be consistent Evangelical at this deeper level.

The Inerrancy Debate

Third, *when you encounter the current Evangelical debate on Holy Scripture, you are encountering an awkwardly confused situation.* What is it all about? Professedly, it is about inerrancy. Men like Harold Lindsell and Francis Schaeffer urge the importance of a clear confession that the Bible is totally trustworthy, not erring in any of its declarations. I believe they are right and have done well to raise their voices. But why is this confession important?

Here the awkwardness of cross-purposes and divided values begins to appear. Some predict that once inerrancy as an avowed principle is given up, it is only a matter of time before all the outlines of Christian supernaturalism will be eroded away, as happened in the liberal Presbyterianism of the past half-century, and that institutions and churches that do not insist explicitly on the factual truth of Scripture at all points will soon be unable to maintain a full testimony to the gospel of Christ. Behind this 'domino' thinking lies a sense that once any biblical declaration is disbelieved, the Evangelical methodology is abandoned, the floodgates of scepticism are opened, and biblical authority as a principle runs aground on the sandbank of subjectivism, where it can be expected to break up completely. Others, however, object that what the domino thinkers mean by inerrancy is a body of (1) interpretations of texts, (2) harmonizations of phenomena, (3) argumentations against older types of scepticism, and (4) formulations of the doctrine of Scripture against which the Bible itself sets a question mark; and that the real issue is whether as a matter of Evangelical method, we are free to submit to biblical, historical, and theological analysis the 'inerrancy tradition' of the past one hundred years to see if it is really scriptural enough. Whether there is substantial disagreement about the nature and place of Scripture as such—that is, about God and the Bible—as well as about interpretative techniques and preferred ways of speaking in apologetics and dogmatics—that is, about man and the Bible—is so far unclear. Nor is it yet apparent whether the weight of the debate is on how to approach and handle Scripture or on how to define inerrancy, and how far it is politic to use this term in Christian communication—whether, that is, the argument is essentially about things or about words.

The dim light of the discussion, allied to the heat that it generates, makes clarity hard to achieve, and debate is never easy when the state of the question is unclear. Also, because of the way in which academic faculties have lined up, it is hard to take any position in the debate without seeming to call into question someone else's competence or good name as an Evangelical, and this is most unfortunate. In the present essay, I try to spell out my own position without attempting to adjudicate on that of others.

1. Encountering Liberal Views

What Pinnock calls 'the curious coalition known as conservative Evangelicalism' (why curious? one wishes that he had told us) is, in fact, a transdenominational Protestant family, united by a common faith in Jesus Christ as our sin-bearing Saviour and divine Lord and a common purpose of allowing God in Christ to rule our minds and lives through the Bible. With this purpose goes a common understanding of the Bible's basic contents, which the striking unanimity of Evangelical systematic theology over four centuries reflects.[6] Also, underlying this body of shared convictions is, as we saw, a common recognition that God himself has taught us the principle of biblical authority through the words of our Lord and of the New Testament writers. Squabbles within the family as to how in detail the principle should be applied presuppose agreement on the need to apply it: the arguments have to do only with establishing a proper technique for the task. Thus we find that the worldwide Evangelical constituency today displays an impressive solidarity of conviction and purpose, and with that an impressive and increasing international cohesiveness, of which such a document as the tight-packed Lausanne Covenant, three thousand words long, produced in a congress lasting just over a week and assented to by some four thousand Christians representing 151 countries, is striking proof.[7]

The case with liberal Protestantism, however, is quite different.

What is liberal Protestantism? It really is 'a curious coalition,' for the resemblances that make up the liberal family likeness are more negative than positive. The positive principle that gives liberalism its basic identity is Schleiermacher's view of religion as a sense of God that is caught rather than taught and can be put into words in more than one way. Then a further major element in that identity has been the polemic, more or less explicit, that liberalism has maintained against Evangelical belief in revealed truth. Polemics, however, like adversity, can make strange bedfellows; shared peeves do not guarantee common purposes, and liberals are often at each others' throats, much oftener, it would seem, than Evangelicals. The word *liberal* is usually explained by those who espouse it as voicing their claim to a spirit of liberality, that is, of tolerance, flexibility, openness to new ideas, and freedom from doctrinaire dogmatism; though whether self-styled liberalism always shows this spirit is a question that, if explored, might leave some faces red. But what convictions do liberals as a body share? Three motifs constantly appear, all with a decidedly negative slant.

First, liberal Protestantism affirms, in Pinnock's words, that 'divine truth is not located in an ancient book but in the ongoing work of the Spirit in the community, as discerned by critical rational judgement.'[8] Note, however, that 'divine truth' means to liberals, not God's instruction nor a permanently valid human formulation, but simply an authentic awareness of God, to which no particular form of words is necessary either as a means or as an expression. As J. Gresham Machen pointed out half a century ago in *Christianity and Liberalism*, the liberal position in all its forms is deeply anti-intellectual in both its stance and its thrust, and this explains why it is so consistently hostile to the attempts of both Roman Catholics and Evangelicals to formulate a definitive theology on the basis of a supposedly definitive Bible.

Second, liberal Protestantism espouses a type of Christology that is not 'from above' in the sense of seeing Jesus Christ as the divine Son, the second person of the Godhead, and the eternal Word made flesh, according to John's gospel, Philippians 2, Colossians 1, and Hebrews 1–2, which the Nicene and Chalcedonian formulae follow. Instead, liberal Protestant Christologies are 'from below,' seeing Jesus in 'humanitarian' terms as a prophetic, God-filled man, an archetype of religious insight and excellence, one who, however much he carries for us what Ritschl called the 'value' of God, is not God in person. Such Christologies involve, of course, abandoning all thought of a real ontological Trinity and a real divine sinbearer. They require a reconstructed view of salvation in which Christ's mediation appears as a matter of teaching and trail-blazing only, with no hint of his having borne the Creator's wrath against our sins in order to render him propitious to us—for it would take a divine person to do that. Liberals characteristically cut the knot here by denying that there is any personal wrath of God against us that needs to be quenched, and maintain a barrage of criticism against 'word-made-flesh' Christology as being necessarily docetic, minimizing the true humanness of our Lord.

It seems right to class all existentialist Protestant positions that build on a 'humanitarian' Christology, even those that, like Bultmann's, came out of neo-orthodoxy, and that affirm a real 'Christ of faith' transcending the 'historical Jesus,' as jazzed-up liberal Protestantism rather than anything else.

Third, liberalism highlights human religious greatness, as seen in the Bible, in Jesus, and in all Christian, pagan, and secular pioneers who have in any way contributed to man's 'humanization' by stressing life's spiritual and moral values. Rightly does Pinnock say that liberals have sought to replace the idea of the Bible's infallibility as teaching from God with what they see as 'proper respect for its human greatness' as 'a classical witness of those in whose lives God once worked which can once again serve to alert us to his reality.'[9] But there is need to go further and underline the deep difference between the mystical and moral naturalism of the liberal idea of religious greatness, of God in men's lives, and the redemptive supernaturalism of those who censure these ideas biblically, in terms of fellowship with God through a divine Saviour. A very great gulf is fixed between those who see Jesus' greatness and significance for us in his human God-consciousness (so Schleiermacher), or in his ethics (so Ritschl, Harnack, and Albert Schweitzer), or in his self-understanding as a man in God's hands and his example of loyal and hopeful commitment (so Ernst Fuchs, James Robinson, and the authors of the British symposium *The Myth of God Incarnate*)[10] and those who, with the writer to the Hebrews, see his greatness in terms of his being our divine-human high priest who put away sins and now saves to the uttermost (cf. Heb. 7:4; 9:25–26; 10:21). The width of that gulf must be stressed; it can hardly be exaggerated.

The point needing emphasis is that liberal Protestant views of Scripture, as indeed of all else relating to our redemption, differ from the generic conservative Evangelical view, not just in detail, but in their whole frame of reference. It is naive and misleading to present the theological relationship between the two types of view (as distinct from the partnership they rightly maintain in the pretheological exercise of historical exegesis) in terms of partial agreement and partial disagreement. The deeper insight was and remains that of Machen, who half a century ago saw here two rival religions that at fundamental level relate to each other only by mutual contradiction and in polemical grapple. Even the word *God* has radically different meanings in the two systems. Granted, some moderns call themselves liberals without espousing fully characteristic liberal views; granted, liberals use a biblical and Evangelical vocabulary (though in a changed and diminished sense); granted, some of today's liberals were yesterday's conservative Evangelicals, who see their current views as a natural outgrowth of what they held before. Yet the basic antithesis between the two types of position remains. The Bible that is thought of as man's testament of religious feeling, self-understanding, and ethical inklings is not really the same book as the Bible that is received as God's testimony to himself, even if the sixty-six books with their almost two million words coincide in both cases. The two types of theological interpretation of Scripture do not mesh at all. It would have been helpful if Pinnock had underlined this more clearly.

2. Encountering Neo-orthodox Views

The word *neo-orthodox* has always been somewhat loosely used. For half a century it has stood as a label for that body of theological work that, following the lead of Karl Barth, has sought a way back from liberalism to the revelation-shaped, salvation-centred orthodoxy of the Reformation without returning to belief in the inerrant inspiration of the Bible on which that orthodoxy rested. The fact that, though far from unanimous on matters of substance, neo-orthodox theologians shared this common purpose justifies Pinnock's reference to neo-orthodoxy as 'a trend in contemporary theology.'[11] 'Contemporary,' however, coming from an author writing in 1977 is not quite right. It is true that for something like a generation after 1930 the neo-orthodox programme was a matter of prominent, perhaps dominant, concern among Protestant theologians; but by about 1965 interest had clearly moved to the problems of ontology, epistemology, and hermeneutics pinpointed by Bultmann's call to demythologize in order to communicate, and there it remains. Also, while it is true that positions characteristic of neo-orthodoxy are still held, the neo-orthodox pilgrim trail is empty today, simply because the old liberalism that was its starting point is now a thing of the past. It is from other places in the wilderness that theologians travelling toward the gospel start today.

In the following paragraphs, Karl Barth is the main object of attention. That is because he was not only the first but also in many ways the greatest of neo-orthodox teachers; also because, being a 'dazzlingly brilliant'[12] writer who gave the world, along with some five hundred other items, the *Church Dogmatics,* an unfinished *summa theologiae* of over seven thousand pages, he is likely to have more long-term influence than other theologians of this type; also because neo-orthodoxy appears at its strongest intellectually and its noblest spiritually in the writings of Barth, and his weaknesses, however great, are comparatively less than the corresponding defects of others on the same trail. It should, however, be realized that Barth stands at the extreme right of the neo-orthodox spectrum; that others who shared his overall purpose (Emil Brunner and Reinhold Niebuhr, for instance) did not backtrack so far from the man-centred liberalism in which they were reared as Barth did; that some who were with him at the start in hoisting the banner of God's transcendence with the ropes of Kierkegaard's existentialism, and were thought of as neo-orthodox in consequence, never got through to anything like Reformation faith in Christ (Rudolf Bultmann and Friedrich Gogarten, for instance), so that their views, if thought of as in any sense standard, make Barth's look utterly perverse (and vice versa, of course); and finally that in Barth's account of Jesus Christ the Word, the God-man, Creator and Redeemer, presupposition and determinant of all that is not God and representative of all mankind both as reprobate and as elect, there really are major eccentricities of his own, by which his otherwise impressive teaching is deeply flawed.[13]

It is to Barth's credit that he laid constant stress on God's sovereign freedom and lordship in grace, on man's incapacity in his sin to feel after God and find him, on the reality of God's communion with us through the Word that he speaks to us in Christ, and on the instrumentality of the Scriptures in conveying to us the knowledge of Christ and of grace that they exhibit. It is to Barth's credit too that the 'Procrustean bed' of his theological method, whereby he collapses all doctrines concerning God and his creation into Christology, whatever its short-comings in other ways, presupposes and builds on a substantially Nicene Trini-tarianism, a Chalcedonian Christology, an acknowledgement of Jesus' death and resurrection as the work of God saving mankind, and a robust confidence that the biblical witness to Jesus Christ, which is God's own witness given through man's, can be truly and precisely expressed in the propositions and theses of rational, disciplined theological discourse. The irrationalism, scepticism, arbitrariness, and ultimate incoherence involved in Emil Brunner's so-called dialectical method, which keeps our minds perpetually in unstable equilibrium as they fly between poles of assertion and denial of the same truth, and of belief and disbelief of biblical teachings,[14] were abandoned by Barth at an early stage and became more and more conspicuous by their absence from successive volumes of the *Church Dogmatics*.

Since Barth never repudiated liberal scepticism about the space-time fac-tuality of some biblically recorded events, choosing rather to ignore and bypass it, and since he never developed a rational apologetic making ontological and epistemological links between what Scripture tells us and the rest of our knowl-edge, but derided such ventures as vicious, his teaching is beclouded with mists of ambiguity. Though it seems clear that he meant to define and describe a Christ whose virgin birth, crucifixion, and resurrection were, and whose future return will be, facts of public space-time history, it is an open question whether his ex-clusively kerygmatic method, allied to his use of phenomenological categories for expressing the contents of revelation, enables him to anchor his Christ in the world of objective reality as well as in that of the theologian's fertile mind.[15] But even if we think that the answer to this question is no, there is much to admire in and learn from Barth's treatment of particular themes.

What does Barth say about the Bible?[16] His basic idea is that the Bible is the means whereby the event of revelation takes place, for in and through its human witness to God, God constantly discloses himself to us. The confession of biblical inspiration (*theopneustia*) concerns in the first instance not its divine origin in the past but its divine instrumentality in the present. This view may reflect a doubtful exegesis of *theopneustos* in 2 Timothy 3:16 and involve something of a false antithesis, but its positive thrust is welcome, and merits our approval. And though, as Pinnock notes, Barth makes quite a meal of rejecting any formal ascription of inerrancy to the Bible and of affirming its 'capacity for errors,' he declines to identify particular mistakes in it, although he declares in general terms that there are some, both factual and religious.[17] However, 'while preaching the errancy of the Bible, Barth practices its inerrancy':[18] his interpretations, while sometimes novel and unconvincing, are always presented as elucidations of the witness the text actually bears, without any suggestion that anything it says should be discounted as false. Evangelicals will applaud Barth's exegesis as correct in method, if not always in substance; but we must realize that by stating that the prophets and apostles erred in their writings even if we cannot say where, Barth himself has made his exegetical method seem hazardous, arbitrary, and untrustworthy. There is ruinous irrationality here. As Colin Brown says (twice!), 'It is impossible to maintain high doctrines of revelation and inspiration without at the same time being willing to defend in detail the veracity and historicity of the biblical writings.'[19] But here Barth fails us, and the effect of his failure is to make it seem unreasonable for anyone, himself included, to trust the texts as he does. Sadly, it must be recorded that other neo-orthodox thinkers see this very clearly, and therefore do not so trust them.

The truth is that the neo-orthodox enterprise of trying to re-establish the authority of biblical teaching on salvation while rejecting biblical teaching on Scripture is inherently inconsistent and self-contradictory; thus, all versions of neo-orthodoxy, like all versions of liberalism before them, exhibit a built-in arbitrariness that it is not possible to eliminate. There is no road to rational faith this way. Barth's exegesis shows him ready in practice to treat the testimony of all texts as divine truth, but his general statement that the human authors made errors in Scripture, even in its religious and theological content, can be squared with his practice only if we suppose that in his view *either* some biblical statements are true in their character as God's Word but erroneous in their character as man's word (which is surely incoherent nonsense, though some who have looked to Barth for inspiration have talked this way), *or*—and this is the way Barth himself seems to lean—the divine message of the passage does not always coincide with the human writer's meaning, since God is free in the event of revelation to use the human words any way he pleases. But that opens the door to allegorizing and turns God's gift of insight into Scripture into the bestowal of uncheckable private revelations. There seems no way out of this dilemma.

Something similar must be said from a methodological standpoint about 'biblical theology' as practiced by such teachers as Sir Edwyn Hoskyns, Oscar Cullmann, Gabriel Hebert, Michael Ramsey, and John Bright during the past half-century. Like neo-orthodoxy, with which indeed it has conscious links, this movement has sought to reapprehend the faith of the biblical writers, reading the Bible 'from within,' and, like neo-orthodoxy, it has highlighted the character of Scripture as witness to God in history and its instrumentality in communicating God and his Word to human hearts today. The method of identifying with biblical faith is impeccable, but it is inconsistently applied, for biblical faith includes the conviction that Scripture as such, being God's Word (both what he *said* and what he *says*), is wholly true and trustworthy, and 'biblical theology' has regularly allowed itself to 'criticise the Bible by the Bible,' as the procedure has been described; that is, to set up a privately selected 'canon within the canon' as a standard for determining what biblical teaching is valid and what is not. It has to be said, however, that nothing in biblical faith itself justifies one's doing this; on the contrary, one who does it parts company, methodologically at least, with biblical faith, and throws doubt on the seriousness of his announced intention always to 'be biblical.'

Nor is it only exponents of neo-orthodoxy and 'biblical theology' who lapse in this way. Pinnock detects the same faulty method in Dewey Beegle, who identified himself as an 'Evangelical critic of inerrancy,' and in Paul King Jewett, who sets out to correct Paul's supposedly sub-Christian utterances on the relation of the sexes in Christ by his Christian ones. As Pinnock says, the natural implication of this method is that 'in Scripture God does not always speak, requiring the reader to determine where he speaks and where he does not. In principle this seems to be liberal ... theological methodology.'[20] As an Englishman who can look back over some ninety years of self-styled 'liberal evangelical' British theology, based on just this approach, I can only sigh agreement. The method is arbitrary and false, involving both denial and disruption of the unity of biblical teaching that those who seek find. The method of integrating Scripture with Scripture in interpretation—the method Calvin called the 'analogy of Scripture,' and that the confession of biblical inerrancy safeguards—is the only method with biblical warrant, and the only one that can keep us from the impoverishment to which an unsanctified selectiveness will otherwise lead.

3. *Encountering Roman Catholic Views*

One might have expected that on the topic of biblical inerrancy, if on no others, Evangelicals would be able to look to Roman Catholics as their natural allies, for during the past century official Roman Catholic assertions of inerrancy have been frequent and explicit. In 1957, in his book *The Authority of Scripture*, J. K. S. Reid began his chapter on 'The Roman view' with this statement: 'The Roman Church steadfastly adheres to the doctrine of the infallibility and inerrancy of Holy Scriptures,' followed by a weighty if tortuous quotation from Leo XII's encyclical *Providentissimus Deus* (1893), as follows:

> All the books which the Church receives as sacred and canonical are written wholly and entirely, with all their parts, at the dictation of the Holy Ghost; and so far is it from being possible that any error can co-exist with inspiration, that inspiration not only is essentially incompatible with error, but excludes and rejects it as absolutely and necessarily as it is impossible that God himself, the Supreme Truth, can utter that which is not true.[21]

Rome has always officially held that Scripture has the nature of, among other things, revealed truth and that inspiration entails inerrancy; the historical cleavage between Rome and the Protestant churches over the Bible concerns its interpretation and authority, not its inspiration.

The strength of Rome's past commitment to inerrancy can be gauged from the fact that when the Modernist Abbé Loisy, in the manner of Protestants like Harnack then and Bultmann since, rejected biblical inerrancy in the course of his fundamental questioning of Jesus' divinity and bodily resurrection and the authenticity of Paul's Christianity, the encyclical of 1907, *Pascendi Gregis*, that preceded his excommunication quoted against him the words of Augustine: 'In an authority so high [i.e., Scripture], admit but one officious lie, and there will not remain a single passage of those apparently difficult to practice or to believe, which on the same most pernicious rule may not be explained as a lie uttered by the author wilfully to serve a purpose.'[22] The domino thinking of Lindsell and Schaeffer about inerrancy has thus some striking precedents! Rather than risk further challenges to inerrancy, Roman Catholic authorities largely clamped down on critical biblical scholarship from the time of the Loisy affair to Pius XII's 1943 encyclical, *Divino Afflante Spiritu*, and it is only since then that it has really flowered.

But Roman Catholic biblical criticism has tended to develop as a getting in on the sceptical act that has now been a liberal Protestant speciality for a century and a quarter, and Reid anticipated in 1957 that the Roman Catholic Church would have to 'choose between a recession of sympathy toward criticism and a diminution of the principle of biblical inerrancy.'[23] At the second Vatican Council (1962–65) the choice was clearly if unobtrusively made. The Council affirmed: 'Since everything asserted by the inspired authors or sacred writers must be held to be asserted by the Holy Spirit, it follows that the books of Scripture must be acknowledged as teaching firmly, faithfully and without error that truth which God wanted put in the sacred writings for the sake of our salvation.'[24] This looks at first sight like a reassertion of the older position without change, but it seems to have been drafted with a view to its functioning as a hole in the dike of biblical inerrancy, and that is certainly how Roman Catholic theologians since Vatican II have used it. Bishop B. C. Butler, for instance, in his authoritative book *The Theology of Vatican II*, argues that this statement guarantees as inerrant only truths necessary to salvation, though Scripture contains a great deal more material than this, and his position is typical.[25] Hans Küng has gone so far as to deny that God's saving 'truth' has the nature of divine assertions, that is, revealed truths.[26] Though individual conservatives still maintain the older view, it does not look as if the Church of Rome will ever officially go back to it. The dike has been breached.

The significance of this change should not, however, be exaggerated. After all, the Roman Catholic faithful are required to take their beliefs from the infallible church, as embodying the true interpretation of Scripture, rather than directly from a Bible that they have ventured to interpret for themselves. There is a sense in which Rome, relying on the infallibility of the church, does not need biblical inerrancy to undergird anything. But for Evangelical Protestants the issue is more serious—and this brings us to our last section.

4. The Cruciality of Inerrancy

In the light of what we have seen so far, three matters seem to call for comment as I close.

First, *what does the confession of biblical inerrancy mean?* Pinnock is one for whom *inerrancy* is 'a strong, excellent term when properly understood.'[27] For him it 'declares the conviction that the Bible is our divine teacher by means of which God himself meets, instructs, saves and corrects us.'[28] But because, as commonly used, the word (1) centres attention on the lost autographs of Scripture rather than its present life-giving power in whatever form it meets us; (2) emphasizes 'questions of factual detail—historical, grammatical, cosmological and the like'— rather than the focal point of Scripture, which is Christ and the truth concerning him; and (3) is not usually qualified clearly enough from a hermeneutical standpoint to make plain that it refers only to what each writer meant his readers to gather and learn from what he wrote,[29] Pinnock will not insist on anyone using it, provided one does not 'settle for an alternative which is really weak and permissive, allowing one to side-step the teachings of Scripture.' Pinnock raises a series of questions: Is this notion of inerrancy scriptural? logically entailed by inspiration? capable of clear definition? necessary as a basis for learning from the Bible? a central concept involved in grasping what is central in Scripture? an assertion honestly justifiable in the light of the phenomena of Scripture? a proper criterion of authentic Evangelicalism? Believing, it seems, that one who understood the word in what has become the usual way (see above) could responsibly decline to say yes to any of these questions and yet retain a credible Evangelical identity, Pinnock invites us to conclude that the inerrancy debate is sterile and profitless and that what we should all be doing is working harder together on the factual and theological interpretation of the biblical text and on the task of theological construction in the light of the Scriptures.[30]

If Pinnock's account of what 'inerrancy' has come to mean is taken as the whole truth, his argument might seem to be the last word on its subject; and certainly, I have no quarrel with its positive thrust. But I think there is more to be said. Pinnock has not fully focused the logical function that the word *inerrant*, when applied to the Scriptures, fulfils for Evangelicals in defining, circumscribing, and safeguarding correct theological method. Starting where Pinnock starts, namely with a recognition that words mean what they are used to mean, neither more nor less, I venture to affirm that when Evangelicals call the Bible 'inerrant,' part at least of their meaning is this: that in exegesis and exposition of Scripture and in building up our biblical theology from the fruits of our Bible study, we may not (1) deny, disregard, or arbitrarily relativize, anything that the biblical writers teach, nor (2) discount any of the practical implications for worship and service that their teaching carries, nor (3) cut the knot of any problem of Bible harmony, factual or theological, by allowing ourselves to assume that the inspired authors were not necessarily consistent either with themselves or with each other. It is because the word *inerrant* makes these methodological points about handling the Bible, ruling out in advance the use of mental procedures that can only lead to reduced and distorted versions of Christianity, that it is so valuable and, I think, so much valued by those who embrace it.

The second matter requiring comment is: *What does the confession of biblical inerrancy accomplish?*

What has just been said shows the answer. Where this confession is not made, Scripture will not all be taken with all seriousness, elements of its teaching will inevitably be ignored, and the result, as Lindsell and Schaeffer with others correctly foresee, is bound to be a certain diminution of supernatural Christian faith—as we have seen in the various versions of liberalism, neo-orthodoxy, and 'biblical theology,' and as we must now expect to see in new forms in tomorrow's Roman Catholicism. But the confession of inerrancy, though it cannot guarantee sound exegesis or agreement among scholars on just what this or that text means, does make a full and faithful articulation of biblical Christianity possible in principle, whereas apart from this confession it is not possible even in principle.

A warning should perhaps be voiced here against the psychological trap (for it is psychological, a matter of falsely associated feelings, rather than logical, a formal mistake in inference) of supposing that the confession of inerrancy involves a commitment to treat all narrative and predictive passages in Scripture as if they were written according to the conventions that would apply to ordinary English prose used today for these purposes, rather than the conventions of their own age and literary genre. Put thus, the mistake sounds too silly for anyone to make, but in fact it is made frequently: hence Pinnock's complaint that not enough care is

taken to attach the necessary hermeneutical qualifications to inerrancy as
And one can see how the mistake happens: people feel, sincerely if confusedly,
that the only natural, straightforward way to express their certainty that the contents of Scripture are contemporary in their application is to treat Scripture as
contemporary in its literary form. So, for example, Genesis 1 is read as if it were
answering the same questions as today's scientific textbooks aim to answer, and
Genesis 2 and 3 are read as if they were at every point prosaic eyewitness narratives of what we would have seen if we had been there, ignoring the reasons for
thinking that in these chapters 'real events may be recorded in a highly symbolic
manner,'[31] and books like Daniel, Zechariah, and Revelation are expounded in
total disregard of the imaginative conventions of apocalyptic. But it does not
follow that because Scripture records matters of fact, therefore it does so in what
we should call matter-of-fact language.

We have to realize that the confession of inerrancy, like that of the inspiration that entails it, implies nothing at all about the literary character of particular
passages. The style and sense of each passage must be determined inductively in
each case, by getting to know its language, history, and cultural background and
by attending to its own internal characteristics. Some Bible narratives are written
in plain, unvarnished, eyewitness prose, and some are not. Which are which? We
will find out only as we go and look.

But my point is that though the confession of inerrancy does not help us
to make the literary judgements that interpretation involves, it commits us in
advance to harmonize and integrate all that we find Scripture teaching, without remainder, and so makes possible a theological grasp of Christianity that
is altogether believing and altogether obedient. Without this commitment, no
such grasp of Christianity is possible. So, despite its negative form, this disputed
word fulfils in Evangelical theology a most positive, enriching, and indeed vital
function, comparable with that fulfilled by the Chalcedonian negatives concerning the union of our Lord's two natures in his one person ('without confusion,
without change, without division, without separation'). In both cases the negative
words operate as a methodological barrier-fence that keeps us from straying out
of bounds at the behest of unruly rationalistic instincts and digging for the gold
of understanding where no gold is to be found.

The third matter requiring comment is: *Why is the confession of inerrancy
important?*

Again, the answer is clear from what has already been said. It is important
that we should embrace a fully believing method of biblical interpretation and
theological construction and it is equally important that the fellowship of Evangelical theologians—of all theologians, as far as possible—should be based on a
common commitment to such a method. The point is surely plain enough by now,
and need not be argued further. And let it be added that this point is a substantial
rather than a verbal one. Words are not magic; each man has a right to use them

in the way that best expresses what he has in mind. So if with, for instance, G. C. Berkouwer[32] and, as it seems, teachers at Fuller Seminary[33] we think the word *inerrant* tainted through its past associations with literary insensitiveness and an improper rationalism in interpreting Scripture, and so prefer not to use it but to say 'infallible' instead, that is our privilege. But what, in that case, our colleagues in Evangelical theology have a right to expect from us is a clear demonstration in both word and action that we are nonetheless committed to what, in the light of the foregoing paragraphs, may be called the 'inerrancy method.' Given this, we shall be able to walk together, whatever words we elect to use—not, however, otherwise.

CHAPTER 2

The Adequacy of Human Language

Can human language, specifically the language of the Bible, be divine language also—God's own verbal utterance, whereby he gives us factual information about himself? Can words of men really be words of God, conveying to us the Word—that is, the message—of God? Historically, the Christian answer has been yes. The common inclination among today's professed believers to say no appears, to say the least, to be an eccentricity. When we ask the reason for this shift, which seems something of an aberration, we find a clear case of failure to think straight. It is worth showing this failure in some detail as we begin.

God's Word Spoken, Written, and Understood

Four preliminary and foundational points should be clearly stated.

1. If, as the New Testament writers and the Nicene Creed say, the Holy Spirit 'spoke . . . through the prophets,'[1] and if the Galilean rabbi Jesus, the teacher who, though more than a prophet, was not less than a prophet (cf. Luke 13:33), was God incarnate, so that his teaching (given him by his father,[2] but at the same time set forth in his own authority)[3] was in the most direct and obvious sense teaching, speech, witness, and instruction from God, then the question whether God uses human language to tell man things is, in principle, settled. He does. The phenomena of prophecy and incarnation prove this decisively.

2. The concept of biblical inspiration is essentially identical with that of prophetic inspiration. No new difficulty arises in acknowledging the former if one acknowledges the latter, for no new element is involved. God's statement to Jeremiah, 'I have put my words in your mouth' (1:9), gives the theological paradigm of what is involved: God causes his message to enter into a man's mind, by psychological processes that are in part opaque to us, so that the man may then faithfully relay the message to others. It is evident that inspiration could, and did, take different psychological forms from one writer to another, and for the same writer at different times. The *dualistic* inspiration of prophets and seers produced in them a sustained awareness of the distinction between their own thoughts and the visions and specific messages that God gave them.

This is psychologically different from the state of mind resulting from the *di-dactic* inspiration of the biblical historians, wisdom teachers, and New Testament apostles. For them the effect of inspiration was that after observation, research, reflection, and prayer they knew just what they should say in God's name, as witnesses and interpreters of his work. Also, it is psychologically different from the *lyric* inspiration of the poets, who wrote the Psalms and the Song of Songs in responsive celebration of what they had come to know of God's goodness in creation, providence, and redemption.

Subjectively, as all versifiers and hymn writers know, the experience of a poem 'coming on' (cf. Pss. 39:3; 45:1), of its gradually taking form in conscious-ness, differs both from the way in which an oracle is received and from the way di-dactic certainty is given. But—and this is the point to note—in the Bible writers' view, which almost all the church shared from apostolic days until quite recently, the theological reality of inspiration is the same in each case. God so controlled the process of communication to and through his servants that, in the last analysis, he is the source and speaker not merely of biblical prophecy but also of biblical history, wisdom, and doctrine, and also of the poems, whose giant-size delinea-tions of adoration and devotion set worshippers of every age a standard for what their own praise and prayer should be.

It makes no difference to inspiration (how could it?) whether its product is oral or written. When in the past Evangelical theologians defined God's work of inspiration as the producing of God-breathed Scriptures, they were not denying that God inspired words uttered orally as well. Indeed, in the case of prophets and apostles, the biblical way to put the point is to urge that the words which these men wrote or dictated are no less God-given than the words in which they shared orally with individuals and congregations, for the spoken word came first.

Jeremiah's oracles, when written, were still 'the words of the LORD' (Jer. 36:6, 8, 11) as well as being 'the words of Jeremiah' (v. 10). Paul, having claimed to speak (λαλέω) what the Spirit had revealed 'in words taught by the Spirit' (1 Cor. 2:13), tells his readers that they should 'acknowledge that what I am writing to you' (the immediate reference is to his set of directions about worship and the silence of women) is a command of the Lord (1 Cor. 14:37). He does not mean that he is quoting what Jesus said on earth (as in 7:10ff.), but that he, as an apostle, is actually speaking (here as elsewhere) in Jesus' name and under the power of inspiration.

Whether spoken viva voce or written, and whether dualistic or didactic or lyric in its psychological mode, inspiration—that divine combination of prompt-ing and control that secures precise communication of God's mind by God's mes-senger—remains theologically the same thing. Of Scripture in particular we must say that, while it is the product of powerful religious experiences and has most inspiring effects, to call it *inspired* is directly to affirm neither of these things. In 2 Timothy 3:16, 'inspired' represents the Greek adjective *theopneustos*, a word that means not, as the lexicons of Cremer and Bauer have said (and Barth after them),[4] 'breathing out God' but, as Warfield proved long ago,[5] 'breathed out by God.' All Scripture, therefore, is a product of his creative power, and so is an authentic disclosure of his mind and presentation of his message.

3. It is clear (1) that our Lord and the apostles saw both their Bible (our Old Testament) and their own teaching as divinely authoritative for faith and life; (2) that they saw their own teaching as complementary and subordinate to that of their Bible, and indeed as expository of it; and (3) that they believed that both their Bible and their own teaching gave factual information about God. Thus they bequeathed to the church, in effect, the idea of the two Testaments, Old and New together, as constituting a *canon,* that is, a rule of belief and behaviour, for all of God's people at all times. The idea of Scripture as a canon in this sense is made explicit by the dominical and apostolic attitude to the Old Testament. Indeed, Paul's statement in 2 Timothy 3:16, 'All Scripture is God-breathed and is [therefore] useful for teaching, rebuking, correcting, and training in righteousness,' is an analysis of the meaning of canonicity in precise terms.[6]

The witness of our Lord to the canonical status of his Bible is especially striking. In the Gospels we find him affirming the divine authority of teaching given in both the indicative and the imperative moods in many Old Testament passages. For example, in Matthew 19:4–5 he quotes Genesis 2:24 as the word of the Creator (because, presumably, it is a scriptural statement, for in context it is not a direct utterance of God) and deduces from it the impropriety of divorce.

Moreover, we find Jesus declaring, categorically and comprehensively, that his ministry would be entirely misunderstood were it thought that he came to cancel or set aside the Law and the Prophets (i.e., the Old Testament). On the contrary, he had come to fulfil both. And clearly, for him to let the Law and the Prophets shape his life and teaching (this is what 'fulfil' implies) was an acknowledgement of their authority over him. How complete that acknowledgement was appears from the temptation story, where Jesus three times embraces the God-prescribed counter to Satan's suggestions, and from the passion story, where we see him going up to Jerusalem to die, because this scriptural prediction of the Messiah's destiny had to be fulfilled.[7] That Jesus, being God in person, taught with divine authority and that his teaching constitutes a rule for his disciples is a Christian commonplace (cf. Matt. 7:21–29; 28:19, et al.); only by following Jesus' teaching can one be his disciple. Part of his teaching was that our Old Testament was canonical for him and is to be so for his followers. A good deal of his teaching derived factual information about God from it. What sort of disciples are we if we decline to receive this basic strand of our Master's teaching?

Of the New Testament canon it need only be said that (1) apostolic witness to Christ, being Spirit-inspired, was always meant to function, in conjunction with the Old Testament, as a rule of faith;[8] (2) the only problem, therefore, at any stage was to identify the documents in which genuine apostolic instruction was given, either directly by apostles themselves or by their immediate and accredited associates (cf. 2 Thess. 2:2); (3) we have no good reason to question the twenty-seven books that the early church identified as apostolic in the required sense—for their external credentials are impressive, their doctrine is homogeneous,[9] and Christians of all generations have found in them that unique, transforming light and power that are the hallmarks of divinity on the biblical canon as a whole, evidencing it to be God's Word and thereby setting it apart from all other writings that the world has seen.

4. It is true that biblical revelation takes the form of an interpretive record of God's will, works, and ways as these were disclosed in a series of episodes in which he dealt with men of the ancient Near East. It is also true that the universally valid truths this record gives us as applied to particular Near Eastern folk of the far-off past, up to the first century A.D., need to be reapplied today. But since these universal truths are intrinsically clear and rational, such reapplication is always a practical possibility.

The essential and continuing task of biblical interpretation is to reapply biblical principles to ourselves, having discerned through historical exegesis what the human author meant his contemporaries to gather from what he said, and having distinguished between principle and application within his message. Historical exegesis is only the preliminary part of interpretation; application is its essence. Exegesis without application should not be called interpretation at all. The fear sometimes felt that, because of the distance between the cultures and outlooks of the biblical period and our own, these ancient Near Eastern documents cannot communicate God's mind and will for our lives in our own day, is groundless.

God is rational and unchanging, and all men in every generation, being made in God's image, are capable of being addressed by him. Within every culture in every age it is possible, through overhearing God's words of instruction to men of long ago, to hear God speaking to ourselves, as the Holy Spirit causes these words of long ago to be reapplied in our own minds and consciences. The proof that this is possible is that it actually happens. No proof can be more compelling than that!

Present-Day Doubts about Language

It is clear, however, that some today find difficulty with the line of thought I have set out because their minds are already possessed by deep-rooted uncertainties about the power of human language to convey information (as distinct from evoking attitudes) in the realm of what philosophers might call the supersensible or transcendent and Christians would call the divine. Until these doubts are exorcised, the straightforward belief that in the Bible God tells us things will seem naive and hazardous.

The temptation will be to follow the example of liberal and radical Protestant thinkers from Schleiermacher to Bultmann, Tillich, and their latter-day disciples and to turn the flank of the above exposition by agreeing that it states the Bible's own view. The Bible is treated as a collection of culturally conditioned myths, which for us can function only as symbols of nonverbal pressure that God exerts on the human spirit by evoking experiences of mystical, emotional, and ethical insight. So we need to take the measure of this fashionable scepticism about religious language—in particular, about biblical language. It appears to draw its strength from four features of today's sceptical culture.

The first source of scepticism is *a widespread sense of the inadequacy of all language as a means of personal communication.* This attitude, which finds vivid expression in poets like Stein, in novelists like Kafka, and in playwrights like Beckett, appears to be a symptom of a pervasive failure of nerve from which Western culture has conspicuously suffered in this century. Whereas writers from Shakespeare, Donne, and Milton to Hopkins, Housman, and Hardy celebrated and explored the resourcefulness of language as a means of communication at all levels, their successors show themselves burdened and oppressed at the isolation of each individual and the inadequacy of anyone's words to make known to others what is really going on in his innermost life. Ludwig Wittgenstein was very much a modern man when he declared that what can be said can be said clearly, that what we cannot say clearly we had best not try to say at all, and that the existential questions that matter most to us (*unsere Lebensprobleme*) are inexpressible.[10] T. S. Eliot was voicing what many today feel when he wrote in *Four Quartets* ("Burnt Norton" V) that in personal communication

> Words strain,
> Crash and sometimes break under the burden,
> Under the tension, slip, slide, perish,
> Decay with imprecision, will not stay in place,
> Will not stay still.

Moods do not always express either great insight or strong logic, but they are potent things while they last, and undoubtedly the modern mood is one of deep scepticism as to whether words can ever articulate the realities of personal existence and convey to others what is in the depth of one's own heart. And if this is true (so it is felt) among us who share a common human nature, surely it is much more true when God, who is so different from us, is the communicator. He can, no doubt, give us flashes of insight and illumination about ourselves, but precise information about his own will and purpose, his own thoughts and outlook?—surely not. Our post-Christian monotheistic paganism, which disbelieves the incarnation and stresses God's remoteness, serves merely to reinforce this mood, and unless and until true faith in Christ revives in Western culture, belief that God, in Scripture, specifically tells us things about himself is likely to go on being thought crude, unsophisticated, and naive.

The second source of scepticism is *widespread doubt as to whether language can convey transcendent realities at all.* At the presuppositional level, this doubt runs through much of the intensive study of language in which philosophers (mostly empiricists) and exponents of linguistics (a new academic discipline, developed mainly as a department of sociology) have been engaged for over half a century. While it is clear that the doubt was brought to this study rather than derived from it, it has so shaped professional procedures and techniques that, to casual observers, linguistic philosophy and semantic theory, with their stress on defining things by pointing to them, seem to confirm the doubt. Logically, of course, this is nonsense, just as the idea that naturalistic natural science can confirm its own uniformitarian presuppositions is nonsense. There is no denying, however, that it is, at present, potent nonsense.

The fountainheads of linguistic philosophy were Ludwig Wittgenstein's *Tractatus Logico-Philosophicus* (1922) and Alfred J. Ayer's *Language, Truth and Logic* (1935). Wittgenstein's book was deeply sceptical, and Ayer's reflected the positivist views of Rudolf Carnap's 'Vienna Circle,' whose members held that all facts are public and observable and therefore the ideal universal language is that of physics. Wittgenstein moved on to acknowledge a multiplicity of universes of discourse ('language games'), and Ayer's tract went down in history as logical positivism's last manifesto as well as its first.

Yet interest in the logic of language, 'syntactics' as it is sometimes called, remains, and with it the convention, basic in both books just mentioned, of treating as eccentric any view that holds that language can connote, denote, and give information about anything that transcends the world of the senses. The study of semantics, that is, of the way language works as a means of expression and communication, stems from Ferdinand de Saussure's sociologically oriented pioneer work, *A Course in General Linguistics* (English translation, 1960; French original, 1915), and has tended to operate throughout its history in terms of a similar convention. The convention is arbitrary enough, but while it exists among the learned it cannot but create a climate of opinion in its own favour among those who, as students, seek to benefit from the professionals' expertise. Students naturally soak up what their teachers take for granted.

The third source of scepticism is *the widespread unwillingness of Christian teachers to allow that in and through the teaching of Scripture God is informing us about himself.* Since liberalism took hold a century and a half ago, Protestant theologians, while remaining sure that Scripture mediates conscious, life-giving contact with God, have for the most part been equally sure that Scripture is not his Word in the sense expressed by Augustine's 'what thy Scripture says, thou dost say.'

Kant, whose Deism controlled his philosophy in a rather obvious way, had denied both the possibility and the need of verbal revelation from God, and liberal theologians took their cue from him. From the start, their thought was that Scripture is a product of religious and moral insight, which triggers similar insight in those who are capable of it. The actual theology of the Bible writers, however, is no more than culture-bound human witness to these awarenesses of God, awarenesses that in any case were essentially ineffable, as are all religious experiences.

Schleiermacher, with his belief that the essence of all religion is an intuition (feeling) of dependence on God and that Christianity is distinctive only because in it this feeling was and is mediated through the impact of the historical figure of Jesus, is the archetypal liberal teacher and was in fact the fountainhead of this whole development. Ritschl is usually thought of as a liberal patriarch because he denied verbal revelation and miracles and was deeply agnostic about God, but his hostility to mysticism was uncharacteristic of the movement generally.

In this century, neo-orthodoxy has stressed that through the Bible God's Word comes to us but has declined to conceive of that Word as simply Bible teaching applied to our situation. On the right wing, Barth viewed the Word as a breaking forth of something that Scripture 'intends' and that the church needs to hear, rather than as a systematic and integrated application to us of what Scripture actually says. At the centre, Brunner spent much time urging that, since God's revelation of himself is personal, it cannot be in any sense propositional—a curious false antithesis that makes God's method of self-disclosure analogous to the nonverbal communication of Harpo Marx.

On the left wing, Bultmann insisted that our life-transforming encounter with the Word of God yields no factual information whatever, and that the nature of true faith is to trust God, knowing that, in the strict sense, one knows nothing about him at all. The practitioners of the new hermeneutic follow Bultmann in exploring the nature of 'language-events' that alter our self-understanding without bringing us any direct understanding of God.

When leaders of theology thus decline to treat any of the statements of our thousand-plus-page, two-million word Bible as information from God to us and trumpet abroad that there can be no such thing as God-given information and that it is an intellectual mistake to look for any, it is no wonder if folk lose faith in the capacity of biblical speech to tell us facts about our Maker. Were we all clearheadedly logical, we should see ourselves as called by this situation to choose between such modern theologians as those just mentioned and such older ones as Moses and the prophets, Jesus Christ, Peter, Paul, John, and the author of Hebrews. Seeing the issue that way we might resolve that, on this point at least, we should ditch the moderns. But because many people are muddle headedly conventional, it is not always realized that this is the choice that faces us; nor, even when it is realized, is the right decision always made.

The fourth source of scepticism is *the widespread influence of Eastern religious ideas, all stressing that God is inexpressible by man.* Thus, for example, Lao-tse begins his treatise by saying: 'The tao [way] that can be trodden is not the enduring and unchanging tao. The name that can be named is not the enduring and unchanging name.' 'In Lao-tse and in Eastern mysticism generally,' comments John Macquarrie, 'the thought seems to be . . . of a primal undifferentiated Being, which we cannot even name without giving it a determinate character, and so making it some particular thing.'[11] In Eastern thinking, as in the neo-platonism that circled like smog around early Christianity, the ultimate being does not have a determinate character, in fact is not a particular being at all.

Christians believe that God made man in his own image, so that he and man might talk together; and, furthermore, that Jesus is God incarnate, come to us to show us what God eternally is; so the above-mentioned transcendentalist hang-up does not touch us. Eastern faiths, however, lacking these biblical truths and leaning as they do to either pantheistic or deistic conceptions (e.g., Hinduism in the former case, Islam in the latter) can hardly avoid it. To Westerners, for whom Christianity is old hat and Eastern religion is a novelty, and who, like the Athenians, are always going for new things, the thought of God as wholly remote from the categories of human language may seem, like Tennyson's white-clothed arm that grasped Excalibur, 'mystic, wonderful.' Christians, however, will see the idea as an embracing of darkness instead of light. But the Eastern notion of God as wholly inconceivable and inexpressible certainly infects many minds today and reinforces the common sceptical reaction when Christians claim that God has used human language—Hebrew, Aramaic, and Greek, to be precise—to give us specific information about himself.

Our Language-Using God

Such scepticism, however, is as far from the world of biblical religion as it is from the historic faith of the church. As we have already seen, Christianity from the start has been based on the biblical conviction that in and through words spoken to and by prophets and apostles, and supremely by Jesus Christ, the Word made flesh, as well as by the voice heard from heaven (Mark 1:11; 9:7; John 12:28ff.; 2 Pet. 1:17), God has spoken, in the precise sense of using language to tell people things. To assume, with the liberals, that the biblical vocabulary of divine speech is metaphorical, in the sense of signifying nonverbal communication, or is simply the spontaneous discernment by sensitive souls of spiritual values, is incorrect.

We may take the very explicit witness of the letter to the Hebrews as proof. The writer opens with the great 'In time past God spoke to our forefathers at many times and in various ways, but in these last days he has spoken to us by his Son' (Heb. 1:1–2). The phrase 'various ways' recalls the visions, dreams, theophanies, angelic messages, and other forms of direct locution whereby God revealed his mind to his Old Testament messengers. It also indicates the occasional and fragmentary nature of the revelations themselves, at least when seen in the light of the final and definitive self-disclosure that God gave through his incarnate Son, Jesus Christ. But when the writer says that God *spoke* by his Son, what he has in mind is precisely verbal communication, just as when he says that God spoke through the prophets. His argument continues with the inference that, because of the Son's supreme dignity, we must pay all the greater attention to the message of the great salvation that he declared and that his first hearers, the apostles, relayed in their spoken testimony (Heb. 2:1–3).

The author proceeds to make, or at least to buttress, every positive theological point in his whole exposition, up to the final chapter of the letter, by exposition and application of Old Testament passages—which he cites as what the Father or the Son or the Holy Spirit says to Christian believers (see 1:5–13; 5:5ff.; 8:3–12; 10:30, 37ff.; 12:26; 13:5 for the Father as speaker; 2:11–13; 10:5–9 for Christ as speaker; and 3:7–11; 9:8; 10:15–17 for the Holy Spirit as speaker).

We cannot here go into the fascinating question of the principles by which the writer of Hebrews interprets the meaning of these passages. Our present concern is simply with his conviction that the words of his Bible (our Old Testament), along with the words of Christ and the apostles, express both what God said on the public stage of the space-time continuum that we call world history and also what he says now, in personal application to all to whom the message comes and in a way that is decisive for their eternal destiny.

This is the characteristic biblical conviction, found not only in Hebrews but wherever in Scripture the words of the Law, or the Prophets, or the apostles, or the Lord Jesus Christ are mentioned. It is this conviction that we must now examine.

As we have already seen, it is a conviction about authority, that is, about God's way of exerting his rightful claim to direct his rational human creatures into acknowledgement of his truth and obedience to his will. As such, it is a conviction both about the reality of communication from God to us, whereby he tells us what otherwise we could not have known, and about God's gracious plan to make us sinners his friends—which is the end to which the knowledge he gives us is meant to lead.

Formally, the conviction is made up of these three strands:

(1) God's word of direct self-disclosure to individuals in history—to Noah, Abraham, Moses, Jonah, Elijah, Jeremiah, Peter, Paul, and others—was directly authoritative for their own belief and behaviour. God having spoken to them, they were bound to believe what he had told them, knowing it to be true (because he is a God of truth), and bound also to do all that God had told them to do.

(2) The same direct divine authority attached to all that God prompted his chosen spokesmen—prophets, wisdom writers, poets, apostles, and Jesus Christ himself—to declare orally to others in his name. Their authority was not just that of deep human religious insight, deep though their religious insight was. Primarily and fundamentally, their authority was that of the God whose truth they were relaying in the verbal form to which he himself had led them. Paul declares that 'we (apostles] have . . . received . . . the Spirit who is from God, that we may understand what God has freely given us. This is what we speak . . . in words taught by the Spirit' (1 Cor. 2:2–13). Verbal inspiration, as here defined, conferred direct

divine authority on the words that God's messengers spoke, authority that required their hearers to receive what they heard as from God himself.

(3) The same divine authority belongs to what they wrote, in the books that now constitute our canonical Scriptures.

As our God-inspired canon, the rule for faith and life, Holy Scripture may properly be called *law* (understanding that word in the sense of the Hebrew *torah,* which signifies the kind of authoritative instruction a father gives to his children). But this statement must not be taken to imply that all Scripture has the uniform linguistic quality of civil statutes or lawyers' textbooks, or that it all consists of simple factual assertions (propositions), with appended commands of a single logical type. The uses of language in the Bible are at least as varied as one would find in any sixty-six other books, and it is important to do justice to their complexity.

In ordinary communication, language appears to have five main functions at least. First, it may be *informative* conveying factual data of one sort or another that the persons addressed are assumed not to know. Second, it may be *imperative,* communicating commands and calling for action. Third, it may be *illuminative,* using various devices to stir our imaginations into empathetic activity and so deepen our insight into, and understanding of, facts that at the conceptual level we know already. Thus poems about nature—sunny days, snow, rain, flowers, trees, and so on—are offered, not as versified meteorology or botany, but as transmitting the poet's vision of the significance of these familiar things. The analogies, metaphors, and parables with which we pepper our own prose are meant to be illuminative in a similar way.

Fourth, language may be *performative,* actually bringing about states of affairs by announcing them to be the case. By saying, 'I declare this road open,' the mayor actually opens the new highway. By writing, 'His name is John,' Zacharias actually settled what his son should be called (Luke 1:63). Fifth, language may be *celebratory,* focusing on a shared apprehension of things in a way that confirms that it is shared and so binds together more closely those who share it. Much ritual and ceremonial language, many speeches in many contexts, and all such utterances as 'Isn't this lovely?' or 'Look at that!' or even 'Wow!' come in this category. Now, God's instruction given to sinful men as we find it set before us in Holy Scripture involves all five of these uses of language.

Informative language is basic, for every book of Scripture, in its own way, is didactic—making affirmations, implicit if not explicit, about God. This is true even of Esther, which celebrates God's providence, though the book does not mention his name, and also of the Song, which is a love duet celebrating in parable form the mutual devotion and affection of the Lord and his people. He who, in face of this, is still resolved to deny that revelation is informative—that is, to use the word that has been fashionable since the forties, 'prepositional'—ought logically, therefore, to deny outright that Holy Scripture is in any sense revelation.

This view, being a departure from dominical and apostolic teaching, has no claim to be taken seriously. What believing Christians should hold, rather, is this: every assertion that the Bible, soundly exegeted, proves to be making, whether about matters of natural and historical fact within the created order or about the Creator's own plans and actions, should be received as information given and taught by God as part of the total presentation, interpretation, and celebration of redemption that Scripture essentially is.

Imperative language is equally basic. The Mosaic law, the wisdom literature, the moral teaching of the prophets, of Christ, and of the apostles, and abundant other particular narratives set forth God's commands: 'You shall . . . you shall not; . . .' (Exod. 20:3–17); 'Do not . . .' (Matt. 5:34, 36, 39, 42, 6:3, 7ff., 16, 19, 25, 31, 34; 7:6, 35; et al.); 'Go and do likewise' (Luke 10:37); 'Watch' (Mark 13:33–37); and so on. This point needs no further illustration.

Illuminative language appears when such literary devices as analogy, allegory, imagery, or parable are used by God's spokesmen to help us grasp imaginatively and existentially, sometimes through traumatic self-judgement, the deep significance for them of events in their lives, and in particular how these events bear on their relationship with God. New facts are not here being communicated, but listeners are nudged into seeing old facts in a new light.

Examples are Jotham's parable of the trees, spoken to the men of Shechem (Judg. 9:7ff.); Nathan's parable of the ewe lamb, directed to David (2 Sam. 12:1ff.); Ezekiel's allegories of the two eagles and the two sisters (Ezek. 17; 23); and Jesus' parables, whereby he sought to startle his popular-minded, prejudiced, uncommitted audience into grasping the revolutionary realities of his gospel of the kingdom. Jesus' parables 'work' by vividly invoking everyday realities, sometimes with a built-in surprise (as in the stories of the labourers in the vineyard, of the great supper, and of the Pharisee and the publican) and sometimes not (as in the stories of the sowers, the mustard seed, and the lost sheep). They always challenge the hearer to face with all seriousness God's ways in relation to him personally and to examine his own response to God in the matter of the kingdom.

In other words (to use once more the language of an earlier generation), these parables have less to do with teaching doctrine than with applying doctrine already taught. They are an imaginative device for making folk see the personal bearing of what conceptually they knew before.

Performative language appears also, as when God, having told Abraham that he will make his covenant with him, proceeds to say, 'This is my covenant with you' (Gen. 17:2–4). The use of these words causes the state of affairs spoken of to exist.

Celebratory language is found in the Psalms, Exodus 15, and similar passages, where known facts of God's work in his people's history are turned into themes of gratitude and praise.

Another important issue should be discussed before going on to the next section. When biblical inspiration is said to be *plenary* (as opposed to partial) and *verbal* (as opposed to the idea that God gives only inklings and insights, without determining in what words they should be expressed), this does not imply a Koranic view of inspiration, whereby translations of the original are precisely not the Holy Book. As Reformation theology used to say, it is the sense of Scripture that is Scripture, and all translations are in truth the Bible, at least to the extent that they are accurate.

Nor does this view imply, as it is persistently thought to do, that because biblical words are God's words we may lawfully seek or find in Scripture meanings unrelated to what the human writers were conveying to those whom they were immediately addressing. The Bible is as fully human as it is divine, and the way to get into the present mind of God the Holy Spirit is by getting into the expressed mind of his human agents—the biblical authors, God's penmen—and by making appropriate application to ourselves of what they say. Allegorizing, and everything like it, is illegitimate.

The point that *plenary* and *verbal* make is that the biblical words themselves (in Hebrew, Aramaic, or Greek) are to be seen as God-given. Men were not left to articulate information about, and interpretations of, God's ways with men apart from his superintending providence. On the contrary, the Lord who gave the Word also gave the words. It was not just the writers' thinking but 'all Scripture,' the written product, that is inspired by God (2 Tim. 3:16; cf. 2 Pet. 1:21).

It is critically important, therefore, that, so far as possible, we make certain that we know what the God-given words are. Words, after all, are the vehicles and guardians of meaning; if we lose the words, we shall have lost the sense too. So the science of textual ('lower') criticism becomes a matter of key significance. When, for instance, the Basis of Faith of the British Inter-Varsity Fellowship (now the Universities and Colleges Christian Fellowship; UCCF) ascribes inspiration and authority to Holy Scripture *as originally given,* the point of this phrase is not, as is sometimes thought, to give unrestricted licence for suspecting textual corruption whenever an apparent discrepancy between passages arises. Its point is simply to make clear that mistranslations and demonstrable copyists' slips are not to be revered as God's truth but are rather to be detected and amended.

It has often been said, and rightly, that not one word in a thousand in the Greek text of the New Testament is open to serious doubt, and that there is no place at all in either Testament where uncertainty about the text raises a question of doctrinal substance.

Also, it is often said, and surely rightly again, that no honest translation of the Bible has ever been so bad that God's life-giving message could not reach men through it. Nonetheless, human mistakes in translation and transmission can only obscure the divine message, and therefore we ought to try to weed them out, just as proofreaders ought to try to weed out all misprints, even if what is printed would be intelligible and generally reliable with the misprints there.

However, in thus stressing the importance of the particular words that the human authors, and through them God the Spirit, gave us, we must not forget that the semantic units (i.e., units of meaning) in the Bible, as in all other literature, include sentences, paragraphs, chapters, and ultimately whole books. It is always wrong to think of interpreting any document by combining all the possible meanings of each individual word as the dictionaries define it. It is doubly wrong when, in interpreting Scripture, we assume that each word that we think is theologically significant will always have the same acreage of meaning, and when we then define that meaning by reference to the way the word is used elsewhere in Scripture.

The monumental mistake of Luther, in taking for granted that James meant by 'justify,' 'works,' and 'faith' exactly what Paul meant by these words (and on this basis wishing to see James dropped from the canon because Jas. 2:14–26 seemed to contradict Romans and Galatians) stands as a warning for all time against the danger of this false method. The ambiguous and easily misused dictum that the Bible should be read like any other book is true at least in this sense, that the ordinary rules of semantics must be recognized as applying to it, and any interpretative technique that violates them must be ruled out.[12] Docetic interpretations of Scripture (those that query the reality of its apparent humanness) are as objectionable as are docetic understandings—misunderstandings, rather—of the personal, human experiences of the incarnate Lord.

The Problem of Theological Language

We should now take notice that the position spelled out in the foregoing paragraphs—a position learned, as we believe, from the Bible itself—solves in principle two of the knottiest problems in current philosophy of religion; namely, how theological language can have any definite meaning, and how in particular it can be a means of revelation, in the sense of communicating true information about God.

During the past half-century, linguistic philosophers have frequently tried to show, on various logical grounds, that language cannot possibly carry knowledge about God. Answers to them have been given, with some success, in terms of the philosophers' own assumption that our language is an evolutionary development, for which reference to physical sense-experience is, if not exclusive, at least primary.

Ian Ramsey has shown how, by attaching well-chosen 'qualifiers' to verbal 'models' ('heavenly' to 'Father,' for instance), we can so 'stretch' language as to direct men's minds to a transcendent object of reference and thereby, under God, precipitate a 'disclosure' to them of its reality.[13] John Macquarrie has analysed theological language ('God-talk' as he calls it) as stemming from reflection on existentially significant encounters with Holy Being.[14] Austin Farrer has displayed biblical language as 'working' in the manner of poetic imagery.[15] Eric Mascall, among others, has laboured to give new life to the classical doctrine on which Thomist natural theology rests, namely, that God, being One whom we resemble in some ways though not in others, can be known metaphysically through the construction of analogies.[16] Basil Mitchell, Ian Crombie, and others have exhibited biblical and ecclesiastical phraseology as a combining and balancing of parables.[17] Frederick Ferré, having worked his way conscientiously through various forms of scepticism and agnosticism concerning the objective reference point of theological language, ends his argument by affirming that if, as is claimed, the personal linguistic 'models' of Christian theism unify and make sense of our experience as a whole, that will decisively vindicate the claim that they are both meaningful and true to reality.[18]

As *ad hominem* responses to the sceptics, starting from the ground that scepticism occupies with regard to human language, these expositions have merit. But their authors fail to query the sceptical assumption that the systems of arbitrary signs, vocal and visual, that we call language are 'from below,' i.e., are an evolutionary development in which the signification of physical entities is basic to everything else. This omission leaves their job half-done, so that their apologia is only at half-strength.

Lack of both space and competence make it impossible to explore here the many problems that arise concerning the origin and development of human language. But the main point is this: The opening chapters of Genesis—one *obiter dictum* (incidental comment) from which was quoted, we saw, by our Lord as the Creator's own word (Matt. 19:4ff., citing Gen. 2:24)—teach us that human beings were created in God's image (1:26ff.) and proceed on the basis that both a sense of God and a language in which to converse with him were given to men as ingredients in, or perhaps preconditions of, the divine image from the start.

By depicting God as the first language user (1:3, 6, et al.), Genesis shows us that human thought and speech have their counterparts and archetypes in him. By telling us of Adam, Eve, and their descendants listening and responding to God, Genesis shows us that references to the Creator do not 'stretch' ordinary language in an unnatural way; rather, such 'stretching' is actually language's primary use.

What is unnatural is the 'shrinking' of language reflected in the supposition that it can talk easily and naturally only of physical objects. By making us aware that, from the start, God has used language to tell men things and so to teach them what to think about him and how to talk to him, Genesis both vindicates the language of theology and worship as meaningful and establishes God's own utterances as the standard of truth to which our theological notions must always conform.

Thus the biblical position that God's speaking and God's image in man imply a human capacity to grasp and respond to his verbal address shows up the arbitrariness, and indeed provincialism, of the post-Christian, positivistic theory of language on which the scepticism of linguistic philosophers rests. The final proof that human language can speak intelligibly of God is that God has actually spoken intelligibly about himself in it. This intelligibility flows from the so-called anthropomorphism (man likeness) of his account of himself. But such anthropomorphism is primarily a witness to the essential theomorphism (Godlikeness) of man. The fact that God's self-disclosure is couched linguistically in the same personal terms in which we talk about ourselves and is therefore intelligible to us does not mean that God must have misrepresented himself in what he has said. What it means, rather, is that in our personhood and in our capacity to give and receive verbal communication, we are less unlike God than perhaps we thought.

The conviction of latter-day Western philosophers is that the supposed difficulty of believing that human theological language can actually refer to God and express factual truth ('true truth,' as Francis Schaeffer calls it) about him springs from two sources. First, it is assumed that God (if real) must so differ from us that we can never be sure that any of our statements or concepts really fit him. Second, he must be assumed to be silent, not helping us see what to say about him by saying things to us about himself. In these two convictions we meet the baleful legacy of Kant, as theologized in the liberal tradition from Schleiermacher on.

It was Kant, with his lethal combination of a priori Deism and a posteriori agnosticism (for this was the ultimate epistemological issue of his critical philosophy), who put abroad the ideas that no serious philosopher could believe in a God who speaks and that religion should be shaped by reflection 'within the bounds of pure reason.' While God might be a necessary postulate, he cannot strictly be *known* in any sense, by any means, at any time, any more than can be the *Ding-an-sich* (thing-in-itself) in the natural order. Kant hereby bequeathed to us the now chronic misunderstanding of God's transcendence and incomprehensibility as implying that, in his personal existence, he is both remote and unintelligible.

Some of the greatest of the moderns have been infected by this misunderstanding. 'To Barth,' wrote John Frame, 'God's transcendence implies that he cannot be clearly revealed to men, clearly represented by human words and concepts.' That is because Barth's thinking ran on good Kantian lines. But, notes Frame, 'Scripture itself never deduces from God's transcendence the inadequacy and fallibility of all verbal revelation. Quite the contrary: in Scripture, verbal revelation is to be obeyed without question, because of the divine transcendence . . . God's lordship, transcendence, demands unconditional belief in and obedience to the words of revelation; it never relativizes or softens the authority of these words.'

Is this an idolizing of human words, as Barth, blinkered by his Kantianism, would urge? No, says Frame, for the words of Scripture are no less the Word of God than they are the word of man, and divine authority is intrinsic to their message.[19] This is the proper correction of the Kantian mistake. Anglo-Saxon philosophers, no less than continental theologians, would do well to take note. Since

God, though really transcendent, really says what Scripture says, and since man, being really theomorphic, as God's image bearer, really does apprehend what God in Scripture says, philosophical scepticism about the capacity of language to carry truth about the true God must be dismissed as an unhappy and indeed rather ludicrous mistake.

The Condescension of God

Paul calls the divine ordaining and encompassing of the cross of Jesus Christ *the foolishness* and *weakness* of God (1 Cor. 1:25). He is being ironical, of course, for he knows Christ to be God's wisdom and power (1 Cor. 1:25). He is insisting that the word of the cross only appears as folly to those who have not understood it. He is also making a positive theological point as well, namely, that the death of God's Son on Calvary shows how completely God, in love to mankind, was willing to hide his glory and become vulnerable to shame and dishonour. Now God in love calls men to embrace and boast of this foolish-seeming, weak-looking, disreputable event of the Cross as the means of their salvation. It is a challenge to sinful pride of both mind and heart.

Similarly (and this is our next point) God in love calls us to humble ourselves by bowing to Holy Scripture, which also has an appearance of foolishness and weakness when judged by some human standards, yet is truly his Word and the means of our knowing him as Saviour. God first humbled himself for our salvation in the incarnation and on the cross and now he humbles himself for our knowledge of salvation by addressing us in and through the often humanly unimpressive words of the Bible.

We are here confronted by that quality in God of which C. S. Lewis wrote: 'The same divine humility which decreed that God should become a baby at a peasant woman's breast, and later an arrested field preacher in the hands of the Roman police, decreed also that he should be preached [and, we may add, written about] in a vulgar, prosaic and unliterary language.'[20] For this quality in God whereby he lovingly identifies with what is beneath him—the quality of which the incarnation is the paradigm, though all his gracious dealings with men show it—the classical name is *condescension* (Greek, *synkatabasis*) and the etymological significance is 'coming-down-to-be-with.'

Calvin, who was perhaps over-conscious of the literary limitations of some parts of the Bible, spoke emphatically of God's condescension in deigning, out of love, to talk to us in earthy and homespun language 'with a contemptible meanness of words' (*sub contemptibili verborum humilitate*).[21] In this, as Calvin saw it, God's first aim is not so much to keep us humble, though that comes into it, as to help us understand. His simple mode of speech to us, in and through the words of the largely unsophisticated writers whom he used as his human penmen, is in itself a gesture of love. 'God . . . condescends [*se demittit*] to our immaturity [*ru-ditatem*]. . . . When God prattles to us [*balbutit*] in Scripture in a clumsy, homely style [*crasse et plebeio stylo*], let us know that this is done on account of the love he bears us.'[22] One sign of love to a child is adapting to the child's language when talking to him, and so, says Calvin, God in his love to us adapts to our childishness in spiritual things. Far from causing obscurity, therefore, God's 'baby talk' (what Calvin calls his prattling) dispels it, making everything plainer to us than it could be otherwise.

Surely Calvin is right. The genuine human weaknesses and limitations that Scripture sometimes exhibits—from Paul's forgetfulness (1 Cor. 1:16) and coarseness (Gal. 5:12) to the bad Greek of Revelation and the wild, pain-wrenched rhetoric of Job do in fact contribute to the communication that Scripture (i.e., God in and through Scripture) effects. That communication comprises not simply doctrinal truths but demonstrations of how divine grace works in the lives, not of paragons and plaster saints, but in those of all sorts of earthy, flesh-and-blood human beings. Just as God chose 'undignified' mortals (even sinners like you and me!) to save, so he was ready to become 'undignified' in both incarnation and inspiration in order to bring about our salvation. The condescension of God in becoming a baby Jew, in being executed on a Roman gibbet, and in proclaiming his goodness and his gospel to us via the down-to-earth, unliterary, often rustic words of the sixty-six canonical books, is one and the same and spells the same reality throughout—love to the uttermost.

But God's humility offends man's pride, and hence both incarnation and inspiration are rejected by some as incredible. It is instructive to note the parallel here. The pagan philosopher Celsus (ca. A.D. 150) led the van in ridiculing the incarnation. How could God the Son, the supposedly infinite, eternal, and un-changeable Creator become man—let alone become a Jew!—and make himself known within the limitations of human finitude? Surely the idea is absurd! Scrip-turally instructed Christians are content to reply that it must be possible, since God has actually done it. The incarnation is a wise and glorious mystery, despite its attendant weakness and shame, and from it comes salvation.

At the end of the eighteenth century the Deist philosopher Kant, as we have seen, turned away in comparable contempt from belief in inspiration, and thus pioneered a stance that has become typical of Western intellectual culture ever since. How could the infinite, transcendent, and incomprehensible Creator reveal himself in the words of folk from the primitive Near East thousands of years ago? This, too, seems absurd! Again the Christian will reply, as in regard to the incarna-tion, that it must be possible, since God has done it. In fact he still reveals himself by so applying to us what he said to others in the past that we come to know with certainty what he says to us in the present. This also is a wise and glorious mystery, and from it flows saving knowledge. In both cases, the correct reply to criticism is found in confession of God's salvation: how it was wrought in the first case, and how it is grasped and enjoyed in the second. In neither case, however, does the correct answer remove the offence that the criticism expresses.

God's condescension, we now see, is one aspect of his saving grace, whereby both in the Son's incarnation and in the Bible's inspiration he brought about a full union and identity of divine with human, our salvation being his goal. Such condescension gloriously displays his self-humbling, self-giving love. Any suggestion, therefore, that the unity of divine and human, whether in Jesus or in Scripture, is less than complete will reduce our apprehension of this love, and thus in reality dishonour it.

When patristic writers urged that the Christ of the Gospels suffered impassibly (i.e., without feeling all the pain that we should have felt) or when they said that he suffered in his human nature apart from the divine (and wrought miracles in his divine nature apart from the human), they meant to honour him by highlighting his deity. Actually, however, they took away his honour by questioning whether his condescension in becoming man was all that it seemed to be—whether, that is, Jesus was one fully divine-human person living a fully divine-human life throughout, or whether he was less than this. So, too, if it is urged that the parts of Scripture we think worthy of God are inspired and that the parts we think unworthy are not, the glory of his condescension (in so inspiring human witness to him that it becomes his own witness to himself) is at once blurred.

Biblical passages that are mundane and raw in matter or manner or both are not any less inspired on that account, just as the baby talk of a genius like Einstein chatting to young children is not any less his speech because it is baby talk. What needs to be said here is that, just as all of Jesus' words, works, and experiences were words, works, and experiences of God the Son, so all the words of Scripture testifying to the God of grace—words of praise, prayer, narrative, celebration, teaching, and so on—are words of God testifying by these means to himself. Only in light of this truth can the full glory of divine condescension, in inspiration as in incarnation, be grasped.

So now it appears that the confession of biblical *infallibility* and *inerrancy* (which words I treat as substantially synonymous) is important, not simply as undergirding Scripture's function as our divine authority for faith and practice, the whole teaching of which we receive as from the Lord, but also as showing the measure and extent of God's gracious condescension in bringing us to know him savingly. For inerrancy and infallibility are entailed by inspiration; and inspiration, like incarnation, is a fruit of divine condescension. From this standpoint, biblical inerrancy is part of the doctrine of grace, and God's action in giving us a totally trustworthy Bible is a marvellous benefit.

We may sense a certain lack of credibility in folk who question inerrancy while still claiming to be grateful for the Bible despite their uncertainty as to how much of it they can trust. Certainly, however, those who know they have received—as it were from their Saviour's own hand—a Bible they can trust absolutely, as imparting to them the mind and knowledge and will of their God, will thank him for this his second unspeakable gift with joy that knows no bounds.

The Adequacy of Biblical Language

It is asked whether biblical language is adequate to communicate knowledge about God. In the foregoing pages we have tried to spell out the principles that entitle us to affirm that it is. The key fact, as we saw, is the theomorphism of created man, whom God made a language user, able to receive God's linguistic communication and to respond in kind. But it is important, in saying this, not to appear to claim too much.

If we ask what knowledge about God biblical language communicates, the answer is, not exhaustive knowledge of himself and of all things in relation to him—the knowledge that is distinctively his—but only such knowledge of those matters as he sees to be adequate (i.e., sufficient) for our life of faith and obedience. 'The secret things belong to the LORD our God, but the things revealed belong to us and to our children forever, that we may follow all the words of this law' (Deut. 29:29). This, in concrete terms, is the adequacy of biblical language: it suffices, not indeed to make us omniscient in any area, but as 'a lamp to [our] feet and a light for [our] path' in discipleship (Ps. 119:105).

Those who doubt biblical inerrancy certainly claim too little with regard to the certainties that Bible readers may have, but it will not right the boat for those who affirm inerrancy to claim too much. All of us may need a warning here. What we know is that, as Jesus Christ is adequate to bring us to God, so Holy Scripture is adequate to bring us to Jesus Christ. Where acknowledgement of Scripture as adequate verbal communication from God is lacking, adequate acknowledgement of Jesus Christ is likely to be lacking too. If we can make plain to the church and to the world that our concern in contending for biblical inerrancy is in the first instance soteriological, obediential, doxological, and devotional—not rationalistic, but religious—we shall do well; if not, we shall do much less well. Failure here would be tragic! May it not be.

Appendix: Notes on Some Technical Questions about Biblical and Christian Language

If the argument in this chapter is right, the apt model for understanding how God communicates with us is our own verbal communication with each other, by oral and written discourse, and we should approach the Bible in the light of the following principles:

1. God made us in his own image (i.e., among other things, reasoners and language users) so that he could address us through the medium of language, the means by which we address each other, and so draw us into a genuinely personal response to himself, in which we in turn use language to address him, namely the language of prayer and praise. The supreme demonstration of this is the preaching and teaching ministry of Jesus Christ, the Son of God incarnate.

2. Scripture, which in its character as human witness to God records many direct verbal communications from God to particular men, is through similar inspiration, equally and indeed primarily God's own witness to himself. Imagine your boss handing to you, one of his employees, a policy memorandum written by some of his personal staff and assuring you as he does so that it exactly expresses his mind. This situation is parallel to that in which a Christian comes by God's providence to possess a Bible. The employee no doubt has some general idea of the boss's goals and strategy before he reads the memo, inasmuch as he belongs to the firm, but by studying the memo he comes to know the boss's mind with a precision not otherwise attainable. So it is with members of the Christian church as they study their Bibles.

3. The men who wrote the biblical books had in view a readership contemporary with themselves and wrote to be understood by that readership. So our task in biblical interpretation is twofold: first, to fix the historical meaning of each book (what it was saying to its first intended readers) and second, to apply to ourselves the truths about God and man that the original message embodies. We go to school with Abraham, Moses, David, Job, Jeremiah, Paul, the Israelites in the wilderness and before and after the exile, and the churches at Corinth, Colossae, Laodicea, and other places. We watch God dealing with these folk, overhearing what he said to them and seeing what he did to and for them. Hence, in the manner of observers in the classroom, we learn by inference his mind and will concerning us.

Through the understanding God gives us of his ways with, and his will for, these biblical characters he draws near to call, correct, and challenge us today. Through the Spirit's agency, Jesus Christ, who is the same yesterday, today, and forever (Heb. 13:8), steps out of the gospel stories to confront us with the same issues of faith, obedience, repentance, righteousness, and discipleship with which he confronted men when he was on earth. This is biblical interpretation: seeing first what the text *meant* and then what it *means*—that is, how what it says touches our lives.

4. While commentaries supply historical meanings, only the Holy Spirit can enable our sin-darkened minds to discern how biblical teaching applies to us. Prayerful dependence on the Spirit's help is therefore necessary if our attempts at interpretation are ever to succeed. Historical exegesis becomes interpretation only when the application is truly made.

5. Since all Scripture is God preaching in and through the preaching of his servants (for every biblical book is edificatory in intention and therefore

homiletical in thrust), it is through being preached, and being heard and read as preaching, that it is most fully understood.

On the basis of these principles, more or less clearly focused and kept in view, the international, multiracial, multicultural community called the church, consisting of educated and uneducated, clever and less clever folk together, has sought to learn of God and hear his voice speaking in and through his Word. The solid testimony of the centuries is that precisely this has happened.

Against the background of these centuries of worldwide Christian experience one would not expect to find the assertion that it is impossible to talk significantly about God or to treat any biblical or ecclesiastical utterances that purport to refer to him as fact-stating. This, however, as we have indicated, is exactly what certain teachers of philosophy in Western universities during the past half-century have claimed. They do not deny that such utterances may express and communicate the speaker's emotional or volitional attitudes (see, for instance, R. G. Braithwaite's analysis of religious assertions as expressing commitment to a behaviour policy—in the case of Christian assertions, commitment to an agapeistic way of life).[23] What they deny is that these utterances can state public facts about God, that is, inform us of things concerning him that are true irrespective of what any particular person thinks, feels, or intends.

What are their reasons for taking this position? The essential claim that all these teachers make in some form is that statements about God cannot fulfil the conditions of significant fact-stating speech. These conditions, it is urged, are (1) *speciality*—you must be able to show that you are talking about something real and to show how that something is to be identified and distinguished from all other realities, and (2) *verifiability* or, at least, *falsifiability*—you must be able to show what would confirm the statement as true, or at least what would count against it. These conditions, it is urged, God-talk can never meet.[24]

Let us look at these two points in order.

1. It is argued that God is not specifiable; that is, when one speaks of him there is no way of telling what one is talking about. There are two questions here: whether the word *God* connotes a specific being, distinguishable in thought from all other beings, and whether, if so, such a being exists, as distinct from being an insubstantial fantasy. The following responses suggest themselves.

First, the word *God* on Christian lips refers to the Creator-Redeemer whose actions and character are described in canonical Scripture.

Second, there are two sorts of realities that, at least *prima facie,* point to the real existence of a Creator-Redeemer corresponding to this description. For one thing, there are historical facts that seem inexplicable on any other hypothesis, notably the existence and character of the Christian church and the existence and contents of the Holy Scriptures. For another thing, there are the facts of religious experience, whereby countless human lives have been changed morally in such a way that facets of Christlikeness now appear in them that previously seemed out of their reach.

Two things may have given colour to the idea that God is not specifiable. The first is the unwillingness of much Protestant theology in this century to treat biblical statements about God as revealed descriptions rather than high-minded guesses. The second is the observed defects of the classical Thomist doctrine of analogy, which was supposed to enable us to specify God in fundamental ways on the basis of natural theology alone, without appeal to the Bible (an intrinsically invalid method for fallen minds, some Protestants would think).

A word about these defects may be in order. Analogy was thought of as a kind and degree of likeness or correspondence of creature and Creator to each other. Two sorts of analogy were posited: the analogy of *attribution,* whereby formal qualities in man were held to correspond to qualities in God that ontologically were their creative cause, and the analogy of *proportionality,* whereby it was affirmed that God and man shared common qualities in a way appropriate to their distinct natures (as in the quality of existence: necessary and underived in God, contingent and derived in man). But neither of these modes of analogy, when pursued in the classical Thomist manner, on the basis of a cosmological 'proof' of God's reality alone (apart from reference to his self-presentation in Scripture), yields determinate positive knowledge of what God is.

The analogy of attribution requires us to ascribe to God all conceivable predicates, at least virtually, and thus proves to be saying only that God somehow causes everything that we are. The analogy of proportionality likewise fails to tell us how the characteristic predicated of both God and man is differentiated in the former from what it is in the latter. The classical doctrine of analogy does indeed seem to leave God unspecified and unspecifiable.[25]

There is, however, another use for the word *analogy* altogether, namely, as a description of the way in which the Bible—and Christian theological and liturgical speech, following the Bible—uses of God such predicates as 'father,' 'loving,' 'wise,' and 'just,' which are normally used of human beings who are finite. They are said to be used in reference to God not *univocally* (i.e., in exactly the same sense as that in which they are used of man) nor *equivocally* (i.e., in an entirely different sense) but *analogically. Analogically* here means 'univocally up to a certain point.' Only *some* of the implications of the normal use of these predicates, therefore, carry over.

To the question, How much of the original (human) meaning of each word remains when it is applied to God, Basil Mitchell replies by giving the following rule:

> A word should be presumed to carry with it as many of the original entailments as the new context allows, and this is determined by their compatibility with the other descriptions which there is reason to believe also applied to God. That God is incorporeal dictates that 'father' does not mean 'physical progenitor,' but the word continues to bear the connotation of tender protective care. Similarly, God's 'wisdom' is qualified by the totality of other descriptions which are applicable to him; it does not, for example, have to be learned, since he is omniscient and eternal.[26]

This rule seems correct and valuable as a guide both for apprehending what God tells us of himself through the biblical writers, and for learning to shape our own speech in a way that reproduces the substance of the biblical witness.

2. It is also argued, as noted above, that statements about God are neither *verifiable* nor *falsifiable*, and that this renders them vacuous. The fact that you do not know (so it is argued) what would tend to confirm or disprove such statements shows that they can have no determinative meaning, even to the one who makes them. (There is a strong element of putting the Christian on the spot in all expositions of this point known to me, hence my *ad hominem* way of putting it here.) To this general thesis, a five-point reply may be made:

(1) If, as is often the case in discussions of this point, very general statements about God (e.g., 'God loves men') are considered in isolation, it can be made to look very hard to determine what they mean when a Christian asserts them. Because they are being considered out of context, their implications have to be laboriously beaten out as the discussion proceeds, and the impression is easily given that rigorous logical analysis hounds the Christians from pillar to post. At the start, therefore, it should be said that any assertions about God that Christians make are part of a coherent system of thought learned at each point from the testimony of the Bible (which is itself demonstrably coherent in its teaching), and the meaning of these assertions is finally fixed by the system as a whole.

(2) If it can be said, in the manner of early logical positivism, that the meaning of an empirical statement (as distinct from an analytic statement, which is true by definition) is the method of its verification, or that it depends on knowing what would have to be done to verify the statement, the sufficient answer is that this verification principle, which is itself offered as an empirical statement, cannot itself be empirically verified. The positivist position self-destructs as being, by its own standards, meaningless.[27]

(3) A great deal that Christians, echoing Scripture, affirm about God has to do with future experiences of weal or woe, stretching ultimately beyond this life, which he will bring about. In the nature of the case such assertions (which at this point are like our own promises) can be verified only by future events fulfilling them. But the conceivability of this eschatological verification shows that they are entirely meaningful, in the strictest verificationist terms.

(4) If it be said, as later logical empiricists allow, that the question of meaning depends on the statement in question is held to presuppose and to imply and that the question of its truth, once its meaning is determined, is a matter of evidence, then it will not be hard to say either what the various assertions of which Christian belief is made up mean or what states of affairs would in principle tend to verify or falsify them. If, for instance, there were reason to think that Jesus never existed or, if he did, that he never rose from the dead, this would effectively falsify the Christian claim. But in fact there is no reason to think this and every reason to think the opposite.

(5) If it be allowed, as it should be, that verification can take the form of trustworthy assurance as well as of actual or possible experiences or observations, then it may properly be said that the testimony of our truth-telling God in Holy Scripture is itself the most cogent verification of what we believe.

The burden of these all-too-brief notes is to show that the logical grounds sometimes alleged for discounting Christian and biblical language about God as not being fact-stating are not cogent. The details of the philosophical doctrines that underlie this scepticism have not been exposed at all. Suffice it to have shown that, so far as criticism of Christian discourse is concerned, the sceptics have not established their points.

CHAPTER 3

The Bible and the Authority of Reason

This title is in itself highly provocative. We may expect it to draw forth strong reactions from two quite different types of people.

On the one hand, those who speak for the post-Christian humanism of the West will not like it. They will object to it for seeming to imply that the Bible takes precedence over the authority of reason. This implication, they will say, is false; the authority of reason is absolute and sacrosanct, and is subject to nothing that is external to reason itself. And they will wish to change our title to 'The Authority of Reason and the Bible,' in order to make it express their view that reason ought to judge Scripture, but not vice versa.

On the other hand, the alert Evangelical Christian will not like our title either. He will complain of it for seeming to imply that the authority of reason is a reality with which the Bible in some way comes to terms. But this, he will say, is not so: the authoritative Scriptures do not regard the authority of reason as any more of a reality than is the power of an idol, or the truth of a lie. And he will go on to tell us that the word *authority* in our title ought to stand in inverted commas, or be followed by a bracketed question mark, so as to show that the real issue here is whether the Bible will allow us to speak of the 'authority' of reason at all.

So here we have two diametrically opposed positions. The humanist asserts that all authority belongs to human reason; and if there be a god, his status is merely that of patron for the truths which reason determines. The Evangelical Christian asserts that all authority belongs to God the Creator, and not, therefore, to human reason; for human reason is not God. The seat of authority is not in the minds of men, but in the Word of God before which human reason must bow.

From this difference of principle flows a difference of intellectual method. The humanist subjects all things, the teaching of Scripture included, to his own critical judgement. The Evangelical Christian subjects all things, including his own thoughts and those of other men, to the critical judgement of Holy Scripture. Hence, when the humanist and the Evangelical Christian meet in discussion, head-on collisions are inevitable.

But someone will say: surely there is a way of avoiding them? Can we not eliminate these collisions by partitioning the fields of life and truth into two watertight compartments? Can we not mark off the realm of religion from the secular realm, and let the Bible hold sway in the first, while reason rules in the second? Can we not in this way arrange a working agreement—a limited mutual recognition, a concordat—between the Bible and reason? Can we not thus keep the two principles of authority from clashing, by ensuring that they are never both applied to the same subject matter?

No, we cannot. The solution is not feasible, for two reasons. In the first place: how are we to fix the line of demarcation between the two realms? By appealing to the Bible, or to reason? The very act of appealing to one rather than the other is in effect a recognition that the one to which we appeal has authority over the other. Thus we cannot fix any line of demarcation without prejudging the very issue which we were trying to evade. And then, in the second place: neither the Bible nor reason will allow us to partition life and truth in this way. The Evangelical Christian cannot concede that there is any department of life or thought in which the Creator does not demand to rule through his written Word. The Christian will therefore wish to tell the humanist that the Bible, or, rather, the God of the Bible claims to exercise authority over all human thinking, and all human conduct, and that nothing may be exempted from his sway.

Our humanist friends will, I think, be equally anxious to assure us that reason claims to rule the whole of life, and that all we believe and do needs to be brought into line with its dictates. Discussion will show that each side is committed to a programme which includes the conversion of the other. Our humanist friends will tell us that they want to bring us to their way of thinking, because ours is obscurantist and outmoded. We shall reply that we want, under God, to convert them to our way of thinking, because theirs is sin. In other words, the conflict here is between two rival views of life, two totalitarian ideologies, each of which necessarily condemns the other and seeks to overthrow it. And the idea that one could stop this conflict by partitioning life between the two combatants is foolish. One might as well hope to stop two boxers from trying to knock each other out by drawing a chalk line across the ring!

The directness of the opposition between these two outlooks has become clearer in recent years than once it was. A century ago, in Europe and America, post-Christian humanism in its various forms was in an advanced state of growth, but for the most part it had not yet cut loose from the Christian church. By and large, its status was still that of a cuckoo in the church's nest; it was still vaguely theistic, and represented its opinions as a reinterpretation of Christianity rather than as an alternative to it. Only a few bolder spokesmen of the humanistic move-ment, like Nietzsche, ventured as yet to challenge the Christian outlook as a whole; and within the churches only a few prophetic spirits, like Abraham Kuyper, saw the magnitude of the ideological conflict which was brewing. Today, however, things are different. The humanists are now for the most part outside the church, and attacking it; and the trend of modern theology, with its renewed stress on divine revelation and man's bondage to sin, has been such as to make it clear that humanistic self-sufficiency and biblical Christianity will not mix. The conflict between Christianity and humanism in all its many shapes—idealist, materialist, and existentialist—is now generally realized to be a war to the death. It can only end with the collapse or capitulation of one or both of the contending parties.

What I have said has already shown that the Western humanist is in revolt against his Christian cultural heritage. Accordingly, his claim that final authority for life resides in human reason must be understood as a defiant denial of the historic Christian view on which the post-Reformation culture of Europe and America was founded—the view, namely, that final authority for man's life resides in the statements of Holy Scripture. Our humanist friend, whether he calls himself a theist or an atheist, will deny categorically that Holy Scripture is authoritative divine truth in writing. This denial is the foundation on which his whole position rests. It is worth our while to consider at this point how he would justify his view of Holy Scripture.

If faced with this question, our humanist friend will probably think it enough simply to say that the older view of Holy Scripture was overthrown a century ago by the literary, historical, and philosophical critique to which the Bible was then subjected. The Bible, he will say, emerged from this ordeal a discredited oracle, a fallen idol. The view that all biblical assertions were authoritative divine utterances presupposed that all biblical assertions were true. But the effect of criticism was to show that not all biblical assertions are true. The critics taught the Western world to see the Bible as a strange mixture of fact with fancy, and of truth with error. Thus they made it impossible for modern man to go on treating the Bible as God's infallible truth. And thus they made it impossible for modern man to regard biblical statements, as such, as possessing final authority; for final authority cannot attach to statements which are not certainly true.

So our humanist friend will tell us that the old Protestant claim, that final authority for faith and life resides in the teaching of Holy Scripture, has now been exploded, just as the similar claim on behalf of the 'teaching church' was exploded at the time of the Reformation. But this, he will say, compels modern man to make his own reason his final authority for determining belief and behaviour, since no valid external principle of authority now presents itself. As claimants to final authority, both the church and the Bible have demonstrably failed; from now on, therefore, willy-nilly, modern man must find his principle of final authority in himself. This, our humanist friend will say, is as true of the modern Christian as it is of the modern atheist. Henceforth, the theist must ground his theism and the Christian his Christianity on the same appeal to the final authority of reason as the arbiter of fact and the judge of truth that the atheist makes. And the debate between Christians and non-Christians must henceforth be understood as a debate between two kinds of rationalists, two brands of subjectivists, two groups which, however much their tenets differ, do at least find common ground in their common appeal to the authority of the human intellect. And if our humanist friend is knowledgeable in the realm of theology, he may well try to clinch his point by observing that many theological leaders in Western Protestantism do themselves accept this, and are labouring accordingly to reinterpret the biblical faith on rationalistic lines: which observation is, alas, only too true.

It is beyond our present scope to discuss the phenomenon of nineteenth-century biblical criticism in detail; but we cannot let this view of its significance pass unchallenged. What we are being told here is that the historic view of biblical authority was refuted, and the final authority of reason as a judge of truth was established, by the (alleged) collapse of the Bible under critical probing. But this is a mistake. It cannot be said that these positions were established by the last-century critique of Holy Scripture, for the very good reason that they were in fact the concealed presuppositions of that critique itself. Let us demonstrate this.

Consider the two principles on which the critique was avowedly founded. The first was that the biblical record needs to be tested by the ordinary methods of historical research, and that we should not accept them as true further than they can be verified by this means. What does this principle imply? It implies that it is an open question whether biblical assertions are true or not. It implies that we are under no obligation to accept what is in the Bible as truth guaranteed to us by the fact of the Bible's divine authorship. In other words, we may regard ourselves as free to discount the testimony of Scripture to its own inspiration, truth, and authority, and to evaluate Scripture in a way which involves denying these aspects of Scripture's evaluation of itself. So the first principle amounts to this: that we are to proceed on the presupposition—we are, in other words, to take it for granted—that the historic view of biblical authority is false.

Such was the first principle. What of the second? The second principle was that the critical intellect of the scholar has power to discern where the biblical presentation of things is false, and to make a truer reconstruction of what 'really' happened, or what God's thoughts and intentions 'really' were. In other words, we may set reason to the task of correcting Scripture. So the second principle amounts to this: that we are to proceed on the presupposition—we are, that is, to take it for granted—that reason has final authority as a judge of truth, whereas Holy Scripture has not.

Thus it appears that the conclusions supposed to have been established by last-century biblical criticism were really the presuppositions on which it was based. Therefore they cannot be held to have been proved by biblical criticism at all.

How can a presupposition be established? Only by showing that no other presupposition is possible, because all other presuppositions lead to self-contradictory conclusions. Have the presuppositions of the fallibility of Holy Scripture, and the final authority of reason, been established in this way? They have not. Conservative Protestant scholarship has shown abundantly during the past hundred years that the phenomena of Holy Scripture can be accounted for without recourse to these presuppositions, or to any other presuppositions which are not yielded directly by Holy Scripture. It cannot be maintained, therefore, that the presuppositions which underlay last-century biblical criticism were the only possible ones. They were neither necessary nor obligatory; and the mere use of them cannot be held to have established them.

So the significance of last-century biblical criticism was not that it refuted the principle of biblical authority and established the authority of reason in its place. Its real significance was rather as a sign of the times. The fact that rationalistic criticism could establish itself in Protestant Christendom so triumphantly, and win so many of the best minds in the churches to its support, showed how deeply and thoroughly secular assumptions were permeating the nineteenth-century Western mind as a whole. The truth is that secularism laid hold of the entire Western outlook during the last century; science, philosophy, politics, art, all fell under its influence; and its grip has hardly been loosened yet. The appeal to the authority of reason is, of course, the root-principle of secularism. Hence our present subject has a direct relevance to the troubles of our times. For of this we may be sure: that the apostasy of the Western world will not be brought to an end till the authority of reason is rejected, and the authority of God in Holy Scripture is acknowledged once more.

Such, then, is the contemporary background against which our subject must be set. In the light of it, I want to devote the rest of my time to discussing three themes: (1) the idea of the authority of reason in religion; (2) the appeal to the authority of reason in Protestant theology; (3) the estimate of the authority of reason in Holy Scripture.

The Idea of the Authority of Reason in Religion

Our aim in this section is to analyse more closely what is meant by the claim that reason has final authority in the realm of divine things and to show what is involved in making this claim. We begin by defining our terms.

First, then: what is *reason*? In ordinary speech, reason means, first and fundamentally, the power of abstract, analytical thinking. When we speak of the possession of reason as distinguishing man from other animate beings, what we mean is not that animals have no mental processes at all, but that man is the only animate being that can form an abstract idea, construct a definition, analyse a concept, make a generalization, classify, draw inferences, make deductions, conceive hypotheses and means to verify them—in short, do all the things that we lump together under the umbrella-word *ratiocination*. Reason is the faculty whereby man *ratiocinates*.

Why does man ratiocinate? In obedience to the characteristically human impulse to gain knowledge, to find things out, to understand the how and the why and the wherefore of happenings and phenomena, to make sense of his environment, and, if possible, to learn to control it. The object of reason's quest, in a word, is truth. And the fundamental notion of truth is that of correspondence between man's thoughts and that which is objectively the case.

In the realm where statements can be verified by direct observation, the pursuit of truth presents no apparent theoretical problem. It is not hard, for instance, to verify assertions like 'there are more than 80 people in this room,' or 'the date today is August 14th'; nor is it hard to find out the truth about, say, the way that a washing machine works. But in the realm of ultimate meanings, explanations, and values—the realm to which, of course, all theological statements belong—direct observation cannot guide us, and the determination of truth becomes a theoretical problem at once. Is it possible, we ask, for human reason, unaided, to probe this realm? Here is our humanist friend, who regards the Bible as an exploded fairy story and approaches life without reference to the Word of God—has he a right to assume that his own unaided reason can lead him to truth, and keep him from error, in the realm of ultimate realities and values? I submit that two factors in his situation ought to convince him that he has no right to make any such assumption.

The first is his *lack of a criterion of ultimate truth*. He has no final rational test for truth and falsity in the realm of meaning and value. The principle of coherence—the principle, that is, that all truths are consistent both with themselves and with all other truths—is sometimes invoked as if it could provide such a criterion; but it cannot. It does not follow that because a statement, or set of statements, is internally consistent, and contradicts no truth that we know of, therefore it is true. For it is always possible that it contradicts other truths that we do not yet know of. There was a time when Newton's physics passed the coherence test and were regarded as final; but then further truths about planetary movements were discovered with which Newtonian formulae were not consistent, and as a result Newton's physics had to be modified by Einstein. There is no guarantee that any man-made view of anything will not sooner or later share a similar fate. Thus it appears that, because we lack omniscience and so never know what facts we shall stumble on next, we are never entitled to regard the coherence test as a final criterion of truth. Later discoveries may force us to abandon the most seemingly solid hypotheses. But if this is so, our humanist friend is evidently left without any conclusive test of ultimate truth at all. Thus he has no right to assume that it is within his power to find out ultimate truth and avoid fundamental error.

Then, in the second place, he needs to bear in mind *the reality of non-rational influences upon his own thinking,* especially in the realm of morality, ideals, and religion. The point here is that reason is not an abstract cosmic principle, pure and inflexible in all its operations, as the Greeks and Hegel, and many after Hegel, supposed; the reason which operates is always some particular person's reason, and the way that each man thinks will depend to a greater or less degree—certainly more than he himself realizes—on the kind of man that he is. Professor Dooyeweerd of Amsterdam and his colleagues are not the only twentieth-century thinkers to emphasize that each man's point of view and deepest convictions come out of his *heart,* and express and reveal his inmost being.

Modern psychology, in its way, has taught us the same lesson. It has shown us that human ratiocination is profoundly conditioned by unrecognized non-rational factors: temperament and character, physical condition, traumatic experiences which scar the soul, repressions, complexes, reaction to one's upbringing, and the rest. It has made us aware that much of what passes for ratiocination is really rationalization of non-rational impulses. And it has made it plain that no man living can assess adequately the influence which non-rational factors of this kind are exercising upon his total outlook and way of thinking. Freud interpreted Jewish monotheism as a neurotic obsession, but there are grounds for suspecting that it is rather Freud's own atheism that should be accounted for in this way. Who can tell how far his deepest conscious convictions about God and duty have been determined for him by unconscious factors over which in principle he could exercise no control? Our humanist friend, in particular, has no right to assume that he is exempt from such biasing and deflecting influences. And this is a further reason why he is not entitled to assume that the attainment of ultimate truth lies within his power.

But if there is substance in what we have just said, then the claim that final authority in religion belongs to reason begins to sound rather forlorn. Consider what this claim means.

The word *authority* expresses the idea of a rule that is exercised as of right. That which has authority is entitled to legislate and govern. So the claim that final authority in religion belongs to reason must mean this: that when questions arise concerning God, and our relationship to him, each man should set up his own reason as judge, and bow to what it says. He must call before him the various witnesses whose testimony bears on the issue—the biblical authors, the church's tradition, and such individual opinions as seem to him important—and hear them all. But he is to listen to them as a judge listens to evidence, giving no more credence to any of them than the quality of their testimony seems to merit. Man's reason—that is, the thinking individual himself—stands in an autonomous, critical relationship to all the opinions that pass before him. Having heard them, it is now his responsibility to make up his own mind, on the basis of his assessment of the views expressed, and in the light of any relevant convictions and principles of judgement that he may himself have brought to the inquiry. Then he must live by the conclusions he reaches. To claim that final authority in religion belongs to reason is to assert that this is the method by which religious truth is to be sought, and that no other method is legitimate. The claim, in other words, is a demand that every man should act in this way when religious questions press upon him.

Upon this proposed intellectual method we would pass just four comments:

(1) *See what it presupposes.* It assumes that there is no such thing as immediately accessible revelation from God the Creator. For if there were, then it would at once become man's duty to believe and obey it, to renounce this recommended critical autonomy, and to become a humble pupil of the Word of God. In other words, the claim that reason has final authority in religion presupposes, as we pointed out earlier, that the Bible is not infallible and authoritative Divine truth, but something less.

(2) *See where this method leads.* Sooner or later, it is bound to issue in a new authoritarianism. This sounds paradoxical, for the envisaged method purports to be the antithesis of all authoritarianism; but it is nonetheless an inevitable development. Why? Well, for this reason. Sooner or later, each individual thinker will reach the point where he has to acknowledge that in certain departments of religious study he is not expert enough to have a right to an opinion. Therefore he will resolve to defer to those who in his judgement are experts in it. So before long we shall find our champions of freedom from external authority coming to regard the professional biblical critic, or the religious philosopher, or the oracular ecclesiastic, or the confident preacher, or even the pontifical schoolmaster, in precisely the same way in which Roman Catholics regard the priest and the Pope: namely, as persons whose word is to be taken without demur because they know what they are talking about. Here is a further illustration of the inexorable law that those who cast off the authority of the Word of God always end up in bondage to the thoughts and words of their fellow men.

(3) *See how little hope of success this method has.* From what has been said of the limitations of human reason as a tool for discovering truth, and without reference as yet to the mental effects of sin (that will come later), we are already entitled to ask: is it likely that those who trust to the critical authority of reason will be led by it into all religious truth? Is it not, rather, certain that at the end of their explorations they will find themselves in the state described in 1 Corinthians 1:21—'the world by wisdom knew not God'? And is it not, therefore, certain, too, that the only fruit of such experiments will be a collapse into scepticism and nihilism, under a crushing sense of reason's failure and bankruptcy? Indeed, we have only to look around us to see proof of this: for did not the intellectual heroics of last-century philosophy in the realm of religion give rise to just such a temper of disillusionment in European culture? And is not that temper with us to this day?

(4) *See how this method differs* from that which will be followed by the Evangelical Christian, on whose heart God has sealed the authority of his own inspired Word by the testimony of his Holy Spirit. When facing religious questions, the Evangelical Christian also will use his reason, and think hard; but he will not appeal to his own thoughts as in any way authoritative. In all his thinking, the part he seeks to play will be that of a pupil, not a judge. The whole purpose of his intellectual efforts will be to learn of God, to receive what the Bible teaches, to

understand and apply Holy Scripture. He will listen to the words of the biblical writers, not as expressing merely human views of truth, possibly right and possibly wrong, but as God's own words, spoken through human lips: words to be believed, treasured, applied, and obeyed. In all this, he will not dare to lean to his own understanding, but will pray constantly for divine teaching; and his hope of gaining truth from his study of Holy Scripture will rest, not on any confidence in the powers of his own critical intellect, but on his confidence in the power of the Holy Spirit, who inspired the Bible, to interpret it to him. His critical activity in Bible study, therefore, will take the form, not of judging Holy Scripture by his own thoughts, but of correcting his own thoughts in the light of what the Holy Spirit teaches him through the written Word. There could not be a greater contrast in the realm of intellectual method than that between the consistent Evangelical Christian and the protagonist of the authority of reason. And it is now clearer than ever that no compromise is possible between them. To accept either is really to repudiate the other.

This leads us on to the second of our three subjects:

The Appeal to the Authority of Reason in Protestant Theology

Clearly, from what we have said, no such appeal ought ever to be made by Protestant theologians. In fact, however, it has been made, and made in most far-reaching ways, almost since Protestant theology was born. The pattern each time has been the same: current philosophical principles have been taken as axiomatic, without being first tested and corrected by exegesis of Holy Scripture, and then the task of exegesis has itself been reconceived as one of learning to read the Bible in the light of these principles. In other words, reason has been appealed to provide the basic categories for biblical interpretation. Exegetes have brought to the Bible a philosophical strait-jacket and squeezed the Bible into it; or—to illustrate differently—they have played Procrustes, building a bed of philosophical principles, compelling the Bible to lie on it, and ruthlessly twisting and hacking it about, if necessary, in order to make it fit.

The basic perplexities of modern Protestant theology are the direct result of three such episodes—three successive mutilations of the doctrine of God through the intrusion of philosophical principles into biblical exegesis. We may briefly sketch out what these were.

First, at the beginning of the seventeenth century, came the movement of thought which *made God stand back from man.* This was, of course, Arminianism, which read Scripture in the light of the philosophical axiom that man's moral freedom and responsibility are not compatible with divine control of his actions. The Arminians insisted that man acts independently of God, and that man has power to thwart God's plan for his life, and, indeed, for history as a whole, by non-cooperation with God. This was to deny what Reformed theology, following Scripture, had previously taught, namely, that God is Absolute Lord even of free and responsible human actions, as he is of all things beside.

Then, at the end of the seventeenth and in the eighteenth century, came the movement of thought which *made God stand back from his world.* This was English Deism, later exported to provide a theological foundation for the continental Enlightenment. The Deists presupposed the Arminian position, and went further. They read Scripture in the light of the philosophical axiom, drawn from current science, that the universe was to be conceived as a machine, running according to fixed, built-in laws. They pictured God as the Great Mechanic who built the machine, and now stands idle, watching it go. Not only does he not directly control man's actions; he does not directly control anything. His role in history is merely that of an interested spectator. This was to deny a further principle which Reformed theology, following Scripture, had previously taught, namely, that God actively energizes and controls all that comes to pass in his world.

This effective dethroning of God was not reversed when later theologians stressed God's immanent presence in his world rather than his transcendent separation from it; for they did nothing to restore his active lordship over it. The change, therefore, was no improvement. It does not, after all, make much difference in practice whether I bar an unwelcome guest from the house, or lock him in the cellar: and this was really all that the change meant.

Then, in the nineteenth century, the third step was taken: *God was silenced.* This was the contribution of Kant, Schleiermacher, and the Liberals. Liberalism in effect abolished the idea of revelation. It read Scripture in the light of the philosophical axiom that religion is a universal human phenomenon, consisting essentially in a sense of God, having no communicated intellectual content, but evolving as man evolves, and producing in the course of its evolution sacred books in which this sense of God finds more or less adequate expression. This was to deny the historic Reformed and biblical view, namely, that God has spoken to man, and the Bible is, quite simply, his own written account of what, by word and action, he has said. For this view was substituted the idea that the Bible is a human testament of religion—a record of pious impressions and human thoughts about God, but no more.

Thus the authority of reason, intruding into Protestant theology, in effect forbade the Creator to do or say anything in his own world. And this was the intellectual legacy—the combined legacy of Arminianism, Deism, and Liberalism—that twentieth-century theologians inherited. Hence their perplexities. The dominant figures in modern theology—men like Barth, Brunner, Niebuhr, and even Bultmann and Tillich—profess to have reconstruction as their aim, and to be recapturing the lost essence of the biblical faith. But to do this effectively, it is clear that they need to disown the authority of reason, and to repair these breaches in the walls of the Christian faith which a sinful deference to reason has occasioned. Are they, we ask, successfully doing this?

It must be said with regret that on the whole they are not. If I may venture on some provocative generalizations, modern theology presents the spectacle of a kind of intellectual antinomianism. It recognizes its sins, but is not prepared to put them entirely away. It is attempting to recover faith without a complete repentance; to recover the ground that was lost through the three invasions mentioned above without properly repairing the walls, or turning out the invaders. Thus, modern theologians want to recover the reality of revelation in the Bible, and yet they do not want to break with the last-century view of the Bible as a fallible and partly untrue record, nor do they want to part company with the philosopher Kant, whose teaching seemed to rule out any possibility of prepositional revelation. They want to recapture the knowledge of God's sovereignty in the world, and yet they do not want to break with the accepted modern scientific world-view although this view has no time, or is supposed, at least, to have no time, for any concept of miracle. In short, the authority of reason has not yet been thoroughly challenged in modern theology; and until it is, evasive interpretations of Scripture and ambiguous theological syntheses will inevitably continue to be the order of the day. No theologian can serve two masters, and not even Bultmann can convince us that it is possible to maintain faith in God the Redeemer while denying God the Creator and the Lord. But we cannot develop these thoughts here.

We proceed, then, to our third and final subject.

The Estimate of the Authority of Reason in Holy Scripture

Here we raise three questions. First: Whence comes the impulse, common, as we have seen, to our humanist friends outside the church and to a great number of theologians within the church—common, indeed, to us all, though some of us try to resist it—to trust and follow the leading of human reason in matters of religion, rather than be content simply to take God's word for things? Whence, in other words, comes the impulse to exalt reason over revelation, and the sense of outrage which is so widely felt when the authority of reason in religion is challenged? Answer: This spirit springs from *sin*.

To doubt revelation in favour of a private hunch was the sin into which Satan led Eve, and Eve's children have been committing the same sin ever since the fall. The impulse to indulge oneself in believing something other than what God has said is an expression of the craving to be independent of God, which is the essence of sin. The attempt to know all things, including God, by reason, without reference to revelation, is the form that this craving for independence takes in the intellectual realm, just as the attempt to win heaven by works and effort, without grace, is the form that it takes in the moral realm. Pride prompts fallen mankind to go about, not merely to establish their own righteousness, but also to manufacture their own wisdom. The quest all along is for self-sufficiency: our sinful arrogance prompts us to aspire after independence of God in the realm of knowledge. We want to be intellectually autonomous, intellectually self-made men.

This is a sin of which we need to repent and of which the gospel commands us to repent. The gospel not only tells us that it is useless to seek righteousness by works, and commands us to stop doing it, and to put faith in the Lord Jesus Christ as our righteousness with God; the gospel also, and fundamentally, is a message that tells us that it is useless to seek the truth about God by speculation, and it comes to us as a command to stop speculating, and to put faith in what God has said, simply on the grounds that it is he, the God of truth, who has said it.

The gospel, in other words, repudiates absolutely the authority of reason, and demands implicit subjection to God's revealed truth. It is a summons to repentance on the intellectual plane no less than on the moral plane. And this is why it appeared 'foolishness' to the Greeks (1 Cor. 1:23), and why it still appears foolishness to their intellectual descendants in the modern world.

Second: What results from setting up the authority of human reason in the realm of religion? Answer: The result is *ignorance of God*, and *idolatry*—nothing more, and nothing less. In the pagan Gentile world, possessing only God's general revelation of himself through nature and conscience, this ignorance becomes complete, and this idolatry absolute. So it was in the pagan world of Paul's day, and so it is among unevangelized pagan tribes today. The formula that covers this state of affairs is that of 1 Corinthians 1:21: 'The world by wisdom knew not God.' 'Professing themselves to be wise, they became fools, and changed the glory of the incorruptible God into an image made like to corruptible man, and four-footed beasts, and creeping things' (Rom. 1:22f.). Whether the pagans are cultured, like the Greeks, or uncultured, like the South American Indians, makes no significant difference to the situation.

Fallen man's reason is blind through sin, so that no amount of reasoning unaided by the Holy Spirit can find out God. Fallen man's reason is, moreover, the servant of a sinful heart, which does not like to retain God in its knowledge (Rom. 1:28), and labours accordingly to turn the light of general revelation into darkness. Thus men 'hold down the truth in unrighteousness' (Rom. 1:18 RV), and out of their hearts, through the perverting of general revelation, come false gods of all sorts. The hands and minds of men make gods in man's own image, or in the image of something lower than man; and the service of such gods leads to self-debasement, and immorality, and crime, and shame (Rom. 1:26–32).

And in the churches, where gospel light has shone, the only result of paying attention to speculative theology, and allowing private guesses and hunches to determine one's faith to any degree, is ignorance of God, misconceptions of Christ, misdirection of worship, and ethical aberrations, so that one's Christianity is more or less impoverished and distorted. The second chapter of the Epistle to the Colossians bears much pondering in this connection.

Third: What will break men of the habit of looking to the authority of reason in religion? Answer: Only *regeneration* will break it in the natural man, and only *revival* will break it in a regenerate church. Fallen man cannot of himself escape from bondage to sin. Sin he must, whatever he does. It is not in him to acknowledge God's authority; it is not in him to receive God's truth when it is presented to him. 'The natural man receiveth not the things of the Spirit of God, for they are foolishness unto him; neither can he know them, because they are spiritually discerned' (1 Cor. 2:14 KJV). What can cure his condition? Only *regeneration*. Only the man who is born again of the Spirit of God will repent of the sin of intellectual self-sufficiency, and consent to be taught of God through his written Word. As Calvin insisted, it is one of the marks of the Christian man that he is convinced, through the Spirit's inner witness, of the divinity and authority of Holy Scripture, and subjects his mind and binds his conscience to it.

But sin remains in the regenerate, in the mind no less than in the members. And when the fires of spiritual life burn low in the church, the sinful lust for intellectual autonomy reasserts itself. The intellectual apostasy of Western Christendom in recent years is not unconnected with its spiritual lethargy and barrenness: each has both fostered, and been fostered by, the other. What can cure this condition? Only *revival*.

Only a new outpouring of spiritual life can clear the spiritual vision, and bring home to the minds of Christians the power, the authority, and the meaning of 'God's Word written' and enable them to see their mental sins, their intellectual compromises and betrayals of truth, for what they are, and give them strength of mind to repent and cast the sinful ways of thinking out. Only revival will bring a moribund church to subject its thoughts effectively to Holy Scripture, and enable it to apprehend truly and deeply the riches of Christ, 'in whom are hid all the treasures of wisdom and knowledge' (Col. 2:3), and to bring 'every thought into captivity to Christ' (2 Cor. 10:5). There is no question that this is the most urgent and crying need of Protestant Christendom today.

May God revive his work in his Church in this day of wrath, that his people may once again learn to think and live to his honour and glory.

CHAPTER 4

Contemporary Views of Revelation

'What do we mean by revelation? It is a question to which much hard thinking and careful writing are being devoted in our time, and there is a general awareness among us that it is being answered in a way that sounds very differently from the traditional formulations.' These are the opening words of Dr. John Baillie's book *The Idea of Revelation in Recent Thought,*[1] and they are true. Indeed, the point could be stated much more emphatically than this. The question of revelation is at the very heart of the modern theological debate. And, just because Christianity purports to be a revealed religion, whose content and character must be determined from the revelation on which it rests, this means that the real subject under discussion is the essential nature of Christianity. The modern debate is carried on with a measure of awareness of this fact among all parties, though the depth of the cleavage between the Evangelical position and its alternatives within modern Protestantism is not always seen.

The aim of this essay is to survey, from the standpoint of Evangelical faith, some influential lines of thought which are being prosecuted today concerning the nature of God's saving revelation of himself to man and the place of the Bible in that revelation. While limitations of space will preclude a full assessment of representative theologians, we hope to clarify the trends of the day in terms of underlying principles. It would not, in any case, be fair to take isolated statements by modern theologians, on this or any other topic, as purporting to be final. Theologians generally write today in hope of furthering discussions rather than of finishing them, for modern theology is well aware of its own fluid and transitional character. The Barthian hopes that a new epoch of church science is beginning; the liberal has never doubted that the Christian apprehension of God requires constant reassimilation and restatement in terms of shifting cultural forms; and theologians of all sympathies within the ecumenical movement envisage the synthesizing of the scattered insights of a fragmented Christendom as a task that claims urgent attention. None doubts that theology is on the move, however much disagreement there may be as to where it is going. In this situation, it would be risky to regard any particular expressions of view as other than exploratory and provisional. Our aim in this chapter must rather be to understand the tendencies which individual modern views embody, and to ask how far these represent progress along the right lines.

Historical Antecedents of the Modern Debate

We shall best understand the modern debate if we first remind ourselves of its historical antecedents.

From the earliest days of Christianity, the whole church regarded the Bible as a web of revealed truths, the recorded utterances of God bearing witness to himself. Theologians varied in the significance which they attached to the historical character of Scripture (Irenaeus, for instance, allowed it more than Origen). Nor were they all agreed on the limits of the canon, or on the value of allegorical modes of exegesis. But these differences concerned only the meaning and content of Scripture, and presupposed a common view of its character. In the Middle Ages, it came to be held that Scripture needed to be authenticated, interpreted and supplemented by the *ecclesia docens* and that faith (here conceived as *fides*—credence—merely) had as its proper object the teaching of the church as such; but this did not mean any change of view as to the nature of Scripture. The Reformers broke with the Roman position at many points. They enthroned the Spirit in place of the church as the authenticator and interpreter of Scripture; and, since they recognized that the Spirit's testimony to Scripture is given in and through the statements of Scripture itself, they expressed their position by speaking of Scripture as self-authenticating (*autopistos* was Calvin's word) and self-interpreting. As self-interpreting, they held, Scripture must be allowed to fix its own sense from within; arbitrary modes of interpretation, such as were practiced by the medieval allegorists, may not be imposed upon it. Scripture has only one sense: the literal (i.e., natural). This insight made possible for the first time a just appreciation of the literary categories of Scripture, and, guided by it, the Reformers laid the foundations of scientific exegesis. Concern for the literal sense in turn led them to a new understanding of the real contents of Scripture—Law and Gospel, saving history and gracious promise, the love of God revealed in Christ. The self-sufficiency of Scripture was also recognized, and the Bible was set up, according to its own demand, as judge of those traditions which had previously been supposed to supplement it. Faith was now correlated with Scripture, both formally and materially; as a result, the concept of faith was enlarged so as to include, along with credence, *fiducia*—personal trust and reliance upon the biblical promises and the biblical Christ; and the task of theology came to be conceived, not as a matter of systematizing the agglomerated contents of the church's teaching (the medieval view), but as, on the one hand, receiving, studying, and expounding the written Word and, on the other, reforming the belief and practice of the church by it. These changes of view as to the place and use of Scripture in the church were radical and far-reaching; but—and this is the point that now concerns us—there was in all this no break with the historic conception of Scripture as a unified web of revealed truths. Witness to this was borne as eloquently by Luther's doubts about the canonicity of James and Hebrews, on the grounds of their teaching, as by the proliferation of confessions in which the new-found biblical doctrines were set out in creedal form.

From the seventeenth to the nineteenth century, however, the history of Protestant thought was one of steady inroads made into the Reformers' position by the forces of subjectivism. By subjectivism we mean the attitude which posits final authority for faith and life in human reason, conscience or religious sentiment. It is the application to theology of Protagoras' dictum: 'Man is the measure of all things'; defined in terms of the Reformers' position, it means failure to recognize the need of submitting oneself to the correcting judgement of Scripture, and betrays an unwarrantable confidence in the power of the unaided human mind to work out religious truth for itself. It perverts the Reformers' principle of the right of private judgement from a demand for freedom to be subject to Scripture into a demand for freedom from such subjection: freedom, that is, to disagree with Scripture where it does not fit in with our previous ideas. Subjectivism has taken two characteristic forms: *rationalistic* and *mystical*. In the first, final appeal in matters of faith is made to the verdict of speculative reason, informed by extra-biblical principles of judgement; in the second, to the content of the empirical religious consciousness. The first appeared on the circumference of seventeenth-century Protestant orthodoxy, in certain a priori developments and modifications of the doctrine of Scripture and in a widespread reversion to the Scholastic belief in the validity of natural theology. But the great efflorescence of rationalistic subjectivism came in the eighteenth-century Enlightenment. The 'age of reason' forced Christianity on to the Procrustes' bed of Deism. The Enlightenment was avowedly naturalistic in temper, being as hostile to the idea of supernatural interruptions of the ordered course of nature as to that of supernatural revelation. Accordingly, it whittled down Christianity, as the English Deists had done earlier, to a mere republication of the religion of nature. Kant, the greatest philosopher of the movement, denied the very possibility of factual knowledge concerning a super sensible order, and this appeared to seal the fate of the historic doctrine of revelation. The legacy of the Enlightenment to the church of later days was the axiom that certainly some biblical teaching, and perhaps all, is not revealed truth; biblical affirmations, therefore, should not be received except as confirmed by reason. Modern Protestantism has not yet fully rid itself of the incubus of this rationalistic axiom, as we shall see.

At this point Schleiermacher, the father of modern liberal theology, introduced the mystical type of subjectivism into Christian thought. He sought thereby to save Christianity from rationalistic malaise, but, despite all the skill of his ministrations, the cure was in some ways worse than the disease. To side-step Kant's critique of the idea of revealed truth, he abandoned the notion altogether, and argued that Christianity is essentially not knowledge but a feeling of dependence on God through Christ. The Christian faith is simply an infectious historical mysticism, 'caught' (like measles) from contact with others who have it. Doctrine does not create Christian experience, but is created by it. Doctrinal statements are attempts to express in words borrowed from the culture of the day the contents of the corporate Christian consciousness, and theology is the systematic examination of this consciousness as thus expressed. The proper study of theologians is man; theology is an account of certain human feelings, and its method is that of a psychological science. Man's self-consciousness is the reference point of all theological statements; to make them is simply a way of talking about oneself; they tell us nothing of God, but only what men feel about God. Theology is thus dogmatically agnostic about God and his world. As a science, it knows nothing of any events but states of mind. For information about the nature of the world and the course of history—including the historical process out of which Christianity came—it looks to other sciences. It reads the Bible as a classic expression of religious experiences, but is not concerned with it as anything more. Schleiermacher's position made the idea of revelation really superfluous, for it actually amounted to a denial that anything is revealed. On his principles, divine revelation must be simply equated with human advance into God-consciousness. Thus, his legacy to the church can be summed up in the axiom that, whatever else revelation may be, it is not a communication of truth from God to man. This, too, is an incubus which the church has not yet succeeded in throwing off.

The vacuum left by Schleiermacher's denial that Christianity involves any positive world-view or historical affirmations was swiftly filled by nineteenth-century science. The devotees of 'scientific' history practiced 'higher criticism' on the biblical records and rewrote the story of Hebrew-Christian religion in terms of the naturalistic principle of unilinear evolution. The supernaturalism which, in fact, determines the whole biblical outlook was eliminated as a matter of method; that miracles happen was not considered a permissible hypothesis, and miracle-stories in the Bible, it was held, should be dismissed as superstitious accretions, just as such stories should be if found in any other document. The question-begging character of this procedure was not seriously considered. Meanwhile, the 'scientific' concept of evolution was pressed into service to provide a clue to the meaning of history, sacred and secular alike, and a glowing eschatology of inevitable progress. These rationalistic developments had the blessing of Schleiermacher's disciples, for they did not in any way impoverish Christianity as this school conceived it. And the liberal understanding of Christianity grew increasingly dominant throughout the nineteenth century.

Rise of 'Post-Liberal' Theology

The First World War seemed to explode quite decisively the eschatology of inevitable progress, and led to a deep-seated uncertainty as to the rightness of the anthropocentric view of religion which had so gaily sponsored it. In this situation, two significant theological movements appeared, both stressing from complementary angles of approach the reality of the revealing action whereby God speaks to sinful man in judgement and mercy. The first was the dialectical 'crisis-theology' of Karl Barth, which summoned the church in the name of God to humble herself and listen to his catastrophic Word. The second was the 'biblical theology' movement, which first became articulate in English through the work of Sir Edwyn Hoskyns, calling the biblical scholar in the name of historical objectivity to recognize that the Bible cannot warrantably be treated as a book of mystical devotion, nor as a hard core of non-supernatural history overlaid with inauthentic theology, but that it must be read as a churchly confession of faith in a God who has spoken and speaks still. These two movements, linked together in all manner of combinations, are the parent stems from which the theology of the past generation has grown. Taking as their own starting point the reality of divine revelation, they have forced the church to reconsider this theme with renewed seriousness, and to recognize that the proper task of theology is not reading off the surface level of the mind of man, as subjectivism supposed, but receiving, expounding and obeying the Word of God.

But this raises a crucial and complex problem for the theologian of the 'post-liberal' age: how are we to conceive of the Word of God? In what relation does it stand to the Bible, and the Bible to it? The complexity of this issue in the minds of present-day theologians arises from the fact that they suppose themselves to be standing amid the wreckage of two fallen idols. On the one hand, the older orthodoxy, which recognized the reality of revelation and sought to build on it, was founded on belief in verbal inspiration and inerrancy; but these beliefs, it is said, have collapsed before the onslaught of biblical criticism, and are no longer tenable. On the other hand, nineteenth-century liberalism, with all its devotion to biblical science and the study of the religious consciousness, left no room for revelation at all; and that is seen not to be satisfactory either. A new synthesis is held to be required, incorporating what was right and avoiding what was wrong in both the older views. The problem, therefore, as modern theology conceives it, is this: how can the concept of divine revelation through the Bible be reintroduced without reverting to the old, 'unscientific' equation of the Bible with the Word of God? It is admitted that the biblical idea of revelation must be in some sense normative; and the main strands in the biblical idea—that revelation is a gracious act of God causing men to know him; that his self-communication has an objective content; that faith and unbelief are correlative to revelation, the former meaning reception of it, the latter, rejection; that the subject matter of revelation concerns Jesus Christ; and that the act of revelation is effected, and its content mediated, through Scripture, are matters of general recognition. It is seen, too, that Schleiermacherian mysticism, which denies the reality of revelation *in toto,* and naturalistic rationalism, which substitutes for faith in what God has said faith in what I think, are both wrong in principle. Yet, it is said, we cannot go back on the liberal view of the Bible. Hence the problem crystallizes itself as follows: how can we do justice to the reality and intelligibility of revelation without recourse to the concept of revealed truth? How can we affirm the accessibility of revelation in Scripture without committing ourselves to belief in the absolute trustworthiness of the biblical record? How can we assert the divine authority of biblical revelation without foreclosing the possibility—indeed, it would be said, the proved reality—of human error in Scripture? Or, putting it the other way round, how on the basis of the nineteenth-century view of the Bible can we vindicate the objectivity and givenness of revelation, and so keep out of the pitfalls of mysticism and rationalism? Plainly, this is a problem of some difficulty. *Prima facie,* it would seem to be an inquiry after ways and means of having one's cake and eating it. The aim proposed is, not to withdraw the Bible from the acid-bath of rationalistic criticism, but to find something to add to the bath to neutralize its corrosive effects. The problem is how to enthrone the Bible once more as judge of the errors of man while leaving man enthroned as judge of the errors of the Bible; how to commend the Bible as a true witness while continuing to charge it with falsehood. One cannot help thinking that it would be something of a tour de force to give a convincing solution of a problem like this. However, such is the task attempted by modern theology. It is proposed, by drawing certain distinctions and introducing certain new motifs, so to refashion the doctrine of revelation that the orthodox subjection of heart and mind to biblical authority and the liberal subjection of Scripture to the authority of rationalistic criticism appear, not as contradictory, but as complementary principles, each presupposing and vindicating the other. We are now to examine some of the main ideas about the nature of revelation and its relation to Scripture which have been put forward in recent years for the furtherance of this enterprise.

Current Views of Revelation and Scripture

Before going further, however, it is worth pausing to see on what grounds modern theology bases its rejection of the historic view that biblical revelation is prepositional in character; for, though this rejection has become almost a commonplace of modern discussion, and is, of course, axiomatic for those who accept Schleiermacher's interpretation of Christianity, it is clearly not something that can just be taken for granted by those who profess to reject his view.

J. K. S. Reid recognizes that 'there is no a priori reason why the Bible should not have this . . . character' (viz., that of being a corpus of divinely guaranteed truths).[2] But if that is so, the a posteriori arguments brought against this view must be judged very far from decisive.

Archbishop Temple, in his much-quoted discussions of our subject,[3] rejected this conception of Scripture on three counts: first, that little of it seems to consist of formal theological propositions; second, that little or none of it seems to have been produced by mechanical 'dictation,' or anything like it; third, that if we are to regard the Bible as a body of infallible doctrine we shall need an infallible human interpreter to tell us what it means; and 'in whatever degree reliance upon such infallible direction comes in, spirituality goes out.'[4] But, we reply, the first two points are irrelevant, and the third false. To assert prepositional revelation involves no assertions or expectations a priori as to the literary categories to which the parts of Scripture will belong (only study of the text can tell us that); what is asserted is merely that all affirmations which Scripture is found to make, and all other statements which demonstrably embody scriptural teaching, are to be received as truths from God. Nor does this position involve any a priori assertions as to the psychology of inspiration, let alone the mechanical 'dictation-theory,' which no Protestant theologian seems ever to have held.[5] Temple's third point we deny; we look to Scripture itself to teach us the rules for its own interpretation, and to the Holy Spirit, the church's only infallible teacher, to guide us into its meaning, and we measure all human pronouncements on Scripture by Scripture's own statements.

Others raise other objections to our view of the nature of Scripture. It is said, for instance, that modern study has proved that Scripture errs. But *proved* is quite the wrong word: the truth is, rather, that modern critical scholarship has allowed itself to assume that the presence of error in Scripture is a valid hypothesis, and to interpret the phenomena of Scripture in line with this assumption. However, the hypothesis has never in any case been shown to be necessary, nor is it clear how it could be; and the biblical doctrine of Scripture would rule it out as invalid in principle. Again, it is held that to regard the Bible as written revelation is bibliolatry, diverting to Scripture honour due only to God. But the truth is rather that we honour God precisely by honouring Scripture as his written Word. Nor is there more substance in the claim that to assert the normative authority of Scripture is to inhibit the freedom of the Spirit, who is Lord of the Word; for the Spirit exercises his lordship precisely in causing the church to hear and reverence Scripture as the Word of God, as Calvin reminded the Anabaptists more than four centuries ago.

However, despite the inconclusiveness of the arguments for taking this line and the Bible's self-testimony on the other side, modern theology finds its starting point in a denial that Scripture, as such, is revealed truth. The generic character which this common denial imparts to the various modern views is clearly brought out by Daniel Day Williams in the following passage:

In brief this is the new understanding of what revelation is ... Revelation as the 'self-disclosure of God' is understood as the actual and personal meeting of man and God on the plane of history. Out of that meeting we develop our formulations of Christian truth in literal propositions ... Revelation is disclosure through personal encounter with God's work in his concrete action in history. It is never to be identified with any human words which we utter in response to the revelation. In *Nature, Man and God*, William Temple described revelation as 'intercourse of mind and event, not the communication of doctrine distilled from that intercourse.'

Doctrines, on this view, are not revelation, though they are formulated on the basis of revelation. As Temple put it elsewhere,

There is no such thing as revealed truth ... There are truths of revelation, that is to say, propositions which express the results of correct thinking concerning revelation; but they are not themselves directly revealed.[6]

What this really means is that the historic Christian idea of revelation has been truncated; the old notion that one part of God's complex activity of giving us knowledge of himself is his teaching us truths about himself is hereby ruled out, and we are forbidden any more to read what is written in Scripture as though it were God who had written it. We are to regard Scripture as a human response and witness to revelation, but not in any sense revelation itself. After observing that nearly all theologians today take this view, Williams goes on, in the passage from which we have already quoted, to explain the significance of this change:

What it means [he writes] is that Christian thought can be set free from the intolerable dogmatism which results from claiming that God's truth is identical with some human formulation of it [scriptural no less than later creedal, apparently] ... It gives freedom for critical re-examination of every Christian statement in the light of further experience, and in the light of a fresh encounter with the personal and historical act of God in Christ.[7]

Professor Williams' statement well sums up the modern approach, and its wording suggests at once the basic problem which this approach raises: namely, the problem of objectivity in our knowledge of God. What is the criterion whereby revelation is to be known? If there is no revealed truth, and the Bible is no more than human witness to revelations, fallible and faulty, as all things human are, what guarantee can we have that our apprehensions of revelation correspond to the reality of revelation itself? We are sinful men, and have no reason to doubt that our own thoughts about revelation are as fallible and faulty as any; by what standard, then, are we to test and correct them? Is there a standard, the use of which opens in principle a possibility of conforming our ideas of revelation to the real thing? Historic Christianity said yes: the biblical presentation of, and pattern of thinking about, revelation-facts is such a standard. Modern theology, however, cannot say this; for the characteristic modern position really boils down to saying that the only standard we have for testing our own fallible judgements is our own fallible judgement. It tells us that what we study in Scripture is not revelation but the witness of faith to revelation; and that what as Christian students we have to do is critically to examine and assess the biblical witness by the light, not of extra-biblical principles (that, it is agreed, would be illegitimate rationalism), but of the contents of revelation itself, which the church by faith has some idea of already, and which it seeks to clarify to itself by this very study. Such, we are told, is the existential situation in which, and the basic motive for which, the church studies Scripture. And the 'critical re-examination of every Christian statement in the light of further experience' which is here in view is a reciprocal process of reconsidering and reinterpreting the faith of the church and the faith of the Bible in terms of each other: not making either universally normative for the other, but evolving a series of working approximations which are offered as attempts to do justice to what seems essential and constitutive in both.

Theology pursued in this fashion is held to be 'scientific,' and that on two accounts. In the first place, it is said, theology is hereby established as the 'science of faith,' a strictly empirical discipline of analysing the contents of Christian faith in its actual manifestations in order to elucidate the nature of the relationship which faith is, and of the object to which it is a response. (Reference in these terms to the reality of the object of faith is thought to parry the charge that this is just Schleiermacher over again.) Then, in the second place, this theological method is held to vindicate its scientific character by the fact that, in interpreting and restating the faith of the Bible, it takes account of the 'scientific' critical contention that the biblical witness contains errors and untruths, both factual and theological—a contention which, no doubt, is generally regarded these days as part of the faith of the church. But it is clear that theology, so conceived, is no more than a dexterous attempt to play off two brands of subjectivism against each other. On the one hand, the subject proposed for study is still the church's witness to its own experience, as such, and the contents of Scripture are still treated simply as important material within this category. It is true that (at the prompting of critical reason) the *prima facie* character of this experience, as one of objective relationship with a sovereign living God, is now taken seriously, and that due respect is paid to the church's conviction that the biblically recorded experience of prophets and apostles marks a limit outside which valid Christian experience is not found, but this does not affect the basic continuity between the modern approach and that of Schleiermacher. On the other hand, autonomous reason still acts as arbiter in the realm of theological methodology, following only those principles of judgement which it can justify to itself as 'scientific' on the basis of its own independent assessment of the real nature of Christianity. It is true that (out of regard for the distinctive character of Christian experience) this 'scientific' method recognizes the uniqueness of Christianity and resists all attempts to minimize it; and to this end it requires us to master the biblical thought-forms, in terms of which this unique experience received its classical expression. But it does not require us to accept the biblical view of their objective significance except insofar as our reason, judging independently, endorses that view; and in this respect it simply perpetuates the theological method of the Enlightenment. The effect of following the modern approach has naturally been to encourage a kind of biblical double-talk, in which great play is made with biblical terms, and biblical categories are insisted on as the proper medium for voicing Christian faith, but these are then subjected to a rationalistic principle of interpretation which eliminates from them their basic biblical meaning (e.g., a story such as that of the fall is treated as *mythical,* significant and true as a symbol revealing the actual state of men today, but false if treated as the record of an objective historical happening). Thus theological currency has been debased, and a cloud of ambiguity now broods over much modern 'biblicism.' This, at least, is to the credit of Bultmann that, having pursued this approach so radically as to categorize the whole New Testament doctrine of redemption as mythical, he has seen, with a clear-headedness denied to many, that the most sensible thing to do next is to drop the mythology entirely and preach simply that brand of existentialism which, in his view, represents the New Testament's real 'meaning.'

It is clear that, 'scientific' or not, this nicely balanced synthesis of two forms of subjectivism is not in any way a transcending of subjectivism. It leaves us still to speculate as to what the biblical symbols and experiences mean, and what is the revelation which they reflect and to which they point. It leaves us, indeed, in a state of utter uncertainty; for, if it is true (as Scripture says, and modern theology mostly agrees) that men are sinful creatures, unable to know God without revelation, and prone habitually to pervert revelation when given, how can we have confidence that the biblical witness, and the church's experience, and our own ideas are not all wrong? Why should we think that by a 'scientific' amalgam of the three we shall get nearer to the reality of revelation than we were before? What trust can we put in our own ability to see behind the biblical witness to revelation so surely that we can pick out its mistakes and correct them? Such questions did not trouble the subjectivist theologians of the eighteenth and nineteenth centuries, who assumed the infallibility of the human intellect and wholly overlooked the noetic effects of sin; but the mid-twentieth century, haunted by memories of shattered philosophies and exploded ideals, and bitterly aware of the power of propaganda and brain-washing, and the control that non-rational factors can have over our thinking, is tempted to despair of gaining objective knowledge of anything, and demands from the church reasoned reassurance as to the accessibility of divine revelation to blind, bedevilled sinners. But such reassurance cannot in principle be given by those who on scriptural grounds acknowledge the reality of sin in the mind, and hence the bankruptcy of rationalism, and yet on rationalistic grounds jettison the notion of inscripturated divine truth. For unless at some point we have direct access to revelation normatively presented, by which we may test and correct our own fallible notions, we sinners will be left to drift on a sea of speculations and doubts forever. And when modern theology tells us that we can trust neither the Bible nor ourselves, it condemns us to this fate without hope of reprieve.

Modern theology is, indeed, fully aware of the scriptural and churchly conviction that revelation is objectively and normatively presented in and by the biblical witness to it. In an attempt to do justice to this conviction while still holding Scripture to be no more than fallible human testimony, theologians focus attention on two 'moments' in the divine self-revealing activity in which, they affirm, revelation does in fact confront us directly and authoritatively. These are, on the one hand, the sequence of historical events in which revelation was given, once for all, to its first witnesses; and, on the other, the repeated 'encounter' in which the content of that original revelation is mediated to each successive generation of believers. Both 'moments,' of course, have a proper place in the biblical concept of revelation; what is distinctive about the modern view is not its insistence on them, as such, but its attempt to do justice to them while dispensing with that which in fact links them together and is integral to the true notion of each—namely, the concept of infallible Scriptures, given as part of the historical revelatory process and conveying that which is mediated in the 'encounter.' Most modern statements make mention of both 'moments' in combination (compare Williams' reference to 'a fresh encounter with the personal and historical act of God in Christ'), but they vary in the emphasis given to each. Scholars whose main interest is in biblical history, such as C. H. Dodd and H. Wheeler Robinson, naturally stress the first.[8] Those chiefly concerned with systematic theology and apologetics, such as (reading from the right wing to the left) Karl Barth, Emil Brunner, H. Richard and Reinhold Niebuhr, Paul Tillich, and Rudolph Bultmann lay more stress on the second.[9] These theologians all agree that what is communicated in the 'encounter' is that which was given once for all in Christ; where they differ is in their views as to the essential content of the primary revelation and the precise nature of the existential 'encounter.' A third group of more philosophically minded theologians have devoted themselves to fixing and holding a balance between these two emphases: among them, the late Archbishop Temple, Alan Richardson, and John Baillie.[10]

Can the objective accessibility of revelation be vindicated in these terms? We think not. Consider first the idea that revelation, imperfectly mirrored in the Bible, is directly available in the historical events of which the Bible bears witness. Temple expounded this idea very clearly. He thought of revelation as God's disclosure of his mind and character in the 'revealing situations' of redemptive history. At no stage does God give a full verbal explanation of what he is doing, but he enlightens prophetic spirits to discern it. (The notion somewhat suggests a divine charade, to be solved by the God-inspired guesswork of human spectators.) The biblical authors were prophetic men, and made roughly the right deductions from what they observed; though their recounting and explaining of revelation is marred throughout by errors due to human frailty. Our task is critically to work over the records which they left, checking and where necessary correcting their representations; and the facts themselves, thus discerned, will speak their own proper meaning to us.

But (not to dwell on the arbitrary and unbiblical features of this view, and the fact that, if true, it would create a new authoritarianism, by making the expert historian final arbiter of the church's faith) we must insist that, on this showing, so far from being able to use historical revelation as a norm, we can only have access to it at all through prior acceptance of another norm. For, as Alan Richardson points out, commenting on Temple, all our study of the past is decisively controlled by the principle of interpretation which we bring to it; that is, by our antecedent ideas as to the limits of possibility, the criteria of probability and the nature of historical 'meaning' and explanation. In this case, if we do not already share the supernaturalism of the biblical writers' faith about God and his work in his world, we shall be debarred from sharing their convictions as to what happened in redemptive history. So the revealing facts of history are only accessible to those who are already sure that Christianity is true. And how do we become sure of this? By faith, says Richardson. But what is faith? Receiving what God has said, on his authority, is the basic biblical idea. But Richardson cannot say this, for he has already told us that until we have faith we are in no position to gather from the human records of Scripture what it is that God has said. He wishes (rightly) to correlate faith with spiritual illumination. But he cannot depict this illumination as an opening of blind eyes to see what objectively was always the case—that the Bible is God's Word written, and its teaching is his revealed truth; for to his mind this is not the case. He is therefore forced back into illuminism. He has to represent faith as a private revelation, a divine disclosure of new information not objectively accessible—namely, that what certain human writers said about God is in fact true. On his assumption that Scripture, as such, is no more than human witness, there is nothing else he can say. So we see that the idea of an objective presentation of revelation in history, when divorced from the idea of a divinely authoritative record, can only in principle be maintained on an illuministic basis. Before I can find revelation in history, I must first receive a private communication from God: and by what objective standard can anyone check this? There is no norm for testing private revelations. We are back in subjectivism with a vengeance.

At this point, however, appeal will be made to the concept of 'personal encounter.' This, as generally expounded, attempts to parry the charge of illuminism by the contention that God, in sovereign freedom, causes the biblical word of man to become his word of personal address in the moment of revelation. Brunner has, perhaps, made more of this line of thought than anyone else. Basing it on an axiomatic refusal to equate the teaching of Scripture, as such, with the Word of God, he treats the concept of personal encounter as excluding that of prepositional communication absolutely. God's Word in the encounter comes to me, not as information, but as demand, and faith is not mental assent, but the response of obedience. Truth becomes mine through the encounter; but this truth consists, not in any impersonal correspondence of my thoughts with God's facts, but in the personal correspondence of my decision with God's demand. Truth is that which happens in the response of faith, rather than anything that is said to evoke that response; 'truth' is an event, correlative to the event of revelation which creates it. But this is a very difficult conception. If we are to take seriously Brunner's Pickwickian use of the word 'truth,' then his idea is one of a communion in which nothing is communicated save a command. God speaks only in the imperative, not at all in the indicative. But is it a recognizable statement of the Christian view of revelation to say that God tells us nothing about himself, but only issues orders? And what is the relation between the command given in the encounter and what is written in Scripture? Never one of identity, according to Brunner; Scripture is human witness proceeding from and pointing to communication in encounter; but not embodying its content; for that which is given in the encounter is ineffable, and no form of words can properly express it. So, where Augustine said: 'What thy Scripture says, that (only that, but all that) thou dost say,' Brunner says: 'What thy Scripture says, that is precisely not what thou dost say.' But how, in this case, can Brunner parry the charge of uncontrolled and uncontrollable mysticism? Nor would he be better off if he said that what is spoken by God in the encounter is the exact content of Scripture texts, that and no more; for then he would either have to abandon the idea that Scripture is throughout nothing but fallible and erring human testimony, or else to say that God speaks human error as his truth, which is either nonsense or blasphemy.

Has the objectivity of revelation been vindicated by this appeal to the 'encounter'? Has anything yet been said to make intelligible the claim that, though we regard Scripture as no more than fallible human witness, we still have available an objective criterion, external to our own subjective impressions, by which our erring human ideas about revelation can be measured and tested? It seems not. By deserting Richardson for Brunner, we seem merely to have exchanged a doctrine of illuminism (private communication of something expressible) for one of mysticism (private communication of something inexpressible). The problem of objectivity is still not solved; and, we think, never can be on these terms.

Lessons from the Contemporary Situation

From this survey, sketchy as it is, we learn three things.

First, we see the essential kinship of the various modern views of revelation. They differ in detail, but all begin from the same starting point and have the same aim: to restore essential biblical dimensions to the older liberal position.

Second, we see the dilemmas in which modern theology hereby involves itself. 'Post-liberal' thought turns out to be liberalism trying to assimilate into itself certain biblical convictions which, once accepted, actually spell its doom. The spectacle which it provides is that of liberalism destroying itself by poisoning its own system. For liberalism, as such, rests, as we saw, on a rationalistic approach to the Bible; and the acceptance of these new insights makes it as irrational in terms of rationalism as it always was unwarrantable in terms of Christianity to continue following such an approach. By recognizing the incomprehensibility of God and his sovereign freedom in revelation, while retaining its peculiar view of Scripture—by trying, that is, to find room for supra-rational factors on its own rationalistic basis—liberalism simply lapses from coherent rationalism into incoherent irrationalism. For the axiom of rationalism in all its forms is that man's mind is the measure of all things; what is real is rational, and only what is rational is real, so that in terms of rationalism the supra-rational is necessarily equated with the irrational and unreal. By allowing for the reality of God who in himself and in his works passes our comprehension, theological rationalism declares its own bankruptcy, and thereby forfeits its quondam claim to interpret and evaluate Scripture, with the rest of God's works, on rationalistic principles: a claim which it could only make on the assumption of its own intellectual solvency. It is simply self-contradictory for modern theology still to cling to the liberal concept of Scripture while professing to have substituted the biblical for the liberal doctrine of God. And the fact that it continues to do the former cannot but create doubt as to whether it has really done the latter.

Again, by admitting the noetic effects of sin, and the natural incompetence of the human mind in spiritual things, without denying the liberal assumption that reason has both the right and the power to test and explode the Bible's view of its own character as revealed truth, modern theology is in effect telling us that now we know, not merely that we cannot trust Scripture, but also that we cannot trust ourselves; which combination of convictions, if taken seriously, will lead us straight to dogmatic scepticism. Thus, through trying to both have our cake and eat it, we shall be left with nothing to eat at all. Modern theology only obscures this situation, without remedying it, when it talks here of paradox and dialectical tension. The truth is that, by trying to hold these two self-contradictory positions together, modern theology has condemned itself to an endless sequence of arbitrary oscillations between affirming and denying the trustworthiness of human speculations and biblical assertions respectively. It could only in principle find stability in the sceptical conclusion that we can have no sure knowledge of God at all.

Thirdly, we see that the only way to avoid this conclusion is to return to the historic Christian doctrine of Scripture, the Bible's own view of itself, as embraced and taught by Jesus and the apostles, which this book[11] is concerned to present. Only when we abandon the liberal view that Scripture is no more than fallible human witness, needing correction by us, and put in its place the biblical conviction that Scripture is in its nature revealed truth in writing, an authoritative norm for human thought about God, can we in principle vindicate the Christian knowledge of God from the charge of being the incorrigibly arbitrary product of our own subjective fancy. Reconstructed liberalism, by calling attention to the reality of sin, has shown very clearly our need of an objective guarantee of the possibility of right and true thinking about God; but its conception of revelation through historical events and personal encounter with the speaking God ends, as we saw, in illuminism or mysticism, and is quite unable to provide us with such a guarantee. No guarantee can, in fact, be provided except by a return to the old paths, that is, by a renewed acknowledgement of, and submission to, the Bible as an infallible written revelation from God.

CHAPTER 5

An Evangelical View of Progressive Revelation

Of 'progressive revelation' (the quotation marks are his), James Barr writes, 'Everything depends on what is meant by the term.'[1] It does indeed. Both 'revelation' and 'progress' mean different things to different people. Put them together and the result, semantically speaking, is most slippery. You have been warned!

We hear less of 'progressive revelation' today than we once did. The more recent theological fashions (Biblicist neo-orthodoxy, Tillich's new gnosticism, the existentialism of the demythologizers, neo-Romanism, and neo-Evangelicalism) bypass the theme. Why? Because they are all, in their different ways, anti-evolutionary and anti-historicist. They view Scripture functionally, as a means of revelation in the present, rather than as a revelatory record of a revelatory process in the past. Whether this approach is well balanced can be and often is questioned, but for the moment it remains dominant; hence, interest in 'progressive revelation' is small, save among exponents of older points of view. The situation has changed strikingly over half a century since C. H. Dodd took 'Progressive Revelation' (in quotation marks) as the title for a key chapter in his book *The Authority of the Bible* (1928; revised 1938, 1960), calling it 'a current phrase.'[2]

It was a phrase liberal Protestants had coined; during the generation before Dodd's book, they had repeatedly urged it as the clue needed for understanding the Bible. What did they mean by it?

Liberal Protestant Views

The liberal notion was that the religious process the Bible reflects should be explained in terms of evolution. Evolutionary explanatory concepts (models, we should call them) were much in vogue a century ago in biology, cosmology, anthropology, politics, and sociology; and it was only natural that they should also be tried out in the field of religion. Evolutionary thinking had two roots, Hegel's philosophical account of spirit (*Geist*) unfolding from within and Darwin's biological theory of the origin of species from a primitive cell. Evolutionary hypotheses assumed that under stimulation from outside, things grow and diversify from within by realizing their built-in potential, and that with complexity comes value. Out of the 'lower' comes the 'higher'; the 'primitive' yields to the developed'; and the end product is more adequate in its meshing with reality than that which went before. The intellectual counterpart is that a truer grasp of things comes to replace 'crude' notions that were less true. 'Progress' was the name given to each process thus conceived.

Evolutionary hypotheses did not claim that such processes were always free from false starts and wrong turnings; they only claimed that what finally emerged in each case was a developed realization of potential within an existing system, as distinct from a divine creative intrusion. The only theological frame into which evolutionary hypotheses would fit was a thoroughgoing immanency ('some call it evolution, some call it God'); and even so, by dogmatically denying unique works of God within the created order, these hypotheses set themselves apart from and indeed against biblical theism. Philosophically, they took for granted a natural affinity between man's mind and ultimate reality, according to the idealist slogan that the real is the rational and the rational is the real. For liberals it was axiomatic that what our minds and hearts at their best think about God is actual knowledge of God, truer and more trustworthy than 'lower' views, wherever found, even in the Bible. Sadly, the liberal criterion of 'hearts and minds at their best' was secular, relativist, and provincial; 'at their best' meant, in practice, 'most in line with the perspectives (partly Christianized, partly de-Christianized) of western European intellectual culture today.'

On the basis of the redating of the Pentateuch and Joshua, which is now part of 'critical orthodoxy' in the schools, liberal Protestants considered the writing prophets from Amos and Hosea to Jeremiah and 'second-Isaiah,' and then Jesus and his apostles as marking the two crucial stages of advance from lower to higher in the biblical religious process. Moses, the Robin Hood of Israelite folklore, was a murky figure about whose actual achievements nothing certain could be shown; but the ethical monotheism which the prophets were held to have developed within Israel, and which Jesus was held to have universalized by announcing God's fatherhood and man's brotherhood, was solid historical fact. Whether, as Schleiermacher had thought, Jesus represents an all-time climax of religious development, the topmost rung of the evolutionary ladder as far as God-consciousness was concerned, or whether, as Troeltsch urged, a higher syncretism must be in the pipeline of the ongoing religious world process were details of debate within the liberal camp. But the evolutionary reading of the Bible sketched above was the manifesto and rallying ground for all liberal forces.

Within this framework, the words 'progressive revelation' came to bear a quite precise meaning. They signified an initial discernment by the eighth-, seventh-, and sixth-century writing prophets, followed, after a temporary regression under Judaism, by Jesus' purer distillation of the best and truest ideas of God and goodness that the world has yet seen. The fact that the graph of advance, after running up from earlier crudities to the prophets, then stayed level or turned down for more than five hundred years was not held to invalidate the 'progressive' character of the process, and the fact that what developed was true understanding of God seemed ample warrant for calling the entire process 'revelation.'

Value of 'Progressive Revelation'

The doctrine of 'progressive revelation' was valued in its day for critical, interpretive, apologetic, and theological reasons. First, from the critical standpoint, it seemed to give religious sanction and support to the scepticism about Moses and the patriarchs that flowed from the fashionable Graf-Wellhausen hypothesis that the Pentateuch is late and unauthentic, constantly reading back later ideas into an idealized past. The 'progressive revelation' concept showed that one can embrace this scepticism without loss, since what matters is the ideas themselves rather than the date of their first arrival, and that one will grasp them better by seeing the real course of their historical growth.

Second, from the interpretive standpoint, 'progressive revelation' seemed to map a highway through the Bible, pinpointing what mattered most, giving criteria by which the rest might be judged, and enabling us to see which parts must now be held to lack authority for Christians, being relatively 'primitive' and falling short of full and final vision.

Third, from the apologetic standpoint, 'progressive revelation' would excuse and justify elements in Scripture that are so 'primitive,' morally and religiously speaking, as to embarrass cultured men (two generations ago, anyway; cultured men are perhaps less easily embarrassed today). Embarrassment could be removed by arguing, first, that this discreditable material which sees God as ferocious, capricious, and so on had been effectively negated and corrected by later biblical emphases; and second, that its presence in the Bible was still needed so that the greatness of God's achievement in the revelatory process might be grasped (compare the way advertisements show what difference a product makes by pictures of 'before' and 'after').

Fourth, from the theological standpoint, 'progressive revelation' was welcomed as substantiating a view of authority in Christianity as the claim of superior insight—the insight of spiritual experts, pundits, or gurus. This is a far cry from the biblical idea of the authority of God's own words, but it was the only concept of an authority external to ourselves that Kant's denial of a speaking God (the basis of all liberal Protestantism) had left viable.

The shrewdest account of 'progressive revelation' was by C. H. Dodd, who presented 'the work and influence of Jesus' as 'the climax of the whole complex process which we have traced in the Bible,' and argued that because it is 'of the highest spiritual worth . . . we must recognize it in the fullest sense as a revelation of God.'[3] Dodd allowed that one could not take for granted that 'the phenomena of biblical history can all be brought under the formula of "the evolution of religion," but must build the case for this view from factual evidence.'[4] He admitted too the oddity of giving the name 'revelation' to a process of discovery by insight, but justified this by interpreting the insight as a function of God-given genius. Seeing the 'revelation' that progressed as a general clarification of God's character and his scale of values rather than a communication of specific information or commands, Dodd did not think it inappropriate to give this name to a process which at all stages save the last involved the holding of beliefs that were partly wrong. He summed up the matter thus:

> We observe a process which as a whole must be called progressive. At each stage of the process we observe individuals who gathered up in themselves the tendencies of the process, criticized them by some spontaneous power of insight, and redirected the process in its successive stages. That which these individuals contributed was a vision of God, determined by what they themselves were. This they were by the grace of God, for we cannot give any other account of their experience. Whether we say that men progressively discovered a revelation which in God's intention is eternally complete and unalterable, or that God himself proportioned the measure of his revelation to the stages of human progress, is perhaps no more than a matter of verbal expression.[5]

Criticism of 'Progressive Revelation'

Views of this kind are open, however, to at least the following criticisms. The first has to do with the *agents* of revelation. The theory interprets the experience of the geniuses through whose insight the process went on in a way they themselves would not accept. No doubt they were geniuses, and it is no doubt true that the profoundest insights of human genius really do feel as if they had been given from outside rather than distilled by one's own mind, but it is nonetheless clear that when prophets and apostles—to say nothing of Jesus Christ—said that the God whom they served had given them their message to deliver they meant more than 'Of this I am sure . . .' After all, false prophets were sure of things too, and the difference between false and true was not that either was more sure than the other, but that God had sent the latter and not the former (cf. Jer. 14:13–16; 23:40).

What warrant is there for supposing that 'Amos, being a religious genius, realized' is deeper and truer than 'the LORD took me . . . said to me . . . showed me . . . and he said . . .' (Amos 7:14ff.; 8:1)? Today, Kant's certainty that reason, pure and practical, must discount all thought of God speaking looks more like a deistic a priori than a demonstrated conclusion. May not the genius of Amos instruct the genius of Kant on this matter, rather than vice versa?

The second criticism has to do with the *content* of revelation. According to prophets, apostles, psalmists, the Christ of the Gospels, and exponents of 'biblical theology' who displaced the older liberalism, the revelatory process has yielded more than general truths about God's character and values.

He declares his word to Jacob, his statutes and ordinances to Israel (Ps. 147:19).

He has made known to us in all wisdom and insight the mystery of his will, according to his purpose which he set forth in Christ as a plan for the fullness of time, to unite all things in him, things in heaven and things on earth (Eph. 1:9–10).

Divine disclosures by word and sign, confirmed by the solid reality of historical events (Exodus; conquest; kingdom; exile; return; life, death, and resurrection of Jesus; outpouring of the Spirit; expansion of the church), have disclosed God in purposive action, saving and teaching his people and renewing his world through the Saviour who has come and will come again. Moreover, it is precisely by reference to particular historical events, understood as acts of God, that the qualities of his character are known and defined.

Thus, for instance, John explains 'God is love' in terms not of a mere generalized benevolence without regard for our ill-desert, as is often done today, but of Jesus' historical death on the cross: 'In this is love, not that we loved God but that he loved us and sent his Son to be the expiation [better, propitiation, as in KJV] for our sins' (1 John 4:10). God showed his love, not just by disregarding our sins, but by taking costly action to put them away.

The backbone of the Bible story is the sequence of history and the new-creative events it records. The basic theology of the Bible writers, as is often pointed out, takes the form of reciting the mighty works of God in creation, providence, and redemption, for it is these that show who and what God is.

Here we see highlighted a further weakness of the 'progressive revelation' theory, a weakness so fundamental that it cannot be corrected until this whole frame of reference is given up. The theory assumes that the revelatory process, first to last, took the form of creative brooding by religious geniuses, out of which there crystalized moral and spiritual insights. In days when the dominant idealist philosophy—ignoring sin—took for granted a natural affinity between man's mind and God's, this was a congenial concept, and it is obvious that a great deal of creative brooding went into the ministry of the prophets and the writing of the Bible.

But the snag is that the mental model of the revelatory process as *meditation* is asserted to the exclusion of all thought that the revelatory process, whatever its psychological form, had the nature of *meeting*. This is where the weakness comes. The God of this theory does not cause particular events to become, as such, his communicative encounters with men. He does not meet us to tell us things, and anything in Scripture that suggests otherwise should be taken as picturing only the general fact that reflection intensifies one's sense of God.

So this approach, consistently applied, must limit the content of revelation to a *general awareness* of divine absolutes (about which, it was held, man's mind can rise to certainty), plus *guesswork*—it cannot be more—regarding God's purposes in history. Dodd went further than most in stressing that revelation is through history, but even he ends up finding revelation not in events, but in their interpretation by enlightened men. It seems inescapable upon analysis that the content of revelation was for Dodd a compound of certainties about ethics and the transcendent, plus likelihoods (good guesses!) about God's plan for his kingdom.

What follows? The Bible's exhibition of knowledge of God, both in the lives of its characters and in the teaching of its authors, as a person-to-person relationship based on receiving God's instruction, knowing his plan and his work, trusting his promises, obeying his commands, following his leading, and expecting experience of his guidance and power, can no longer be taken seriously; the theory has no room for the directness of communication between God and man on which this view of knowing God is based. It is small wonder that exponents of 'progressive revelation' fail to assert knowledge of God in biblical terms. In addition, the biblical gospel cannot be taken seriously either, for the gospel proclaims revelation in the form of a cosmically significant redemptive act of God in the death and resurrection of Jesus Christ, an act God himself has explained to us in terms of sacrificial atonement; and the categories of divine act and divine explanation are precisely those with which 'progressive revelation' cannot cope.

It is small wonder that exponents of this theory have usually held an Abelardian view of the atonement as a non-transactional disclosure of God's love, based on a view of Jesus, the Teacher who died, as a God-indwelt man who was not, in the sense of John's gospel and the Chalcedon formula of 451, God incarnate. After all, to allow that Jesus' words were the words of God in person would blow Kantian scepticism and all theories based on it sky high! But in fact God *has* spoken, both in the person of his incarnate Son and in the words of prophets and apostles, and he has told us a great deal more than 'progressive revelation' will allow us to know.

The third criticism has to do with the *record* of revelation, Holy Scripture. Scripture is God's own revelatory record which by its interpretive account of God's self-revelation in history becomes the means of God's applicatory revelation of himself here and now in the human heart. The criticism is not merely that 'progressive revelation' as expounded involves wholesale querying of the historical and theological truth of what the Bible says, although this is true. The deeper trouble is that the theory operates as a new Marcionism, making great sections of Scripture, including most of the Old Testament, seem substandard and hence irrelevant for Christian people. By urging the need to distinguish higher religious ideas from lower and cleave to the higher only, the theory diverts attention from the true thread that binds the canon of Scripture together and makes every book important in its place. What is that thread? It is the theme of promise and fulfilment, the fulfilment in world history and individual lives of the manifold purposes announced by the sovereign Creator, the God who reigns, speaks, and renews. But by harping on the need to find the 'higher' and leave behind the 'lower,' the 'progressive revelation' theory, far from clarifying the process recorded in Scripture and furthering a sound understanding of the text, actually darkens counsel and obstructs comprehension at both points.

The fourth criticism, which concerns the *author* of revelation, is that this theory involves an unworthy view of God, in two ways. First, it denies that the Creator can address messages or communicate thoughts to men whom he made in his own image. This denial is unworthy; prophets, apostles, and Jesus Christ all speak against it. Second, assuming that the revelatory process is one of providentially ordered human discovery, the theory accounts for the progressiveness of revelation in terms that query God's sovereignty in his world.

It is suggested constantly by exponents of 'progressive revelation' that God was restricted throughout by the slow-moving process of natural religious evolution and that he was limited in what he could do at each stage by the limits of men's natural receptiveness at that stage, so that he could not give all he would have liked to give in the way of ideas of himself. Obviously, this calls into question God's sovereignty. But does he not create the hearing heart just as he does the clean heart? (Ps. 51:10; cf. Acts 16:14.) Surely he does; and the fact that throughout the biblical period he chose to reveal himself to his people in terms of the culture which by his providence was theirs at the time does not in the least mean that he was at any stage hampered and frustrated in communicating with them, any more than it means we should now apologise(!) on his behalf for unavoidable inadequacies in the early stages of his self-disclosure. 'Whatever the LORD pleases he does, in heaven and on earth' (Ps. 135:6), in revelation of himself and his mind as in all other matters, and sound theology takes account of this fact.

The Evangelical Alternative

We need not go further into reasons for rejecting liberal ideas of 'progressive revelation.' The evolutionary understanding of how God's self-revelation advanced is plainly inadequate, however stated, and has few supporters today. But the phrase 'progressive revelation' is one which Evangelical theology may with advantage reclaim for its own use. A real development (though not an evolutionary one) is plain to see not only in the history of revelation that the Bible writers record, but also in their grasp of God's purpose in and through that history. The letter to the Hebrews opens by telling us, 'In many and various ways God spoke of old to our fathers by the prophets . . . he has spoken to us by a Son' (1:1, 2 RSV). Here is a series of successive revelations leading to a climactic disclosure of a 'great salvation . . . declared . . . by the Lord.'

May not this revelatory process rightly be called progressive? In considering this question, we must bear in mind, first, that advance was not uniform in either the disclosing or the apprehension and application of God's truth but also, second, that God's disclosures to the prophets and other bearers of revelation were more than, and indeed of a different order from, human insights crystalizing in men's minds through the power of their natural genius. Surely, in light of this second point, the proper conclusion is that, overall, 'progressive revelation' is a label that fits.

Admittedly, some Evangelical teachers have seen the phrase as tainted by liberal use (misuse, rather) and have therefore avoided it. Others, however, have adopted it without inhibitions. Thus, W. H. Griffith Thomas wrote in the 1920s, 'Revelation having been mediated through history has of necessity been progressive. The first stage was primitive Revelation . . . Then followed in due course the Revelation of God in the Old Testament . . . The New Testament Revelation was the crown and culmination of the Divine self-manifestation.'[6]

And in 1961, Bernard Ramm wrote,

> Revelation . . . unfolds as an organic whole with a measure of progressive development . . . What is meant in saying that revelation is progressive is that in its main sweep, in its broad outlines, it moves on to clearer expression and higher notions of God and more refined ethical teachings. Of course, the root of the progress in revelation is the progress in divine redemption. This is the stream which carries it along.[7]

We agree that revelation has progressed in this way, and we shall spend the rest of this essay considering how the nature of this progress is best spelled out.

First, how should we define revelation? The word can be used broadly, encompassing God's total activity in bringing men to know him, or narrowly, focusing on a particular disclosure of or about him made in the course of that total activity. We are concerned here with the broader sense. The first point to underline is that while God's work in revelation certainly includes the imparting of truths and commands, it is he himself, their source, who is thereby revealed. What God makes known to us is God, not just theology! Revelation of God and knowledge of God are correlative. Just as the latter is in essence personal, relational knowledge, to which factual knowledge about God leads up, so the essential object of the former, over and above facts about God, is God himself.

It has long been Christian custom to equate revelation with the Bible. This equation is not wrong, but it is so foreshortened and over-simplified that it hinders clear analysis and thus is misleading. Certainly the Bible is central and crucial to divine communication, but that is because first, it records, interprets, and shows the right response to God's revelation of himself in history, and second, it is the means whereby God brings all subsequent believers to recognize, receive, and respond to that revelation for themselves. For clear thought about revelation from the beginning to the present day, we need to distinguish within the revelatory process three interconnected stages.

First, *God's redemption revealed in world history*. Scripture records a long series of saving acts of God which, as a sequence, had the world's blessing in view. These acts range from the promise to Adam, the preservation of Noah, the call of Abraham, the rescue from Egypt, the many deliverances of Israel, and the various presentations of messianic hope, to the life, death, and resurrection of Jesus Christ and the outpouring of the Holy Spirit.

What preceded Christ in this sequence was revelation of God in redemptive action as truly as was the death and resurrection of Christ himself; but it was all preparatory and in various ways provisional, whereas the work of Christ has achieved a redemption from sin that is final, definitive, adequate, and available for all mankind throughout all time. The story and offer of this redemption constitute the Christian gospel. God still acts in his world, but not in a way that reveals anything new about him as Redeemer that the history from Adam to Christ does not already reveal. For further disclosures of unknown divine things, the world must wait for 'the revelation of Jesus Christ' in his glory at the end of the age (1 Pet. 1:7; Col. 3:4), when our redemption will finally be complete (Rom. 8:23; Eph. 1:14; 4:30).

Second, *God's redemption recounted in public records*. 'Public records' is a phrase of John Calvin's and it indicates the significance of Holy Scripture as a testimony and memorial for all time of God's redemptive work in Christ, and all that led up to it and now flows from it. So that all men, always and everywhere, might be able to profit by what he had done, God prompted the writing of a great deal of miscellaneous material—history books, law-codes, letters, poems, sermons, meditations, records of visions, and hymns—which, when compiled, constitute an interpretive presentation of the whole process.

Though it is true that the Bible contains, at least in embryo, a complete perspective on all aspects of God's relation to his world, what is central in Scripture is redemption; everything else is looked at in its light. Since canonical Scripture is divinely inspired, it is more than human witness to God; it is also and equally God's own witness to himself, a complex organism of divine-human instruction on life under God's redeeming sway. As such, the Bible is in and of itself revelation.

Holy Scripture, we might say, is in essence God preaching—God our Creator and Redeemer telling us through human agency, yet in the deepest sense in his own words, who he is, what he has done, what he will do, and what we must do. By giving us the Bible, God opens his mind and his heart to us.

Third, *God's redemption revealed to, and received by, individuals in the church*. 'Reveal' in Matthew 16:17 and Galatians 1:16, 'revelation' in Ephesians 1:17, and God's 'shining in our hearts' in 2 Corinthians 4:6, all relate to inward enlightenment from God whereby the meaning and truth of divinely inspired witness to redemptive realities are grasped and those realities are themselves embraced in responsive faith. This is the third stage in the process of divine communication, without which neither of the first two would constitute actual revelation to anyone. Revelation in this subjective sense (illumination, as it is often called) is the work of the Holy Spirit, whereby he fulfils his teaching ministry (John 14:26; 1 John 2:27). Whatever may have been true regarding direct revelation in the first generation of the church's life, he fulfils his teaching role to us today by using the inspired Scriptures as his textbook, either directly or indirectly (through someone's reproduction of what they say). In this sense (but in no other it seems) revelation continues at the present time.

These three elements in the work of revelation must be bound together in the mind, for they are three stages in the single process whereby God in mercy brings spiritually blind sinners to know him. Just as Paul would say '[He] loved me and gave himself for *me*' (Gal. 2:20 RSV, emphasis mine), thus considering redemption as the reason his life had been made new, so every believer can and should say, 'He wrought redemption, and inspired the Bible, and sent the Spirit to teach through the Word, for *me*,' thus giving revelation in its full threefold sense as the source and explanation of the fact that he now knows God.

In what sense, then, is God's revelatory work *progressive*? Once the basic distinctions are drawn, the answer is clear.

True Progressive Revelation

The historical process leading to Christ was progressive in the sense that one thing followed another until the climax came. God chose a man, made his family into a nation, gave that nation a land, gave them a religious culture in which prophets, priests, and kings were leaders and sin was highlighted as the hindrance to fellowship with God, and out of the frustrations of their national life raised their minds to a messianic hope. All this was progressive preparation for Christ.

The process of inspiration that produced the Scriptures, a process which from early days kept pace, more or less, with ongoing historical developments, was progressive in the sense that God's ways and purposes, and particularly his central saving purpose for the world, were blocked in and illustrated more and more clearly as time went on.

> In progressive revelation [writes Ramm, referring to the biblical process] the former revelation lays the foundation for later revelation. The law prepares the way for the prophets; the earlier prophets lay the foundation for later prophets; the total Old Testament is the preparation for the total New Testament.[8]

To understand the Bible thoroughly as the organism of divine truth that it is, it is important that these inner links of development be followed out and that each writer's prior knowledge and assumptions be accurately gauged.

The Spirit's work of illumination and instruction is also progressive, in the sense that those whom the Spirit teaches learn one thing after another. This principle applies not only to the individual but also to the church, within which a 'progressive orthodoxy' appears as one doctrinal issue after another is raised and resolved. But since the concept of 'progressive revelation' has never yet been linked with these matters, we say no more about them here.

By spawning the concept of 'progressive revelation,' liberalism presented Evangelicalism with a question: If evolutionary progress is not the correct explanation of the overall historical process, and within it, the particular literary process that led up to Christ and left us the Bible as its legacy, then what is? We are answering that question by stating that the historical process that led up to Christ and left us the Bible should be viewed in terms of an organic sequence of divine words, events that correspond to those words, and written products that commemorate them. Together they carried forward and elucidated a historical panorama of preparation and promise, coming in due time to consummation and fulfilment in Jesus Christ, for the redemption of the church and ultimately the renewal of the world through Christ's final triumph. 'Progressive revelation,' thus understood, speaks to us not of an evolutionary process within which God is present as prisoner rather than as Lord, but of the mighty cosmic purpose which an absolutely sovereign God is bringing toward completion even now. Salutary doctrine? Yes, indeed! Hallelujah!

CHAPTER 6

The Necessity of the Revealed Word

By 'The Revealed Word' is meant Holy Scripture, and this phrase is used as a pointer to the high estimate of Holy Scripture as written revelation from God, authoritative divine teaching for all men at all times. Acceptance of this estimate marks off our position from that of much contemporary Protestantism and the present argument requires clarification of the difference.

Revelation and the Bible: Modern Views

It is true that Protestant divines generally during the past fifty years have highlighted the themes of revelation and the Word of God; but they have commonly defined revelation in a way that excludes the thought of verbal or conceptual communication, and the Word of God in a way that opposes it to the written Scriptures. They assert that revelation is illumination but not instruction, so that, in William Temple's formula, though there are 'truths of revelation' (the results of correct thinking concerning revelation) there are no 'revealed truths' (statements of fact communicated by God).[1] Similarly they contend that the Word of God is either Jesus Christ himself, or man's encounter with Jesus Christ, or an event of self-understanding in the light of Jesus Christ, while the Bible is simply a human record through which, indeed, the Word is graciously mediated but with which it must not be identified.

We, however, reject these polarizations. Without denying that revelation, biblically conceived, involves illumination,[2] or questioning John's identification of Jesus with the eternal personal Word of the Father,[3] we hold, first, that the essence of revelation is conceptual communication, whereby God makes known his own nature, thoughts, and knowledge, and, second, that Holy Scripture may yet be called the revealed Word of God in the most proper sense, inasmuch as it is in its totality God's own utterance and message. Holy Scripture is God's witness to himself no less than it is man's witness to him. It is both human and divine. What it says, God says. It is simultaneously man's responsive testimony to God and God's revealed Word to men.

The Word of God and the Word of Man

In affirming the divine origin of Holy Scripture, we do not deny the validity of the human characterizations on which the scholars of the past century have laboured so hard, and in some ways so successfully. One may freely admit that Holy Scripture is partly an interpretive record of, and partly a meditative response to, the words and deeds of God in saving history from the first Adam to the last. It is both true and faithful to recognize that both as record and as interpretation (for the two are ultimately one) it has been shaped by its writers' didactic aim, personal interests, and overall theology. Such clarifications have high value, for they afford a basis not only for exact historical exegesis, which is vital, but also for impressive a posteriori demonstrations of the unity of saving history on the one hand, and of biblical theology on the other.

One sometimes hears it said that by continuing to maintain the plenary divine inspiration, and hence the entire trustworthiness of the Scriptures, Evangelicals are throwing away the gains of a hundred years of scientific inquiry into the Bible. This is not so. The true gains of the 'critical' era lie in the field of Near Eastern background studies, through which the understanding of biblical languages, cultural, and literary forms, and religious orientations has made enormous strides forward.

We hold no brief for a docetic approach to Scripture, which bases its hermeneutic, in the manner of ancient allegorism, on an arbitrary disregard of the historical humanity of the texts. Neither can we accept the quasi-Nestorian approach to Scripture which hesitates to affirm direct identity between the instruction in divine things given by the biblical writers and God's own instruction given through them. It is this non-identification, which all hypotheses of error in biblical narrative and teaching presuppose, that Evangelical theology is basically concerned to controvert. Evangelical Protestants, in company with both Vatican Councils and Roman Catholic biblical scholars generally, are concerned to reject this presuppositional disfigurement of the 'critical' movement in biblical study. This rejection we advertise when we call the Bible God's revealed Word.

Sources of Scepticism

This is not the place to set out reasons for regarding as part of the given essence of Christianity the concept of Scripture as divine truth. We have done that elsewhere,[4] and others do it on other pages of this symposium of Dr. Tenney's. It is, however, worth noting why so many modern Protestants find this view incredible.

The basic reason is not, as it is sometimes thought, the existence of problems in harmonizing the Bible both with itself and with extra-biblical knowledge. Most of these problems were known, and more or less satisfactory solutions were offered, long before modern scepticism about the truth of Scripture arose. Why was it that at a particular point in the history of the Protestant West—between 1860 and 1890, to be exact—many thoughtful Christians came to feel that they could no longer assume the divine inspiration, truth, and authority of the Scriptures, and on this basis tackle their problems as their fathers had done?

The change cannot be ascribed simply to the arrival during the period of the Graf-Wellhausen hypothesis about the Pentateuch, the prophets, and the emergence of ethical monotheism. This hypothesis, though impressive in the range of phenomena for which it purports to account, has no compelling force unless it be assumed in advance that a theory of religious evolution is likely to be the true explanation of the Old Testament, or, in other words, unless the concept of biblical inerrancy has already become problematical. The welcome which the Graf-Wellhausen hypothesis received from the start showed that the concept of biblical inerrancy already had become problematical. Why was this?

The answer seems to lie in the combined effect on the thought about God of three movements of intellectual apostasy in European and American culture. These movements were English Deism, which was prolonged in the continental Enlightenment and in eighteenth-century America; Kant's critical philosophy, by which all subsequent Western philosophy was marked; and the man-centred panentheistic teaching of 'the father of modern theology,' Friedrich Schleiermacher. Each of these, in different ways, challenged the very possibility of a 'revealed Word'—that is, an inspired and infallible Bible.

The deistic denial of 'particular providence' made it seem impossible that God should have controlled the biblical writers so directly as to guard them from all error. Deistic writers freely suggested that biblical miracle-stories and doctrinal formulations sprang from faulty observation and understanding. The Kantian theory of knowledge invalidated any sort of supernatural communication from God, and Kant, ignoring the greater part of the Bible, reduced religion to 'the bounds of pure reason'—that is, to ethics without dogma. Schleiermacher, accepting that there were no supernatural communications, denied all knowledge of God except that distilled from the Christian religious consciousness, and taught men to read the Bible as a testament of man's religious sensibility, rather than as a testimony from a living, speaking, personal Creator.

With attitudes bred by these theories as part of his cultural heritage, it is no wonder that modern Western man, inside as well as outside the church, finds it hard to believe that God can speak to man intelligibly in any sense at all. Still less can he admit that God could cause to be written over more than a thousand years a set of documents making a wholly faithful and trustworthy account of his revelation, all of which, whatever their human character, date, and literary form, are equally to be treated as instruction from himself.

On the other hand, the possibilities that philosophers and theologians of a particular age can envisage should not be taken as the measure of what God can or cannot do. Man's Creator is not limited by man's thoughts about him. Now that the arguments for Deism, Kantianism, and Schleiermacherian liberalism have become mere historical curiosities, it behoves us to shake off prejudices against the possibility of a 'revealed Word' to which these positions formerly gave rise.

The Crucial Question

The question before us is whether the revealed Word of Scripture was, and is, *necessary*. What does the question mean? Necessary for whom? and for what? Protestant divines of the sixteenth and seventeenth centuries wrote against a background of controversy with Rome, in which the claim was frequently heard that the church without the Bible was guide enough for the faithful. They took the question to mean: Is the Bible necessary for the preservation and propagation of the gospel, the securing and spreading of true knowledge of God? They answered this question with an emphatic 'yes.' By way of illustration, we cite the opening chapters of Calvin's *Institutio*, which are concerned to establish this very point.

1. Calvin on the Need for Scripture

The first of the *Institutio's* four books is entitled 'Of the knowledge of God the Creator.' Having first characterized true knowledge of God as issuing in self-knowledge and practical godliness, Calvin next shows that, though 'a sense of deity is indelibly engraved on the human heart' (I.iii.3) by general revelation, this sense of God is 'stifled or corrupted, ignorantly or maliciously' (I.iv, title) by dull and perverse man, so that none truly grasps, let alone responds to, God's self-disclosure in the created order.

This leads Calvin to a powerful chapter (I.vi) entitled 'The need of Scripture, as a guide and teacher, in coming to God as a Creator.' Viewing Scripture explicitly as teaching (*doctrina*) from God, first given directly to men of Bible times and then 'consigned, as it were, to public records' (I.vi.2) for the instruction of later generations, Calvin argues that without its aid we shall never know our Creator as Creator, let alone as Redeemer. We quote some of the key sentences of this chapter.

> As the aged, or those whose sight is detective, when any book, however fair, is set before them, though they perceive that there is something written, are scarce able to make out two consecutive words, but, when aided by glasses, begin to read distinctly, so Scripture, gathering together the impressions of deity which, till then, lay confused in their minds, dissipates the darkness, and shows us the true God clearly (I.vi.1).

> Therefore, while it becomes man seriously to use his eyes in considering the works of God, since a place has been assigned to him in this most glorious theatre that he may

be a spectator of them, his special duty is to give ear to the Word . . . If true religion is to beam on us, our principle must be that it is necessary to begin with heavenly teaching, and that it is impossible for any man to obtain even the tiniest portion of right and sound doctrine without being a disciple of Scripture (I.vi.2).

If we reflect how prone the human mind is to lapse into forgetfulness of God, how readily inclined to every kind of error, how bent at the same time on fashioning new and fictitious religions, it will easily be realised how necessary such a sealing of heavenly doctrine has been, to prevent it from either perishing by the neglect, vanishing away amid the errors, or being corrupted by the presumptuous audacity of men. It being thus manifest that God, foreseeing the ineffectiveness of his image imprinted on the fair form of the universe, has given the aid of his Word to all whom he has ever been pleased to instruct effectually, we too must pursue this straight path, if we aspire in earnest to a genuine contemplation of God (I.vi.3).

The argument is that the revealed Word is necessary for the knowledge of God, because, on the one hand, God has given and appointed it for this purpose, and commands that it be used accordingly. On the other hand, sin has so darkened human minds that they cannot know God apart from the light (information plus inner illumination) that Scripture brings; or rather (to indicate Calvin's full thought) apart from the light that the Holy Spirit brings by sealing Scripture on men's hearts. It is clear that for Calvin this line of reasoning, which is developed in the *Institutio* in specific relation to knowing God as Creator, has double force when it comes to knowing him as Redeemer through Christ, for here there is no general revelation at all. The Scriptures, which are the literary embodiment of the historical manifestation of Christ, are, so Calvin insists, the only fount from which knowledge of salvation can be derived.

2. Later Views

Most Protestant writers of the age of orthodoxy took the same line, affirming the necessity of Scripture explicitly, and stressing the impossibility of true knowledge of the gospel being attained or retained where the Bible was not functioning as a canon or rule of faith.[5] Turretin (*Institutio Theologiae Elencticae*, II.ii.6) added the point that Scripture is also necessary for the propagation of the true faith, 'that it might more conveniently be spread and transmitted, not only to the absent, but also to posterity.'

In modern times the question of the necessity of Scripture has not received much formal discussion, but the Reformation position has been, in effect, assumed and enforced every time Evangelicals have expressed their mind on the destructive tendency of 'higher critical'—that is, naturalistic—views of the Bible, or extolled Bible reading as a vital means of grace, or demanded and developed expository preaching, Bible schools, and Bible conferences.

A pervasive conviction of the necessity of Scripture lies at the heart of Evangelicalism, and it is no accident that Evangelicals have always been the backbone of the world's Bible Societies, and the pioneers of Bible translation, a field in which the work of the Wycliffe Bible Translators is only the latest in a long series of distinguished developments. The self-conscious Bible-centredness of Evangelical culture in all its forms during the past three centuries is further testimony to the strength of the Evangelical conviction that Scripture, and Scripture alone, can and must guide us in living to the praise and pleasure of God.

Nor is it only among Evangelicals that this conviction is found at the present time. The current renewed interest in the Bible and the reappearance of biblical theology and dogmatics in liberal Protestant circles may be cited as proof that a sense of the necessity of Scripture is actually spreading in our time. Even more striking is the biblical revival in the Roman Church, which seems now to have dispelled fully the idea that the Bible is a Protestant book which Roman Catholics need not read. Although by comparison with Reformation theology this new awareness may seem for the most part not to be perfectly focused or thought through as yet, its presence in the churches is a most hopeful sign for the future.

The Purpose of Our Argument

Our purpose in this essay is to confirm the Reformation position by further argument. Before attempting this, however, for the sake of clarity, we must analyse the meaning of the thesis that Scripture is *necessary* a little further than Evangelical writers of earlier times were wont to do.

1. The Question of Necessity

First, it should be made clear what kind or kinds of necessity are being considered. 'Necessary' in this context might mean necessary for God, or for man. Reformation theology, as we have seen, concentrated on showing that Scripture is necessary for man if he is to know God truly, but a further question waits to be asked: Was, then, the giving of Scripture, and the use of it for the church's instruction, in any way necessary for God?

It is clear that God was under no absolute necessity to reveal himself savingly to sinful men. God owes sinners nothing; if he does them good, it is an exercise of free grace on his part, the freedom and freeness of which consist precisely in the fact that he was not obliged to show it. One may still ask, however, whether God's plan of redeeming, calling, sanctifying, and perfecting a worldwide church through the mediation of one man, Christ Jesus, whose universally significant ministry took place at one particular point in the total space-time structure of world history, did not require the giving of the Scriptures as a necessary means to God's end.

In other words, did God's plan to bring men in every place and every age to know Jesus of Nazareth as their God and Saviour necessarily involve the giving of written testimony to Jesus through inspiration, just as it necessarily involved the sending of the Son from heaven to acquire the identity of Jesus through incarnation? A further question is whether one should distinguish degrees of accuracy and adequacy in the knowledge of God in Christ. Should one conclude that the necessity of Scripture will become increasingly apparent as concern rises from a general desire that men should in some degree know Christ to a specific desire that their knowledge of him should be perfect, full in content and free from distortion and mistakes?

2. The Necessity of the Record

Second, one must be clear as to what is and what is not in view when he speaks of the revealed Word. In the first part of this essay this phrase is used to denote the inspired Scriptures, in which the saving words and deeds of God are recorded and explained in a way that is wholly true, trustworthy, and therefore normative for faith. By way of further qualification, it is used henceforth to refer only to the Scriptures, and not to God's historical acts of revelation and redemption, as such, which the Scriptures record. It would not, however, be improper to call God's messages to the patriarchs, Moses, or to any of his people at any later time between Moses and the apostolic age, his 'revealed Word.'

So far from this usage being improper, it is primary: had God not spoken in history to reveal his redemptive plan, and then fulfilled his words by saving action, there would be nothing for Scripture to record. But it is important to distinguish between the testimony and the events to which testimony is borne. Both are necessary to salvation, but not in the same way. God's historical messages about his saving intentions, and the redemptive events which fulfilled them, are necessary to the essence of salvation. The inspired record, however, is necessary, not for the being of salvation, but for the full and exact knowledge of it. This distinction must be kept clear; hence the deliberately restricted usage.

3. Is Inspiration Necessary?

If, however, belief in the supernatural inspiration of the revealed Word is, for whatever reason, discarded, and the biblical documents are regarded as no more than human records written by good men in good faith, is knowledge of salvation then jeopardized? Does Jesus Christ then vanish in the mists of historical doubt?

Watchers of the left-wing liberals of Germany and America at the end of the last century who, with their denials of scriptural inspiration denied also much of the factual and doctrinal substance of biblical faith (such as the ontological reality of the Trinity, the uniqueness of the incarnation, the transactional atonement, the virgin birth, miracles, and physical resurrection of Jesus), were tempted to conclude that the answer to these questions was 'yes.' They contended that once inspiration was surrendered, then by some kind of logical necessity everything must fall. B. B. Warfield, however, among others, denied this very strongly:

> Let it not be said that . . . we found the whole Christian system upon the doctrine of plenary inspiration . . . Were there no such thing as inspiration, Christianity would be true, and all its essential doctrines would be credibly witnessed to us in the generally trustworthy reports of the teaching of our Lord and of His authoritative agents in founding the Church, preserved in the writings of the apostles and their first followers, and in the historical witness of the living Church. Inspiration is not the most fundamental of Christian doctrines, nor even the first thing we prove about the Scriptures . . .

> These we first prove authentic, historically credible, generally trustworthy, before we prove them inspired. And the proof of their authenticity, credibility, general trustworthiness would give us a firm base for Christianity prior to any knowledge on our part of their inspiration, and apart indeed from the existence of inspiration . . . The verities of our faith would remain historically proven to us—so bountiful has God been in his fostering care—even had we no Bible; and through those verities, salvation.[6]

Warfield's statement prompts two comments.

First, we could not endorse the abstract, Butlerian, anti-deistic, and basically rationalistic structure of Warfield's formal apologetics without qualifications so heavy as to change the whole character of his system. We could admit the thesis that as things are, Christian faith could in principle survive in some form, under the good hand of God, 'even had we no Bible'—even, that is, if the writings that survived from the age of the inspired apostles had clearly not been themselves inspired, and had never become a canon for faith because they were not fit for this purpose (which is what Warfield seems to mean).

It is likely that any initial reluctance to concede this will prove to reflect only our habitual underestimate of the evidential significance of sub-apostolic and patristic Christianity, not to mention later Christian history and experience. Indeed, Christianity did survive, after a fashion, in the Dark Ages and the medieval period under conditions of biblical ignorance which created a situation not dissimilar to that which Warfield envisages.

Certainly, it was right to resist the suggestion that the rejecting of plenary inspiration must mean the end of the historic Christian faith. The right-wing versions of neo-orthodoxy and biblical theology in our own day have shown this clearly, for, whatever distortions may appear to be built into them, it can hardly be denied that the systems of Barth, Brunner, Niebuhr, Hebert, and A. M. Ramsey—to name no more—represent a recognizable recovery, in conscious opposition to liberalism, of a Christ-centred, redemption-rooted faith in the living God; yet no one of these writers holds to the plenary inspiration and inerrancy of the Bible.

Second, however, it must be stressed that to say that under certain circumstances Christianity can survive is not to say that it can survive healthily. Warfield himself in a footnote[7] points to facts which show that without the acknowledgement of Scripture as God's revealed Word, Christianity cannot survive healthily. Inspiration, he writes, is

> (1) the element [of the Christian faith] which gives *detailed certitude* to the delivery of doctrine in the New Testament, and (2) the element *by which the individual Christian is brought into immediate relation to God* in the revelation of truth through the prophets and apostles (italics ours).

The point that must be grasped is that faith, viewed both as trust in the truth of God and as communion with the God of truth (and both aspects are essential), has as its primary object the speech and teaching of God, the Creator, as such.

The truths of God's Son as Saviour, and of his Father as our Father, being *consequent* objects of faith, owe this status formally to the fact that God in his teaching has so set them forth. Hence, as physical life is enfeebled when proper food and drink are withheld, so faith is impoverished and our whole relation to God with it, just to the extent to which God's revealed Word—his own account of the facts and acts of faith—is unknown to us, or denied by us. The reason for this is that such ignorance or denial obstructs the covenanted work of the Holy Spirit in sealing God's truth on our hearts and eliciting response to it.

God's truth, indeed, evidences itself as such through the inward illumination of the Spirit, but inadequate or mistaken notions about Holy Scripture will so clutter and prejudice our minds that its divine authentication and authority as God's truth will not be felt. Not only, therefore, is there, as Warfield argued, logical failure in a professed Christian super-naturalism which rejects a supernatural Bible; which claims to revere Christ and his apostles as teachers from God yet disregards their testimony to Scripture as itself the speech of God; but also there is spiritual failure. Some degree of definiteness and fullness of conviction, and some due exercises of spirit in dealing with God are bound to be lacking where faith in the Bible as the revealed Word of God is absent. This will be exemplified below.

4. The Necessity for a Scriptural Revelation

There are three lines of thought which show the necessity of the inscripturated Word if God's purpose of saving and sanctifying a worldwide church during the centuries between Christ's two comings is to be fully accomplished. First, the revealed Word of which we speak is the Bible as we have it, the sixty-six books of the canonical Old and New Testaments, composed by many authors over more than a thousand years. Second, it is precisely from the Christianity which we learn from this source that we infer the need for this source to exist to teach it. Whether any other revealed word would have been necessary for other purposes under other circumstances is not the question; we are affirming, third, that the Bible was, and is, a necessary element in the Christianity we have received. We argue that it is, for the reasons that follow.

(i) The revealed Word is necessary because of the complexity of revealed truth

From the moment man sinned, God the Creator began to show himself a God of grace, accepting responsibility to do all that was necessary to restore, not merely individuals, but, in a real sense, the whole human race, to himself. This restoration, being essentially a reversal of the effects of sin, necessarily involved the redeeming of sinners out of their negative status. He raised them from guilt, alienation, ignorance, and exposure to the first and second death under his wrath, into a positive relation with him in which they knew and enjoyed reconciliation, forgiveness, and fatherly love and care.

Their restoration also involved, by equal necessity, the renewal in them of the divine image. God the Creator is rational and righteous, and his image in man consisted of a derived and dependent rationality expressed in responsive righteousness, a rational righteousness comprising both worshipful obedience to God and sacrificial service of man. It is evident that both the enjoyment of a restored status and the practice of rational righteousness presuppose knowledge of the will, works, and ways of God.

It was necessary that the work of restoration should have an educational, in-structional aspect. In addition to making redemptive provision for sinners, God must speak to them, not only in the imperative but also in the indicative mode, not only in directive but in didactic speech, to teach them his character, aims, standards, and proposals. He must explain to them what his purpose is both for themselves as individuals, and also for the church, the redeemed community, and the whole cosmos, so that they may know his mind at least in principle regarding every issue and situation with which they have to deal, and in which he has to deal with them.

To move us by external physical force alone, as men move sticks or stones, would not answer God's restorative purpose. Only as he addresses us directly, and works on and in us in conjunction with his message can our activity take the form of rational, personal response to himself. Therefore a revealed Word from God to mankind, embracing a wide range of instruction, was necessary from the start. Such a revealed Word cannot avoid being complex if it is to deal adequately with the complexity of human life, 'that the man of God may be complete, furnished completely unto every good work' (2 Tim. 3:17 ASV).

Furthermore, all God's instruction to sinful men had to be given correctively, in contradistinction both to their false ways and also to their distorted ideas about God and life. Sin has intellectual as well as moral effects, so that, as Calvin rightly insisted in the passages quoted earlier, we are all now dull and perverse in spiritual matters, prone to miss the point and to misunderstand, and very slow to see how God's truth applies to ourselves. Sin by thus corrupting mental life has complicated it.

In place of the childlike receptiveness and simplicity in the face of God's Word which was part of his image, there is now the fathomless complexity of self-regarding rationalization and moral dishonesty which prompted Jeremiah to cry, 'The heart is deceitful above all things, and it is desperately sick: who can know it,' and to confess that none but God can search its depths (Jer. 17:9f.). It was necessary, therefore, that God should set forth his Word in corrective application to the manifold misconceptions and oversights of man in the realm of moral and spiritual reality.

A great deal of the Bible is in fact devoted to detecting and correcting errors; 'reproof' and 'correction' are specified as part of the purpose for which Scripture was given (2 Tim. 3:16). A corrective presentation cannot help being as complex in form as are the aberrations which it seeks to correct, as a moment's thought about Isaiah's polemics against idolatry, or Christ's against the manners and mentality of the Pharisees, or Paul's against the Galatian and Colossian heresies will show.

Furthermore—and this is the weightiest factor of all—the divinely decreed way of restoration was by means of an ordered historical process exalting the Lord Jesus Christ, the God-man, as Saviour of God's people and reintegrator of all creation, and bringing sinners to worship, trust and love him as such. The heart of the knowledge which God now seeks to impart is, as the New Testament shows, knowledge of the risen Jesus of Nazareth as a living person, who is to be understood in terms of thought-modes for which the theological labels are the triunity of God, the incarnation of the Son, the mediatorial office, and saving union with Christ—perhaps the most complex and elusive concepts in the whole history of human thought.

The Bible indicates that to enable men to rise to these thoughts when Jesus came, God spent literally centuries preparing the way by teaching the Jewish people through the instruction of priests and prophets, through typical institutions of ministry, leadership, and worship, and through the revealed Word of the Old Testament writings, the basic concepts that they needed for this task. Thus the Old Testament now stands as a divine lexicon and phrasebook for the New.

The New Testament teachers themselves proclaimed Christ and the Christian economy as the fulfilment of the Old Testament, and expounded the significance of Christ in Old Testament terms (prophet, priest, king, judge, sacrifice, covenant, etc.). In this way the revealed Word of both Testaments forms a single organism of revelation, the New building on the Old and the Old buttressing the New, each incomplete without the other. And it appears true to say that, just as the Old Testament was necessary to make possible the gigantic intellectual achievement of the apostles in comprehending Jesus Christ, so both Testaments together are necessary to the church in its equally gigantic intellectual task of grasping their message, and restating and reapplying it in terms of the cultural shifts and mutations of each successive age.

The complexity of this message, in its full New Testament presentation, makes it inconceivable that the church could retain it intact were not the revealed Word constantly at hand to be pored over and consulted in cases of doubt and uncertainty, and as a safeguard against forgetfulness. We conclude, therefore, that the complexity of human life which it covers, the variety of deviations which it seeks to correct, and the theological depths and demands of the apostolic confession of Christ, made the provision of God's Word in writing a necessity if God's restorative purpose was to be carried through.

(ii) The revealed Word is necessary because the church constantly needs its renewing impact

The psalmist's statement 'Thy word hath quickened me' (Ps. 119:50) points to the fact that the way the Spirit of God creates, sustains, and renews our fellowship with our Creator is by applying to us the Word of God—that is, God's message, as his inspired messengers set it forth, whether orally or in writing. The Old Testament use of the phrase 'the word of the Lord' for each prophetic oracle points to the organic unity of all the particular 'words' of God, as part of a single composite manifestation of a single speaker's mind.

> Each individual revelation is not *a* word, but *the* word of Jahweh . . . In every single revelation it is always the whole word of God that expresses itself.[8]

In the New Testament, apart from its Johannine application to the Son of God (John 1:1–14, cf. 1 John 1:1), the phrase 'the word of God' denotes specifically the Christian message as a whole, the many-sided good news of divine grace through Jesus Christ, as proclaimed by Jesus and his apostles. The New Testament itself, and, indeed, in a large sense the whole Bible, may properly be called 'the Word of God' in this material sense, as being proclamation of the gospel, no less than in the formal sense of having God as its source and speaker.

As in the Old Testament the Word of God is said to go out into the world with power to produce its intended effect (Isa. 55:10f., cf. Jer. 1:9f.) so in the New Testament the Word of God—that is, the Gospel—is declared to be the means whereby God searches hearts (Heb. 4:12), creates faith (Rom. 10:17, cf. John 17:20), effects new birth (Jas. 1:18, 1 Pet. 1:23), cleanses (John 15:3, Eph. 5:26), sanctifies (John 17:17), gives wisdom (Col. 3:16), builds up Christians in faith and brings them to their final heritage (Acts 20:32)—in short, saves their souls (Jas. 1:21).

Two principles emerge. The first is that what God blesses to us is his truth, and only his truth—that is, the teaching of Scripture, as faithfully echoed and reproduced in the preaching and witness of the church. The argument that some particular Christian point of view (Roman Catholic, Calvinist, Arminian, Pentecostal, for instance) must be true because God has demonstrably blessed people who hold it cannot ever be conclusive, because God in mercy blesses his truth to us despite errors that may be mixed with it. But it is not the errors that he blesses—it is only with his truth that he feeds our souls.

The second principle is that God's Word, whether viewed as a whole or from the standpoint of the particular 'words' that make it up (cf. Mic. 2:7, Ps. 119:103, John 14:24, 15:7), has the nature of a call (cf. Ps. 50:1, Jer. 7:13). It comes as a summons to each hearer to respond to God in the light of its application to himself, and the way the Holy Spirit blesses it is precisely by causing us to understand and receive it as God's call, and to answer accordingly.

If the church could be trusted to transmit apostolic teaching undistorted, the need for Scripture would be less. But the church, being made up of sinners who are not yet perfectly delivered from inbred intellectual perversity, cannot be relied on to do this. Whenever the church attempts to rethink its message in order to relate it effectively to current non-Christian movements of thought, a spirit of intellectual worldliness operates to induce assimilation of the gospel to that which it should be challenging and correcting.

This occurred in connection with Gnosticism during the apostolic age itself, as the New Testament bears witness; again with Platonism at Alexandria through Origen; and with Aristotelianism in the Middle Ages through Thomas Aquinas; with Newtonian physics in the Enlightenment; with Kant's theory of knowledge and Hegel's metaphysic of 'spirit' in the nineteenth century; and with existentialism in the twentieth. Moreover, the temptation to revert from grace to works is constant, as witness the Judaizing movement in New Testament times, the sacramental and juridical legalism of the patristic period, the amalgam of merit and magic in medieval popular piety, the moralism of liberal Protestants, and the ecclesiastical legalism of Roman Catholics since Trent.

Always vulnerable to these tendencies and likely to petrify in external formalism, the church's life presents a pattern of constant decline, reversed, however, from time to time by fresh outpourings of the Spirit of God. What does the Spirit do at these times? The answer can be stated with precision. He confronts the church afresh with the revealed Word of God from which it has drifted, and causes professed Christians to hear again the biblical message of grace as God's promise and call to themselves. This has been the real essence of all movements of genuine reformation and revival in the church. Were there no revealed Word of God by which degenerate traditional forms of faith and worship could be corrected, the renewal that is constantly needed in the church on earth would never be possible. Thus, from this angle also, the necessity of the revealed Word appears.

(iii) The revealed Word is necessary as the foundation for our life of faith

We have already said that faith, according to the Bible, is correlative primarily to God's Word as such, and consequently to the various realities set forth in God's Word—chiefly, the living God himself, and his Son, the living Christ, and the promises of his covenant. The focal centre of faith, according to the Bible, is the promise of mercy to sinners which is confirmed by Christ's mediation and shed blood. 'How many soever be the promises of God, *in him is the yea*' (2 Cor. 1:20).

In God's promises, thus guaranteed—promises of forgiveness, of guidance, of protection, of help, of glory—God's people are to trust. *Standing on the promises of God* is the essential exercise of faith, as appears from Romans 4, where Paul pointed to Abraham as the exemplar of justifying faith. 'Abraham believed God, and it was counted unto him for righteousness' (Rom. 4:3 ASV).

Wherein did his faith consist? It was manifested in his tenacious, God-honouring adherence, against all reason and probability, to the divine promise that he should have an heir and a host of descendants. 'Without being weakened in faith he considered his own body now as good as dead . . . and the deadness of Sarah's womb: yet, *looking unto the promise of God*, he wavered not through unbelief, but waxed strong through faith, giving glory to God, and being fully assured that what he had promised, he was able also to perform. *Wherefore it was reckoned unto him for righteousness*' (Rom. 4:19ff. ASV italics for emphasis).

Abraham's faith, the faith whereby he was justified and blessed, and which Paul proclaimed as a standard and a model, was essentially an unyielding trust in God's promise. The same principle is taught in Hebrews 11, where faith is depicted as a spirit of obedient loyalty to God on the basis of trust in his promises, both general (the promise of reward, v. 6) and particular (such as the promise of a child to Sarah, who 'counted him faithful who had promised,' v. 11).

Where shall we find the promises which we are to trust? Abraham received God's promise by immediate revelation, but what of us, living nineteen centuries after immediate revelations ended? It must be emphasized that, if the Bible were not God's revealed Word in the sense explained in the opening section—if, that is, no one could be sure that everything which the biblical writers say of God, God also says of himself—we could not be sure either that any single statement in the Bible purporting to be a promise of God to Christian believers is really valid.

No critical cross-examination on earth can tell us whether such statements are genuine divine commitments to which God has pledged himself to stand to all eternity, or whether the human writers were not perhaps astray in the words of promise which they put into the mouths of Jesus and his Father, and the assurances which they gave in God's name. If the canonical Scriptures were not

God's revealed Word, but only a mere fallible human witness to God's Word, no present-day Christian could emulate Abraham's faith, because none could be sure that he had a single definite promise from God on which to rest. The historic Evangelical concept of the life of faith as a matter of living and dying in the strength which God's promises give would then have to be thrown away as a beautiful pipedream. Those who jettison the Evangelical concept of a totally trustworthy inspired Scripture must exchange the rational biblical notion of faith as walking in the light of God for the irrational existential idea of faith as a leap in the dark, and must abandon the firm foundation of the divine promises for the yawning abyss of a foggy uncertainty. Surely it is plain that we do in fact need the revealed Word that God has given, just as our ancestors in the faith supposed.

An old hymn (by Bernard Barton) crystallizes this truth:

> Lamp of our feet, whereby we trace
> Our path when want to stray;
> Stream from the fount of heavenly grace,
> Brook by the traveller's way;
>
> Word of the ever-living God,
> Will of his glorious Son,
> *Without thee how could earth be trod,*
> *Or heaven itself be won?*

The appropriate application follows:

> Lord, grant that we aright may learn
> The wisdom it imports,
> And to its heavenly teaching turn
> With simple, childlike hearts.

Bibliography

Kuyper, A., *Principles of Sacred Theology* (Grand Rapids: Eerdmans, 1954).

Ramm, B., *Special Revelation and the Word of God* (Grand Rapids: Eerdmans, 1961).

Works by Warfield, B. B., and Calvin, J., as cited.

CHAPTER 7

Our Lord's Understanding
of the Law of God

On June 10th, 1953, Professor R. V. G. Tasker delivered an admirable Campbell Morgan Bible Lecture on the subject of 'Our Lord's Use of the Old Testament.' In his introduction he described his subject as 'one which we may be very sure would have appealed to him whose memory this lectureship was founded to perpetuate.' I hope that the same can be said of my own subject. What I have to put before you is, from one standpoint, a supplement to Professor Tasker's lecture, exploring further some of the lines of thought which he opened up on that occasion and confirming some of his conclusions. My aim is to examine our Lord's view of the authority and meaning of the law of God which is set forth in the Old Testament. And I think that such a study may be of value to us in two special ways.

First, it may contribute to *the maintaining of Evangelical faith.*

The foundation of the historic Evangelical faith is the doctrine of the inspiration, clarity, sufficiency, and authority of the Holy Scriptures. The first mark of an Evangelical is that he believes that version of the Christian message which he finds in the Bible, and no other. Also, he thinks himself bound to believe everything that he finds taught in the Bible, and to order his life in accordance with it. Why is this? Because he regards the Bible, as a whole and in all its parts, as the true and trustworthy Word of God, given to be an authoritative rule of faith and practice for the church. This is the historic Evangelical position.

But, as we know, many Protestants today, both liberals of the older type and spokesmen for the current Barthian and 'biblical theology' movements, reject the Evangelical view of Scripture, and maintain against it that there are in the Bible both records of fact and statements of doctrine which, though purporting to be true, are in reality false. In face of this, Evangelicals are accustomed to insist that their faith in the truth and authority of all Scripture rests upon the explicit testimony of our Lord Jesus Christ himself to the inspiration and authority of the Old Testament. This was the thrust of Professor Tasker's own lecture, and it is a point on which many have laid stress in recent years. Sometimes, however, it is met with the following reply: that whatever our Lord may have said about the Old Testament in general terms, and whatever use he may have made of it when arguing *ad hominem* with his Jewish opponents, he clearly did not regard it as entirely authoritative, since he publicly criticised it and parted company with it on such matters as divorce, oath taking, revenge, the treatment of one's enemies, and the food laws. On all these matters (it is said) our Lord consciously and deliberately went against the Mosaic enactments. So we cannot justifiably invoke any of Christ's statements as grounds for holding that the Bible is always right and to be followed, because the Christ who made these statements sometimes insisted that the Old Testament was in fact wrong, and to be disregarded.

It is clearly important for Evangelicals to determine whether there is substance in this contention or not. Did Christ really set aside the Old Testament in the manner alleged? Was he really a proto-liberal in his handling of the sacred text? Clearly, we need to look again at the relevant evidence in the four gospels to see if this is the right construction to put on it. That is one of the things that we are going to do now. And if it appears, as I think it will, that in reality our Lord never set the law aside at all, then we shall at once have in our hands the answer to this argument for discounting the significance of our Lord's testimony to Holy Scripture.

Then, secondly, this study may also contribute to *the strengthening of Evangelical life.*

It is often said that standards of conduct and integrity among Evangelical Christians today are not as high as they were in days gone by. Few, I think, would feel able to dispute the justice of this accusation. But why should it be so? Some might point to the way in which standards of honesty, purity, and general decency have fallen in society around us, and find in this the cause of our own moral decline. And there would no doubt be an element of truth in such a diagnosis: certainly, when the ideals and values of our callous and immodest culture are constantly being shouted at us by newspapers, novels, radio, television, and public advertisements, it is impossible for us to avoid feeling their impact, however much we might wish to. Yet the root of our trouble must surely lie deeper than this. After all, what the Bible calls 'the world' and 'the spirit of the world' is not essentially different today from what it always has been. And it is just a fact of history that in the days when Puritan laymen and the early Evangelicals became a byword, as they did, for sheer goodness and integrity, the general standards of public morality were no higher than they are now, and in some cases even lower. What was it, then, we ask, that made the difference between their lives and ours? Why were they so outstanding for righteousness while we are so feeble at this point? Even a cursory study of their life and thought will show us that what made the difference was this: not that the pull of the world on them was any less strong or insidious than it is on us, but rather that their minds and hearts were more deeply exercised in the law of God than ours are.

The root of our trouble, putting it quite plainly, seems to be that we neither know nor care much about the law of our God. On the one hand, we do not give ourselves to studying and applying the law in the way that our Evangelical forefathers did. Our neglect of the Old Testament in particular bears witness to this. On the other hand, our thinking, unlike theirs, has a lawless tinge. There is an antinomian streak running through it. We act as if our freedom from the law has made it a matter of comparative unimportance whether we keep the law in daily life or not. We appear to care more for right faith than we do for right living. We show a greater concern to be orthodox than to be upright. We seem to be more anxious to know the truth than we are to adorn it by our behaviour; we are, it appears, more interested in feeding our own souls than in doing good to our neighbours. We lap up the doctrinal chapters of the epistles, but we skate over the ethical ones. Our Lord accused the Pharisees of antinomianism, telling them that they had 'neglected the weightier matters of the law, justice and mercy and faith' (Matt. 23:23 RSV); would he not have reason to bring a similar accusation against us? Here, then, is the root cause of our present moral flabbiness: we have neglected God's law.

What we need, therefore, is a quickening of conscience with regard to the moral demands of the New Testament. One means to this would be a deepened understanding of the Old Testament moral teaching in which those demands are rooted. It is my hope that this present study of our Lord's understanding of the Mosaic law, however sketchy and selective, may, under God, contribute a little at both these points.

The exposition will proceed in three stages. In the first section, we shall lay down some general principles about the place of Christ's ethical teaching in his total ministry. In the second section, we shall examine in some detail Christ's view of the authority of the Old Testament law. In the third section, we shall pass in brief review his own positive exposition of that law.

The Place of Christ's Ethical Teaching in His Ministry as a Whole

A view which has been widely current during the past eighty years is that the real Jesus of Nazareth was never more than a moral instructor: all that he sought to do was to teach, and all that he sought to teach was ethics. This idea originally formed part of the larger theory that there is a fundamental cleavage between the historical Jesus, whom we meet in the gospels of Matthew, Mark, and Luke, and the Jesus of New Testament theology, the Jesus whom we meet in the epistles and the gospel of John. Those who held this theory usually blamed Paul for turning the Rabbi of Galilee into a divine Saviour, and they often described the cleavage which they postulated as being between 'the Jesus of history' and 'the Christ of Paul.' Naturally, they sought to separate the ethical teaching of Jesus from the supposedly inauthentic theology about his person and work in which the New Testament writers had embedded it. And this was the conclusion that they reached: that Jesus' teaching boils down simply to the universal duty of loving our neighbour, on the basis of a belief in God's universal fatherhood. In other words, we are to regard every man, irrespective of class, colour, or creed, as God's child and therefore our own brother, and treat him accordingly. This, they held, was to Jesus' mind the whole duty of man. Thus, Jesus' teaching finds its full and complete expression in the 'golden rule' of Matthew 7:12, 'do as you would be done by,' and its perfect illustration in the parable of the Good Samaritan.

(One supposes that it is because the Sermon on the Mount contains the 'golden rule,' together with a passage on loving one's enemies, Matt. 5:43–47, that it was claimed so often by the advocates of this theory as the classic summary of Jesus' teaching. From their point of view, however, the claim was somewhat inept, since the other 101 of the Sermon's 107 verses are demonstrably about matters which their own theory ignored—salvation from sin, and the life of faith: as the minister of this chapel showed in detail between the years 1950 and 1952.[1])

It will be seen that the theory which we have outlined involves the assumption that the moral teaching of Jesus stands, as it were, on its own feet, not depending for its interpretation or validity on any knowledge at all about the teacher who gave it. It would have made no difference to its meaning, or its claim upon us, if it had been given by Mohammed or Confucius. The theory that the Jesus of history was not the Christ of Paul is now generally abandoned, but this assumption, that our Lord's ethical teaching can be understood without reference to the rest of his ministry, still lingers on in many places. Our first step, therefore, must be to challenge it. For in fact the moral teaching of Jesus does not, and never did, stand alone, and if we isolate it from the larger context to which it belongs we are certain to misunderstand it. What is that larger context? It is precisely the same context as that to which the ethical teaching of the epistles belongs—the context, namely, of redemption. Christ's ethics, like those of the apostolic writers, are corollaries of the gospel which sets him forth as the divine Saviour.

Since this point is fundamental to my whole argument, I propose to spend a little time explaining and confirming it. To this end, I shall lay down two propositions. The first has to do with the relation of Christ's spoken ministry, as such, to the rest of his work on earth: the second has to do with the relation of his ethical teaching to his preaching of the gospel. The first proposition is that all Christ's preaching and teaching presupposed his atonement. The second is that all Christ's ethical teaching presupposed his preaching of the gospel.

The first proposition affirms that Christ's work of redemption appointed from eternity, foreshadowed and guaranteed at his baptism, and finally accomplished at Calvary, was the basis upon which his entire spoken ministry rested. The Gospels make this very clear. They tell us that Christ's preaching ministry began with the announcement 'The time is fulfilled, and the kingdom of God is at hand: repent ye, and believe the gospel' (Mark 1:15 KJV). The gospel referred to was the good news of the nearness of the kingdom: for the kingdom of God was the state of affairs, foretold by the prophets, in which God's people would enjoy peace, safety, and happiness in the fullest measure under the rule of the Messiah. How was it, we ask, that Jesus could announce that this kingdom was at hand? Why, because he himself was at hand, the divine-human King of Old Testament prophecy. For he was not just a Galilean Rabbi; he was God the Son made flesh; and he had come to reign. The reason, therefore, why he could announce the presence of God's promised salvation was that he, the promised King, was now present in person to bestow that salvation on all who submitted to his rule. Thus his preaching of the kingdom was based directly upon the fact of his own kingship. But kingship was not the whole of Messiahship. The Gospels indicate that Christ's kingly rule was itself based on something more fundamental, namely, the ministry of atonement. That which the Gospels show to have been really primary in Jesus' Messianic vocation was the action which he performed at the end of his earthly ministry—the offering of himself as a sacrifice for sin, according to the prophecy of Isaiah 53; for it was his atoning death that actually secured for sinners the blessings of the new relationship with God into which as King he had been leading them throughout his public ministry. The reason why he had been able during those three years to forgive men's sins and make them God's sons was because he was already pledged to die for them on Calvary's cross; he could not have done it otherwise. This was what lay behind his quotation from Isaiah 53 in the upper room: 'this that is written must yet be accomplished in me. And he was reckoned among the transgressors' (Luke 22:37 KJV). The new covenant, which he had for three years been ministering, must now be sealed by his blood (v. 30). Earlier, he had told his disciples that the basic reason why he was in the world was to die for sinners: 'The Son of Man came not to be ministered unto, but to minister, and to give his life a ransom for many' (Mark 10:45). We see, then, that Christ came, not only as a prophet, to announce salvation; not only as king, to bestow the salvation he announced; but first and foremost as priest and sacrifice, to lay the foundation of the salvation he bestowed by bearing away men's sins. All his ministry of directing and leading sinners into a knowledge of the grace of the kingdom—a knowledge, that is, of forgiveness of sin and adoption into the family of God—presupposed his forthcoming atonement as its basis, and apart from that basis it could not have been performed at all. So if we fail to interpret his preaching and teaching about the kingdom in the light of the atonement, we are bound to misconstrue it. And since all his public preaching and teaching had to do, in one way or another, with the kingdom, we can go so far as to say that nothing he ever taught can be properly understood without reference to his redemptive death. So much for the first proposition.

The second proposition is that all Christ's ethical instruction presupposed his preaching of what Mark calls 'the gospel of the kingdom of God' (Mark 1:14)—preaching, that is, by which he summoned sinners to enter into this new relationship of peace and fellowship with God through faith in himself. This amounts simply to saying that all the teaching he gave on how to live was meant for people who had already received 'the gospel of the kingdom,' who had already trusted him as their Saviour and Lord, and who thus had already been forgiven, and born again, and adopted into God's family. The Gospels give proof of this proposition by telling us specifically that all our Lord's set discourses on ethical themes—principally, the Sermon on the Mount, the Sermon on the Plain, and the sermons in Luke 12 and Matthew 18—were directed, not to the listening crowds, but to his own disciples (see Matt. 5:1; 18:1; Luke 6:20; 12:1, 22), whom he addresses as already children of God and heirs of the kingdom (cf. Matt. 5:45, 48; Luke 12:32). (It would seem that the disciples did in fact enter the kingdom when first they gave Jesus unreserved allegiance as Messiah [cf. John 1:40ff.] even though it was not till much later that they understood either the meaning of his Messiahship or the nature and blessings of the kingdom into which they had come.) Jesus' moral teaching, then, was meant for believers; hence it follows that it presupposed his preaching of the gospel of the kingdom, through which men become believers.

Once we see this, the nature of Christ's ethical teaching becomes clear. Jesus legislated, not for men as such, nor for men in the state of sin, but for Christians, for men in the state of grace, for those who had given their hearts to him and so had come to know themselves as forgiven sinners, sons and heirs of God. Jesus' ethics are not the ethics of the Garden of Eden, nor the ethics of Egypt and Babylon, but the ethics of the kingdom of God. Again, Jesus legislated, not for society, but for the individual Christian. As entry into the kingdom by faith is a personal and individual matter, so living in the kingdom by grace under the King's royal law is a personal and individual matter; and so our Lord treats it. His ethics are therefore not a code for a statute-book, but an ideal for the individual citizen of God's kingdom. Christ's ethics are Christian in the fundamental sense of being ethics for Christians, and for Christians only. In other words, Christ's ethics are a corollary of Christ's gospel, and cannot be understood except in terms of it. What Paul calls 'the law of Christ' (Gal. 6:2) is specifically and concretely a law for the redeemed. By saying this, we do not, of course, mean to deny that in one sense the law of Christ binds all men, as embodying a definitive expression of God's unchanging demands upon mankind. But we do mean to assert that Christ's exposition of God's eternal law is given in terms of the particular situation of the believer, and of nobody else. It is a statement of God's law as it applies to the citizen of God's kingdom. The only person to whose condition it speaks directly is the born-again Christian.

From this we can see what was new about the law of Christ, as compared with the law of the old covenant. Christ's law was new in the same sense in which Christ's gospel of the kingdom was new. As the kingdom was not a new departure, but a fulfilment of prophecy, according to the redemptive pattern established at the Exodus, so the law of Christ was not a new departure, but a filling-out of the law which Moses gave to God's redeemed people in the wilderness, and a re-stating of its demands in terms of the new situation which the coming of the kingdom had created.

What new factors, then, appear in Christ's re-statement of the law? Chiefly, two. First, we find a *new depth of exposition*. This follows directly from the enlarged and deepened revelation of God's grace to the individual sinner which the gospel of the kingdom contains.

A basic principle of all biblical ethics is the principle of the family likeness—the principle, that is, that those who are God's by right of creation and redemption must strive to imitate him, so that their character will reflect his. This principle was announced to Israel in the wilderness, after their deliverance from Egypt: 'You shall be holy: for I the LORD your God am holy' (Lev. 19:2). The principle was re-stated by Christ, in slightly different terms, to his own disciples, the children of the kingdom: 'Be ye therefore perfect, even as your Father which is in heaven is perfect' (Matt. 5:48 KJV). In form, these two commands correspond, but in meaning the second, in its gospel context, goes further than the first. For Christians, through their personal knowledge of forgiveness, new birth, and God's fatherhood, know more of the riches of God's free love to sinners than individual Israelites knew, or could know, in Old Testament days. The words 'your Father which is in heaven' in our Lord's statement of the principle point to the difference. Israel knew God as the Father of the nation, it is true (cf. Exod. 4:22; Hos. 11:1; Mal. 2:10), but nowhere in the Old Testament did God reveal himself as the Father of the individual believer, in the way that the gospel of the kingdom reveals him. The Christian knows much more of the height, and depth, and length, and breadth of God's free love to him personally than the Old Testament saint knew. Therefore the imitating of God will require of him correspondingly more in the way of generous and spontaneous love to others than was demanded of Israel.

Hence we find in the law of Christ emphases relating to the love of others which go beyond anything that the Old Testament law contained. For instance, the Christian must love his enemies. Again, the Christian must be infinitely forgiving, because of the infinite debt of sin that has been forgiven him (Matt. 18:21ff.). Again, the Christian must keep a 'new' commandment—he must love his fellow-Christians as Christ loved him (John 13:34). What is new about this is not the demand for love to one's brother, on which the Old Testament has a good deal to say, but the standard of love that Christ sets; the commandment is 'new' simply because the love of Christ dying to redeem the ungodly creates an entirely new ideal of what mutual care and service among Christians ought to mean. These three examples are typical illustrations of how the subject matter of the gospel imparted a new depth and richness to our Lord's exposition of the law.

The second fresh feature in Christ's re-statement of the law is a new *stress in application*. This was due to the change of circumstances under which the law was then being set forth.

The Mosaic law as a whole is stated in a predominantly negative form. It contains a mass of prohibitions and what the Puritans would have called 'dehortations,' and even the Decalogue is cast into the mould of 'thou-shalt-not.' Also, the whole exposition of the law from Exodus to Deuteronomy is punctuated with tremendous threats and warnings about the consequences of disobedience. The law was given to Israel in this way for three main reasons.

First, it was intended to function as a code regulating the national life of the Old Testament church; and it is natural when expounding a law-code to centre attention upon the defining of crime and of penalties for crime.

Second, the law was intended, as Paul tells us in Galatians 3:19–24, to prepare the Jews for the coming of Christ. This it did, says Paul, by acting as gaoler and tutor. As gaoler, it kept men 'shut up' in custody, under bondage, forced to shoulder a burden of observances which, as Peter said, 'neither our fathers nor we were able to bear' (Acts 15:10; Gal. 3:23). As tutor, it made them ready for Christ by convincing them that they were sinners needing a Saviour (v. 24). It was natural that, in order that the law might serve this purpose, stress should have been laid in the giving of it upon the forbidding of ritual omissions and the detecting of moral lapses, and the detailing of God's judgements upon both.

And then, third, the law was meant to act as a 'wall of partition' (Eph. 2:14) between Jew and Gentile, keeping the Jews from the pagan ways of surrounding nations and isolating them for the moral and spiritual training that God planned to give them. Naturally, therefore, emphasis was laid on prohibiting the evils in which Israel's neighbours indulged and laying down penal sanctions against them.

These three factors explain why prohibitions and threats should have dominated the Old Testament law in the way that they did. When the kingdom of God came, however, these factors ceased to apply, and when Christ re-stated the law, his sole purpose was to teach the sons of God how life in the kingdom ought to be lived. The result was a complete shift of emphasis. To start with, the law as Christ taught it is predominantly positive: he lays the stress directly upon love to God and man. Also, the law of Christ concerns itself with character, and underlines the importance of a right attitude and motive in one's heart. Christ calls repeatedly for humility (Matt. 5:3; 18:1ff.), a single eye to God and the things of God (Matt. 6:22ff.), uncalculating generosity (Matt. 5:42; Luke 14:12ff.), unconquerable meekness (Matt. 5:5, 38ff.), heavenly-mindedness (Matt. 6:19ff.), and unselfconsciousness in well-doing (Matt. 6:3, 25, 37ff.); and he reserves his fiercest denunciations for pride (Luke 14:11), hypocrisy (Matt. 6:1–18; 7:1ff.; 23:13ff.; Luke 12:1), and covetousness, the service of mammon (Matt. 6:24; Luke 12:15ff.). These things are not stressed in the Old Testament as our Lord stresses them. We see, then, that when Christ re-stated the law in the light of the coming of the kingdom, he shifted the whole centre of interest and emphasis away from the externals of correct or conventional conduct to the heart and character of the child of God. In all his teaching on the Christian life, it is with this that he was supremely concerned. And we who call ourselves his disciples can hardly excuse ourselves if we do not share his concern.

Christ's View of the Authority of the Old Testament Law

From what has been said thus far, we might expect to find that our Lord brushed aside the Old Testament legislation as no longer having any relevance for Christian people. It is striking, therefore, to observe that in fact he did exactly the opposite, and asserted in categorical terms its abiding validity. 'It is easier for heaven and earth to pass, than one tittle (tiny letter) of the law to fail' (Luke 16:17 KJV), Till heaven and earth pass, 'one jot or one tittle shall in no wise pass from the law, till all be fulfilled' (Matt. 5:18 KJV). The law, he added, retains its binding force specifically over those who have entered the kingdom. 'Whosoever therefore shall break one of these least commandments, and shall teach men so, he shall be called least in *the kingdom of heaven* (i.e., of God); but whosoever shall do and teach them, the same shall be called great *in the kingdom of heaven*' (v. 19 KJV). He scathingly dismisses the oral law, 'the tradition of the elders,' by which the Pharisees set such store, as unauthoritative 'commandments of men' (Mark 7:7), but by contrast he insists that the written Mosaic injunctions are 'the commandment *of God*,' 'the word *of God*' (Mark 7:8f., 13), and must therefore be obeyed.

He tells us further that we should radically misunderstand his own ministry if we thought that the new order which he was bringing in involved any annulment, relaxing, or cancellation of the Old Testament law. 'Think not that I am come to destroy the law, or the prophets; I am not come to destroy, but to fulfil' (Matt. 5:17 KJV). From this statement it would appear that, just as in his life and death he was consciously fulfilling the pattern of the Messianic ministry which he found laid down in the Old Testament prophets, so in his moral teaching he was consciously reaffirming, in its new and final application, what he discerned to be the substance of the Old Testament law. It is significant that he should have made the statement at all; clearly, he thought it important to guard against misunderstanding at this point, and to make it clear that, though he had come to change much in the life of God's people, he had not come to set aside the Scriptures. In John 10:35, arguing from the statement 'ye are gods' in Psalm 82:6, he lays it down as a premise common to himself and his Jewish critics that 'the Scripture cannot be broken' (that is, refuted, confuted, or overthrown). That this was his genuine conviction, and that, like other Jews of his day, he held that the written Scriptures of the Old Testament were verbally inspired, would seem to be the natural conclusion to draw from this statement, and from the other texts which we have quoted in the preceding paragraph.

But it is just here, as we said earlier, that a problem arises. There appear at first sight to be five points at which Christ brushes aside, on his own personal authority, the teaching of the Old Testament law. The first is his denial of the legitimacy of divorce for any cause but adultery (if, indeed, that), despite the existence of a Mosaic procedural regulation for divorce in Deuteronomy 24:1ff. (see Matt. 5:32; 19:3ff.; Mark 10:2f.; Luke 16:18). The second, third, and fourth are the sections in the Sermon on the Mount where he appears to criticise the Mosaic regulations about swearing, revenge, and benevolence ('ye have heard that it was said ... but I say unto you, Swear not at all ... resist not evil ... love your enemies'). The fifth is the passage in which he lays it down that man is defiled, not by the food that goes into him, but by the evil that comes out of him; a statement which seems to deny the assumption that underlay Moses' list of unclean meats in Leviticus 11. Mark, reporting the episode, comments on the significance of Christ's words in this connection—'Thus he declared all foods clean' (Mark 7:19 RSV). In these five cases. Christ's attitude to Old Testament teaching appears inconsistent with that which he seems to profess elsewhere. And this creates a problem.

But what exactly is the problem? It might be either one of two quite different problems. On the one hand, if in the passages cited Christ really rejects Old Testament teaching because he disapproves of it, then the problem is to explain what he meant when he asserted in general terms the law's unqualified authority. On the other hand, if we accept these general assertions at their face value, then the problem is to explain what he meant in the five cases quoted. Which of these two ways of formulating the problem is the right one?

Let us for a moment explore the first view of the problem. Those who take it would presumably wish to hold that Christ's real attitude to the Old Testament all along was one of critical independence. Christ, in their view, was a proto-liberal: he set himself above Scripture as judge of its teaching, accepting what he approved and rejecting what he did not. As the late C. J. Cadoux put it, Christ always followed 'his own direct awareness of what was true and good'; hence he 'took the liberty of freely setting aside one injunction of Scripture in favour of another, and even of appealing from the Mosaic law itself to ultimate principles grasped intuitively. This independent attitude to the law did not prevent him quoting as divine and authoritative those parts of it which he felt to be eternally valid'—but it did stop him from endorsing those parts with which he disagreed.[2] As we have said, the problem on this view is to explain the presence in the Gospels of such statements as 'the Scripture cannot be broken,' and our Lord's twice-repeated insistence that not the smallest detail of the law shall pass away (i.e., lose its force) as long as time lasts (Luke 16:17; Matt. 5:18). If these statements did not express our Lord's mind, what are they doing in the text?

Only two answers to this question are really possible. The first is to say that the statements are not genuine. But there is no evidence to warrant such a verdict. The second answer is to say, as Cadoux did, that when our Lord made these statements he did not really mean what he said: not that he sought deliberately to deceive his hearers as to his own views (that idea is surely quite incredible), but rather that he did not fully know his own mind. Either his view of the authority of Scripture altered, or oscillated, during the course of his ministry, or else he simply failed to see that his treatment of particular texts was inconsistent with his own professed principles. Cadoux allowed for both possibilities. But our Lord himself would seem to rule them both out when he assures us that 'my doctrine is not mine, but his that sent me' (John 7:16); 'as my Father hath taught me, I speak these things' (John 8:28); 'I have not spoken of myself; but the Father ... gave me a commandment, what I should say' (John 12:49), and therefore 'heaven and earth shall pass away; but my words shall not pass away' (Mark 13:31). If we accept our Lord's testimony that all his teaching was divinely given and abidingly true, we can hardly be content with Cadoux's theory that this part of it, at any rate, was the product of an unstable or muddled mind.

Moreover, if it were really the case that Christ parted company with Moses in the five cases under discussion, why did not his enemies make this a ground of accusation against him? When he threw out his challenge, 'Which of you convicts me of sin?' (John 8:46), why did not somebody cite the fact that at certain points he would not accept the authority of the Mosaic law? Why was it that at his trial the Jews had to invoke the aid of false witnesses in order to trump up any sort of charge against him? Clearly, not even his bitterest foes thought that he had at any point denied the authority of the Mosaic law, much as they would have liked to think it. And it is certain that Matthew, Mark, and Luke did not think so. For they report Christ as preceding his teaching on the five points in question by the most emphatic vindications of the authority of the law. Thus, in Matthew 5 Christ's teaching about divorce, oaths, revenge, and loving one's enemies follows straight upon verses 17–19, in which, as we saw, Christ affirms that the entire law stands for ever as a rule of life, even in the kingdom of God. In Luke 16, Christ's denial of the lawfulness of divorce and remarriage (v. 18: 'Every one who divorces his wife and marries another commits adultery, and he who marries a woman divorced from her husband commits adultery;' RSV) directly follows the statement that 'it is easier for heaven and earth to pass away, than for one dot of the law to become void' (v. 17). And in Mark 7, the words in which Christ 'declared all foods clean' come straight after a slashing attack on the Pharisees for setting aside the law of Moses, and the fifth commandment in particular, in order that they might keep their own unauthoritative tradition (vv. 6–13). These juxtapositions, in which Matthew, Mark, and Luke clearly saw no inconsistency, are in reality most significant; for they make it virtually incredible that in the five matters under discussion our Lord was really, as we should say, 'writing off' the Mosaic law. The idea that on each of these occasions Christ should have gone straight from vindicating the law as the authoritative word of God to criticising and repudiating something it prescribed is surely fantastic.

The only possible conclusion seems to be that in his treatment of these five points our Lord was in fact doing something quite consistent with his assertions that the law continues in force. Can we see what this was? I think so. It appears that in each case he was seeking to bring out the true meaning of the law against the negative, legalistic, external interpretation put upon it by the Pharisees. If we look at the passages in question, we shall see this clearly.

Look first at Matthew 5:21–48, a famous passage from the Sermon on the Mount in which four of our five problem cases are dealt with. The passage is a unit consisting of six sections, each of which is introduced by a version of the formula 'you have heard that it was said . . . but I say unto you.' Since each of our Lord's statements of what was 'said' starts with words from the Mosaic law, some have thought that it was the law of Moses, as such, that he was criticising. But two considerations make it clear that it was not.

First: this whole passage is introduced, and the key to its interpretation is given, by verses 17–20, on which we have commented already. In these verses, as we saw, Christ says (a) that he has come, not to destroy the law, but to fulfil it; (b) that any disciple of his who disregards 'one of these least commandments' will suffer loss in the kingdom as a result; (c) that unless his professed disciples go beyond the righteousness of the Pharisees, they will never enter the kingdom. These verses lead us to expect that Christ's motive throughout the coming discussion will be to vindicate the law by showing the full range of its demands, and to show the incompleteness of the Pharisaic exposition of it. They are quite inconsistent with the idea that he is going to show that the law itself is in error.

Second: the introductory formula to each section is not 'you have *read* that it was *written*—as we would expect if our Lord's intention had been to discuss the Mosaic law as such—but 'you have *heard* (from your scribal instructors) that it was *said*.' This also indicates that Christ is contrasting what others have said that the law of Moses means and what 'I say unto you' that it means. He is challenging, not the law, but misinterpretations of the law. A final proof of this is the wording of verse 43, where our Lord says, 'You have heard that it was said, "You shall love your neighbour and hate your enemy."' The words 'and hate your enemy' expressed part of the Pharisaic understanding of the law, no doubt, but they are not in the Old Testament at all. This shows conclusively that what Christ is criticising is the Pharisaic exposition of the law, not the law itself.

Each of the sections into which the passage falls, when studied, bears this out. Let us glance at them.

The first two sections (vv. 21–30) deal with the sixth and seventh commandments. Christ does not find fault with either, but simply points out that they cover much more than outward acts of murder and adultery. This is evidently a hit at the externalism and lack of concern about motives that marked the Pharisaic exposition of these commandments.

The third section (vv. 31f.) deals with divorce. Here Christ simply points out that if a man divorces his partner for any cause other than adultery and she remarries, her new husband commits adultery with her and her old husband must take the blame. He cites the Mosaic procedure for divorce ('Whoever divorces his wife, let him give her a certificate of divorce,' cf. Deut. 24:1), but he does not find fault with Moses for enacting it. He had no cause to: for the enactment of itself did not confer the right to divorce upon anyone. In Matthew 19:8 our Lord tells us how he understood Moses' action. Moses, he said, 'suffered' (allowed) you to put away your wives 'because of the hardness of your heart.' In a situation in which unfaithfulness to the marriage bond was already rampant, and wives were being irresponsibly abandoned, Moses instituted a set procedure to regulate divorce. His aim, presumably, was to keep this evil under control, and to safeguard the status of the woman by ensuring that she should have proper legal evidence that she had been put away, so that her former husband could make no further claims upon her. But Moses did not condone this evil by his endeavours to control it. Divorce was not made any the less undesirable by the introduction of a legal procedure for effecting it. And what our Lord is condemning in Matthew 5:31ff. and 19:8–9 is not the law which fixed this procedure, but the idea (common, we know, among the rabbis) that divorce for other causes than adultery is permissible on the basis of this Mosaic regulation. Christ counters this idea by insisting that the existence of the regulation in no way implies God's approval of such practice. As Genesis 2:24 (quoted in Matt. 19:5) makes clear, God's order is lifelong monogamy, and any breach of this order, however procedurally correct, remains the highroad to adultery.

The fourth section (vv. 33–37) deals with oaths. The law on which the Pharisees laid stress (Lev. 19:12; cf. Deut. 23:21) demanded that oaths taken in God's name should be kept. Christ finds no fault with this principle. The point he is concerned to make is simply that his disciples ought to be the kind of persons whose plain word, unadorned by oaths, will stand sufficiently firm. Also, he wants to warn them against getting entangled in the Pharisaic casuistry of swearing. The Pharisees held that oaths not taken in God's name need not be kept (a dishonest subterfuge which Christ attacks directly in Matt. 23:16ff.). Here, Christ seeks to undercut this principle by showing that every oath is an implicit invocation of God. Again, however, our Lord is not in this criticising the law, but its expositors.

The fifth section (vv. 38–42) is a dissuasive from living by the principle of tit for tat. The law says that an eye for an eye and a tooth for a tooth is a right penal proportion, and Christ does not dispute this. What he does dispute, rather, is the rightness of invoking this principle (originally laid down, no doubt, to restrain disproportionate private revenges) as an incentive for trying to extract the eye and the tooth on every possible occasion. It is the vindictive spirit, the spirit that always demands reparation, that Christ is criticising. Instead of being vindictive and standing on your rights, he says, cultivate the spirit of unconquerable meekness so that you may overcome evil with good.

In the final section (vv. 43–47), on loving one's neighbour, the words 'and hate thine enemy,' with which Christ finds fault, are not biblical at all, as we observed earlier; so that there is no ground whatever for supposing that Christ is here criticising anything other than Pharisaic misinterpretation of the law.

From our brief survey, we conclude that any suggestion that in this passage Christ rejects certain Mosaic laws as unauthoritative is quite groundless. What he is doing is simply exhibiting the true meaning of the law as a rule for life in the kingdom of God.

Nor can we fairly treat the words by which (according to Mark's later interpretative comment) Christ declared all food clean as implying that he rejected the Old Testament food-law as uninspired and unauthoritative. The subject about which he was speaking was not, after all, food, but defilement; and what he was saying about defilement was that the thing that makes a man unclean in God's sight is not what he eats, but what comes out of his heart. This only shows that our Lord saw that the uncleanness with which the food-laws dealt was merely ceremonial, not moral or spiritual. It typified the real defilement of sin, but was not to be equated with it. That it was God who had instituted the food-law, presumably to be a constant reminder to his people of the reality of spiritual defilement, Christ was not denying in the least. The effect of his statement was thus to interpret the food-law and throw light on its real significance, but not in any way to impugn its divine origin, or its binding authority over himself and his fellow-Israelites.

It seems, then, that all the problem passages in which Christ appears to cast doubt on the inspiration and authority of parts of the Mosaic legislation can be explained and, indeed, demand to be explained, in a way that is entirely consistent with Christ's assertion that no jot or tittle should ever pass from the law. Christ knew, of course, that the civil and ritual part of the law, which had been given specifically for the ordering of Israel's national life in Palestine until Christ should come, would soon cease to apply, when the Israelite state passed away. But when he spoke of the perpetuity of the law, what he had in mind was the moral law, which in different ways both the civil and ritual law had subserved. This, he maintained, was an abidingly authoritative word from the Lord, which, in the final form and application which he himself had given it, would stand for ever as the law of God for his own people.

Our Lord's Exposition of the Law

What was the essential content of this law, as our Lord understood it? Very briefly, as we close, we will try to sketch out the answer to this question.

The heart of the law, in Christ's estimation, was the two great commandments. When the lawyer asked him which was 'the great commandment in the law' (a perennial topic of rabbinic debate), Christ replied by giving, not merely one, but a pair: 'You shall love the Lord your God with all your heart, and with all your soul, and with all your mind. This is the great and first commandment. And a second is like it. You shall love your neighbour as yourself' (Matt. 22:37ff.). What it meant to love God with all one's powers, Christ showed throughout his ministry by a mass of teaching on self-denial, the single eye, loyalty to God, prayer, trust, joy, and Christian contentment. What it meant to love one's neighbour as oneself, he explained parabolically on the occasion when, in answer to the question 'Who is my neighbour?' he told the story of the Good Samaritan. That there was a necessary link between loving God and loving one's neighbour he showed on two occasions by quoting against the Pharisees God's word in Hosea 6:6: 'I desire mercy, and not sacrifice' (Matt. 9:13; 12:17). Active compassion for one's needy fellow-men, Christ means, is more acceptable in God's sight than any number of pious acts without compassion can ever be.

On the two great commandments, said our Lord, 'hang all the law and the prophets' (Matt. 22:40)—in other words, the rest of the Old Testament moral teaching merely expounds and applies what these two commandments say. It is here, therefore, that the Decalogue comes in, as the central core of this exposition. Our Lord himself discussed the meaning of some of the commandments, and it is notable how in each case he penetrates to the positive requirement which underlies their negative, prohibitionary form. Thus, in dealing with the fourth commandment to keep holy the Sabbath day, Christ treated the Pharisaic approach, based as it was simply upon a casuistry of abstinence, as altogether wrong, and argued, on biblical grounds, that the Sabbath was made for man's good, and that not only works of personal necessity, but also acts of love and kindness to others, might be performed on the Sabbath with the greatest propriety (cf. Matt. 12:1ff.; John 7:23f.; Luke 13:10ff.). Again, in commenting on the sixth commandment, as we have seen, Christ's concern was to prohibit the spirit of hate, which rules out love; indeed, at the end of Matthew 5 he shows that what he really wanted to do was to bring his disciples to a frame of mind in which the spirit of love, even to their enemies, would rule them in everything, so that there would be no room in their hearts for hatred at all. Again, in dealing with the seventh commandment, he finds underlying the prohibition of adultery and lustful thoughts a positive demand for purity and singleness of heart toward God, which it is worth any amount of effort and self-denial to enter into, because of the vastness of the issues that hang on it. 'If your right eye causes you to sin, pluck it out and throw it away; it is better that you lose one of your members than that your whole body be thrown into hell . . .' (Matt. 5:29 rsv). At all costs, the disciple must become a whole-hearted, single-eyed, utterly devoted lover of God and of men.

Such are the lines on which our Lord's exposition of God's law proceeds. It is, as we have said already, an ethic for the redeemed, those who love God because he has forgiven and adopted them, and they have known his saving grace. It is, as Christ himself implies, an ethic for the regenerate; the good fruit of a life according to this pattern can only grow on a good tree, a tree that has been made good by the new birth. And it is, above all, an ethic for disciples, for the ideal which it sets forth was incarnate in the Master himself, and if we want to know what obedience to the two great commandments really means the most effective way to find out is to turn our eyes upon him and watch how he walked. He himself, in life and conduct, in the love and humility with which he served God by serving and dying for men, was the clearest exposition of his own understanding of God's law, and it is most of all by observing him that we shall learn of him to walk in the way of righteousness.

CHAPTER 8

A Lamp in a Dark Place

A Sermon

My text is in 2 Peter, chapter one, verses 19–21. The apostle writes:

We have the word of the prophets made more certain, and you will do well to pay attention to it, as to a light shining in a dark place, until the day dawns and the morning star rises in your hearts. Above all, you must understand that no prophecy of Scripture came about by the prophet's own interpretation. For prophecy never had its origin in the will of man, but men spoke from God as they were carried along by the Holy Spirit.

If, like myself, you have inspected the redwoods in northern California, you will have noticed that in the redwood preserves the trees are carefully fenced off. Perhaps you wondered why. The answer is that though they are enormous, they have a very shallow root system. And the constant tramp of visitors' feet can so loosen their roots as to make them very vulnerable to any wind that blows. That is why the fences are put up: to keep the visitors from coming too near to them just in case they become too unstable and go over.

That says something to me. For a third of a century now, [1979] I have been a Christian, an Evangelical Christian watching Evangelicalism. And I have come to think that in many ways, Evangelicalism today is like the redwoods. I have seen marvellous growth in the Church of England, my own mother church. Something like a quarter of ministers in local churches have a definite Evangelical commitment. That's utterly different from how it was thirty years ago. Here in the U.S.A. something like a fifth of the total population professes to be born again. That, I am sure, too, is a new thing. I've seen Christian literature prosper and expand, increase in quantity and deepen in quality, both at popular and specialist levels. There was nothing like present-day Christian literature when my Christian pilgrimage began. I've seen great movements of evangelism. I've seen exciting movements of church renewal. I've lived through the period of the great congresses at Berlin and more recently at Lausanne. There has been great and wonderful growth.

But also, it seems to me, there has been an unmistakable shallowness. And as the years have gone by and the growth has increased, it seems to me that the shallowness, if anything, has become shallower, rather than being eliminated as the growth went on.

You say, 'What do you mean?' I mean this. I am sure I have seen over this past generation a real weakening in doctrinal concern in favour of an almost exclusive concentration on experience. If you feel right and you act zealous, well, doctrine doesn't matter. I have seen uncertainty and confusion in all sorts of surprising places with regard to quite basic beliefs; and in particular, with regard to the nature and use of the Bible, which is the source of all our beliefs. Of course when there is uncertainty here, you must expect to find uncertainty everywhere else. I have seen in my time major churches and teaching institutions slip away from the Bible. And I have been troubled.

I believe that the work that we are doing at this summit could, under God, do much for the rootage of Evangelicalism in our time. The alternative I fear to some effective concern for the roots is that we shall continue to get shallower and shallower. And what will the outcome of that be? Soon I fear we may get swept away. I am sorry to start on such a gloomy note, but this is how I see it.

I believe such a statement on inerrancy as we aim to produce, with its corollaries drawn out, is a most strategic thing in seeking to re-establish the authority of the Word of God in the lives of Christians and of the Christian church. We've got to go deep if we are going to touch the heart of the biblical problem in our time. In the context of modern discussion, the inerrancy theme takes us to the heart of things.

Maybe you've heard the story of the doctor who was called in to a patient with acute abdominal pains, and straightaway he gave him a pill. A person looking after him said, 'Oh, doctor, is that going to make him better?' And the doctor said, 'No, but it's going to give him a fit and I can cure fits.' God forbid that we should ever handle the real needs of the church in our time like that. We must zero in on the actual problem area, which is our attitude to the Bible.

Look at the words of our text. They are words of the Apostle Peter, the anchorman of the early church. They are words from the second letter that he wrote, using, I think, a different *amanuensis* to compose it for him from Silvanus, the man whose help he employed in the first letter. (And that, be it said, explains why the style of 2 Peter is different from the style of the first letter, and why the difference gives no support to fashionable doubts about Peter's authorship.) It is Peter writing, as he believes, his very last words of testimony and instruction to those who have been the recipients of his ministry, those for whom he has been carrying recognized pastoral responsibilities, those to whom he has sought to minister the things of God over the years.

He knows that his death is near. He speaks of it in 1:14. 'I know,' he says, that I will soon put it aside [the tent of this body], as our Lord Jesus Christ has made clear to me.' And so he writes the second letter to remind them of things that he has taught them already and to confirm them in those things. He says in verse 12, 'I will always remind you of these things, even though you know them and are firmly established in the truth you now have.' And again, in verse 15: 'I will make every effort to see that after my departure you will always be able to remember these things.'

And you say, 'What are these things?' The answer is clear. They are the things concerning the knowledge of Jesus Christ the Lord, 'Jesus Christ our Lord and Saviour,' as Peter says in verse 2. And again in verse 3, and again in verse 8 of this chapter. It's a favourite phrase of this letter and it comes again in the very last words that Peter speaks, in 3:18, where he summons his readers to 'grow in the grace and knowledge of our Lord and Saviour Jesus Christ.' This has been the burden of Peter's ministry all along, and it's these things concerning Jesus Christ the Saviour and Lord that he wants to enforce in this last letter.

And here in the section from which our text comes, he is dwelling on 'the power and coming of our Lord Jesus Christ.' You have that phrase in verse 16. In verse 3, Peter spoke of the power of Christ, whereby he gives life—how his power has given us everything we need for life and godliness. And the coming of our Lord Jesus Christ, that great climactic event of human history, in the light of which all of God's people must live, and which they should look forward to every day.

In verses 16–18, speaking of these things, he has been confirming the reality, the truth, the reliability of the things he has taught them concerning Jesus Christ, God's Son, by referring to the transfiguration, that great event of which he himself was an eyewitness. 'We did not follow cleverly invented stories,' he says in verse 16. [Incidentally, that word for stories is *myths* and that word *myths* in the first century, just as today, meant 'a story which whatever its significance for you hasn't got a factual basis.'] That is the point that Peter is making here. 'We didn't follow cleverly invented myths.' 'We didn't stuff you up with stories that have no factual basis when we told you about the power and coming of our Lord Jesus Christ,' he says. 'No, we were eyewitnesses of his majesty. We saw and heard. He received honour and glory from God the Father; a voice came to him from the majestic glory saying, "This is my Son, whom I love; with him I am well pleased." We saw it, we heard it,' says Peter. 'Take it from me.'

And then, amazingly, in verse 19 he goes on to say, 'Don't just take it from me. And don't even *primarily* take it from me. We have a more sure source of knowledge about Christ even than eyewitness testimony; we have something more firm, more sure, more reliable.' He does say, you note, 'We have,' putting himself alongside them. 'Something more sure for me,' says Peter, 'although I saw and heard. Something more sure for you, although I've been telling you what I saw and heard.' Do you see what he is doing?

His thought is running in entirely the opposite direction to the way that we so often commend the faith today. We say, 'Yes, it's written in the Bible. Let me show you; let us turn to the text; read it with me. And more than that, it works. Let me tell you my experience and I'll show you how it works.' And we move from Scripture to personal witness, to personal experience, as if that were the more sure thing, and the real basis on which we are commending biblical truth. But Peter here is doing exactly the reverse. 'Now,' he says, 'we have something more sure than any testimony that you can hear from me. We have the word of the prophets, which is more certain.'

You will notice that I do not say '*made* more certain,' as modern translations and commentaries generally do. They think Peter means that the voice from heaven at the transfiguration made the prophetic word more trustworthy than it was before. But 'made' is not in the Greek, which reads: 'We have something surer, (namely) the prophetic word (*logos*),' and which would have been written differently had Peter meant what the moderns suppose. With the King James version, I follow the natural sense of the Greek. Back, now, to it.

'The prophetic word,' Peter declares, 'is more sure even than my eyewitness as an apostle to what happened at the transfiguration.' You say, 'That's an amazing thing for Peter to say. Why should he speak of Scripture as "more sure even than this"?' One way to understand his statement is as apostolic modesty; are we to understand it perhaps even as apostolic uncertainty? No, it's not that. Peter's point is rather different.

When he speaks of the word of the prophets, the prophetic word, what he is thinking of is, as all the commentators agree, the Old Testament as a whole. All of it was regarded as prophetic. Moses was a prophet and the historians were thought of as prophets, the former prophets as they were called, and all the teachers and psalmists and wisdom writers in the Old Testament were prophets too, as those first-century men understood the matter. And the nature of the prophetic word was that it was, in truth, God teaching, God preaching, God addressing men, God instructing men in the most direct way through, to be sure, the utterance of human agents. But the word that they spoke was most directly and most categorically his word and not their own. 'Thus saith the Lord' the prophets would say, and this was to alert all who heard them, and later all who read what they wrote, that what was now to be presented was not the private idea of Jeremiah, or Isaiah, or Ezekiel, or whomever, but it was the word of the Lord God himself, speaking directly through his prophetic spokesman. And the way Jesus and the New Testament writers quote and echo and apply texts from the psalms and wisdom books show that they thought them prophetic in the same sense, even though the prophets' introductory formula was not used.

Now the point Peter is making is this: 'God has spoken in the prophetic word. And what I say, and what the voice that I heard from heaven said, can only be right if it is in line with that prophetic word.' The prophetic word confirms it. It is not the other way around. The prophetic word confirms that Peter's experience is right, that the voice that he heard from heaven was indeed the voice of God.

That word is more sure, more certain, more reliable. That word confirms all our experience now. That's the point that Peter is making. Take everything ultimately, he says, from the written word that God has given us.

And that suggests three matters about which I invite you to reflect with me a little further now. First, how much does Peter's statement cover?

Well, as I have already said, it covers the whole of the Old Testament, for all the Old Testament was understood as prophetic in those days. Taking the total testimony of Peter's letter, however, we are made to realize that it covered apostolic writings, too. For in 2 Peter 3:15, in a passage which by implication is exhorting all his readers to study of the Scriptures, Peter speaks of 'what our dear brother Paul also wrote with the wisdom that God gave him.' 'He writes the same way in all his letters,' Peter continues, 'speaking in them of these matters. His letters contain some things that are hard to understand.' Yes, we can agree with that. 'Things which are hard to understand, which ignorant and unstable people distort, as they do the other Scriptures, to their own destruction.' Isn't that striking? Here in the apostolic age, Peter is already comparing the letters of his fellow-apostle, Paul, with 'the other Scriptures,' classifying them as Scripture themselves.

And really there is nothing unnatural in that. Peter knew what apostolic inspiration was. Peter, after all, enjoyed it himself. And Peter understood that apostolic inspiration under the New Testament corresponded to prophetic inspiration under the Old. The psychological mode might be different, but the effect—men spelling out the heart of God in words which God himself gave them—was identical in both cases. So, we may take what Peter says about the prophetic word, that sure word, more sure than anything one sees or hears or experiences, indeed, the test of all that one experiences—and we can apply that to the New Testament writings no less than to the Old. In other words, the prophetic word for us comprises all the canonical Scriptures.

Second, whence does the absolute sureness of the sure word derive? Here again the answer is clear. From its divine origin; from the fact that it is God's word. It has, if you like, a dual authorship. The men are its secondary authors; God is its primary author. This is, of course, how Peter himself explains the matter in verses 20, 21. 'You must understand,' says Peter, '[this is very important], that no prophecy of Scripture came about by the prophet's own interpretation of things.' This wasn't his own private idea; nothing of the kind.

'Prophecy never had its origin in the will of man, but men spoke from God as they were carried along by the Holy Spirit'—carried along in the way that a ship is carried along by the wind. The Greek verb would be used for a ship with the wind in its sails. Scripture is more sure than any other source of knowledge, just because it is directly and essentially, the testimony, word, or witness of God. When we read of Jeremiah receiving God's promise in the first chapter of his book, 'I have put my words in your mouth,' we with Jeremiah are being told what divine inspiration means.

In Acts 4:25, the story of the first recorded Christian prayer meeting, you have the early church praying, 'Sovereign Lord . . . You spoke by the Holy Spirit through the mouth of your servant, our father David: "Why do the nations rage, and the people plot in vain?" In Acts 28:25 you have Paul saying to the Jews in Rome, 'The Holy Spirit spoke the truth . . . through Isaiah the prophet.' You have New Testament Christians acknowledging that God put his word in the mouth of these Old Testament men. You have the writer to the Hebrews quoting Scripture as the word directly of the Father and the Son and the Holy Spirit. And you have our Lord Jesus himself saying in Mark 12:36: 'David himself, speaking by the Holy Spirit, declared, "The Lord said to my Lord: Sit at my right hand until I put your enemies under your feet."' When these words are spoken in the New Testament record, witness is being borne that the nature of Scripture is in truth God's words in men's mouths.

This view of the nature of the Scriptures, please note, is not the instrumental view of inspiration which is so popular today: the view that Scripture is essentially no more than human witness, sincere but fallible, to God and his grace. This view allows you to discount details of what the biblical witnesses say. That is not the view that Peter is putting forward. He doesn't start with the Bible's humanity. He starts with its divinity. And his view of the nature of Scripture is not simply instrumental, human witness which God uses despite its flaws; rather his view of the nature of Scripture can be called incarnational. For to Peter the words of Scripture are simply the human form, the human nature, we might say, of God's own witness to himself.

Peter starts with the testifying God. And he says the reason why God speaks through these biblical writings to us now is because he spoke through them once for all, when he gave them. They are therefore the means of God's instruction to us now, the most sure source of spiritual knowledge that we have. The view which we must take of inspiration, according to Peter, is an incarnational view in this sense: that just as in the person of Jesus Christ we see the Son of God having taken to himself human nature, while his essential identity remains his divine identity; so in the Scriptures we see the human form which God's word took to itself, but its essential identity is that it is God's word, in no way diminished by its human embodiment.

Men spoke from God, being borne along by the Holy Spirit. Their word was and is the word of God, because of its divine origin. It is so before ever God uses it to communicate to us today. And because it is God's own word, it is universal in its relevance, even though it is particular in its form. The Bible is a set of particular writings from the ancient world just as Jesus Christ is a particular Jew of the first century A.D. But just as Jesus Christ is God's Son and Saviour for the world, so Holy Scripture is God's word and wisdom for the world. In this particular reality there is the universality of God. Because the Bible is the Word of God, it is utterly trustworthy and utterly authoritative for our lives—not just relatively so, as being the best source we have, but absolutely so, as being God's pure word of address to all mankind which stands for all eternity.

My third question is: what is all this saying to us, here and now?

I believe it comes to us from God as a word of positive and definite encouragement, telling us that we are right to be here and right to be seeking to do together the thing that we are doing. Our concern revolves around the word *inerrancy*. We are saying that the authority of Scripture lacks substance unless the inerrancy of Scripture is affirmed as its basis. Some folk today question whether the word *inerrancy* is helpful. I value it and I would like to tell you why.

It is in truth, in the scriptural sense of the word, a 'Shibboleth'; that is to say, a touchstone whereby things are known. I know that the word *Shibboleth* has bad vibrations and has been cheapened today, but you will remember how that word originally came to be used. In Judges 12 we read how the Gileadites and Jephthah possessed themselves of the fords of the River Jordan, and when an Ephraimite, one of their enemies, came across, they would ask him if he was an Ephraimite. Well, of course, he would say 'No.' But then they would ask him to say the word *Shibboleth*. And if he was an Ephraimite, he couldn't say it, and then they knew who he really was, and they dealt with him accordingly.

The word *Shibboleth*, which Ephraimites couldn't pronounce, thus became a touchstone of identity. Now I want to put it to you that this word *inerrancy* is similarly a touchstone of identity. Reactions to it tell us what people really mean when they speak of the authority of the Bible. If inerrancy is denied, as it tends to be by those of our friends who think of the inspiration of Scripture in instrumental terms only, then that which has authority for them is only a privately edited Scripture, a Scripture minus those bits and pieces which they think are wrong. And of course, there is no higher court of appeal for them than what they think; and what they think today, they may change their mind about tomorrow. And it has to be said by their friends, for their friends see it more clearly, I think, than they themselves, that once you start along this line, all certainty is gone. This I have seen before.

I come to this conference as one who has been ministering in the Church of England. In the Church of England in the first decade of this century, there were a group of folk brought up in the good, old Evangelical way who began to call themselves Liberal Evangelicals because, they said, 'We can allow ourselves to doubt the total truth of Scripture and the biblical view of the atonement and the death of Christ, and we shall not lose anything of the vitality of Evangelical faith, but we shall be able to make adjustment to modern theology, and that will give us greater influence.' Two generations have passed. The pioneer Liberal Evangelicals truly had the root of the matter in them. In the 1940s, when spiritually I began to sit up and take notice, they were still at the helm and appeared to be carrying everything before them, while Evangelicals of the older type were a very small minority in the Church of England, with a very poor public image.

In the 1970s, however, the situation is reversed. The children and the grand-children of the first Liberal Evangelicals have mostly now ceased to call them-selves Evangelical in any form at all. Most of them are in the radical camp of those who doubt the deity and the resurrection of Jesus and call in question the Trinity and do not expect the personal return of Jesus and have no doctrine of the atonement. They understand new birth not in terms of entering into a new life but simply of turning over a new leaf. Naturalism has come in and swallowed them up. That's the way it goes. And when I hear Francis Schaeffer asking apropos of the weakened view of biblical authority and biblical inspiration that's going the rounds today, 'What is this going to do for our grandchildren?' I say, 'Brother, you are asking the right question!' My English experience enables me to answer it. I know what it will do for our grandchildren if in fact it isn't scotched.

Peter affirms ontological inspiration—inspiration comparable to the incarna-tion of Christ himself. He is the Son of God; the Bible is the Word of God. There-fore, Peter affirms that the whole of Scripture is authoritative, and its authority is the authority of God. Now he says, and surely we can begin to see something of the weight of what he is saying now, 'We have that which is utterly sure, the biblical word, and you will do well to pay attention to it, as to a light shining in a dark place.'

I think I know why some of my brethren have abandoned biblical inerrancy. Partly they have been offended by unhappy things which believers in biblical iner-rancy have sometimes done in interpreting the Bible, and partly they have been bothered by those minor discrepancies of detail which still are with us, though, may I say, not the same ones that bothered our fathers and our grandfathers. The law of the study of discrepancies seems to be that one generation's problems come to be solved in the next generation and a fresh crop of little problems emerge for that generation to pass on to the next generation and so it goes. Certainly, there are these little discrepancies and it seems to be part of the discipline of the life of faith that we should be living with them and acknowledging that because the Bible is the Word of God, these things must be optical illusions. If we can't see it now, we should believe it, and maybe our children will see it to be so as knowledge increases, just as we in our day have seen the removal of some little problems (the exact dating of the Kings of Israel, for instance) which bothered our fathers.

On this matter of discrepancies I remember something which I read in an old seventeenth-century Puritan named William Bridge, in a passage where he says that harping on discrepancies shows a very bad heart. (I cite it from memory.) 'For the godly man,' he says, 'it should be as it was with Moses.' Then he appeals to Exodus 2. 'When a Godly man sees the Bible and secular data apparently at odds, well, he does as Moses did when he saw an Egyptian fighting an Israelite; he kills the Egyptian, that is, he calls in question the secular testimony, knowing God's word to be true.' But, says Bridge, 'When he sees an apparent inconsistency between two passages of Scripture, he does as Moses did when he found two

Israelites quarrelling. He tries to reconcile them. He says, "Aha, these are brethren. I must make peace between them."' It's quaint, but sweet, and I think very true. It is a word from three hundred years ago for us.

But, as I say, though I understand how it is that some of my brethren have abandoned inerrancy in these days, I think it a tragic weakening of their witness. Inevitably it means that the Bible, which they profess to acknowledge as their authority, becomes a nose of wax for them. They can bend it any way they like; there is no certainty for them in what it says. But Peter's words must encourage us to go on seeking to bear our witness in line with his witness to the divinity of God's word written.

There is a final matter on which I invite you to meditate with me the darkness of the dark place. 'You do well to pay attention to the Scripture, the prophetic word, the word which men spoke from God, as they were carried along by the Holy Spirit. For,' says Peter, 'it's like a light shining in a dark place.' That word *dark* is one which is used in Greek for a dingy place, like a cellar, cowshed, or mine. And you can see, straightaway, the thought that Peter is picking up here. It's a thought parallel to that which is given in Psalm 119:105, that well-known verse where the psalmist says, 'Your word is a lamp to my feet and a light for my path.' By its light I can see to go. Without its light I could never see to go, and would be bound to lose my way.

That's the point that the psalmist is making here. It's a picture. Here he is and it's dark and he's got a journey to take, and in the dark he can't see the path. The country is rough and if he tries to travel in the dark, he'll slip and stumble and fall, and he'll hurt himself. Someone kindly gives him a light. And you know what happens when you've got a light. You hold it up in front of you, your flashlight, your lamp, whatever it is. It isn't the same as the sun coming up; it doesn't banish all the darkness that surrounds you; but it does banish that little bit of darkness in front of you so that you can see the way to go. That's what your flashlight is for.

Well, that, I believe, is Peter's thought here. You do well to pay attention to the word, he says, as 'to a light shining in a dark, dingy place.' The place, I think, is indoors rather than out, though the Greek word doesn't make that absolutely certain: but Peter is, I think, speaking about our hearts (as he is explicitly in the next clause), rather than about the world around us—though that, in all conscience, is dark and dingy too. The human heart is regularly a place that is actually dirty, where the muck and the dirt needs to be shown up so that it can be removed. And it is a place, certainly where there are many obstacles to well-being—prejudices, biases, complexes, obsessions, and the like—which you need the light in order to avoid being tripped by. You know what it's like trying to make your way through a furnished room in total darkness. You don't know where the furniture is—you fall over it; you bang your legs; you can hurt yourself quite considerably by running into things. Your heart needs a light, and, says Peter, 'you do well to pay attention to God's word. God's written word is as a light that shines in a dark place to enable you to avoid falling victim to the obstacles and see your way and maybe clean it up and remove the dirt.'

Three nights ago I was in a student meeting. A young man said to me afterward, 'I was talking to a friend of mine last week and I didn't know how to answer him. He was urging that it's perfectly all right to be a minister and a practicing homosexual. What was I to say to him?' The man had never thought that he would be asked such a question. He had been completely dumbfounded by hearing it. I said, 'Well, would he think it right to be a minister if he were a practicing fornicator?' I went on with him along that line, which I think is the scriptural line to take. But these things, we know, are being said in the church. And indeed, there are some who are acting on these principles. It's a dark world. It's a dark church. People's hearts are dark, even Christian people's hearts, and no wonder. It's bewildering. We need light. Thank God, we have in the written Word of God the light that we need.

If anyone should say to you or me, 'Is it you, you troubler of Israel, stirring up dust, forcing people to argue and debate about inerrancy?' we should have to reply, as Elijah replied when a similar thing was said to him, 'It's not we that trouble Israel, but the trouble comes with those who are leading Israel astray over the truth and authority of the Word of God.' Who is putting out the light? And who is seeking to put on the light? I don't think I need to debate that point, as if there could be any doubt.

Bless God for the light that he has given us for our journey through this dark world. That light is the Holy Scriptures, the inspired Word of canonical instruction on God and godliness which shines as a light in this very dark place. Learn to thank God for the Word and to commend what we believe about it, by the way in which you treasure it, read, mark, learn, and inwardly digest it. I remember a book of mine in which the contents page carried this precious misprint, 'RSVP means Revised Standard Version,' but RSVP—*répondez s'il vous plaît*, reply if you please—is in truth what God has in effect written in the front of our Bibles for us all. The Word is for us to treasure up in our hearts and respond to in faith, as the day-star of spiritual understanding arises within us. God give us grace so to do, to say with Isaac Watts, 'My hiding place, my refuge, tower, and shield art thou, O Lord; I firmly anchor all my hope in thy unerring Word.' Let this be the word of our hearts as we attend to the light which God has given to us to shine in this dark place, and by God's grace we shall do well.

CHAPTER 9

Upholding the Unity of Scripture Today

As it is natural for pendulums to swing, so it is also for academic opinion. Critiquing conventional wisdom and exploring alternatives that might fit the facts better is after all the name of the game, once our classes and grading are through. So it should cause no surprise that this century should have seen brisk oscillations of view regarding the unity and diversity of Scripture.

Seventy years ago the liberal idea of an ultimate evolutionary pluralism in Scripture was in the ascendant. Reacting against that, Karl Barth and the pioneer British biblical theologians developed theologically unitive hermeneutics based on Chalcedonian Christology and the concept of *Heilsgeschichte* respectively, and such theologians as T. F. Torrance on the Barthian side and Brevard Childs on the biblical theology side still carry the torch for these approaches. (They have a good deal in common, of course.) But both these unitive approaches to interpretation are currently in eclipse, and the interest of academic Biblicists has come to centre once more on forms and items of diversity in the canonical material. The common view, it seems, is that there is more to be learned from studying differences between the things that biblical authors say than from noting their similarities. The pendulum has not swung back to unitive theologizing as yet.

So I may as well say at once that the views that I am going to express now are somewhat at a distance from the mainstream of professional theological thought in the West today. (I see no reason why that need worry either you or me, but I thought it best to come clean about it right at the start.)

I begin, now, by observing that in both East and West, in both reformed and unreformed churches, the traditional emphasis has been on the harmonious unity of the canonical Scriptures. Historically this emphasis went with a stress on their divinity as being in truth God's message to the world, his instruction in faith and life—in other words, as being throughout God's law (*torah*) in the biblical sense of that term. Showing the internal unity of the Scriptures was then seen as part of the interpreter's task. Interpretation accordingly was practiced, really if not always self-consciously, in terms of a specific model found both in Scripture and in all the cultures to which Christianity came—the model, namely, of the law of the land; and four ideas shaped and controlled the interpretative enterprise.

The first idea was of normative content. Scripture was the heavenly legislator's *didache*, his teaching, his *doctrina* (to use the Latin equivalent beloved of Augustine and Calvin), from the explicit statements of which, both narrative and explanatory, we learn what is true orthodoxy, true worship, and true obedience.

The second idea was of internal coherence. As law codes are to be presumed consistent, so all the contents of Scripture, originating as they were held to do from God's mind as their single source, were to be treated as harmonious and were to be interpreted in terms of the principle that the Reformers called *the analogy of Scripture* or *the analogy of the faith* (*analogia fidei*). Accordingly, Anglican Article 20 states that the Church may not 'so expound one place of Scripture that it be repugnant to another'—for such exposition would necessarily be wrong somewhere.

The third idea was of continuing and multiple application. What the books of Scripture said to their original recipients they were thought of as continuing to say in application to each successive generation, just as unrepealed secular legislation continues to bind each generation of citizens. As applications of secular law are made by bringing its principles to bear on particular cases under the guidance of its overall purpose and are valid whether or not the terms of the law explicitly envisage the cases in point, so it was held to be with the Bible.

The fourth idea was of the legislator maintaining his law. God was believed to watch over his word to perform it, keeping his promises, blessing those who trusted and obeyed him, and judging any who failed to tremble at his word.

The locus of authority on this view was quite specific. Authority belonged to texts—that is, to the specific things that God tells us in the words of texts.

The model is of course familiar, for all conservative Protestant theology assumes it, and I imagine that most of us here would rise to defend it from the way in which the Bible in both Testaments interprets itself.

By contrast, contemporary emphasis on the diversity of Scripture goes with a stress on Scripture as man's witness to God, a multiform collection of materials that emerged from what can only be called a sustained struggle between God and his people. As such it embodies perceptions and presentations of God that are neither consistent nor coherent. The model in terms of which Scripture ought consciously to be read is the complex traditional process that occurs in any large continuing community, a process in which elements of tradition regularly get reinterpreted and revised.

This model is offered, to be sure, more as a definition of the unity of Scripture than as a denial of it. Clearly, however, it negates something that the other model affirmed and sought to justify—namely, the real possibility of applying Scripture (that is, of moving from the particularity of biblical statements to the particularity of present-day situations and questions) with genuinely normative force. On the modern view there is no way through this theological Northwest Passage, though there are many hermeneutical Frobishers who have opined the contrary and made voyages of intellectual exploration to try to prove their point. But if you start with fallible human witness in Scripture you end up with fallible human guesses from its expositors, and no more. That is surely inescapable.

Looking more closely at the diversity-based approach, we see four emphases characterizing it. The first is on the conceptual variety, both diachronic and synchronic, of the teaching and traditions that the two Testaments contain.

The second is on the comprehensiveness of the historic canon, which includes so much of this diverse material. The third is on the actual selectiveness and one-sidedness of all biblical expositors, each working with a 'canon within a canon' (a fact that, though doubtless undeniable, should surely be regretted as a weakness of the flesh rather than paraded as if it were a theological virtue). The fourth emphasis is on the instrumental effectiveness of the biblical material in all its diversity for triggering ethical and relational insights, even if not for teaching doctrine in the sense of factual truth about the work of God. In all of this the Kantian cloven hoof shows—namely, the denial that there is such a thing as revealed truth.

Authority on this view is not specific. It belongs to the tradition as a whole viewed as a matrix of insights, and accepting its authority means only committing oneself to reaching one's final views in dialogue with the biblical material.

On this approach methodological perplexities arise if norms for faith and life, authoritative truths for evangelistic proclamation and pastoral direction, are sought. Thus:

(1) How can biblical theology as a discipline yield norms? How can study of the thought of biblical authors ever be more than phenomenological description, a chapter in the history of ideas?

(2) How can systematic theology as a discipline yield norms? How can study of alternative conceptual grids for formulating the faith ever be more than phenomenological description?

(3) How can hermeneutical endeavours yield norms? The so-called 'new hermeneutic' of Ernst Fuchs makes the text interpret you creatively, in such a way that what emerges from it is not intelligibly controlled by what is meant historically. That might be thought extreme. E. D. Hirsch assures us that no utterance means more than its writer thought he meant by it at the time, which would rule out all forms of *sensus plenior* and all forms of the claim that the meaning of some OT prophecies was unclear to the prophets themselves and is only made clear by NT facts and teaching, and would call in question the apostle John's declaration about Caiaphas unwittingly prophesying salvation when he spoke of one man dying for the people (John 11:49–52). This might be thought extreme too. But where between these extremes can norms ever appear if no text is in itself the normative message of God?

Many exponents of the modern approach see that it can never answer these questions, and so they conclude that the quest for norms of truth is inherently improper and that any attempt to derive norms from Scripture is an abuse of the intellect and something of a confidence trick. Conservative theologians battle against this attitude in liberal circles all the time.

Such then are the two models, side by side. Now my question is: How should those who embrace the first, as I do, believing that there are good and necessary reasons for doing so, respond to the emphasis on the internal diversity of Scripture that marks model number two? To this question I offer the following answer.

The first main point is that all the observable differences between theologians and theologies in the canon to which attention has been called ought to be acknowledged and assimilated. That, for instance, the Gospels draw four distinct theological portraits of Jesus, and that Paul and John and the writer to the Hebrews had different vocabularies and thought forms, and that all three possessed architectural minds whereas Peter and James did not, are facts of importance about the form in which God's instruction reaches us. But if within this material contradictions of theology or empirical fact are alleged, the proper reply (so I judge) is that the allegations are unwarranted. Here let me voice three of my own convictions.

First, as regards theology in Scripture, I think that the differences between the expressed thought of the NT writers in particular are often absurdly exaggerated through concentrating exclusively on matters of linguistic form and neglecting to study the directional thrust and persuasive purpose (for specific pastoral situations) of the things they wrote. It is the implications that a man draws from his own statements rather than their verbal form as such that show what he meant, and the implications for faith and life that the various NT authors draw from their doctrinal statements are strikingly homogeneous and consistent—which surely suggests that the theologies on which those practical inferences rest cannot really be so very different in meaning.

Second, as regards statements of empirical fact and detail in Scripture, I am sure that we often make difficulties for ourselves in two ways: (1) by not seeing that the question of the truth of these statements relates precisely and specifically to what they were meant to communicate to their own first readers in their own culture; (2) by not realizing that the meaning-content of these statements was less in the ancient oriental world than would be the case in a history book written in the modern manner, where every detail counts, and also by failing to realize that we really cannot know how much or how little each such statement asserts without logical and literary, over and above merely grammatical and philological, study of the larger semantic unit—that is, the book—to which it belongs.

Third, as regards our inerrancy claim itself, I judge that, while inerrancy ought always to be held as an article of faith not capable of demonstrative proof but entailed by dominical and apostolic teaching about the nature of Scripture, we have now reached a point in technical Evangelical scholarship at which the possibility of an entirely harmonious exegesis of the whole Bible has been shown in such conclusive detail that the century-old liberal assertion that this position cannot be held with intellectual integrity may safely be dismissed as refuted.

It is not an adequate response to the questions that the emphasis on diversity raises, however, merely to reassert the inerrancy of Scripture, and so I move on.

The second main point is that while appreciating the phenomenological, descriptive method of studying canonical material, which highlights its diverse literary types—sermons, songs, poems, prayers, works of theological history, prophecy, wisdom and pastoral didactics, letters, lists, statistics, liturgies, laws, visions, etc.—as well as highlighting the different emphases, interests, nuances and purposes of each item, I think we need to see this method—which I am sure we all of us use—as calling us to renewed reflection on the idea of canonicity. Model two treats the canon as essentially a human compilation, a sort of heritage collection of literature, brought together in the interests of maintaining and deepening a sense of group identity by constantly presenting to the group (in this case, the church) the traditions that made it what it is, and that are to be valued now because of their proven power to trigger insights about living to God. But model one, which sees Scripture as divine communication—God's revealed witness to his own work, will and ways in the form of human responsive witness to these things—entails that God himself created the canon as one of his saving acts, a stage in *Heilsgeschichte,* and that he did this first by inspiring the various books and then by enabling the church to discern them as being inspired and therefore to acknowledge them as the divinely given rule of faith and life. From this it follows that Scripture as a whole, with all its internal diversity, must be viewed as an organism of divine instruction, and that along with proper recognition of the historical particularity of each biblical book and its contents, a canonical style of interpretation must be consciously developed, as by Irenaeus and Augustine and Calvin and Barth and Brevard Childs in their different ways, and that we must frankly admit that Jews studying the OT as a closed literary unit and Christians studying it as the foundational and preparatory section of a two-part literary unit will not have the same overall view of the significance of its contents, however far they may be able to walk together in the formal descriptive exercises of phenomenological analysis. Can this approach to the phenomenon of the canon be vindicated today? I am persuaded that it both can be and must be, though Evangelical scholars seem slow to take the task in hand.

Let me add explicitly that this approach does not forbid us to distinguish and compare and contrast the theologies of different periods and different biblical authors, nor to abjure the stimulus of finding relatively polar emphases in these different theologies, as for instance Paul D. Hanson does in his book *The Diversity of Scripture* where he works with the form/reform and visionary/pragmatic polarities that he sees emerging in the OT.

Nor does it forbid us to recognize that particular emphases in this or that biblical writer may become specially relevant at particular times, over and above the general relevance that they have at all times—as did Paul's teaching on justification by faith without works in the sixteenth century, and as I think his teaching on the revelation of the mystery of the cross in 1 Corinthians 1–2 has become today. The approach I describe does, however, require that we recognize as complementary rather than contradictory all the different emphases and theologies that Scripture yields, and that we finally seek to integrate them all into a single texture of thought about the living God whose character and purpose do not change, whose value system for human life remains constant, and whose work is ever to be understood within the paradigms and parameters of interpretation that the canonical Scriptures yield.

The third main point is this: When we emphasize the internal diversity of Scripture, and in particular the difficulty of blending all that Scripture tells us about God himself (so that sometimes we have to throw in the towel here, as did Calvin when he said of the Creator-turned-Redeemer: 'In an ineffable way [ineffabili quodam modo] he loved us while he hated us') we are alerted to the inescapable inadequacy of all theology in this world. 'Now I know in part; then I shall understand fully, even as I have been fully understood' (1 Cor. 13:12)—said Paul, and if that was the truth about him, much more is it the truth about us.

Now I am not implying that theology does not in fact advance. The contrary is true. Certainly there is a sense in which, in the great John Robinson's phrase, fresh light and truth break forth again and again from God's holy Word, as new existential questions get brought to it. Then, as Gadamer states the matter, its horizons mesh with ours at points not explored hitherto, and fresh light does indeed come our way.

In our day, for instance, it seems that fresh light has broken forth from the Word on ecological ethics, a matter on which Scripture was not interrogated till very recently. And perhaps (though here I speak less confidently) light is currently breaking forth also on the meaning of womanhood, and the place of women in the church and the world. Certainly, too, God uses controversy to stir up the questioning through which deeper insight comes, as happened when Paul challenged the Galatian and Colossian heresies, and Irenaeus challenged Gnostic dualism, and Athanasius challenged Arianism, and Augustine challenged Pelagianism, and Luther challenged medieval works-religion, all working with insights that had come to them, as it seems, through the provocation of the error they attacked.

Perhaps Christians of the twenty-second century, if the world lasts that long, will perceive that fresh light and deeper insight broke forth from the Word through the debates of the past hundred years about revelation and the Bible. Who knows?

Certainly, also, insight into divine things is deepened through dialogue with the historic traditions of Christian thought, as we see the cases of, for instance, Thomas Aquinas, John Calvin, and Karl Barth. And here I feel bound to say that I wish some of the exponents of my model two, described earlier, would dialogue more deeply with the traditional expositions of my model one rather than march on in resolute disregard of the older view, taking it for granted as good evolutionists that they must be better and wiser than their fathers because they arrived later. Tradition, after all, is the fruit of the Spirit's teaching activity through the ages as God's people have sought understanding of Scripture. It is not infallible, but neither is it negligible, and we impoverish ourselves if we disregard it. I am bold to say that Evangelicals, even those of Anabaptist polity, should be turned by their own belief in the Spirit as the church's teacher into men of tradition, and that if we all dialogued with Christian tradition more we should all end up wiser than we are.

But when all is said and done, surely Barth was right to say that 'the dogma' (he meant the definitive understanding of God's revealed Word) is an eschatological concept. Here we are on the way to it; it is only in glory that we shall actually have attained to it. Though it is possible (as I think) for our theology to be true as far as it goes, we can be sure that we do not at present understand anything about God perfectly. Here we know only in part. God is to us mystery, a reality that transcends our understanding, and in the same sense so is Scripture.

When we look at either we cannot see all that we are looking at, since the light that shines forth from both is too bright for our spiritually dim eyes. Highlighting the diversity of Scripture will remind us that this is so, and that our theological reach exceeds our present grasp, just as Romans 7 shows us that the moral reach of men of the Spirit also exceeds their present grasp, and by thus reminding us it will keep us humble and hard at work, theologizing in hope. Therefore we should be grateful for it. In truth, such highlighting serves us well and does us good.

PART TWO

INTERPRETING THE WORD

CHAPTER 10

Understanding the Bible: Evangelical Hermeneutics

To discuss hermeneutics today is to open a can of worms. Though worms have their uses—birds thrive on them, and anglers catch more with worms than they could without them—most people find them uninteresting; and similarly, few people get fired up by hermeneutical questions. But hermeneutical questions, though abstract, complex, and tedious, have to be faced, for our answers to them bear on our interpretation and understanding, not just of the Bible, but of all documents and data, of whatever kind. We live in an age in which intellectual pluralism in the global village has made hermeneutics central to top-level academic discussion throughout the whole range of the humanities and human sciences, and the first thing to say as we approach the theme of Evangelical hermeneutics is that it pitchforks us, willy-nilly, into this larger debate.

The Hermeneutical Debate

What, we ask, is the debate about? It is about three things together, on which all civilization, scholarship, and social life depend: communication, interpretation, and understanding. *Communication* may be defined for present purposes as our attempt to share, one way or another, our thoughts, perceptions, and feelings; *interpretation* then means our attempt to gather from words used, signs made, and signals displayed, what is meant and how it applies to us; and *understanding* denotes our state of mind when interpretation has so succeeded that meaning and application—*significance* as some term it—have been grasped. When that which is communicated is truth, and interpretation is correctly done, then our understanding of the communication will constitute knowledge of truth, something that all serious people want very badly; and that knowledge is the ideal and goal over which the discipline of hermeneutics stands guard.

Do we need hermeneutics? Yes, for problems arise. Truthful communications may be, and often are, misinterpreted, so that only misunderstanding and misconception result from them. A true grasp of communicated content may yet be misapplied. And a true declaration of the true application to us of a true communication may still not be understood, due to our own inner inability to take it seriously. This inability may result either from alien assumptions (presuppositions) shaping and pre-empting our thought processes or from our being unable to internalize the truth imaginatively, and both conditions are effective bars to understanding. The discipline of hermeneutics offers itself as therapy for those various breakdowns.

To put it positively: the art of communication is to avoid needless obscurity, obfuscation, and offence, and to achieve accuracy and clarity of presentation. The art of interpretation is to avoid reading into communications what cannot be read out of them, and to achieve precision in receiving and applying them. The art of understanding is to lay aside prejudice and the wilfully closed mind, and to achieve imaginative as well as conceptual *rapport* with both the communicator and the communication. Hermeneutics is an umbrella study of all the factors involved in practicing the second and third of these fine and useful arts, that is, in interpreting and coming to understand what is presented to us.

It is startling to see how in this century specific disciplines coming under the umbrella of hermeneutics have multiplied. There is *linguistics*, the study of how language functions in the human community in its conveyance of meaning. There is *semantics*, the study of meanings themselves. There are also *semiotics*, the study of signs and processes of signification; *logic*, expanded from its original, Aristotelian focus on the forms and criteria of valid thought into the study of all types of rational expression in speech; *communication theory*, which concerns itself with the processes of 'encoding' and 'decoding' our messages to and from each other; *psychology*, which studies subjective factors bearing on people's actual beliefs; *sociology*, which explores differences between one cultural milieu and another, pinpointing circumstantial hindrances to grasping what is being communicated when it comes out of a culture that contrasts with one's own; and *philosophy*, which studies, among other things, our various concepts of truth. Those who work in hermeneutics cannot but remind observers of the old woman who lived in a shoe; they have so many academic specialisms to look after that it is small wonder if they do not seem always to know what to do. But if interpretation and understanding are themselves to be understood and practiced with success, there is no help for it: the business of hermeneutics, however complex it proves, must go on.

Three Hermeneutical Questions

Every field of study that works with documents and/or data needs, and currently has, its own special hermeneutics. This consists of an attempt to answer, in terms of that particular field of study, the three generic hermeneutical questions, which are as follows. First comes the question of *descriptive analysis*—what really does it mean to understand what is being communicated from the other mind, or the verbal source, or the observed data, that is the object of study? What relation to that object constitutes understanding of it? Next comes the question of *critical criteria*—in what ways, and for what reasons, may persons who think they understand each other, or readers who think they understand documents, or data, actually fail to do so? What goes wrong, and what are the indicators of inadequacy when things have gone wrong? What tests must a proposed understanding pass before it can be accepted as sound and true? Then, third, comes the question of *prescriptive technique*—how, in our across-the-board variety of ventures in interpretation and understanding, can we most effectively programme ourselves for success in the enterprise?

Semiotics, the study of signs and signification, has been whimsically defined as having for its subject matter every device and resource that can be used to lie or mislead; and in the same way hermeneutics can be defined as having for its subject matter everything that can stand in the way of our 'getting the message.' The definition sounds negative, but the aim is positive: hermeneutics seeks to understand understanding in principle in order to clear the path to it in practice, and engages with obstacles to understanding in order to remove them.

Our present concern is with the special hermeneutics of Evangelical Bible study. To this topic we now turn.

How Different Is the Evangelical Approach?

The first thing to say is that Evangelical Bible study, both within Anglicanism and outside it, is a distinctive activity. This is because of the distinctiveness of the Evangelical view on how the Bible should function in the church. To be sure, the Bible is the sacred book of the Christian church as a whole, and all sections of the church study it from one standpoint or another. But, just as Evangelicals believe themselves to be trustees for the most authentic version of the religion that Christ and his apostles founded, and that the New Testament exhibits and explains, so they are self-consciously Bible-based in their believing and behaving in a way that other forms of Christianity characteristically are not. Catholicism, whether Roman, Orthodox, or Anglo-Catholic Anglican, has historically venerated the Bible as the authoritative Word of God, but has trusted tradition (that is, for practical purposes, the say-so of the on-going church itself, voicing its historical consensus through its appointed officers) to interpret the Bible on all major matters. Protestant subjectivism, a movement of thought that has in the past called itself rational, liberal, progressive, and radical by turns, has seen (and apparently settled for!) enormously diversified conclusions among its exponents, but is unified at the level of method by its attitude to the Bible. It refuses to categorize the Bible as God's own testimony to himself and teaching about himself, given in the form of human testimony to him and teaching about him; it knows that this is the historic Christian view, but for various reasons refuses to receive it. Instead, it treats Holy Scripture as a flawed and often unhelpful, though sometimes stimulating and insight-triggering, resource for reconstructing and restating Christianity within the frame of current secular thought. But Evangelicalism has historically affirmed the infallibility and *sufficiency* of the canonical Scriptures as a God-given guide in all matters of faith and life; their *necessity* as a control and corrective of human thought about God, which left to itself will always go astray; and the *clarity* or *perspicuity* of the entire collection, as a body of intrinsically intelligible writings that demonstrably belong together and constantly illuminate each other. These three principles, taken together, yield a functional view of biblical authority that sets Evangelicalism apart from all other forms of Christian faith.

At the risk of seeming to over-simplify, but in order really to clarify, we may state the position this way: Catholicism says that those who want to know the mind and will of God on Christian essentials should listen to the teaching church, and finally let tradition guide them; subjectivists say that they should listen to the expert theologians, and finally let their own thoughts guide them; but Evangelicals say that they should listen to Holy Scripture, and finally let its teaching guide them, however much reordering of their prior ideas and intentions this may involve, and however sharply it may set them at odds with the mind-set of their peers and their times.

Like the Christians of the early centuries, Evangelicals stand at a distance from the fashions of thought and behaviour that mark the culture around them; rather than uncritically endorse that culture, whether in its secular or its ecclesiastical aspects, thus becoming its puppets and its victims, they seek to evaluate its philosophies, presuppositions, and prejudices by the teaching of God's own textbook, and to identify only with what Scripture sanctions. 'My conscience is captive to the Word of God,' cried Luther at Worms; 'to go against conscience is neither right nor safe' (he meant, it imperils the soul); so 'here I stand, there is nothing else I can do; God help me; amen.' Evangelicals have in mind Luther's example of declining unbiblical conformities as they do their Bible study.

The Bible and Belief

To be sure, Evangelicals value the tradition of the church—the whole church, be it said, not just its Evangelical segment! Evangelicals are not stereotypical Anabaptists, imagining that nothing of importance for understanding the Bible happened between the New Testament era and their own day; nor are they stereotypical sectarians who think that all truth flows in their own stream and there is nothing they need to learn from any other source. They know that getting help from the Christian past is a proper form of Christian fellowship, and since they know too that the Holy Spirit has been interpreting God's word to the church from the start, they expect to find church traditions to be full of wisdom; which in fact is what they constantly do find. But they treat tradition as ministerial rather than magisterial, and make a point of testing the various traditions (that is, the church's past efforts to spell out and apply the Bible) by the Bible itself; for they also know that the church can go wrong, so that a position may be traditional and yet not true. Therefore, though Evangelicals respect tradition, they do not regard any of its deliverances as infallible and irreformable, and remain in dispute with Roman Catholicism in particular with regard to this.

Again, Evangelicals respect reason's demand for clarity, coherence, and comprehensiveness, and must not be thought (as sometimes they have been) to sponsor obscurantism, anti-intellectualism, or irrationalism in any form. Evangelicals meet this demand for rationality, however, by showing that what God teaches in Scripture is rational and coherent, both in itself and as a frame and foundation for understanding everything else, and they oppose all speculation that cuts loose from, moves beyond, or goes against biblical truth. Their reasons are, first, that sin has so disoriented the human mind that natural theology, not grounded on Scripture, can never be wholly right, and, second, that loyalty to Jesus Christ requires them to limit their ideas about God and his world to what the Bible explicitly tells them. The rule of faith embedded in Christ's teaching is that belief and behaviour must be ordered by the light of the Jewish Scriptures, supplemented and interpreted by his own words of witness and those of the members of the apostolic circle—in other words (to cut a long story short) by the Bible as we have it. Seeing this, Evangelicals maintain that the rule of embracing biblical teaching without addition, diminution, or deviation, is integral to and indeed, from a formal and methodological standpoint, constitutive of authentic Christianity.

The Bible and Devotion

Nor is this all. It needs to be added that the Bible has a determinative role not only in Evangelical belief but also in Evangelical devotion. Hearing Scripture preached, reading it regularly, memorizing it (as those, past and present, who were not able to read it for themselves have always had to do), masticating and internalizing it by meditation, and applying it to give content to one's personal worship—one's praise and prayer, one's faith, hope and love—as well as to find direction for the living of one's personal life—are characteristic Evangelical procedures for developing one's communion with the Father and the Son. Evangelicalism is conversionist and evangelistic, in the sense of insisting that all human beings need to exercise penitent and obedient faith in the crucified, risen, reigning, and returning Lord Jesus Christ as their Mediator and Master, since only by this means does any adult come to enjoy eternal life; so that all who have not yet turned from sin to trust Christ in a conscious way must be urged to do so at once.

Central to conversion, as Evangelicals understand it, is a living relationship with the living Lord, and the heart of Evangelical testimony to the impact of the Bible on those who soak their souls in it is that the word of the Lord constantly brings home to them the presence and power of the Lord of the word. The transforming impact of devotional commerce with the Bible, as Evangelicals characteristically witness to it, is thus, in the most direct sense, the work of Christ. He walks, as it were, out of the pages of the Bible into our lives. He writes on our hearts the faith set forth by Paul, John, Matthew, Peter, and the rest of the Bible writers, so that again and again we find ourselves turning back to him in contrition, in excitement, in love, and in gratitude. Particular passages search us and leave lasting impressions on us, particular words of praise fire our spirits so that we start praising too, and we know inwardly that it is Christ himself who by his Spirit made this happen. Thus more and more we come to see how much we owe to him and how faithful he is in leading us on with himself.

I do not suggest that such inward experience is peculiar to Evangelicals (it is not); my point is simply that it is characteristic of lively, healthy Evangelicals in every era, every culture, and every part of the world, and that this universal, unitive experience is brought about through taking to heart the written Word of God, through which our heavenly Father and our gracious Saviour communicate with us. So the Bible is truly as basic to Evangelical devotion as it is to Evangelical theology.

The Bible and Evangelical Identity

Evangelicalism, then, stakes its identity (the phrase is not too strong) on the authenticity and authority, which involves the intrinsic coherence and clarity, of canonical Scripture, received as the true and trustworthy witness of God to himself given in the form of man's witness to him as the Redeemer-Lord of history ('his story,' as preachers put it) in the world that he made and sustains. Discernment of the dual character of Scripture as God's word in the form of man's word is basic to the Evangelical position; the characteristic claim that the Bible is infallible and inerrant mirrors this view, and so does Evangelicalism's constant insistence that the only analogy to the sacred mystery of biblical inspiration is the even holier mystery of divine incarnation itself.

Our task now is to outline the hermeneutical principles that guide Evangelicals in their efforts to grasp the biblical message; so we cannot here explore the nature of inspiration, or the place of Scripture in God's self-revealing, world-redeeming strategy, or the warrant for identifying the sixty-six books of the Protestant canon, neither more nor less, as the Word of God, important as these questions are and necessary as it is to speak to them convincingly if the Evangelical handling of Scripture is to be properly justified. Space allows only for a direct statement of the way Evangelicals go about finding what biblical passages *mean* as God's message to us today through learning what they *meant* as the human writer's message to his own envisaged readership. For this is how Evangelicals focus the interpretative enterprise, as we shall now see.

The Principles of Evangelical Hermeneutics

Evangelicals characteristically interpret Scripture, whether in the study, the pulpit, or the closet, by applying four principles. All of these are held to be prescribed from within, as it were, by the character and contents of the books themselves. Evangelical interpretation is inductive from first to last: the books are read as in effect they ask to be, and to read them thus, so that they are allowed to correct and amend our prior ideas about them and the matters with which they deal, is the basic procedure whereby their authority is acknowledged.

The first of the four principles is: biblical passages must be taken to mean *what their human writers were consciously expressing.*

This principle embodies the Renaissance insistence, out of which in a real sense the entire Reformation movement sprang, that all ancient documents, biblical texts among them, should be understood *literally* as opposed to *allegorically.* Medieval preaching had assumed that allegorical meanings were what mattered, and medieval theology had treated biblical books as storehouses of proof-texts rather than units of communication, so that adopting the common-sense Renaissance procedure could not but open a new era in biblical study. The 'literal' sense that Renaissance exegesis sought was the 'literary' sense, the sense that the writer meant his readers to catch, the sense that emerges as one takes account of the literary genre (type, category), the linguistic character, the cultural and historical background, the rhetorical structure and communicative function of each biblical book and each unit of meaning (section, paragraph, sentence) within it. In the mid-sixteenth century John Calvin became a landmark exegete of this type, and today's 'critical' exegesis, as practiced in commentary series and university and college classrooms, follows the same path. This is the method of exegesis to which Anglican Evangelicals have always been wedded, as a study of the preaching and teaching of Reformers like Hooper, Latimer, and Cranmer, Puritans like Perkins and Sibbes, and revival leaders like Whitefield, Wesley, and Newton, the Bible commentary of Thomas Scott and the work of latter-day eminences like Charles Simeon, J. C. Ryle, John Stott, David Watson, Philip Hughes, and Leon Morris will speedily show.

It must be admitted that at a popular level 'literal' interpretation has sometimes been practiced in a way for which 'literalistic' would be a better label.

'Literalistic' interpretation results when from the twin truths that the Bible is for every man, not for priests and scholars only, and that through the Holy Spirit Scripture yields up its wisdom to all prayerful, honest-hearted, and obedient readers, it is inferred that the literary considerations listed above may be disregarded—in other words, that Scripture may properly be read as if it had all been produced within our own contemporary culture, and each subject was being written about as we moderns would write about it in our ordinary everyday letters or news reports.

Such assumptions, which are really a docetic diminishing of the humanness of Scripture, can produce unhappy mistakes: celebrations of the created order get read as lessons in science (e.g., Gen. 1–2), apocalyptic symbolism as prosaic prediction (e.g., Rev. 6–20), the Gospels as ventures in biography; the Scofield Bible builds from scattered texts its eschatological scheme of rapture-tribulation-Jewish millennium; and so on. But today's Evangelicals are increasingly aware of what academic integrity in literal interpretation involves, and are less and less inclined to such hermeneutically flawed views as those mentioned; and the obsessive attempts of such as James Barr to convict Evangelicals, especially those who publish with Inter-Varsity Press, of exegetical crookedness as a way of life must be judged to have failed.[1]

It should be added that the Bible writers unanimously and unambiguously testify to a God who *speaks,* in the straightforward sense of that word—that is, a God who addresses verbal messages to people, states facts, tells us things; and therefore Evangelicals affirm, on the basis of the Bible literally interpreted, that cognitive instruction via Scripture is integral to God's self-disclosure and that biblical teaching, as such, is God's teaching, as such. Therefore they oppose as insufficiently biblical any account of revelation through the Bible that does not finally settle for the proposition of Augustine's prayer: 'What thy Scripture says, thou dost say.' The possibility of misinterpretation makes Evangelical use of the phrase 'The Bible says' as a formula of authority dangerous, as critics often point out; but the fact of inspiration makes this usage, with all its risks, right, proper, and necessary. What Scripture says, God says; this, for all Evangelicals, is a basic reality that everyone must face, and come to terms with.

The second principle is: the *coherence, harmony, and veracity* of all biblical teaching must be taken as our working hypothesis in interpretation. What this means is that Scripture must be expounded in accordance with Scripture. Text must not be set against text, nor must apparent contradictions or inconsistencies be treated as real ones, but we should proceed on the basis that there is in Scripture a perfect agreement between part and part, which careful study will be able to bring out once the relevant facts become accessible; and if at any point we cannot discern that agreement, we should conclude that the problem lies in our lack either of competence or of factual information. 'It is not lawful,' declares Article 20, 'for the church to . . . so expound one place of Scripture, that it be repugnant to another'; nor is it lawful for any individual to do so. The warrant for embracing this principle of harmony, which the Reformers were affirming when they spoke of *the analogy of Scripture,* is the fact of inspiration; for the Holy Spirit, who gave us the Bible through his superintending influence on the human writers, cannot be supposed to have contradicted himself, or vacillated in expression through not knowing his own mind.

The third principle is: interpretation involves *synthesizing* what the various biblical passages teach, so that each item taught finds its proper place and significance in the *organism* of revelation as a whole.

As a physical organism is a complex unit of life, with a given functional pattern, so the canonical Scriptures are a complex unit of divine communication—truth, wisdom, command, promise—with a built-in relationship between one part and another; and the full significance of each part is only appreciated to the extent that we are enabled to grasp that relationship. What is often said of theology, that one must have some knowledge of the whole before one can have adequate knowledge of any single part, is equally true of the Bible. The full significance of each passage appears only in its connection with all the rest of Scripture, and therefore the work of biblical interpretation requires us to move on from exegesis to synthesis, whereby we seek to establish the multiple aspects of this connection.

The contemporary fashion in bibliology (an American word, meaning one's theological account of the Bible) is to view the canon as a many-stranded collection of traditions and thoughts about God which, though not always quite compatible with each other, find their unity in their reference-point, inasmuch as they all point, more or less clearly and instructively, to the one God revealed in Jesus Christ.

Evangelicals, however, think this notion insufficient, and go further. Seeing the sixty-six books of Scripture as God-inspired parts of a God-given whole, they look within this fascinating human plurality of witnessing voices for a perfect unity of divine instruction; and what they seek they believe themselves to find. Thus every Evangelical systematic account of Christian faith and life, from Calvin's *Institutes* to the present day, offers itself, not as a personal statement of personal opinions, but as a global hypothesis as to what God's teaching in the Bible really adds up to, and must accordingly be measured by the Bible itself, the Bible whose own measure this synthetic statement has sought to take.

Two concepts that all Christians embrace in some form, but which Evangelicals understand with distinctive precision, guide the synthetic stage of Evangelical interpretation, namely *the progress of divine revelation* and *the fulfilment of divine promise.* Both need to be defined with some care.

Progressive revelation means for Evangelicals not an evolutionary process of growing spiritual discernment through which cruder notions come to be left behind (which was how the older liberalism saw the matter), but two other things.

The first is a divinely planned sequence of gracious words and works from Eden on leading up to Christ, who was himself the climax of revelation precisely in and through his ministry of redemption. The second is a divinely planned series of written documents (biblical books) recording, interpreting, predicting, and applying the successive steps in God's on-going plan of history that brought to mankind progressively clearer and richer declarations from God himself concerning his kingdom, people, and covenant. Earlier revelation became the foundation for later revelation: the law prepared for the wisdom books and the prophets; the earlier prophets became a foundation for the later prophets; the total Old Testament functioned historically and functions still as the conceptual and didactic basis for the total New Testament.

Fulfilment of promise means more than the bare fact that God keeps his word, though this is where it starts; it is the notion that directs the following out of the thematic links that bind one part of Scripture to another, and notably the Old Testament to the New. Thus Old Testament prophecies are to be understood in light of the New Testament account of their fulfilment; Old Testament types are to be understood in light of the antitypes that the New Testament identifies; the significance of Old Testament characters in their foreshadowings and anticipations of Christ and of the life of faith in him and discipleship under him are to be understood in light of New Testament comments on them and appeals to them; and so on. By following out these two principles a basic frame for synthesizing all the specific teachings of Scripture is established, and within that frame Evangelical testimony, not just from Anglicans but from the whole worldwide community of Bible-believing scholarship, affirms that the organic interconnections of these teachings become plain to see. The proof of the pudding is in the eating; the integrating and unifying value of this perspective evidences itself more and more to those who work with it.

The fourth principle is: *the response for which the text calls* must be made explicit.

All the biblical books were written to build up their readers in faith, obedience, and worship, and interpretation is neither complete nor correct until the material exegeted and synthesized has been so angled in presentation as to further this, its original purpose. God and man have not changed, and neither have the subjective dimensions of this threefold response to the God of grace. What changed from time to time was the specific content of the promises and commands by which God's people were called to live, and the external routines of the worship that he sought from them. But the heart-reality of trusting God's promises, obeying his orders, doing the things he says he loves to see and avoiding what he says he hates to see, celebrating his mercy, and adoring his glory, remained constant throughout Bible history, from Abel outside Eden to John in Patmos, and it remains so still, irrespective of cultural differences between the various locations and eras covered by the Bible story and those of our life today.

So, just as it is possible to identify in all the books of Scripture universal and abiding truths about the will, work, and ways of God, it is equally possible to find in every one of them universal and abiding principles of loyalty and devotion to the holy, gracious Creator; and then to detach these from the particular situations to which, and the cultural frames within which, the books apply them, and to reapply them to ourselves in the places, circumstances, and conditions of our own lives today. Rational application of this kind, acknowledging but transcending cultural differences between the Bible worlds and ours, is the stock-in-trade of the Evangelical pulpit and the recognized goal of the Evangelical discipline of personal meditation on the written text, both in and beyond Anglicanism. (Perhaps this is the moment to observe that Anglicans are only a tiny handful within today's world Evangelical community, and are in no sense its leaders.)

The truth seems to be that the Evangelical heritage enshrines within itself a clearer understanding of the theory of application than can be gleaned from any other source, whatever may be thought of the often over-narrow applications of Scripture principles that particular Evangelicals sometimes make. Evangelicals do not find their models of interpretation in the 'critical' commentaries of the past century and a half, which stop short at offering historical explanations of the text and have no applicatory angle at all; they find them, rather, in the from-faith-to-faith expository style of such older writers as Chrysostom, Luther, Calvin, many Puritans, Matthew Henry, J. A. Bengel, Thomas Scott, and J. C. Ryle, who concerned themselves with what Scripture means as God's word to their own readers as well as with what it meant as religious instruction for the readership originally addressed, and whose supreme skill lay in making appropriate applications of the material that they exegeted by grammatical-historical means.

Hermeneutics and the Holy Spirit

The characteristic procedures and techniques of Evangelical hermeneutics are now before us, and it remains only to add that the Evangelical way of practicing them involves radical dependence on the Holy Spirit, a dependence that is expressed by prayer for wisdom and insight before, during, and after the hermeneutical exercise itself. Evangelicals do not forget that sin, as an inbred anti-God perversity of the soul, disables minds from understanding God no less than it disables wills from obeying him, so that divine help is needed at every stage of the process of receiving the divine message. They therefore seek to practice biblical interpretation spiritually (i.e., looking to and relying on the Spirit of God) as well as scientifically (i.e., with maximum accuracy in historical exegesis and theological synthesis). It is the special genius of Evangelical hermeneutics at its best to hold these concerns together; and it is not too much to say that when this blend is properly achieved, Evangelical hermeneutics becomes a model for the whole Christian world.

Modern Criticism and the Evangelical Position

The current theological debate about hermeneutics, centring on the ideas of Schleiermacher, Heidegger, Bultmann, Gadamer, Fuchs, Ebeling, and Derrida, largely passes Evangelicals by.[2] That should not be wondered at. Adherents of the historic Christian view that God uses language (his own gift to us) to tell us things, a view that biblical inspiration presupposes and the incarnation actually entails, already know the answer to the question. How can communication from God, or about God, reach us through ancient Jewish and Christian documents produced within non-modern cultural frames?

Knowing this, Evangelicals, like other conservative Christians, do not share the perplexities about the mode and content of divine communication that appear in the thought of those for whom Jesus is not personally God, God is not a language-user, and Scripture is a compound of legend, corporate historical memory, and expressions of religious insight, feeling, and fantasy, all couched in more or less alien and transient verbal forms. Here, as in several related matters, Evangelicals march intellectually to a different drumbeat.

When Evangelical scholarship (today, a large-scale international enterprise) tests conventional critical opinions about the non-authenticity and unreliability of much biblical material, it finds them not proven and implausible; when it tests conventional pluralist assertions about the incoherence and incompatibility of the theologies that different biblical writers offer, it finds them wrong-headed and unnecessary; when it surveys the academic mainstream of current biblical studies, it finds itself thinking repeatedly of a flock of eccentric sheep, whose fanciful sophistication and brilliant incomprehension as they follow their leaders call forth wonder and sadness by turns; and when Evangelical scholarship looks at the sub-trinitarian, deincarnationalized wrigglings of modern hermeneutical study, issuing as they do in deepened uncertainty as to whether the God who makes us aware of himself actually gives us any sort of knowledge at all, it finds itself less than excited at the prospect of getting into the game. Instead, Evangelical scholarship, preaching, teaching, and personal Bible study continue in faith and hope along the old methodological paths, on the basis of the following three convictions:

First, God is the Lord of communication, just as he is the Lord of saving grace. He speaks from Scripture, read, preached, explained, and applied, across all cultural gaps and barriers, making Christ known and overcoming all muddles of the mind through the power of the Holy Spirit. He has done it constantly throughout the church's long history, and he will continue to do it, whatever the well-meant misunderstandings of his word among the learned and others.

Second, when God gives insight into Scripture, that insight is for obedience, and it is primarily the practice of obedience that opens us up to further truth. There are moral conditions of understandings as well as intellectual ones, and the former are in fact fundamental: it is those who are willing to do God's will who will be enabled to know what it is. God himself will see to that.

Third, Scripture is meant to do (not less, but) more than inform our minds, and only as, by leading us to Jesus, it fires our imagination, feeds our worship, and changes our ways dare any of us claim to understand it. But a life transformed by Scripture from an ego-trip into an intoxication with Jesus Christ is evidence of understanding at the deepest and truest level.

Thus it appears at last that Evangelical hermeneutics belong to the discipline of Christian discipleship, and the sentiments of Psalm 119:169, 171, 173 should find constant expression in the heart as the believer looks to the Father, the Son, and the Holy Spirit on hermeneutical matters:

> May my cry come before you, O Lord;
>> give me understanding according to your word.
>
> May my lips overflow with praise,
>> for you teach me your decrees.
>
> May your hand be ready to help me,
>> for I have chosen your precepts.

So may it be, increasingly, for all Christians today.

CHAPTER 11

Inerrancy and the Divinity and Humanity of the Bible

It will, I think, help you to assess what I say in this conference if you know a little more about where I come from, theologically and spiritually. Let me ask your indulgence in saying just a word or two about myself.

I was converted at age eighteen through the Inter-Varsity people at Oxford University. They gave me my nurture, and one of the first things that became reality for me in the course of that nurture was what John Calvin some years later taught me to recognize as the inward witness of the Holy Spirit to the divinity of Holy Scripture. I can still remember the gathering at which I went in, not at all sure that the Bible was the Word of God, and came out absolutely certain that it was, though all that had happened was that one visionary chapter of the book of Revelation had been reverently expounded.

It was not, as I said, until long after that I found in Calvin the phrase that fits what had happened to me. Calvin said that this Spirit-given certainty that the Bible is the Word of God is something that every Christian experiences. I rejoiced when I read that, for that was what I had experienced. The conviction that the Bible is as divine as it is human has been with me ever since, and has come out, I am sure, in all the speaking and writing that I have done over the years.

I come to you as one who identifies wholeheartedly with the Evangelical heritage in Christendom. I claim it as my inheritance and I seek to learn from all its many varieties. I believe that in Christendom values and insights are often divided and fragmented so that one needs to go around with one's eyes and ears open, drawing wisdom from every source where wisdom can be found. As a reformed and reforming Episcopalian, I am also, I hope, a learning Episcopalian and I have learned many things, may I say, from the Baptists. It will rejoice my heart if I can now share with my Baptist friends something worthwhile in return in this present in-house discussion about the nature and place of Scripture.

The *Review and Expositor* for winter, 1982, page 11, described me 'as a well-known British fundamentalist.' Where, I wonder, did they get that from? I suppose from the fact that in 1958 I published a response to a sustained two-year denunciation of British Evangelicals as fundamentalists. My defence of those

Evangelicals was entitled 'Fundamentalism' and the Word of God, and there is nothing in it that I have ever wished to withdraw. If, now, you want to tag me as a fundamentalist, you are free to do so. But let me say, my defence of what had been called fundamentalism was offered in the belief that the real issue here was and is the authority of the Bible. I do not take it on me to defend all the things that have been done in the name of fundamentalism, in Britain or anywhere else.

Sometimes I have winced at the indifference of self-styled fundamentalists to issues of scholarship, and at their black-and-white way of reasoning about everything, as if uncertainty or suspended judgement is a great dishonour to God and a sign that your faith is failing. I have sometimes winced, too, at their public style and over their separatist tendencies. But for all that, you may call me a fundamentalist, if you wish. I stand with all those who maintain the full and absolute authority of the Bible. And since the historic fundamentalists maintain this I stand with them rather than apart from them, however little I like some particular things that they say and do.

Rather than identify myself as a fundamentalist, however, I would ask you to think of me as a Puritan: by which I mean, think of me as one who, like those great seventeenth-century leaders on both sides of the Atlantic, seeks to combine in himself the roles of scholar, preacher, and pastor, and speaks to you out of that purpose. The word Puritan, like fundamentalist, is often used in an unfriendly way, but if I am to be given an unfriendly description this is the one I would prefer.

What, now, can I offer you in this biblical inerrancy conference? First, an exposition of what I believe to be true about the truth of the Bible and with it a warning out of my Anglican experience in England. When nowadays I see Christian folk teetering on the edge of what I call biblical relativism, imagining that you can retain all of Christian life and vitality, all of Christian experience and devotion to Christ while yet sitting loose to the final authority of the Bible and the final truth of, for instance, the biblical doctrine of the atonement, I shudder, because observing the Anglican Liberal Evangelical Movement has taught me that this is not so.

It was in the first decade of this century that Liberal Evangelicalism in the Church of England came to birth. Its platform was as stated above. It took two generations for that movement to die, but die it did. When I was converted, at the end of its first generation, it seemed that Liberal Evangelicalism had come to stay. The leaders of the Church of England were saying that this was the only version of Evangelicalism that could contribute anything to the Anglican future, and I was made to feel that in cleaving to the conservatives I was retreating into a backwater.

However, another generation has now gone by and during that generation Liberal Evangelicalism, having killed a number of churches, has itself died. You will not find Liberal Evangelicals in England today; the breed is extinct, for the position had no staying power.

Over the years I was involved in the task of reclaiming two congregations that had been ruined by Liberal Evangelical ministries. In each case, the job took between five and ten years. It was totally tragic that previous ministries had detached these congregations so effectively from their biblical moorings, and it was a hard and painful enterprise to bring them back to their earlier anchorage. I am glad to be able to tell you that their return to authentic Evangelical roots led to new vigour in worship, work, and witness in both cases; and I have since seen the same thing happen in Canada.

It is with all that in my memory and in my heart that I speak to you. If I seem to be warning you against biblical relativism with more passion than you would have thought appropriate, remember I am a burned child who dreads the fire. I do not want to see that liberal evangelical scenario which did so much damage in England rerun in the Southern Baptist Convention, and I intend to say all I can to try and stop that from happening.

I should here explain what I mean when I speak of biblical relativism, lest there be any misunderstanding. Whenever the Bible is not allowed to have the last word on any matter of belief or behaviour, there the Bible is being relativized to human opinion. That is what a certain type of biblical scholarship does all the time, and that is what I wish to warn you against.

The inerrancy of Scripture is the overall theme in this conference, and my next step is to make some comments on both these terms. First, please note that the word *Scripture* is a concertina word—that is to say, one that oscillates in use between broader and narrower meanings, like a concertina that is constantly being either extended or closed.

When you speak of Scripture you may be using the word to refer simply to the sixty-six books of the Protestant canon, as distinct from all other books; or to the seventy-eight-book canon defined by the Council of Trent; or to the original Hebrew and Greek and Aramaic text as distinct from any subsequent translations; or to the Bible in some vernacular translation as distinct from its original languages. Again, you may be using the term to refer to the Bible as the historical tradition of the Judaeo-Christian community of faith, honest narration, celebration and explanation of God's words and works in history, set forth for edificatory purposes by the various biblical writers. The academic discipline called biblical theology always approaches Scripture in this way.

Then, sixthly, you may be using the word *Scripture* to signify universally applicable teaching about God and grace and godliness that emerges from these canonical books when you ask them the question 'What has God to say to us here and now about our life today?' And, seventhly, you may be using the word to articulate your own answer to that question.

None of these uses of Scripture is to be censured. All of them are perfectly proper and legitimate in their place. But if they get mixed up with each other, there can be a mental crossing of wires and a short-circuiting of thought and consequent trouble for both mind and heart, as the distinction between the text that we must ascertain, translate, and interpret and our own actual interpretation gets lost.

Now for a comment on the word *inerrancy*. Quite frankly, I recognize that it is in one way an awkward word, because it is negative in form. I have sympathy with those who say that they would rather not use a negative term to describe the Bible. But sometimes one has to use negative words in order to bar out mistakes. And that I believe is the position here.

In any case, inerrant is only a negative way of saying 'totally true and entirely trustworthy,' and if that is the formula that you prefer to use, by all means do so. We are not tied to particular words as if they were magical. I find that in contemporary theological discussion, the older standard words like *revelation, inspiration, authority,* and even *infallibility* are taken and expounded by some in a way that explicitly allows, and indeed insists, that there are matters on which the Bible ought not to have the last word because what it says is wrong. In response to this, I want a word which nails my colours to the mast as one who holds that there is no point at which the Bible ought to be denied the last word. That is why I personally embrace the word *inerrancy* and make much of it in these days.

Why is this assertion of inerrancy made? I make it to declare a methodological commitment that is perceived as part of a Christian's discipleship. The commitment is to (1) believing and obeying all that Scripture sets forth, (2) exegeting Scripture in a harmonious way, (3) letting Scripture judge and control one's thoughts, and (4) responding to everything said in Scripture as proceeding from God for the instruction of his people.

What does the assertion of inerrancy commit one to? It doesn't oblige one to agree with the domino theory that if inerrancy falls, everything will fall with it. That may or may not be true, but it is not implied by the use of the word *inerrancy*. Equally, using the word does not commit one to any exegetical a priori which would force one's understanding of Scripture into an unscriptural mould.

Belief in inerrancy does not commit me to belief in the inerrancy of any particular interpreter, not even myself. Nor does it commit me to disregarding any aspect of the humanness of Scripture. Acceptance of inerrancy does not commit a person to arbitrary and evasive oscillations between literal and non-literal interpretation, either.

On the positive side, asserting inerrancy does commit one to a radical and rigorous a posteriori procedure whereby great pains are taken not to read into the text anything that cannot certainly be read out of it. Further, one is committed to robustly embracing all that the Scripture affirms when grammatically and historically exegeted. Finally, one is committed to a willingness to live with minor problems. I say minor problems because my testimony on the basis of forty years of fairly detailed biblical study is that there are no major problems for the inerrantist.

There are, indeed, problems for which satisfactory answers are not yet secured, but a commitment to inerrancy does not require, and has never required, that we solve them all. All that is required of us is that we be honest thinkers, striving to solve those problems that we can and admitting when we do not yet have the answer to this or that specific question.

What is gained by asserting the inerrancy of Scripture? The assertion of inerrancy primarily safeguards the Christian approach to Scripture as God's Word. Second, the assertion of inerrancy articulates the proper receptivity of faith, conscious of its own emptiness and ignorance and seeking to be taught by God. Further, the assertion of inerrancy establishes the Christian commitment to biblical authority in a clear way. It proclaims that the Bible is always going to have the last word. And, finally, the inerrancy commitment brings the church's handling of Scripture under critical control, at least in principle.

The word *inerrancy* has a problematical status. Some people are frightened of it for reasons of their own. They fear that it will lead to bad apologetics, bad harmonizing, bad interpretation, or bad theology. Perhaps some inerrantists have dishonoured the word by lapsing in those ways. But for all that, a commitment to biblical inerrancy, it seems to me, is not one which in itself can be anything other than right and good for the Christian and the church.

Turning now to the subject of the divinity of the Bible, I give you a formula: Scripture, though human, is divine. This is where we must begin if we are ever to understand the matter. This is the *mystery* of Scripture; that is to say, here we have a divine reality that has in it more than we can understand, like the mystery of the Trinity or the incarnation.

The mystery of Scripture focuses, first, in the marvellous integration of its sixty-six different books, written over more than a thousand years in widely varied cultures, into a single organism of truth. The second part of the mystery is the way in which God has used, does use, and continually will use, the text of Scripture to communicate his message to his church and to the hearts of each of his people. We go to the Word of God and our testimony is that God speaks. Both of these aspects of the matter come into play as we celebrate the divinity of the Bible.

What is the meaning of the claim that the Bible is divine, that is, that it is the Word of God? The claim means three things together. It means, first, that Holy Scripture has God for its source. This is its inspiration, the *theopneustos* to which Paul makes reference in 2 Timothy 3:16. God gave the documents through the human authors. Scripture is not only man's witness to God; it is God's own witness to himself in and through what has been written.

The second thing that the claim of the divinity of Scripture means is that Scripture has God for its theme. This is one of the marvels of Scripture, the unity of the message in all of the sixty-six books concerning the Creator who becomes Redeemer and makes sinners his friends and establishes his kingdom.

The third thing that the claim of the divinity of Scripture means is that Scripture has God as its user. Scripture mediates God's truth to his people; God communicates through it.

The Barthian way is to explain the inspiration of Scripture in terms of its instrumentality as the means of communicating God's Word, thus collapsing the first of my points into the third. In my opinion, this approach of Karl Barth does not do sufficient justice to the God-givenness of Scripture; therefore, I stress that the claim that Scripture is divine must give equal emphasis to all three points.

The crucial question, of course, is why one should ever claim that Scripture is divine. Christians make this claim because it is integral to the teaching of Jesus Christ and his disciples. The relevant evidence falls into three categories. First, there are the quotation formulae in which Jesus and his apostles cite Old Testament Scripture as coming from God or from the Holy Spirit. For example, Jesus himself quoted an observation by Moses from Genesis 2:24 as the Word of the Creator, and I do not think he was forgetting the context; I think he was showing that he understood all that he read in Scripture to have come from his heavenly Father. Jesus used this quotation on the occasion when his foes sought to ensnare him by means of a trick question on divorce: 'Have you not read how he who made them at the beginning made them male and female and said, For this cause shall a man leave father and mother and be joined to his wife . . .' Jesus cites this as the word of the Creator because he read all of his Bible as the word of his heavenly Father.

There is, second, a whole string of passages asserting the didactic function of Old Testament Scripture for Christians as something which God intended all along. Passages like Romans 15:4, where Paul wrote, 'Whatever was written aforetime was written for our learning' illustrate this, as do 1 Corinthians 9:9–10 and 10:11. First Peter 1:10–12 and 2 Peter 1:19–21 and 3:15–17 say the same. Paul wrote to Timothy that the Holy Scriptures were able to make one wise for salvation through faith in Christ Jesus, all Scripture was breathed out by God. Because of its divine source, Paul continued, Scripture is profitable for teaching the Christian and the church, so that spiritual maturity might be achieved (see 2 Tim. 3:15–17).

Third, there are explicit assertions that Old Testament Scripture has authoritative force for Christians and, indeed, that first it had authoritative force for Christ himself; the divine-human Messiah, who fulfilled the law and the prophets and said that that was what he came to do. Consider Matthew 5:17, 'Don't think I came to set them aside, to destroy them, but to fulfil them.' And he did, fulfilling the law by his teaching and by his life, and the prophets by the enduring of the death that was predicted for the Messiah, because he knew from the Scriptures that that was the path the Father had appointed whereby he should enter into his kingdom.

After his resurrection, Jesus met two of his disciples on the Emmaus road and the rest of them in Jerusalem, and he spoke to them in exactly those terms (see Luke 24:25–27, 32, 44–47). Even Jesus, the incarnate Son of God, lived, it seems, under the authoritative force and direction of the Scriptures (see Matt.

26:53–56; Luke 18:31–33). If he set us that example, how dare we hesitate to follow it? As for the New Testament, it rests on the principle that the teaching of Jesus and his apostles is God-given and carries divine authority exactly as does the prophetic Old Testament.

Apostolic teaching is to be received as given in the name of Christ, just as the Old Testament prophecies were to be received as given in the name of God. The apostolic testimony is written down in the New Testament, and what was true of the oral witness of the apostles applies equally to their written witness. Thus one works one's way to the point of setting the New Testament on the same level on which Christ and his apostles set the Old Testament. When this is done, we have the Christian Bible, the Old Testament and the New Testament, both divine for they both come from God.

The claim that the Bible is divine is an integral element in the doctrine of revelation. Revelation signifies the whole work of God in communicating with sinners redemptively to bring them to saving knowledge of himself. This revelation embraces three levels of activity.

First, there is God's self-revelation on the stage of history as he works redemption for the world. Revelation, at that level, finished when it reached its climax in the coming of Christ and the pouring out of the Spirit to give to the apostles the full understanding of Christ.

Second, so that the knowledge of what God had done once and for all in history might be available for all the world, in every generation, God caused a written record, a celebration, a narration, and an explanation of it all, to be written, and that is the sixty-six books of our Bible. This might be called inscripturation.

The third level of God's action can be called illumination, the work of his Holy Spirit in helping persons understand and receive the message. God's revelatory action continues at this third level but not at either the first or second levels.

Obviously, it was and is necessary that the Bible should be a trustworthy record, adequately presenting the Redeemer and the redemption that are to be known. It would not do to trust the transmitting of historical events to oral tradition; the events would then inevitably become distorted and misunderstood. If such had been the case, the third level of God's revelatory action, that is the work of his Spirit giving understanding of the message, would have been, and would today be, frustrated. We see, therefore, how vital it was that there should be a trustworthy record so that stage three might occur.

By way of balancing this discussion, let me address now the humanity of the Bible. Consider this formula: Scripture, though divine, is human.

It is fully human. The divine method of inspiration involved all of the following items: accommodation to the personal qualities and cultural perspectives of the writers, including their literary styles; setting forth revelation in the form of the human story of how redemption was achieved and made known, and how individuals who were involved fared through their faithfulness or lack of faithfulness to God; using a variety of witnesses and a pluriformity of presentation to exhibit redemption from the many angles from which the human witnesses perceived it; using the creativity of the authors who consulted sources, gave their books careful literary shape, and used poetical and rhetorical forms designed to evoke specific responses from readers; and incorporating all kinds of records (genealogies, liturgies, rubrics, census documents, and so forth) into the narrative.

The combination of immediate revelation, enhanced insight, and providential overruling that constitutes inspiration added something to the factors that constitute fully human writing but in no way subtracted from them. God used the literary creativity which he had given these men; their humanity is part of the reality of the Bible, and it is to be celebrated and acknowledged. We don't honour God by minimizing the humanness of the Bible any more than we honour him by minimizing its divinity.

The divine authorship of Scripture entails the full truth (inerrancy) of all its teaching. The human authorship of Scripture necessitates care in determining what that teaching is. This, of course, leads to the question of exegesis.

Exegesis should be grammatical, historical, culturally aware, empathetic, and self-critical. Cultural conventions of communication (e.g., with regard to numbers and narrative sequence), cultural boundaries of interest (e.g., innocence of the concerns of theoretical science), and the limited focus of each logical flow (e.g., the use of cosmological language without asserting its ontological validity) must be kept in view, lest teaching be read into texts that cannot be read out of them. In addition, the theological and religious purpose and the theocentric and doxological perspective of the biblical material must be kept in mind, for this helps us see the scope and limits of what is being taught.

The value of the brands of critical disciplines lies in the light they throw on the writers' didactic purpose and scope of concerns. What they reveal can help us in our quest to better understand the human writers so that we better understand God himself. The critical disciplines and careful scientific exegesis are developments in the modern church for which, in themselves, we should be grateful. Our concern should only be that they are not misused by being harnessed to a philosophy which already is resolved to set human judgement above what the Bible says. There is no necessary connection between any critical discipline and biblical relativism as a religious philosophy.

Finally, let me address the claim that an illuminating analogy exists between the inspiration of Scripture and the incarnation of the Son of God. In both cases, you have a mysterious union of divine and human. In both cases, you have perfection, as a result, in human form. Is that point valid? I believe that it is valid in at least these three ways.

First, it is valid as a way of dispelling the suspicion that the humanness of Scripture in some way requires fallibility and error on the human side. It was not so with Jesus: why should we suppose that it has to be so with Scripture?

Secondly, the analogy saves us from the temptation to relativize anything that we find the Bible teaching; after all, we most certainly would not allow ourselves to do that to anything that the Lord Jesus taught.

Finally, the analogy serves to dispel the suspicion that the inerrantist view of the Bible is docetic. Infallible Scripture is as fully human as is the infallible Saviour.

In these ways, the analogy between Christ and the Bible is real and true and helpful in our efforts to understand the things God has for us in Holy Scripture.

CHAPTER 12

The Challenge of Biblical Interpretation: Creation

My three presentations at this Conference have a common title, 'The Challenge of Biblical Interpretation.' I think that word *challenge* is not unfair. At an earlier Conference I presented to you my understanding of the inerrancy of Scripture, a revealed truth of God, as I believe.[1] I put it to you that Holy Scripture is totally trustworthy, though it must be correctly interpreted. When, however, it is correctly interpreted, all that it teaches in both the indicative and the imperative moods is, in very truth, God's message, that is, his word which applies to us as truly as it ever applied to anyone.

You may well come back to me now and say 'I would like to see you working out your concept of inerrancy in some of the more difficult questions of biblical interpretation: specifically, in some of the hard subjects over which some biblical interpreters have felt themselves bound to give up inerrancy altogether, believing that the concept is impossible to maintain in these areas. I grant you at once that if I am unable to make a worthwhile effort at interpreting some of these difficult topics, what I have said in this very hall about the inerrancy of Scripture will lose something of its credibility. And I hope you will agree that if I can succeed in finding a way through some of these difficult areas in which Scripture is supposed to speak out of, shall I say, both sides of its mouth, I shall be adding some credibility to the formula that I have given you. So, from this standpoint, Packer on trial becomes our agenda item.

My assigned topics are among the most controversial in the world of biblical interpretation: creation, women, and eschatology. While willing to accept the challenge of elucidating Scripture on these subjects, I ask you to bear in mind four things. First, it is inevitable that you will not all agree with everything that I say, for these are three areas on which biblical inerrantists can and do disagree with each other, as well as with those who are not prepared to believe that all that Scripture says is true.

Second, remember that disagreement about interpretation on subjects of this sort does not necessarily indicate lack of agreement either on the total truthfulness of Scripture or on the method whereby those who believe in the total truthfulness of Scripture should set about discovering its meaning and its message. Belief in biblical inerrancy requires us to seek an account of the total Scripture testimony on each subject that is internally coherent, does justice to all the data, and involves no assumption of error or contradiction, either factual or theological, in the sacred text. This is my understanding of the quest for canonical interpretation of the Word of God. Yet it is possible for folk who agree that this is what we are seeking still to come up with syntheses that differ in detail.

Third, all biblical interpretation is provisional. We must give the task our best, but as the church continues in history fresh questions arise, generated ultimately I believe by the Spirit of God, who then leads as we work with these new questions us to see things in the Bible that were not seen before. Old interpretations of Scripture are then sometimes made to appear not indeed wrong, but inadequate and incomplete. Statements which perhaps were once regarded as the whole truth now are shown as being only part of the truth because there is more to be said. My three presentations will no doubt have that character; they shall represent my best effort but will of necessity remain provisional.

Fourth, please appreciate that the practice of interpreting Scripture, like the confession of the inerrancy of Scripture is, so far as I am concerned, a non-political business. I know that in the Southern Baptist Convention there are political questions which bear directly on and are affected directly by the whole discussion of the inerrancy of Scripture and what it implies. Please understand that I am simply seeking truth and wisdom as best I can. I come to you as an Episcopalian, not a Southern Baptist, and I shall share with you what I think I see without any thought, frankly, of possible political implications. You have asked me to interpret Scripture, and I am trying to keep my eye and my mind on that task.

Let me first state in general terms my approach to biblical interpretation. The goal is to extract from Scripture, the Word of God written, the message that is there for us. The best way of describing the nature of Holy Scripture is to say, 'This is God preaching.' That formula seems to me to catch the communicative dynamism of Holy Scripture along with its divine origin, and I value a phrase that does both those things together. So I listen to Scripture to hear God preaching and instructing me in matters theological and practical, matters of belief and matters of behaviour, matters of doctrine, matters of doxology, matters of devotion, matters of orthodoxy (right belief), and matters of orthopraxy (right living). So, to listen is the churchly way in all Bible study.

When I speak of getting from the written text the message that is there for us, I am thinking of our extracting it by exegesis and exposition, exegesis that avoids exegesis, reading into the text what isn't there, and exposition that avoids being imposition, pushing onto the text things that aren't there. I am thinking of exegesis and exposition as disciplined disciplines that depend on using one's mind aright. Spiritual understanding—that is, our Spirit-given grasp of how God's truth should change and control us—rests upon exegetical and expository rectitude, for God blesses to us only his own revealed truth. So biblical interpretation is a task that makes extraordinary demands upon the mind and the heart. The task of exegesis in itself is, thus, a spiritual no less than an academic discipline.

To interpret Scripture successfully, we have to ask each passage three sets of questions. I call them the exegetical, hermeneutical, and practical questions. The exegetical question focuses on what was meant, what was the writer's message to his envisaged readership. To answer that question, we must practice a discipline which is called the grammatical historical-method. We are seeking what we sometimes call the literal, natural, historical sense of the text, and in order to do that we must put ourselves in the shoes of the writer and his expected readers. We must be aware of the cultural milieu to which they both belonged. We must be aware of their specific situation and, to use a modern word, we must recognize the *distance* between them in their situation and us in ours.

Then we have to ask the hermeneutical question, which takes this form: What then does this message, given long ago by a man of God concerning the worship and service of God in his day, mean as the word of God to us? We have to move from what it meant historically to what it means for us in the present. In addition, we have to ask another question: Is there anything in us that will act as an obstacle to our understanding what it means for us and how it applies to us? Are there any cultural prejudices operating in our lives as distorting spectacles, keeping us from seeing how this message applies to us in our own situation? Have we any cultural blind spots? That is a crucial hermeneutical question that has to be asked over and over again.

The modern theologian Gadamer has used an interesting image. Horizons, he says, must fuse in biblical interpretation. The Bible point of view must come over the horizon, that is to say, engage with the limits of our present outlook on things, and perhaps shatter those limits and reshape our thinking. This means that the Word of God coming over the horizon of our thought into the centre of our outlook must relativize us, relativize our prejudices, relativize our age, for God's Word is the absolute and we sinners are more or less off-centre in relation to it. So it must be allowed to come into our minds and hearts to set us straight. This is the hermeneutical inquiry which used to be expressed, and validly, by the question, 'How does it all apply?'

Third, we have to ask the practical question: What then must we do? How must this message from the Word of God change our ways, our thoughts, our practice? What, in other words, must we start doing now that we have not been doing up to this point, and what must we stop doing now that we have been doing up to this point, both at the level of thought and of behaviour? What should obedience to this Word of God amount to in our thought and action today?

The Holy Spirit is involved in all three inquiries. We shall be more conscious of his operation in the hermeneutical inquiry than in the historical exegetical inquiry; nonetheless, the Holy Spirit must be with us in that also if we are to understand the actual faith in God that the writer, by his style as well as his substance, is expressing. We shall be most conscious of all, I suspect, of the Holy Spirit's activity at level three, when we are asking the practical question of what obedience to this word involves. But let us be clear, the Holy Spirit must be with us in all three stages of the inquiry. Otherwise, it will fail.

I have begun by surveying the entire process of interpretation so that you may understand the method which I am following as we explore our three thorny fields of interpretation. This is the way that we are going to go now as we look together at the theme of creation, as presented in the first two chapters of the book of Genesis.

What do I bring to my task? I bring to it first a theological concept of creation which I have learned not only from the first two chapters of Genesis but also from the book of Job, the Psalms, Isaiah, and many places in the New Testament. It is a concept which one theologian defined pretty much like this (I put it that way because I have amended his definition slightly): 'Creation is a free act or series of acts of the triune God whereby in the beginning, according to his own will and for his own glory, he brought into being the entire universe without use of pre-existing material and gave it an existence dependent on his will but distinct from his own.' That is the biblical notion of creation spelled out in full theological form as the KJV of Psalm 33:6, 9 puts it:

> By the word of the LORD were the heavens made; and all the host of them by the breath of his mouth . . . He spake and it was done; he commanded, and it stood fast.

Hebrews 11:3 speaks in the same terms. The language is non-technical, but the meaning is clear: 'Through faith we understand that the worlds were framed by the word of God, so that things which are seen were not made of things which do appear' (KJV). That is to say, there was no pre-existing material out of which God made the worlds. There is more to creation, in other words, than craftsmanship.

Craftsmanship works on pre-existing material; creation is a matter of God saying as in Genesis, chapter 1, 'Let there be.' And by his very word he calls forth that which he says should be, so that henceforth it exists. Creation is mystery, as all the acts of God in the final analysis are mystery. We don't know how God did it. We couldn't do it ourselves. We must, therefore, stand in awe of it. We don't know how creation can happen. All we know from Scripture is that it did happen. God spoke and it was done. It is a marvel, a matter for praise and adoration, one of the wonderful works of God. He created the world.

The second thing that I bring to my study of these chapters, and this I believe to be very important, is a theological concept of natural science as practiced today. What I have to say here is crucial to me; a great deal hangs on it. The natural sciences grew up under the aegis of Scripture. They began to develop in the Christian West in the late sixteenth and seventeenth centuries. But the sciences neither ask nor answer the questions about the world which the Bible answers.

The sciences study the regularities, the processes, the proportions, the cor-relations, the behaviour patterns that operate within the created system, asking always, 'How does it work?' The sciences only take notice of what used to be called second causes within the system, that is functional regularities within the order of creation.

The sciences have no means of telling how the system started, nor have they any means of telling us how God stands related to it now that it is a going concern. If scientists seek on the basis of science to answer such questions, the proper response is to say, 'Sir, as a scientist none of your data tells you anything about any of this. You would be wiser to keep your mouth shut.' Of course modern cosmologists tell us with great confidence, on the basis of evidence within the system, that the universe cannot be more than ten to twenty billion years old. But even if they are right, that says nothing about where it all came from. Science, as such, cannot do so much. Scientists declare there was a big bang, but they cannot account for the existence of whatever it was that went bang. Science is not able to take us outside, or beyond, the systems that it studies.

Scripture, by contrast with the sciences, deals always with the first cause, God himself, and speaks to concerns that are beyond the scientists' reach. Science tells us how the cosmic order works; Scripture tells us who caused it to be, and why, and how its Maker is involved with it, and where he is taking it, and what significance any of it has for him. Scientific inquiry into how everything works fits easily into the biblical frame, but the sciences cannot approach the who—and why—questions that the Bible answers. Two different ways of gaining knowledge are involved here.

The scientific method is to go and look, guess and check. It is an empirical study. The biblical method is to listen and learn, let God tell you. From science we learn how things did, do, and will happen; from Scripture we learn what they mean. The goals of scientific inquiry and of biblical study are thus different. Sci-ence studies the way that each system works with a view to managing it and de-veloping what we call a technology. Scripture, by contrast, tells about the created cosmos in order to lead us to worship the God who made it, admire his work-manship, praise him for what he has done, and manage everything for his glory.

World-views are brought to the sciences by the scientists. Christians bring a Christian understanding of the world as God's creation, and they make that the frame into which they fit their scientific knowledge. Atheists, Deists, pantheists, and panentheists bring a different view of ultimate reality to their science. These views of God cannot be read out of science but they do get read into science. These days, the scientist is so venerated a member of our society that he is al-lowed to pontificate as a scientist about religion, and people suppose that it is his science which has taught him what he believes about God. It is a confusion, how-ever, to suppose that it ever was so or ever could be so. Science is best described as areligious. It does not of itself speak either for or against religion, and will slot into a wide range of views about ultimate reality. And Scripture is best described as ascientific. It does not speak scientifically, nor does it speak either unscientifically or anti-scientifically. Its sustained focus on the Creator who is behind and beyond the cosmos, transcending it while working in and through it, puts biblical teaching on a different wavelength altogether from that to which the sciences are tuned.

Scripture speaks about created things in non-technical, naive, observational language, the language of ordinary human experience which simply records what things look like and what impressions they make on the ordinary observer. Science has its technical language, but the Bible doesn't talk that technical language. Theology too has its technical language, and the Bible provides a foundation for the forming of that language, but as far as scientific language is concerned, the Bible doesn't take us forward at all. The Bible is not teaching science. This, I think, comes to expression very clearly when you compare the way in which Jesus in the Sermon on the Mount in Matthew 5 spoke about the rain with the way that we speak about the rain.

We say, 'It rains.' And if we were asked to explain how it is that it rains, we would explain that there is evaporation and clouds are formed and then barometric pressure drops and the precipitation is delivered. Jesus did not talk that language. Jesus said, 'God sends his rains on the just and on the unjust, on the evil and on the good.' These are two quite different points of view. They are complementary in relation to each other, but they don't overlap because Jesus is talking about God the first cause of all that happens. We in our scientific culture, by contrast, talk about the natural mechanics that produce the precipitation. These are two different worlds of thought. Biblical and scientific accounts of natural events are complementary, but not contradictory. They supplement each other, but they do not challenge each other because first and second causes do not overlap. I bring that view of natural science to my study of Genesis chapters 1 and 2, and its relevance will soon appear.

Finally, I bring to the study of these chapters theological rules for the exegesis of these texts and all other texts. You must also attend to the writer's expressed meaning and not allegorize. You must attend to the writer's didactic nurturing purpose. Every Bible writer wrote what he did in order to do people good spiritually. You need to be clear as to what effect, what impact, what spiritual fruit he was hoping that his words would have. Otherwise you have not fully understood his meaning.

Then, too, you must attend to the writer's literary strategy, his choice of what is nowadays called genre. That is a French word that means the type of writing that you are doing. Poetry is one basic genre, and prose is another basic genre. Do we understand the difference, I wonder, between prose and poetry? In poetry what you are always doing, whether it is poetry that rhymes or poetry that doesn't, is trying to concentrate your experience and perception in forms that will make them resonate with the reader. Your imagination is very much involved: poetry is that kind of communication.

Prose, by contrast, is connected, factual description or narrative or argument that is intended to enable people simply to know what you saw and learned and fancied and thought. Poetry evokes vision, and grabs the heart; prose passes on information, factual or fictional, thus filling the head. Between the poles of prose, such as we read in our newspapers, and poetry, such as Shakespeare, there are many intermediate positions: pieces of prose that are somewhat poetical, and forms of poetry that are somewhat prosaic. These are all specific types of literary genres, to use that interesting word, and they ask to be appreciated and responded to in different ways. So you have to be clear what sort of material it is that you are handling in the Bible in order to know what you should do with it.

How do you determine the genre of a particular piece? By reading it, of course. You read it, and you reread it, and you keep on rereading it until you can see what kind of material it is. You do not impose anything on the text. You ask it, rather, to classify and unfold itself. That is what we shall try to do now.

There are two units of Scripture which we have to examine, and we will take them separately. There is Genesis 1:1–2:3. Then there is Genesis 2:4–25, which starts another story that goes on to the end of Genesis 3, and is chiefly concerned with the origin of evil in this created world.

Taking the first unit, we start by asking some questions. What is the purpose of this piece of writing? What job is it meant to do for us as readers? Certainly, it is solemn writing, even churchly writing, and what it is evidently doing is celebrating the fact and the glory of creation. It is, in fact, the first unit in the first eleven chapters of Genesis. These chapters form a unit in themselves, a kind of prologue to the rest of the Pentateuch, which is telling the story of how God contemplating the fallenness of the world chose a man, Abram, and made out of that man a nation, and redeemed that nation from captivity in Egypt and entered into covenant with them. Genesis 1 is the prologue to the prologue, the beginning of it all.

Looking again at the chapter, we ask, what was the writer's didactic purpose? To start with, he certainly meant to give knowledge of the Creator. What he is saying is not, 'Meet the creation,' as if you have never seen the sun and the moon and the stars and the animals and human beings before, but 'Meet the Creator.' That is the main burden of Genesis 1: See what he did and from what he did see what sort of being he is!

Furthermore, from Genesis 1 it is plain that the author means to give us knowledge of ourselves, as made in God's image, made then with greater dignity than the rest of the creatures, made, however, in dependence on the God who brought everything into being. We are only his image. We are not gods ourselves. Made in God's image, we reflect and represent him in this world, but only as his servants, not as his equals. The writer wants us to know that God commanded mankind, his noblest creature, to manage this world for him, to replenish the earth and subdue it and be his vice-regent within it.

Finally, it is plain from the story that the writer wants us to understand about the Sabbath. God having made the world rested and sanctified the seventh day, to be our Sabbath of rest, a memorial acting-out of his own contentment at the completion of the good work he had been doing.

These are the three didactic concerns which are here plain on the face of the chapter.

There seems also to be a polemical concern. Writing back in the very early days of the human race this writer, whom I shall call Moses until better instructed, proclaimed the one God who made it all and thus excluded polytheism. In the ancient world most religions were polytheistic, that is, they involved faith in many gods between all of whom worship and loyalty had to be divided. Genesis 1 teaches us that no one creates, and no one is to be worshipped, except the Lord God. All the polytheistic systems and superstitious cults are thus ruled out, and this seems to be deliberate.

Finally, Genesis 1 has a nurturing purpose. As we have seen, this celebration of creation is meant to call forth awe and adoration, an appreciation for the Creator and for the dignity that he has given to man and for the special significance of the Sabbath, and so to promote God's praise. With that it is clear that Genesis 1 is intended to direct all its readers to the cultural task which God gave our race: the task embraced by the command, 'Fill the earth and subdue it . . .' (v. 28). But, says the chapter, we are to undertake that task within a proper rhythm of work and rest, six days' work followed by one day's rest. Experience has proved that this routine makes for health and wisdom, whereas by disregarding the rhythm of six days' work and one day's rest, human beings lay up for themselves trouble with their own physical and psychological systems which get overstrained. God knew what he was doing when he made the Sabbath for man.

Now we have to ask another question, and this is the tricky one: What are we to make of the seven days, the six days of work and the divine day of rest following them?

There are four opinions, basically, about the seven days. The first is the literalist hypothesis which maintains that what we are reading about is twenty-four-hour days by our clocks; what we are being told in Genesis 1 is that the whole world came to be formed within what we would recognize as a working week. The hypothesis assumes that what we have in Genesis is descriptive prose, of newspaper type.

The second view is that each of the days of the creation is an allegorical figure. What each of the references to the evening and the morning represent is a geological epoch, a very, very long period of time, hundreds of thousands of years at least. There has been much effort in this century by those who have understood the days this way to try and show that the order of things in Genesis 1 corresponds to the best scientific account that can be given of how specific items emerged and took their place in the order of the world. A witty Roman Catholic writer described this method of understanding as an attempt to raise Moses' credit by giving him a B.Sc. Those who take this 'concordist' view, as it is called, assume that part of the purpose of Genesis 1 was to give us scientific information about the stages by which things came to be.

Third is what is called the revelation day theory, which takes the six evenings and mornings as signifying that creation was revealed in a story with six instalments, each instalment being given to the inspired writer on a separate day. After the first instalment had been given, the writer said there was evening and there was morning. That is a way of saying that God gave him the next bit of the story the next day.

Fourth there is the so-called framework view, sometimes called the literary hypothesis. This view says that the six days, evening and morning, are part of what we may call a prose poem, that is a total pictorial presentation of the fact of creation in the form of a story of a week's work.

Without going into the details of argument about these different views, let me tell you straightaway that in my judgement this fourth view is the only viable one. Why? Because in this account light appears on the first day while God only makes the sun and the moon and the stars on the fourth day. That fact alone, it seems to me, shows that what we have here is not anything that can be called science, but rather an imaginative pattern of order replacing chaos, as follows:

On the first day light and darkness were separated. On the second day the open expanse of the sky was set between waters below and waters above it. On the third day land, sea, and vegetation were created. Here, so far we have a series of uninhabited locations. Then on days four, five, and six, they are populated. The sun, the moon, and the stars are created to rule the day and the night, that is, to mark off the light and the darkness. 'Rule,' of course, is poetry when you think about it. It is not science. Moses is using the astrologers' verb to dismiss astrology; heavenly bodies do not really rule this world, for the God who made them does. On the fifth day God created birds to fly in the sky and mammals and fish to swim in the sea. As for the dry land, the sixth day tells us how the animals and finally man were set there, with humankind as, so to speak, God's bailiff, running his cosmic estate for him.

This is a beautiful pattern, but on the face of it, it is not science. No, it is a patterned way of presenting the fact of creation as the establishing of the infinitely intricate, well-ordered milieu in which the human race lives, moves, and has its being. It seems to me that this way of understanding the chapter is entirely in line with other Scripture references to the fact of creation and takes full account of the observable literary character of the passage—half-poetical repetitive formalized prose, the style, or genre, in which liturgies and hymns in all religions have been written from the earliest times. Such, then, is Packer's path through the complexities of Genesis 1.

Turning our attention now to Genesis 2:4–25 and portions of chapter 3, I shall proceed by questions and answers.

First question: should the Adam and Eve story be called myth? Modern commentaries generally do call it myth. Is that a proper way to describe it? In tackling this question, the first thing we have to do is define myth because the word is a nose of wax and different people mean very different things when they use it.

I use it to signify a non-historical, non-scientific imaginative story expressing a sense of identity, destiny, and maybe duty in the here and now. Is this a story of that kind? I answer no.

In Genesis 5 and 10 Adam and Eve are connected by genealogy with the rest of the race. That is Moses' way of showing that he sees them as figures in space-time history. We should therefore understand their story as historical fact. So it is presented, and so a Bible believer will regard it. Further, it is clear that neither the Lord Jesus nor Paul had any doubt about the historicity of Adam, and they refer to Adam and Eve on a number of occasions. Those who would categorize this story as myth have regularly said we should understand that Adam is Everyman. There is a sense in which that is true. The story of Genesis 2 and 3 may well be held up as a mirror before us all, in which we see our own sin and learn its consequences. But I want us to see that according to the mind of Moses, Adam is only Everyman because first he was Adam, racial ancestor, whose personal history these chapters records.

That is my answer to the question about myth. Myth is the wrong category. This is history. Different scholars have different ways of expressing this. Some, like Barth, call it saga and *Urgeschichte,* which means primal history of a special sort. Some call it epic. What they are all trying to say is that it is history that goes further back than any independent inquiry by any historian can ever go. But certainly it is history, though presented in its own particular way.

This leads to the next question: What sort of history writing have we here? It is a rather unique sort of history. Unlike the narrative one might hear from the witness stand in a courtroom, this is a story told pictorially and symbolically and interpreted as it's told, interpreted, in fact, by the way it's being told. It's history told by the use of didactic symbols that enable us to understand very well its meaning even though the style keeps us from being able to visualize what we would have seen if we'd been there to watch it happening. How do I know this? From reflecting on details of the story itself.

Consider, for instance, the geography of Eden. Where was it? Look at what is said in verses 10–14. 'A river flowed out of Eden to water the garden and it divided and became four rivers.' A big river becomes four, and their names are given. Two we recognize, the Tigris and the Euphrates. But the other two are Pishon and Gihon, names that no one ever heard before; what are they and where are they?

Some guess that the Gihon is the Nile and the Pishon is the Indus. Others that the Gihon is the Blue Nile and the Pishon is the White Nile. Different

suggestions are made, but the point is that you cannot find that geographical feature of one great river that becomes four, two of which are Tigris and Euphrates.
You cannot find that anywhere in the world, which leads me to suppose that this
way of putting the matter is the writer's way of alerting us, the readers, to the fact
that he is not telling us history in a way which enables us to track it down or locate
it on a map or identify the place where it happened or describe to ourselves all
the details of what took place. His story is not that kind of material. Instead, his
joining of two familiar river names with two unfamiliar ones and some legend-
ary geography is, it seems, his way of conveying the thought that as the historical
Adam is also a picture of everyone, as we all are, so the historical Eden is also a
picture of every good place that our sin spoils. This way of communicating such
an idea may seem strange to us, but in the days of Moses it would have been understood well enough. Parabolic history is the literary genre here.

The generic name Adam, meaning *mankind,* and the generic name Eve, meaning *living,* with the implication of *life-source,* seems to say the same. So does verse
7: 'The LORD God formed the man of dust from the ground and breathed into
his nostrils the breath of life and the man became a living being.' And then, what
about the biology of Eve's formation? I understand the theology of it perfectly
well, and so do you, but what are we to make of God taking the rib out of man's
side, and constructing Eve from it? Also, what are we to make of the snake, identified in the New Testament as Satan (see 2 Cor. 11:3, 4; Rev. 12:9), who in due
course receives a snake's curse? ('You will crawl on your belly and you will eat
dust all the days of your life' [Gen. 3:14]). I think what we meant to do with all
these features is to understand them as symbols chosen in order to express the
meaning and significance of things which we are not able to picture or conceive
physically because they are not being described in a matter-of-fact way.

What am I affirming about Genesis 2 and 3? The events were space-time
events, though their location, date, and visual aspect are veiled from us by Moses'
symbolic, parabolic style. I am being, I believe, faithful to Moses in my view of
why he wrote this way. The symbols, I believe, are given me in order to help me
understand the significance of bits of the story, thus: Eden, the Hebrew word for
delight, pictures the total happiness and fulfilment that the first man and woman
enjoyed before they fell. The tree of life is a symbol of the enjoyment of God and
all things in God that would have been mankind's still had man not fallen. The
rib pictures the truth that the woman is a side—the Hebrew word does literally
mean *side* in a number of metaphorical senses as well as the literal one—of the
man's personal being so that he recognizes in the woman the complement of
himself. That each needs the other for completeness is the deepest truth about
the differentiation of the sexes still.

The nakedness of Adam and Eve is a symbolic detail pointing to the fact that
they had no cause for shame before the face of God. The snake is the perfect
symbol for Satan, a symbol which makes the story immediately intelligible in all

cultures. The human race dislikes snakes, and even where snake gods have been worshipped as in some polytheistic systems, they have been worshipped out of fear and dislike. God's walk in the Garden of Eden conveys the thought of his felt presence coming close and becoming inescapable.

God's curses on Adam and Eve symbolize all those experiences of painful frustration, including those that are specified in the text and others also, in a world that is now felt as hostile, frustrating, and painful. The clothes of skins which God made for Adam and Eve signify God's mercy, and perhaps there is a hint here of atoning sacrifice because animals have to die before coats of skins can be made. That is an old interpretation, and I think there is something in it. In a similar fashion, I think that God's strangely expressed curse on the snake surely means more than that humans will hate and try to kill snakes, which in turn will try to bite back. Surely the church was always right to read the curse as the first promise of the Saviour, and as a pointer to that final victory over Satan that the woman's seed would one day win, even though at great cost and pain to himself.

This, then, is the frame of interpretation of Genesis 2 and 3. Please note that I have been bearing in mind both here and in my handling of Genesis 1 the inerrantist rubric that what the writer tell us is all true, but where no assertion is attempted no error can be made, and exegesis must not try to squeeze out of the text more than the writer meant us to find there. All our exegesis of Scripture should, I urge, be thus controlled.

Finally, the hermeneutical question has to be asked: What is there in our minds and culture which could make it hard for us to appreciate narratives told in this way? I think there are three things in our culture that make it very hard for us to get in tune with this sort of communication.

One barrier is our literary culture. Modern newspapers and works of fiction, written as they are, do not attune us to this kind of highly symbolic, imaginative writing, poetry in prose as it almost is, and we find it hard to appreciate it when we are confronted with it. We want the prose of the Bible to be unimaginative narrative because that is what we are used to.

Second, our scientific mind-set, which is so much a part of our culture, predisposes us to assume that any account of the natural order must be written in order to answer the scientists' questions about it, and that is wrong. But we think it, we assume it, and then we try to demonstrate it. And I think that sets us at cross-purposes with the text itself and gets us into all kinds of trouble.

Third, we are rightly committed in apologetics to countering evolutionism as a philosophy of life. Because evolutionism originates with a particular view about the origin of the species, we try to bring Genesis 1 and 2 into line to become ammunition for countering evolutionism. But I have suggested to you that this was no part of the purpose of Moses, and the two chapters do not really bear on the intricacies of the evolution debate one way or the other. If we could adjust our minds at these three points, then I believe we would hear the word of God in Genesis 1, 2, and 3 more clearly than we sometimes do.

The last question of all is the applicatory question: What, then, should we do, having learned these things from our three chapters? The one-sentence answer is: know God, know ourselves as God made us to be and as we have become, know what sin is, know what God's judgement is, praise the Creator for making the world, praise him for sending his Son to die for our redemption, humble ourselves before him as the God who has mercy on sinners, and learn to hate sin as a style of life.

CHAPTER 13

The Challenge of Biblical Interpretation: Women

It is believed by some today that the Bible is hostile to women, and that an inerrantist interpreter is consequently bound to view women in a way that demeans, restricts, and actually insults them. Let us see if this is so. There are factors in our own milieu that make grouping the Bible viewpoint on womanhood less than easy. The place and role of women in the church and community is a matter of intense discussion throughout the Western world at this present time, and the talk is both often confused and confusing. Why should this be? The discussion appears to have two distinct sources, one of them secular and the other properly Christian and churchly, and we need to distinguish them, for their wavelengths and trajectories are very different.

Take the secular one first. It is the question raised and pressed by many women of securing freedom and justice and equality for themselves and for women generally in the modern world. Why does this question arise? There are a number of reasons.

Homemaking for most women is no longer a full-time job because of the mechanical aids that are available, and therefore life in the home leaves them with energy to spare. Luther's formula that a woman's life should be a matter of children, church, and kitchen (*Kinder, Kirche,* and *Kücher*) is unappealing to many women in the modern West. They become lonely, their homes contain no extended family for fellowship, they have no servants, there isn't a community within the house itself, and homemaking is not felt as a complete vocation. Further, the world welcomes women who leave the home and join the workforce.

The world has been doing that ever since the two world wars when women did such a significant job filling posts which men had left to go to the forces. Since then, single women have been expected to take their place in the workforce and married women are routinely welcomed back into it just as soon as they want to return to work. But it is not always the custom in our culture to pay the women as well as the men are paid, and this is an irritant to career women and also to some mothers who have returned to work in the hope of hoisting the family income to a manageable level.

There is a further fact that we must acknowledge: Women have been hurt. They have been hurt in the world, where again and again they have been treated as second-class citizens to such an extent that a lady like Dorothy Sayers on one occasion wrote a very blunt essay 'Are Women Human?' Women have been hurt in the home as well. There have been frustrating marriages. There have been abusive, neglectful, and domineering husbands, and there have been many abler, stronger, wiser wives who have felt that society was on the side of the husband who abused them, and who have found that they are on the horns of a dilemma in the home as to whether they accept or whether they challenge the inadequate leadership of the man to whom they are married. In either case they are unsatisfied, and their domestic dissatisfaction has spilled over into society. Out of all this has come the so-called women's movement, women's lib as we label it, the crusade for women to achieve freedom and equality and justice. At the heart of it I see hurt women, whose very energy in the cause arises out of the bad experiences that they have had.

And part of their purpose, as I discern it, is to upstage men. To my mind, this is rivalry of a kind that is neither creative nor fulfilling. The church, as we know very well, is alternately attacked as a bastion of patriarchy and male dominance and appealed to help change this situation out of compassion for oppressed women as in the past it has been begged to act on behalf of oppressed Blacks. This plea for socio-political and economic upgrading is the secular question which the world hashes over in relation to the position of women.

Alongside that for us in the Christian church, there is a parallel question that needs to be distinguished quite sharply from the first one: How are we to secure the full use of women's gifts in ministry among the people of God? The New Testament proclaims that to every Christian grace and gifts for service are given by the Lord from his throne through the Holy Spirit. But the discussion of how to find and harness women's gifts in ministry unfortunately gets snarled up and skewed by being confused with the world's call for compassion and justice defined as equality, which has often, I think, created a bad conscience among Christian people because they have been prevailed on to believe that the hurts women feel are their fault. Then in the Christian church extremists rise up, take over the discussion, and lead it into fields of exploration which are not always very fruitful.

At one extreme, the liberal response is as it is on most matters: namely, to call for the church to follow the world, to embrace the world's fashionable thoughts, which some might call its cultural prejudices. Follow the world, climb on the secular bandwagon, labour to adjust biblical truth to the modern mind; that is the path constantly taken by liberal theology and of liberal ethics.

Such action is, of course, undiscerning and worldly in spirit. In this case, what it means is backing the campaign to give women freedom, equality, and justice according to the secular idea of these things. Following the world uncritically in this matter is hardly likely to be the right way to go.

Then, at the other extreme there, is a conservative reaction, which is really no more than a reaction. Sometimes reactions are healthy. But they are not healthy if they remain more negative reactions and do not issue in any constructive alternative. Here I am thinking of the reaction which would say that all this talk about improving the woman's position in world and church is utterly misguided. Keep women in their place! As a response to the fierce propaganda of secular feminism this attitude is understandable, but as a policy for an era of rapid social change, in which the question of how best to channel women's gifts into fruitful ministry has come to stay, it clearly will not do.

However, the combined pressure of the two questions, one secular and the other churchly, has led to a skewed discussion in which well-meaning Christian people have come to believe that the intra-church concern for ministry by women has to do with the secular idea of justice and equality for women. I believe that to be a grave mistake. As a result of thinking in those terms, many say, 'Well, surely the answer is to make able women into clergypersons and thus give them equal status with ministering men. Let them act as substitute men. That will fulfil their aspirations. That is what they want.' My response is to say, first, that though it may be what some of them want, it is not, I believe, what the Bible encourages women to want. Perhaps they do want it, but should they? The question hangs in the air.

Second, it is unlikely that this course of action will be a good solution to the problem despite all the experience garnered from mission sources about how, in emergency situations, women have done a man's job as pastors of young congregations and so forth. This is so for several reasons.

First of all, to make a woman a clergyperson certainly gives her status, but the question is about ministry; and just as in the family the ministry of mother and of father are two quite distinct sorts of ministry, though they belong together, so it is likely to be here. The presbyter's role is defined in Scripture as a man's job of teaching and ruling and we are not honouring the God who made the two sexes distinct and different if we simply draft women to be substitute men. That is not what God ever meant us to do. Secondly, relatively few able women are likely to qualify for the clergyperson's role, so we invite a very demeaning sort of tokenism which the women themselves are bound to feel, just as in the early days of integration, the token Blacks felt it in American society. Third, I observe that the role of ruling and teaching is a role which many honest Bible students in the church believe to be improper for women. They believe, in fact, that the Bible actually forbids some or all of that role to women, and, therefore, if we push ahead with a policy of making women into presbyters, it cannot but be provocative and divisive in the body of Christ. Some churches, of course, have pushed ahead no matter what, and the consequences have been as stated.

My own Anglican communion is divided. There are women presbyters in the Anglican Church of Canada, in the Episcopal Church in the States, and in the Church of England. This has created great strains and tensions. I do not think, frankly, that creating internal tensions through power politics is ever a wise way for the church to go, and I personally hope to see the day when enthusiasm for this course of action reduces to vanishing point.

Reviewing these things, I am conscious of five factors which are bound to be reflected in my approach to the relevant biblical texts. Let me come clean about them before I go any further.

First, I sympathize with women who have been hurt by men, and frankly I am ashamed for my sex. I am ashamed that even some Christian men have contributed to that misery and distress. The inhumanity of man to woman as I have met it over the years appals me.

Second, I am opposed to everything that robs women of the dignity that God gave them when he made them. So I am opposed to pornography, prostitution, sweated female labour, and domestic dictatorship. I am opposed to everything in home and society that falls short of being love in the *agape* sense, specifically on the part of men toward women as such.

Third, concern for the future of the family in the Western world ought to be animating us all. The family is dissolving away, and the nurturing grace of God in the family is thereby being diminished. I think that the spiritual poverty of the Western family calls for fresh investment of ourselves, and that's a word not only to fathers but to mothers also.

Fourth, I am zealous for every member's ministry in the body of Christ, and that means every woman's ministry as well as every man's. I see the question about the ministry of women as a question which God is pressing on us all in these days.

Fifth, I have a total lack of enthusiasm for women presbyters. I don't find myself able to say from Scripture that making women presbyters is explicitly forbidden, although I do think it inappropriate for a woman to be sole pastor of a congregation. Yet to make a woman a presbyter, I think, shows something less than respect for the created order of Genesis 2, of which I shall be speaking in a moment. I do not believe that this course of action is beneficial on the whole to women themselves, and I do believe that the answer to the real and pressing question about women's ministry lies elsewhere.

As I turn to the Scriptures, there are two interpretive guidelines to note. First, we are servants of Jesus Christ, and remember that what we are seeking is the mind of Christ regarding women and their place in ministry in his church. The mind of Christ, when we find it, will take the form of an interpretive scheme that does justice to all the Scripture teaching about women, including Scripture testimony to the way that Jesus regarded women in his earthly life, in which as we know he honoured women as friends and disciples in the same way that he took men as friends and disciples. For Christ, Old and New Testaments go together. Now that he rules us by the Bible as a whole I think it not too much to say that our Lord Jesus tells us, in effect, that if we want to be his faithful disciples, we must become faithful disciples of this Book in its totality, in the fullness of its teaching. Certainly, that is how it must be when our concern is with the question of women. We are New Testament believers; we live in the power of Christ's redemption. By bringing in the reality of redemption and establishing his kingdom, Jesus contextualized all Old Testament teaching which now has to be reapplied in the new situation, the kingdom situation as we may call it. That is one of the things we have to do in our interpreting of the Word. Yet, it is quite wrong to suppose that the order of redemption in any way cancels out the order of creation or that biblical thinking about women's ministry runs counter to the Old Testament pattern reaffirmed in the New Testament of male primacy. Here, therefore, I want to warn against another false trail which some Evangelicals have followed: the attempt to pour the biblical material into a feminist pattern of interpretation which dismisses the creation pattern of male primacy. Paul Jewett in his book *Man as Male and Female* began to explore that route. Feminists like Ruether and Fiorenza have gone further. They all drive a wedge between Jesus and the Old Testament, and in my view seriously misinterpret much of the biblical teaching on our subject. That is not the route to go.

Second, remember that we seek spiritual understanding, understanding, that is, from the Holy Spirit. This understanding will be reached by the route which Godamer has called fusing of the horizons, the correcting and amplifying and deepening and enriching of our thoughts by what comes over our horizon out of the Word of God. We may find that we have prejudices that need to be exposed and corrected, for after all we are children of our culture and have in our minds, inevitably, stereotypes of male and female roles, which may or may not be biblical. We shall have to test them and see. None of us fully knows ourselves. Therefore, none of us fully knows our own sexual identity. None of us fully knows what it means to be either a man or a woman. None of us fully knows any of the dimensions of our own human existence. One day we shall know as we are known. One day these things will be clearer to us than they are now. But since at present we do not as a matter of fact fully understand our own sexual identities, we ought to put our hand on our mouth when we find ourselves tempted, having read something in the Bible that doesn't immediately appeal to us, to say, 'Well, that chap didn't understand about women, or didn't understand about men.' That is to get the matter exactly backward. It is we who don't understand what it means to be men and women, and as with the rest of the law of God, so in this area of relationships, we only find out the truth about our own natures as we obey the Word of God implicitly. I think that is a profound point of wide relevance, with a very specific application here.

All that being clear (I hope), I move now to survey the biblical material. I am going to explore, sketchily, three matters: one, the co-equal responsibilities of women and men before God, a matter on which we shall find that the Scripture is clear; two, the cooperative relations of women with men in society, about which we shall also find that the Bible has definite things to say; and three, the contributing roles of women alongside men in the home and the church.

As to the first of those topics, the co-equal responsibilities of women and men before God, I begin by noting that the inferiority of women, essential or consequent, has in the past been affirmed quite often in the church. Aquinas, for instance, in the thirteenth century affirmed the essential inferiority of women. Listen to this: 'As regards the individual nature, woman is defective and misbegotten, for the active force in the male seed tends to the production of a perfect likeness in the masculine sex, while the production of women comes from a defect in the active force or from some material indisposition or even from some external influence such as a south wind.' In the early third century, Tertullian has already affirmed what I call the consequent inferiority of women, thus: 'God's sentence hangs still over all your sex and his punishment weighs down upon you. You are the devil's gateway. You are she who first violated the forbidden tree and broke the law of God. It was you who coaxed your way around him whom the devil had not the force to attack,' etc. You are Eve and you are a rotter; that is what Tertullian is saying to women.

The Bible does not speak in those terms. Scripture affirms the equality of the sexes both in creation and redemption. Let me cite what seem to me to be the clearest passages. Genesis 1:26–28 in the NIV reads: 'God said, let us make man in our image, in our likeness. So God created man in his own image, in the image of God he created him; male and female he created them. God blessed them and God said to them, "Be fruitful and increase in number; fill the earth and subdue it ..."' This is the story of the making of *Adam, mankind*; the two sexes are both there, and there is no suggestion that the second sex is in any way inferior to the first. Both are made in the image of God, which speaks both of man's dependence because we are only God's image and of man's dignity because we truly are his image. No other creature is made in the image of God.

If we ask what constitutes the image of God, the answer must be gathered exegetically from the presentation of God in the earlier verses of Genesis. The word *image* itself expresses the thought of representing God, both functionally (by ruling for him) and substantially (by doing as he does, rationally, relationally and righteously). To be made in the image of God means, among other things, that we are made for relationships: that is, that as God in creation set himself in affirming, enriching, enabling fellowship with the man and the woman, so must men and women relate to each other and to all their fellow humans, imaging God's love to them hereby. Finally, righteousness in the broadest sense is part of the image, the righteousness that values and does good, which is seen in God making the world and finding it good as he makes it.

The last point here is that we, men and women together, are made in the image of God for tasks of procreation and dominion in God's world. The creation mandate, 'fill the earth and subdue it,' is a shared privilege and a shared responsibility. Man and woman are together then in the tasks that humankind has been given, and as it was righteousness in God to create order at each stage in such a way that everything was good, so it will be righteousness in humankind whenever we replenish and rule according to God's command.

Moving on, we need now to examine Genesis 2:18–23, a narrative that speaks of the way in which the woman was made out of the rib, or side, of the man. According to the picture, she was made to be man's helper, a help meet for him, as the old King James Version put it, a helper who really could help him because as a helper she could be in personal fellowship with him in a way that the animals could not. She is a colleague, in other words. The male is there first according to the story, the primacy is his, and the initiative is going to be his. The woman is going to be his colleague and helper in the task that already God has set him to do. When the woman is brought to him, he says, 'This is now bone of my bones and flesh of my flesh.' This, he means, is the complement and completion of me. 'She shall be called "woman," for she was taken out of man.' Surely Karl Barth is right in saying that what you have here is the doctrine of how the sexes perceive each other. This is not the doctrine of marriage yet. We don't meet the reality of marriage until verses 24–25. This is the two sexes each perceiving the other as having in it that which completes what each individual, male or female, is at present. This is mysterious, but it is also glorious. It is part of the enrichment of life that God gave us. It is part of his good gift to the human race. We call it sexuality. To some that is a bad word, but in truth it ought not to be a bad word. It has become a bad word, of course, because of the abuses which have taken place in the realm of sexuality, especially in the twentieth century. But really it is part of the glory of creation and ought to be seen as such. *Vive la différence!* was God's idea long before the French put it into words for us.

Now we turn to the New Testament: specifically, to Galatians 3:28, where Paul, speaking of the new creation and the order of redemption, declares, 'as many of you as were baptized into Christ have put on Christ. There is neither Jew nor Greek, there is neither slave nor free, there is neither male nor female; for you are all one in Christ Jesus.' Surely the thought there is not that distinctions established by creation and providence are to be treated as if they don't exist. The thought there is only this: that in the Christian fellowship, the divine family, the Christian church, in which we all are vitally united to Christ and on the same level both as sinners hopeless in ourselves and as adopted children of God and as such heirs of glory, we should treat each other as equals in Christ and determine our behaviour toward each other by the fact that we are equals in Christ. Even if in human terms one of us is Jewish, one of us is Greek, one of us is a slave, one of us is a free man, one of us is a male, one of us is a female, in Christ we are all on a level and in love and fellowship and should treat each other so. That is the point that is being made there. Paul doesn't develop it. He simply says this is how it is in the new creation, and this is what you have to live out. But as we shall shortly see, this does not, in Paul's thinking, cut across any of the elements in the creation pattern which he actually reaffirms in the Christian context.

That leads me into my next topic: the cooperative relations of women with men in community. Here we shall look at two subjects which I separate for study, although in fact they belong together and overlap. I shall talk first about the co-operative relations of men with women in marriage and second about the general question of male headship.

Take the marriage relation first. What is the Bible doctrine here? The basic doctrine of marriage is taught in Genesis 2:24–25: 'A man leaves his father and mother and cleaves to his wife and they become one flesh,' so says the writer. The author puts the word *therefore* at the beginning of the statement. Wherefore the therefore, we ask? The reason is that the woman whom a man takes to himself, the woman who lets him take her to himself in this way, is a person in whom he sees very vividly and precisely the complement and completion of what he is. And therefore, he wants togetherness with her as long as life shall last. He doesn't refuse ever to make contact with his father and mother again, but his primary relation now is to his wife. He leaves father and mother in terms of primary affection in order to bond with his wife in terms of primary affection. They become one flesh in the total commitment of a personal covenant sealed by a physical relationship. You can see something of the glory and the beauty of this in the exuberance of the Song of Solomon, which Karl Barth described as the second charter of humanity, having already described these verses in Genesis 2 as the first charter of humanity.

I am among those old shellbacks who believe it is right to read the Song in terms not only of Solomon and a country girl but also of Christ and the church. This is so because the Lord from his throne clearly so read it and wanted the La-odicean Christians so to read it. When in Revelation 3:20 Jesus says, 'Behold, I stand at the door and knock. If any one hears my voice and opens the door, I will come in to him, and eat with him, and he with me;' he is picking up and applying to his own relation to his own people the picture of Song of Solomon 5:2–5. The book functions as a parabolic testament of love between the Lord and his people, the Lord's responsive people and their Saviour, precisely by first being a rather torrid love song about a him and a her, Solomon and the Shulammite. And thus it sets before us the biblical ideal of marriage, as an exuberant, joyous, and whole-hearted relationship, lifelong and unashamedly physical. The Bible warns strongly in both Testaments against physical sexual relationships outside the personal covenant of marriage. Read Proverbs 5, 6, 7, and 1 Corinthians 6. Such relations are destructive, says the Book of God. But on the basis of the total commitment, the personal covenant, of the marriage bond, then the physical relationship is, as Roman Catholic theologians would say, transvalued and becomes one of the most precious things in life. So says the Scripture and so experience proves.

In Ephesians 5:22–33 Paul set up ideal standards for marriage in terms of the noblest model, Christ and his church. The parallel is tremendously significant. The husband is to love his wife as Christ loves the church. He is to cherish her as Christ cherishes the church. He is to love her as he loves his own body. She is to respect him and prove herself a loyal helper, responding to his needs as the church must seek to please in its obedience to Christ. This is mutual subjection, says Paul. The section that begins in verse 22 on wives and husbands is introduced by the participial phrase, 'submitting yourselves one to another out of reverence for Christ.' What Paul has to say about wives and husbands, and then in chapter 6 about children and parents and slaves and masters, is spelling out the concept of mutual submission, each being at the other's service according to the pattern that God has established. I repeat and underline *mutual submission*. This is the key thought. Submission means that you put yourself at the other person's service to act toward him or her in love with a purpose of making that person great in the way that God reveals that he wants that other person to be great. There is an irreversible shape to the mutual submission of husband and wife. It is given already by the order of creation and it is reaffirmed by the parallel of Christ and his church. The roles of Christ and church are not reversible, and in the same way the roles of husband and wife are not reversible. But it is love both ways. That is the point. The husband, playing Christ's role, takes the initiative in love. The wife, playing the church's role, makes her response in love. Love in both parties is the purpose of making the other great. And this is their mutual submission in the body of Christ.

Peter picks up some of this in 1 Peter 3:1–7, where he first exhorts wives as to their attitude toward their husbands, and then in verse 7 tells husbands how they are to live with their wives. He, like Paul, defines a mutual submission that is an expression of love. Peter reaches the point of saying explicitly that it is part of the wife's calling to act sweet, even when her husband acts sour. Then he says immediately to the husbands, verse 7, 'you are to live considerately with your wives, bestowing honour on the woman as the weaker sex.' You must care for her even though you sometimes feel that she is limited and so in Peter's sense weak in certain respects. That is not to stop you loving, cherishing, living with her considerately. Of course, the way of the fallen world is to lose interest in people who seem weak: to despise them, distance yourself from them, and cease to bother about them. That is not, however, says Peter to be the way in Christian marriage. Husbands take note. There is nothing in 1 Peter, incidentally, or Paul in Ephesians 5, to suggest anything that one could call marital passivity on the part of the wife. It is not being suggested that the married woman should resign herself to being her husband's gofer, or lackey, let alone his doormat. Here perhaps it is worth referring to the perfect wife of Proverbs 31 who is very far from being a passive person. She is, in fact, a homemaker and a guardian of the home's prosperity in a very significant and striking way. There is really nothing in Scripture to rule out the thought of women taking major responsibility as wives and mothers in the family circle, and as business people outside it.

Moving now to the issue of headship, in 1 Corinthians 11:3 it is said thus: 'I want you to understand that the head of every man is Christ, the head of a woman is her husband, and the head of Christ is God.' Then in Ephesians 5:23 Paul says, 'The husband is the head of the wife as Christ is the head of the church, his body; and is himself its Saviour.' What does that relation of headship signify? This, as a matter of fact, is still a matter of debate among philologists. Rather than foreclose that discussion, I am going to assume that both the thoughts which are being canvassed are part of the truth: namely, that one of the things that headship means is origin, and that the second thing that headship means is primacy. Whether or not the idea of origin is in Paul's mind at all when he uses the word *head* here, his main thought is certainly of primacy: the sort of primacy that God the Father has in relation to Christ the Son and the sort of primacy that Christ has in relation to each male believer.

So what we should be thinking of when we read that 'the husband is the head of the wife as Christ is the head of the church' is that the responsibility for initiative and leadership in Christian marriage rests on the man. The woman should acknowledge that this is the way God meant it to be and fulfil her role in responsive cooperation and support. I believe that these are truths about human nature as God created it, and that they are reinforced, rather than weakened, in and by the realities of redemption. If that is the right way to view the matter, we have given full weight to the thought of headship without saying anything about what is called hierarchy, or called patriarchy, or female subordination and male domination. Indeed, I do not think that the Bible requires us to think in those terms at all. *Cooperation* is the central biblical requirement as between the sexes in general and as between husband and wife in particular. Cooperation assumes mutual goodwill, which sociological terms like hierarchy and patriarchy, and military terms like subordination, and political terms like domination and dominion, do not. In marriage cooperative purpose should be primary, and love as earlier defined should motivate both partners, and it is within this frame that the (formally unequal) duties and claims of the 'head' relationship as taught by God should be set.

Thus I understand headship, and understanding it so, I now move on to what I have to say about my third and last subject: the contributing roles of women in home and church. In the home it is said specifically that the wife is to be a hard-working homemaker. Again I invoke Proverbs 31, also 1 Timothy 5:14 where Paul says: 'I would have younger widows marry, bear children, rule their households, and give the enemy no occasion to revile us.' And again in Titus 2:4–5, Paul says quite specifically: 'Train the younger women to love their husbands and children, to be sensible, chaste, domestic, kind, and submissive to their husbands, that the word of God may not be discredited.' In both those last texts, Paul is concerned that the way Christians live should project the thought of the dignity, worthwhileness, and excellence of the Christian life before the watching world. Paul is concerned that the way Christians live together in their families should excite admiration from the world rather than contempt, lest evil be spoken of the Word of God.

What now about the church? Let's start with 1 Corinthians. While it is a difficult letter to exegete because Paul is discussing situations that he hasn't fully described, answering questions that he doesn't fully elucidate, and responding to comments by Corinthians that he doesn't clearly identify, it seems tolerably clear that in 1 Corinthians 11:3–16 Paul is saying, apparently repeating one of the traditions that he left the Corinthians, that a woman may lead in prayer and prophesy provided that she is covered in such a way (the precise nature of the covering is disputed) as to show the angels that she knows her place in the order of creation, and by leading in prayer and uttering words of prophecy she is not seeking to upstage men or usurp their role. Whatever else it means, it clearly means that. You have this explicitly in verse 5. In 1 Timothy 2:8 Paul shows that his preference is for the men to be leading in prayer in church meetings. He says, 'I desire then that in every place the men should pray, lifting holy hands.' Clearly he is talking about public prayer, leading the congregation. So you could say that it is permission rather than ideal legislation on Paul's part when he says that the Corinthian women may do it. He says that it is not wrong and it may be done, provided that it is done in a way that makes plain that the women doing it know their place in the created order.

In light of that, consider 1 Corinthians 14:33–35 where Paul says, 'As in all the churches of the saints, the women should keep silence in the churches. For they are not permitted to speak; but should be subordinate as even the law says. If there is anything they desire to know, let them ask their husbands at home. For it is shameful for a woman to speak in church.' Two plausible exegeses are offered. One is that Paul is trying to end an abuse in Corinth, the abuse, namely, of women interrupting worship when something was said that they didn't understand. If so, that is the point of Paul's telling them to ask their husbands at home. It has often been said that inevitably the good news of freedom and equality in the family of God for women, making them feel on a par with men for the first time ever, would have turned the heads of some women and encouraged them, against the background of their very defective or non-existent education which was the pattern for women in the ancient world, to throw their weight about. The suggestion is that this is just one instance of that, and Paul writes as he does to stop it happening. He tells the Corinthians that in all the churches he serves he has this problem and makes the same rule. But it is evidently a rule about interruption and not a rule about leading in prayer and prophesying because in chapter 11 he has already made clear that that is permitted.

The alternative exegesis, which is quite popular these days, is to suppose in verses 33–35 Paul quotes what somebody in Corinth is saying very strongly, and that he quotes these words as something which he wants to refute because he understands them as negating the permission that he has just given for a woman to lead in prayer and prophesy provided she is covered. That, then, would be the point of his indignant exclamation in verse 36, 'What! Did the word of God originate with you, or are you the only ones it has reached?' Do you really think you have a right to make rules like this? And by saying that he sweeps the rule aside. Personally, I think that the first exegesis has much more to be said for it than the second, but the second has a lot of support these days, and either is reasonable and acceptable. In neither case is one doing as has sometimes been done and citing 1 Corinthians 14 as cancelling what was said in 1 Corinthians 11. Rational men don't write letters that way, and Paul was a rational man.

In 1 Timothy 2:12 he specifies that a woman may not teach. Again, more than one exegesis is possible when you get down to details, but the theological basis for the prohibition which is stated is that Eve was deceived in a way that Adam was not. Therefore, for a woman to teach is to increase the likelihood of deception in the church; so Paul, as a rule of prudence presumably, does not allow a woman to teach at all. A clarifying comment is needed here. In a situation where printing and literacy are realities as in North America today, all of us have our own Bibles and the activity of teaching doesn't involve the element of 'take it from me' that it did when Paul wrote these words. In those days, when the canonical New Testament did not yet exist teaching involved being careful not to go beyond what the apostles had been heard to teach and what was clear in the Old Testament, which Paul gave to those Gentile churches as their Bible. Teaching, in other words, is a different exercise today from what it was in Paul's day, and Paul seems to be expressing the view that in his situation the women as he knew them were more likely to be led into mistakes of belief, and therefore of teaching, than the men were; so he lays it down that they should not teach. I think it is an open question whether in our day Paul would have regarded what happened to Eve in the Garden of Eden as sufficient reason for forbidding a woman to teach from the Bible. I cannot see that 1 Timothy 2:12–14 applies to Bible teaching at all. When you teach from the Bible, in any situation, what in effect you are saying to people is: 'Look, I am trying to show you what it says. I speak as to wise men and women. You have your Bibles. You follow along. You judge what I say.' No claim to personal authority with regard to the substance of the message is being made. It seems to me that this significant difference between teaching then and teaching now does, in fact, mean that Paul's prohibition on women preaching and teaching does not apply. And certainly, we should all put out of our minds the thought that anyone preaching from the Bible claims any personal authority at all. Preachers seek to be channels of the spiritual authority of Christ our Lord through the Spirit, but that is a different thing. For substance, the things we teach must always come from the Bible and no other source, for in the realm of spiritual truth it is the Word of God, and that alone, that has authority.

Finally, consider 1 Timothy 3:11, 'The women, likewise, must be serious, not slanderers, but temperate, faithful in all things.' Those words come in the middle of a paragraph which is dealing with the office of the deacon. The only natural way to understand verse 11 is in terms of women deacons. Since the deacon's role, according to the New Testament, is to lead the church in practical care for the needy, I see no inappropriateness whatever in asking women to take charge of that particular sphere of the church's service, and no problem with the fact that this is what Paul seems to be doing, thus by his example authorizing us today to do the same.

By way of conclusion, let me voice my view that women's ministry in the church, whatever the specific role, will ordinarily be maternal rather than paternal in style, motherly rather than fatherly, womanlike rather than manlike. This is simply because women are women, and not men. Therefore, I think that it will always be best done informally in homes with informal groups. Whereas for male pastors ministry will often be best done in front of large groups, that will not ordinarily be the way with the woman's best ministry. In our churches we have hardly begun to think out how to shape and model women's ministry in this informal, maternal style, simply because we have been distracted so long by the question, whether women should be made presbyters, which as you see I regard as basically an irrelevance. Meantime, thank God, countless godly women have simply got on with the job of Christian ministry in all sorts of vital ways. Look again at your churches and you will see, they have done it. Long may they continue to do it while we men scratch our heads trying to work all these things out.

CHAPTER 14

The Challenge of Biblical Interpretation: Eschatology

In my attempt to deal with eschatology, I am trying to offer you a coherent, synthetic view of biblical teaching. I cannot discuss the academic minutiae of any of the texts with which I deal because I am trying to cover a great deal of territory. While I admit that my synthesis is not definitive, I trust it is viable. I want to show you at least one way of putting it all together which is internally consistent, which takes account of all that is in the Scriptures, which doesn't require one to turn one's back on any of the biblical material and doesn't oblige one to say, 'Well, Scripture is irrevocably in contradiction with Scripture at this or that point.'

Eschatology is the study of the last things. It is a very important field of study, for its real theme is the Christian hope, and hope is integral to the New Testament Christian life. Indeed, hope is integral to all life that is worthy of that name. Existence without hope is something less than really living. So the study of the Christian hope is important in itself, and essential indeed to those who would proclaim the gospel in its full glory. My subject is the objective, given content of the Christian hope.

I would like to set what I am going to say under the authority of a single phrase found in 1 Timothy 1:1. It is a little phrase of four words which, to my mind, really says it all. The phrase is this: 'Christ Jesus our hope.' Everything that I say will, one way or another, be revolving round that phrase and seeking to illuminate it in different ways. Christ Jesus is our hope. Let us explore this theme of eschatology and see what that means.

To begin, I want to explain a limit which I have set myself. There are three matters often discussed when eschatology is the theme about which I am not going to speak at all.

They are, first, the state and prospects of the country now called Israel, the country relatively young now inhabited by about 2 million Jews who have made themselves a power in the Middle East, as you well know. I will not say a word about Israel. Nor will I address the rapture of the saints before Christ appears. Nor, thirdly, will I deal with the great tribulation, greater than any that has hit the world before and is expected by some at the end of the age before the public reappearance of the Saviour.

The reason I will not address these three themes is a simple one. As I understand the Bible, it says nothing about any of them. The belief contrary rests, I believe, on the misinterpretation of a whole series of texts. Such a conclusion is bound to offend some, but I must share my position honestly, so I start by cleaning the ground.

Eschatology is the study of the last things, God's future, God's fulfilment of his purpose of perfecting his creation by eliminating from it the disorder brought into it by sin and reconstructing everything in its final perfect form. Further, the biblical presentation of this great theme is like an ellipse with two foci, a single oval figure with two points inside it each of which is just as central in its significance as the other. The two foci are *global eschatology* (which has to do with the future of our Lord Jesus Christ and this whole world) and *personal eschatology* (which has to do with the future of the individual Christian and the individual unbeliever).

The perspective set forth in the New Testament is what is usually called *inaugurated eschatology,* that is, the belief that the kingdom of God is here and the powers of the kingdom are at work already. The gospel is the good news that heaven has already begun here on earth for those who are Christ's. The long expected king of Old Testament prophecy has come. He came in lowliness as the servant Saviour of humankind. Now he is risen and enthroned, and from his throne he still comes to us by the personal presence of his Holy Spirit. One day he will come again publicly in glory as the world's judge. Those who are his have already risen with him out of their spiritual death into the life of his kingdom, the life for which eternal life is the New Testament name. We are risen with Christ. We live with Christ. That is our eternal condition. It will always be so in life, in death, in resurrection, through judgement and on beyond; those who are Christ's will be with him and he with them in love, joy and glory. That is the truth about the destiny of the Christian believer.

We live, according to the New Testament, in the last days. That means the period between the Lord's first coming and the Lord's second coming. Not everyone who uses the phrase 'the last days' realizes that that is the biblical meaning of it, but in fact it is, and it would only take two or three minutes with a concordance to verify this. In these last days, this era of Christ's kingdom and church and gospel and the outworking of his saving purpose for those for whom he died, there is constant conflict with the devil and his forces opposing Christ and his people.

This is how it is going to be in an increasing measure, until the Lord comes again. Spiritual warfare will be unceasing. The devil is a beaten foe, but will keep on fighting to the end. That is the biblical perspective of inaugurated eschatology.

Already the Lord is transforming his own people in his own way. He transforms them from the inside out. That is to say, he changes heart and character, though our physical body, that external aspect of our personal being which is given us for enjoyment and expression, remains for the most part unchanged, and in due course wears out, fails, and is left behind. One day, when the Lord comes again, when we are taken from this world to glory, we who already have been changed inside will be given bodies to match, bodies that are true and adequate expressions of the new persons we are in Christ. That will be the fullness of our personal redemption. When Christ comes again, we shall find that in a moment the whole cosmos, glorious as it is in so many ways in its present form, has been remade into yet greater glory. New heavens, new earth, call it what you will, it will be a wholly new order of things, and the word *perfection* will be the only word that will then describe it. That's the biblical perspective: the future fulfilment and completion of what God has already started.

Come then to the study of eschatology with this overall point of view clearly in your mind. What we are going to study is the details within this frame of reference.

But one more introductory remark before we do so: Never underestimate the theological significance of eschatology. In the schools, very often eschatology has been the poor relation in the theology courses. Coming last it has often been, to speak frankly, skimped in teaching. Partly, I think, this is because professors have not always known what to say. In addition, everyone who works in the classroom knows things often take longer to teach than you anticipate, so that the final bit of any course nearly always gets skimped. That's universal teaching experience. But it is a very sad thing that eschatology should ever be skimped because, as you can already see, it is a matter of enormous importance, very much a part of the glory of the gospel and very important for every Christian to understand. Several points give weight to what I am saying about the significance of eschatology.

Eschatology is first the key to understanding the unity of the Bible. Holy Scripture in its totality is a book of hope looking forward to a final consummation, and finding its unity in all its lines of thought and teaching about the divine action which will bring in that final consummation toward which God is working.

Eschatology is, further, the clue to understanding the nature of the Christian life. That life is essentially a life of hope, a life in which nothing is perfect yet but the hope of perfection is set before us, so that we may forget what is behind and reach out to what lies ahead and press toward the mark for the prize of the high calling of God in Christ Jesus. One of the things we modern Christians are very bad at, it seems to me, is remembering what the whole materialist culture around us encourages us to forget: that there are two worlds not just one, two lives not just one, and heaven really is more important than earth, for heaven's life is the goal for which this life is preparation.

Martyn Lloyd-Jones published a sermon on the early verses of the twelfth chapter of Hebrews called 'Life's Preparatory School.' It is a perfect title, taking you right to the heart of the Christian life as the New Testament views it. Life here and now is preparation for something more glorious that is ahead of us in the future. We need, then, to understand the Christian hope in order to understand the Christian life.

Third, eschatology is the key to understanding the shape of world history. The Bible has a clearly articulated view about world history. The people of God have always been at the centre of world history. The way to read the book of world history is in terms of the life, work, fortunes, and battles first of Old Testament Israel and now of the church of Christ. That is a helpful perspective to bring to the bewildering confusions of world affairs today. Remember that the church under the sovereign hand of God is the real centre of what is going on and always will be. That is the Bible view.

Finally, eschatology is supremely relevant for teaching the gospel in these days, considering what we are up against. On the one hand, there are Utopian hopes, false hopes of different kinds offered by different people—some of them Marxists with secular false hopes, some of them simply American optimists, but again with secular hopes that will prove false. On the other hand, we face a great deal of pessimistic hopelessness on the part of people who feel that they have seen through the false hopes of society and now have no hope at all. To me one of the most pathetic things, which of course becomes increasingly poignant to me as I myself grow older, is to observe so many folk of my age and a little beyond who see and feel their life as mere movement into the increasing darkness of a tunnel with no exit. Their physical strength is going. Their health is failing. They have nothing to which to look forward. Their career is behind them. They are lonely. They are hopeless. We have to minister the gospel to many, many folk in that state of mind. We need to speak loudly and clearly about the glory of the Christian hope. The world needs to hear that word from our lips.

For the first nineteen centuries, personal eschatology was central in the church's thinking about the Christian life. The four last things of medieval preaching (death, judgement, heaven, and hell) occupied much of the attention of the Lord's people. Little thinking was done about what the New Testament calls the parousia, the promised royal visit, the return of our Lord Jesus Christ to his world.

In the nineteenth century, and even more in this twentieth century, the pendulum swung to the opposite extreme. Global eschatology, the future of Jesus Christ and world, has become central in people's attention. A number of factors have contributed to this development. Bible believers have insistently affirmed the parousia of hope against liberals in the church who have denied that we need ever to expect to see Jesus Christ again. Dispensationalist teachers, with their dogmatic cultural pessimism and expectation of history's imminent end, have made the parousia a central reference-point for thought. In addition, now that we have it in our power to blow the world up by nuclear means and run the risk of destroying it by ecological folly, the future of the world and of the human race has become increasingly an existential question for everybody.

In the past century not much thinking has been done about individual destiny. Because of this, what I say about individual destiny may seem a little old-fashioned, for all of it was being said one hundred and more years ago. Concentration on one of the foci in eschatology with insufficient concern for the other is always going to produce imbalance. I want to try and set the balance right.

There are interpretative difficulties as one comes to the biblical text for three reasons at least. First, the events and experiences to which eschatology points are in the nature of the case unimaginable. Therefore biblical testimony to them is inevitably open-textured and elusive. We cannot with any certainty imagine what coming events and coming experiences are going to be like. We can use phrases that refer to these realities, but cannot really conceive them. They are beyond us. We can fantasize about the end of history and life beyond death, but we should never doubt that the reality will utterly outstrip our fancyings. That means that in-depth understanding of the biblical testimony to them is difficult, to put it mildly, to achieve.

Second, the Bible is an Oriental book, and its testimony to the future is given in Oriental fashion. It is given in a pictorial, evocative, evaluative, and imaginative way, rather than in the sort of reportorial prose which is informative in the way that a newspaper report of things is informative. This is the way that the Oriental mind, through which God gave us his Word, focuses and formulates and presents these coming realities. So we read of the worm that doesn't die, and the fire that isn't quenched and, the crowns on the heads of God's people, and the white robes that they wear, and so on. And in Revelation 21:16–21 we read of the city of God, new Jerusalem, which comes down from heaven as a bride adorned for her husband, with walls, foundations, and gates of jewels (lists of jewels are given); and it is as high as it is broad, as it is long, in other words it is a perfect cube, and its breadth and length and height are 12,000 stadia, 1500 miles, each way. Imagery is being used.

This sort of imagery enables us to understand the significance of what is being presented. The thought of comprehensive and majestic perfection is being set before us in a dozen different forms without enabling us to envisage what it will look like and feel like in specific detail when it arrives. God thought it good that we should have his Word given to us via the Oriental imagination. What we have to do is to learn to appreciate this material for what it is.

A third point follows from the second: Much scriptural testimony about the future is given in the idiom of Jewish apocalyptic. Apocalyptic is a specific mode of Oriental imagining; it is a highly imaginative form of communication about the future victory of God which to us in the modern West comes across as a quasi-poetic code. It is prose, but there is in it so much transcendent, mind-blowing, kaleidoscopic imagery that it makes us feel as we often do when we read great poetry: namely, that we are receiving insights into the meaning and value and beauty and nobility of things that plain prose could never convey. Imagery is being used to create a sense of significance which we feel and appreciate, but we simply cannot look through the imagery to envisage the events to which the imagery refers.

When this kind of imagination in the Bible really goes into high gear, it expresses thoughts in terms that I call 'visuals' (that is, units of visual imagery), which are often incompatible with reality and are often further decorated with additional visuals that are there to indicate importance rather than to add to our knowledge. An example of visuals that are intrinsically incompatible, though glorious in their meaning (I move for a moment out of apocalyptic into the world of simple imaginative vision), is Revelation 7:14. 'Who are these? These are they who have washed their robes and made them white in the blood of the lamb.' Now if you have ever cut yourself, you know that blood does not make linen white. You know the theology that this phrase is expressing and you glory in it as I do, but when you analyse it, it is a couple of visuals (blood and dirty robes being washed white) which in literal terms contradict each other. The Bible is not contradicting itself, of course, because this phraseology is not a literal description, but is expressing a theological thought. But the two visual elements combined for the purpose actually don't fit. As visuals, they cancel each other out. As indicators, however, of the significance of Christ's cross for those who feel dirty before God because of their sins, they are magnificent. This is one example of the significant imaginings of literal impossibilities, so as to convey thoughts evocatively, that are apocalyptic's stock-in-trade.

A further example, and one that bears directly on our theme, is Acts 2:16–21. Peter on the Day of Pentecost begins his sermon by saying,

> This is what was spoken by the prophet Joel: 'And in the last days it shall be, God declares, that I will pour out my Spirit upon all flesh, and your sons and your daughters shall prophesy, your young men shall see visions, and your old men shall dream dreams; yea and on my menservants and my maid servants in those days I will pour out my Spirit and they shall prophesy.'

This is that, says Peter. But he hasn't finished his quotation yet. He goes on in verses 19–21 as follows:

> 'And I will show wonders in the heavens above and signs on the earth beneath, blood, and fire, and vapor of smoke; the sun shall be turned into darkness and the moon into blood, before the day of the Lord comes, the great and manifest day. And it shall be that whoever calls on the name of the Lord shall be saved.' (RSV)

Is this that has just happened on the Day of Pentecost the outpouring of the Spirit which was spoken of in Joel 2:16–21? As Peter cites the passage, yes, it is. Is Peter expressing the thought that now has come the day of salvation, according to Joel's prediction? Yes, again. What are we to make of the details, then?

On the Day of Pentecost there were no cosmic convulsions. The sun was not turned into darkness nor the moon into blood on that day. No, these details are decoration added to the main thought in the way that all sorts of decorations were added to the main structure in medieval cathedrals to enhance their dignity and glory. Evidently Peter understands Joel's picture of the sun going out and the moon going red as an imaginative way of expressing the thought that what happens when God pours out his Spirit is something so momentous that the world is never the same again.

That is the thought being expressed by this fantastic imagery of the sun turned into darkness and the moon into blood. As a thought, it declares something of the significance of the prophesied outpouring itself. So the imagery carrying the thought may properly be said to decorate what the text has already told us about the event, since through the imagery our appreciation of it is enhanced. There is much of this cosmic pictorial decoration in apocalyptic prophecy, and in interpreting apocalyptic you have to remember to ask constantly what is the main thought and what is the supportive decoration. That is the only way to discern the meaning that is being expressed.

In the vision in Revelation 21 of new Jerusalem, the details of the gold and precious stones of which walls and foundations are made are also decoration. These specifics are put into focus and underline the thought that the city is a glorious city with every glory that you can imagine being a part of it. But if you supposed each of the twelve different sorts of jewels must stand for some specific excellence in the city, you would be misunderstanding the way that the grammar of apocalyptic works. If these conventions of Jewish imaginative writing are not understood, any amount of what the Bible says about the future will be misunderstood in detail.

Turning now to personal eschatology, consider first and briefly the biblical certainties and then second the biblical questions. There are two central biblical certainties. The prospect for believers who already are alive in Christ, indwelt by the Holy Spirit who is God's seal upon them, marking them out as his, is that he one day will come to claim us. Meanwhile his Spirit in us is his seal indicating ownership.

We who through the Spirit manifest his fruit and his gifts and experience the witness of the Spirit assuring us that we are children of God and heirs of glory with Christ, we and all other believers with us, have before us a prospect of glory. We are assured of full-scale reanimation by Christ in resurrection (John 5:28–29; Phil. 3:20–21). In addition, we can count on acceptance through Christ at whatever judgement we may face in that day. We must all appear before the judgement seat of Christ, says Paul. That could mean loss in some sense for some Christians (see 1 Cor. 3:12–15), but it won't mean loss of salvation. The way to express justification is to say that it is God's last judgement passed on to believers here and now in time, assuring us of our eternal security with him. That last judgement will never be retracted or reversed. So acceptance with Christ is guaranteed through that final accounting and whatever lies beyond it.

In addition, we expect association with Christ forever. We shall be forever with the Lord (1 Thess. 4:17). Remember Jesus' prayer in John 17:24 (KJV), 'Father, I will that they also, whom given me thou hast, be with me where I am; that they may behold my glory.' To the Christian, and this is really a very good test of a Christian, the prospect of being forever with the Lord Jesus, whom we love because he loved us, is glorious, thrilling, and nothing better could be imagined. To the unbeliever it would be a different story, but we are only talking about the destiny of the believer now. So animation by Christ in resurrection, acceptance through Christ at future judgement, association with Christ forever, and finally adoration of Christ as the height of love and joy (Rev. 22:3–5; etc.) are the thoughts, the theological thoughts, that make up the New Testament picture of the joyful prospect that awaits the believer. The crowns and the white robes and the gift of the morning star and so on are trimming, decorations, ancient-world images carrying amplifying thoughts in the way we looked at earlier. The relationship with Jesus is the heart of it. That's what it all means, and you can spell it out under these four headings as I have done.

By contrast, and this is the second certainty regarding personal destiny that the New Testament teaches us, the prospect for unbelievers and apostates is awful, fearful. It has only two elements. The first is resurrection to judgement for condemnation. Read again what Jesus says about that in John 5:28–29: 'all that are in the grave, he tells us, shall hear the voice of the Son of Man and come forth, some for the resurrection of life and those who have done evil for the resurrection of condemnatory judgement.' And following that resurrection comes relegation to a condition described in Matthew 25:41 as eternal punishment and in Revelation 20:15 as the lake of fire. Imagery? Yes, but clearly this imagery is pointing to something exceedingly fearsome.

So according to the New Testament the prospect for believers is very good, and the prospect for unbelievers and apostates is very bad. That is stark stuff, you will agree. I simply lay it on the table and move on, for I now want to look at three more specific biblical questions relating to the destiny of individuals.

First question: Is the resurrection body given at death? It has been argued that perhaps it is. The argument has been based on 2 Corinthians 5:1–4 where Paul expresses the Christian hope in terms of not wanting to be unclothed, that is to be deprived of our present physical dimension of life altogether, but rather to be clothed upon, further clothed, so that what is mortal may be swallowed up in life. Paul goes on to say, 'He who has prepared us for this very thing is God, who has given us the Spirit as a guarantee.'

There are three possible lines of interpretation at this point. There is first the common view that bodily resurrection, further clothing, clothing upon, is awaited by the Christian dead who are consciously and joyfully sustained in what we call the intermediate or interim, that is the disembodied, state by the Holy Spirit. God's gift of the Spirit as a guarantee, referred to in verse 5, remains with us through the intermediate state. Though in one sense we have lost because physically we have no body through which to express ourselves, in another and more fundamental sense we will have gained because we will have departed to be with Christ, which as Paul said in Philippians 1:21 is far better. He means far better than life in this world ever can be. This is common view, and I am not sure that I see reason to depart from it.

An alternative view is preferred by such scholars as F. F. Bruce and Murray Harris: Resurrection bodies are actually received at death, but manifested only at the parousia. That is why Jesus is able to say that those that are in the graves will come forth, some to the resurrection of life, others to the resurrection of condemnation. The resurrection bodies, whatever they are, will only be manifested at the parousia.

Then there is a third view, namely that resurrection is experienced by the believer as immediately following death, either because unconsciousness intervenes between the day of death and the day of resurrection or because the dead, in effect, are now outside time. I am not sure what that last phrase means, so I hesitate to embrace this view. But a biblical scholar like T. F. Torrance has argued for it.

It is healthy to remember that when we look into the future, some things are certain while other things are not certain. What is uncertain here is where and how our future enhanced bodily existence becomes real for us. What is certain, however, is that we creatures of God need a bodily form of existence for expression of ourselves. We need a face with which to smile. We need hands with which to wave and hug people. We use our body for purposes of expression. We need a bodily form of existence equally for communication, of which the smiles and the hugs are past. God who made us with a bodily form of existence for these two purposes will one day raise us into a perfected bodily existence in which expression and communication will also be perfected.

What it will be like is beyond us to imagine. But that it will be so is a matter of divine promise. Many texts could be brought in here, such as 1 Corinthians 15, where Paul relates present to resurrection bodies as seed to plant. It is going to happen; it is certain, even if we are less than certain as to when and how the gift will be given, and how it will feel to be enjoying it.

The second biblical question: Is it possible, as more and more today wish to think, that universalism might be true? I am going to be quick, blunt, and even brutal in dealing with this one, for it seems to me that the question is one to which the Scriptures return a very blunt, firm, and brutal answer. And that answer is no.

No text, to start with, unambiguously asserts universalism, and many texts seem to deny it. Many texts speak of the impossibility of salvation without faith. 'He who does not obey the Son shall not see life. The wrath of God rests upon him' (John 3:36). Therefore, those who wish to affirm universalism have to go beyond the texts and embrace some doctrine of a second chance and a postmortem work of sovereign regenerating grace, for those who leave this world in unbelief, and that is a matter of unbiblical speculation in itself. The supposition that all who are unconverted in this world will be converted in some future life is entirely speculative and altogether hazardous.

Three queries can be raised which together are fatal to the universalist's speculation. First: Does not universalism fly in the face of the biblical evidence on the decisiveness of this life's decisions? What is so awful about Jesus' threat to the Jews that if they do not believe that he is the one who should come, they would die in their sins (John 8:21), if indeed they are going to be converted in a future life and weaned away from their sins there? What did Jesus have in mind, supposing that universalism is true, when he said in Matthew 12:32 that whoever speaks against the Holy Spirit will not be forgiven either in this age or in the age to come? What did Jesus have in mind when in the story of the sheep and the goats, that vision of future judgement, he speaks of the sheep being welcomed into eternal life while the goats are banished into eternal punishment (Matt. 25:46)? Eternal life, the life of the age to come, is at the least life that will never end. Must not the same be true of eternal punishment? What are we going to make of the Lord's words about Judas in Matthew 26:24, 'The Son of Man goes as it is written of him, but woe to that man by whom the Son of Man is betrayed. It would have been better for that man if he had not been born'? Do you think Jesus would have spoken that way of someone he knew would be converted in a future life? And what is Paul meaning when he says in Galatians 6:7 that those who sow to the Spirit will of the Spirit reap eternal life but those who sow to the flesh will reap corruption? Are not all these texts stressing that this life's decisions really are decisive for eternal destiny? If that is so, how can the universalist's hypothesis stand?

Second, the universalist's hypothesis impales those who embrace it on the horns of a dilemma from which, I think, they cannot escape. Supposing that universalism is true, was the preaching of hell for unbelievers by Jesus and the apostles inept ignorance or immoral bluff? If universalism is true and Jesus and the apostles did not know it, it was inept ignorance. If universalism is true and they knew it, then their warnings to turn from the prospect of hell and final misery were simply immoral bluff, the kind of things of which Evangelical preachers are sometimes accused.

The third query: Is not universalism contrary to each man's own conscience? Charity, I grant, prompts it. But hear this word from James Denney, Scottish theologian of ninety years ago. 'I dare not say to myself that if I forfeit the op- portunity this life affords I shall ever have another. And therefore I dare not say so to another man.' Don't you agree with me that that is good thinking? If I am not prepared to risk my eternal destiny by being spiritually negligent in this life because I hope that there will be a second chance in another life, it is not really charity for me to suggest that other people may warrantably do so. But that is what the affirmation of universalism does suggest. It is holding out a hope for others that I dare not hold out for myself.

Surely Denney was right. What is certain here is that there is no salvation without faith; there is no salvation without turning to Christ. According to the consistent witness of Scripture the decisive decision is made in this world. I dare not go beyond that. I do not find universalism a comfortable doctrine with which to live. I find it an unbiblical doctrine which is impossible in good conscience to accept.

Let me now ask a third question which has a link with the second one, and here again I am dealing with an issue which is becoming increasingly popular in Christian circles. Is it possible that annihilationism or, as it is sometimes called, conditional immortality is true? That is, is it possible that those who leave this world in unbelief are simply snuffed out by God, so that they cease to be, and thus there is no eternal distress for them? Again, no text unambiguously asserts this dogma, and many seem to deny it. How one can squeeze this idea out of the New Testament's fire and destruction imagery is not clear. Jesus speaks of the fire that is not quenched. And the language of eternal destruction refers (this is Greek lexicography) not to complete non-existence but to being made permanently unfit and unable to fulfil the purpose for which one was created in the way that a car is destroyed when it is scrapped. All the bits and pieces are still there, but they are so mangled that the car won't run any more, never will, never can. The idea of endlessness does seem then to be there in the awesome and heart-wrenching things that the New Testament says about the future of unbelievers.

A theological argument is offered to the effect that preserving the lost in endless punishment is needless cruelty on God's part. The conditionalists are trying to save God from the suspicion of being cruel. This argument, however, fails. It boomerangs in the following way. If it is right to suppose that any preservation of unbelievers in being after this life is needless cruelty on God's part, then you have to say that his preserving them to the day of judgement, as the New Testament clearly says that he will, is itself needless cruelty on his part. Already, then, the conditionalist's hypothesis has proved God guilty of that of which it wants to clear him. But in both Testaments the demonstration of God's retributive justice is praised as in truth integral to his glory. This is not needless cruelty. This is God displaying his righteousness in a way that makes for his praise. So we have in Revelation the loud voice of a multitude in heaven crying, 'Hallelujah! Salvation and glory and power belong to our God, for his judgements are true and just.' He has judged Babylon, the great harlot. Once more in verse 3, 'They cried, "Hallelujah! The smoke from her goes up for ever and ever."'

A passage like this shows that so far from our being in a world of needless divine cruelty, we are in a world of inexorable divine justice. That is what we are talking about when we think of eternal punishment. That is the consistent witness of the New Testament. It seems certain and inescapable that any speculation diminishing the awfulness of the prospect of a lost eternity frustrates the purpose of all that gruesome New Testament imagery, which is precisely to serve as a warning, a red light flashing, a means therefore of begging and alluring folk not to travel along the road that leads to destruction.

What we don't know is how the saved will think of the lost in the life to come. We know, however, that they will be praising God eternally for his manifested justice in judging those who merited judgement. This seems clear in New Testament theology and surely needs to be underlined as we preach the Christian hope and the Bible doctrine of the future of the individual in these days.

Briefly, let us consider now the issue that most eschatologists have concentrated on in this century: global eschatology. There are certain biblical certainties here. The parousia, that is the personal return of Jesus, will be a bodily return, a visible return, a sudden return, a triumphant return. It will interrupt. It will expose. It will change everything that is going on in the world at the moment when it occurs.

Its purpose is threefold: judgement of all human beings, renewal of the cosmos, and the bringing of the saints into their final joy forever with the Lord. Prior to this public manifesting of Jesus Christ there will have been signs showing grace in action. The specific signs here are the worldwide preaching of the gospel, as foretold in Matthew 24:14 and Mark 13:10, and the coming in of the fullness both of the Gentiles and of Israel (Rom. 11:25–29). Also there will have been signs, that is, significant events showing satanic opposition to Christ and his kingdom. There will have been anti-Christs. There will have been apostasy. There will have been persecution. There will in addition have been signs showing divine judgement in action, such as wars, earthquakes, famine, and the destruction of Jerusalem (see Mark 13:14–20; Rev. 6, among other passages).

In this field of truth also there are uncertainties about which questions may be properly asked. In the interest of brevity, I must be sketchy in addressing the two I select.

Question 1: How should we understand the imminence of the parousia? 'Be ready; the Lord may come at any time.' That seems to be a motif running through the New Testament. How are we to understand it?

It seems that the point of the imminence language in the New Testament is twofold. First, since the coming is certain, we should hope for it steadily. And since the date is unannounced, we do need to be ready for it every day, starting now. But Matthew 24:48 and following hint at the possibility of a longer wait than anyone bargained for. The parable speaks of the servant who says, 'My master delays his coming,' so he begins to become slack and go wild. And recall how in 2 Peter 3 the apostle has to minister to folk who are already discouraged at the time of writing because the Lord hasn't returned already. So we must learn to live packed up and ready to go, and at the same time be plugged soberly into the task of advancing Christ's kingdom and so be ready to stay.

Question 2: How should we understand 'all Israel' in Romans 11:26 where Paul's words are, 'And so all Israel will be saved'? Observe first that Paul is discussing the method of grace, whereby God saves both Jew and Gentile. He is showing that, just as the Gentiles were first of all shut up in sin and shut out of God's covenant fellowship and then were saved by grace out of sin, so the Jews are going to be saved out of sin, the sin of unbelief; bringing exclusion from God's favour, in which they are now shut up. So the method of grace is the same for Gentile and for Jew, and all the praise for salvation in both cases will be God's because it was in each case the salvation of sinners who deserved nothing other than final rejection. That is all that is unambiguously clear in these verses 13–32.

There are three ways of taking the words 'and so all Israel shall be saved.' The first way is to understand the phrase 'all Israel' to mean elect Gentiles and to take the word 'so' as referring back to the full number of the Gentiles coming in, as envisaged in verse 25. If this is the case, Paul is saying that through the coming of the full number of the Gentiles, Jeremiah's prophecy of the deliverer coming to Zion and banishing ungodliness from Jacob will be fulfilled.

The second view is that the coming to faith of the entire Jewish race that is alive when the full number of the Gentiles is made up is what Paul has in view, the eschatological conversion of the whole body of Abraham's genealogical descendants. Then the word 'so' is prospective rather than retrospective, it means that through the blessing bestowed on great numbers of Gentiles all the nation of Israel will be drawn to faith in the last days.

The third view is that the reference of the phrase 'all Israel' is to elect Jews in all ages, who right through the gospel era are being brought to faith through the mercy that God has shown to the Gentiles. Paul's reference on this view is to the continuing incoming of those whom God has chosen among his own people. I think that the third view gives proper emphasis to the phrase '*partial* hardening has come upon Israel' in verse 25, and the other two views do not. But a good argument can be made for each option and it is for each of us to decide which we think fits the context best. The certain thing here is that the only future Paul is foreseeing for Jews is in the Christian church, the present form of the one olive tree in which Jews were the natural branches, from which they have been broken off in unbelief, but into which they could be grafted back again, as many of them have been and will be through the sovereign grace of God.

How does all this apply to the Christian life? All that Scripture teaches about the Christian hope, the future prospects for the Lord Jesus and for the individual believer, admonishes us, each day be ready to go. One day Christ will come for each one of us.

Whether we belong to the terminal generation and will see him in the great public parousia, that unimaginably glorious 'day of the Lord' that is promised, we cannot say. But heart-stop and brain-stop day may come to any of us at any time. And that coming day should be understood as an appointment already entered on the Lord Jesus' calendar. It is the day when he will come for us personally to take us to be with himself. One way or another, he is coming for each one of us and should not find us unprepared.

As wise persons preparing for vacations tidy up, pack their bags and get ready well in advance, so should we prepare for the meeting with Jesus that will close our lives in this world. Keep short accounts with God and 'live each day as if thy last,' just as the hymn says. And while our life continues, let us work and pray for the advancing of the kingdom. When Christ appears publicly in this world, in what posture should he find the church? Praying for revival and planning world evangelism, surely. Let us see that when he comes for us, whether it is soon or late, those are the tasks in which he finds us engaged.

CHAPTER 15

In Quest of Canonical Interpretation

Having been asked for a personal statement on how I use the Bible in theologizing, I shall attempt one—though not without anxiety. Not that asking a theologian for such a statement strikes me as in any way improper. On the contrary, it is a supremely fitting thing to do, for one's answer to the request will at once show how seriously one takes one's trade, and that is something which the church needs, and has a right, to know. Furthermore, any theologizing that has integrity will reflect something of one's Christian identity, as that has been formed in experience, and making that identity explicit should therefore help others to understand and assess one's work. Paul's example in Acts 22, 24, and 26, Romans 7, Galatians 1–2, and Philippians 3 shows that it is no solecism for theologians to say where they come from experientially when that helps them to model or confirm what they want to get across. Professional theologians today hesitate to share their experience, fearing lest the pure objectivity and the transcendent reference point of their God-thoughts be thereby obscured; but this is a great pity, for when they define their role merely in ecclesiastical or academic terms, thus in effect hiding behind their official identity, it renders their theology at best enigmatic and at worst downright boring. For my part (so far as I understand myself), the theology that I 'do' in my churchly and academic roles is a conscious confessional expression of my personal identity and spirituality *coram Deo*, and to be asked to identify that identity, as it relates to my handling of Scripture, is no hardship at all. Nonetheless, I find myself feeling some prickles of anxiety as I turn to the task.

Why so? Because anyone who voices certainties as a Christian in directly personal terms runs the risk of being misheard, as if one saying: 'Believe this, or do that, because it is what I believe and do, and my own experience has proven that it is right'; in other words, 'take it from *me*, as if I were your God and your authority.' It was, I think, Kierkegaard who observed that the greatest misfortune for any person is to have disciples, and anyone who talks in a personal way about his convictions maximizes the risk of disciple-making. I have seen Christians in both academic and pastoral work attracting admirers who then progressively lose the power to distinguish between devotion to their human teacher and loyalty to their divine Lord, and I don't want anything of that kind to happen to me. That is why some folk who have asked to have me as their mentor and role model have received dusty answers. I am a pastoral theologian; my aim is to attach disciples to Jesus Christ my Lord, not to myself; and nobody is going to become a Packerite if I can help it. So I shrink somewhat from highlighting what I believe and do, as distinct from what God says ought to be believed and done.

Moreover, since God is infinitely good to all who truly seek him, I do not see how anyone's experience of grace or formation by grace can settle the truth of one confessional position as against another, and I don't want to look as if I think that the quality of my Christian experience or the strength of my Christian convictions should be decisive in persuading others to accept my views. The truth of theological assertions should be decided by asking whether they faithfully echo Scripture, not whether God has blessed folk who have held them. Certainly, one whose religious experience is lacking does well to inquire whether one knows enough as yet of God's truth about spiritual life, just as one who knows that truth sufficiently does well to take note of how God confirms it in experience. But it is Scripture as such, the written Word of God, that must finally identify God's truth for us—Scripture, and in the last analysis nothing else.

Hence, then, my anxiety. I fear lest by the very act of making a personal statement I risk both obscuring an emphasis which is basic to my own Christian identity and to the message I seek to spread and sounding insufferably egocentric into the bargain. But that risk is unavoidable. All I can do about it is ask my readers in charity to believe that my goal is to celebrate God rather than to project Packer; and that I only talk about Packer because I was asked to; and that I would have felt freer and happier altogether if the title of our symposium could have been, 'How *the Bible uses me* when I do theology.' (That title would have meshed directly with my experience of the Bible during the forty years since my conversion. How often in modern contexts has my heart echoed the protest of John Rogers, the Reformation martyr, against the alleged inertness of the biblical text: 'No, no, the Bible is alive!'). Enough, now, of preliminary remarks. I move into my assignment forthwith.

My Perception of the Bible

The first thing to say is that I perceive the sixty-six books of the Protestant canon to be the Word of God given in and through human words.

Canonical Scripture is divine testimony and instruction in the form of human testimony and instruction. Let me explain.

By 'God' I mean the pervasive personal presence, distinct from me and prior to me, who is the source and support of my existence; who through Scripture makes me realize that he has toward me the nature and name of love—holy, lordly, costly, fatherly, redeeming love; who addresses me, really though indirectly, in all that Scripture shows of his relationship to human beings in history, and especially in the recorded utterances of his Son, Jesus Christ; and who is daily drawing me toward a face-to-face encounter and consummated communion with him beyond this life, by virtue of 'the redemption which is in Christ Jesus' (Rom. 3:24). For academic purposes you may call this my theistic model of God, to be set along-side other models, deistic, pantheistic, panentheistic, or whatever. But it is no mere notion; this is my non-negotiable awareness of the One whom I worship, an awareness that has been relatively clear and steady since I experienced a full-scale pietistic conversion from religious formalism to the living Christ at age eighteen.

By 'Word of God' I mean God's own self-declaration and message about the way of godliness—worship, obedience, and fellowship in God's family—that Jesus Christ made known to the world. Some Evangelicals use 'Word of God' to mean the text of Scripture as such, known to be God's communication but viewed as still uninterpreted. I use the phrase as the Reformers did, to signify not just the text in its God-givenness but also the God-given message that it contains. This is in line with the way that in Scripture itself 'Word of God' means God's message conveyed by God's messenger, whether orally or in writing. The narrower usage really involves a false abstraction, since no one ever has or is entitled to have a clear certainty that Scripture is from God when that person has no inkling of its message. I doubt whether any latter-day Evangelicals ever deserved to be called bibliolaters, worshipers of the written Word of the Lord rather than the living Lord of the Word. But if any did, it was this narrow usage that betrayed them by leading them to focus on the book itself as a sacred object, unrelated to the God of whom it speaks.

Many since Kant have doubted whether God, who gave us language, actu-ally uses language to communicate with us—whether, that is, God's 'speaking' to people is a cognitive event for them as my speaking to you would be, or whether this 'speaking' is a metaphor for some non-cognitive way in which we are made aware of his presence. Here, however, the incarnation is surely decisive. Rabbi Jesus used language (Aramaic, to be exact) in order to teach. But Rabbi Jesus was God come in the flesh. So the principle that God uses language to tell us things is at once established; and the claim that Scripture is a further case in point—a claim, be it said, that is irremovably embedded at foundation level in Jesus' teaching about his Messiahship and God's righteousness[1]—presents no new conceptual problem.

By 'canon' I mean the body of teaching that God gave to be a rule of faith and life for his church. God created the canon by inspiring the books that make it up and by causing the church to recognize their canonical character. The gaps and uncertainties that appear when we try to reconstruct this process need not detain us now. Suffice it to say that I read the historical evidence both as showing that this was how the early church understood the canon (Jesus' Bible) in Jesus' own day and as confirming rather than calling in question the authenticity of our entire New Testament. (Scholars will agree that this is a possible and natural way of reading that evidence, even if it cannot be established as the absolutely necessary way.) Then, theologically, I see the attestation of the Protestant canon by the Holy Spirit growing stronger year by year as more and more Bible readers have the sixty-six books authenticated to them in actual experience. (The problem of the eccentric Tridentine canon, which contains seventy-eight books, cannot be dealt with here.) We have to realize that only one theological question about the canon faces us, namely whether any evidence compels us to challenge its historic bounds. Once we grasp this, it becomes clear how we can accept with rational confidence the canon which the church hands down to us, even though many questions about the origin, circulation, and stages of acceptance of the various books remain unanswered.

Knowing how a belief began never, of course, proves it true, and not all convictions for which the Holy Spirit is invoked stand the test of examination; nonetheless, the following facts may be of interest. C. S. Lewis wrote of a motorcycle ride in 1931 to Whipsnade Zoo, a ride at the start of which he did not believe that Jesus Christ was the Son of God and at the end of which he found he did. Similarly, in 1944 I went to a Bible study at which a vision from the book of Revelation (I forget which one) was expounded, and whereas at the start I did not believe that all the Bible (which I had been assiduously reading since my conversion six weeks before) is God's trustworthy instruction, at the end, slightly to my surprise, I found myself unable to doubt that indeed it is. Nor have I ever been able to doubt this since, any more than I have been able to doubt the reality of the biblical Christ whom I honour as my Saviour, Lord, and God. When, years later, I found Calvin declaring that every Christian experiences the inward witness of the Holy Spirit to the divine authority of Scripture,[2] I rejoiced to think that, without ever having heard a word on this subject, I had long known exactly what Calvin was talking about—as by God's mercy I still do.

My Practice of Theology

The next thing to say is that, as the believer, theologian, and preacher that I am, I read Scripture in the way followed before me by Chrysostom (regularly), Augustine (fitfully), and all Western professional exegetes since Colet, Luther, and Calvin—that is, I approach the books as human documents produced by people of like passions with myself. I read these books as units of responsive, didactic, celebratory, doxological witness to the living God. Those who wrote them, being believers, theologians, and preachers themselves, were seeking to make God and godliness known to their original envisaged audience, and the first question to be asked about each book has to do with what its writer saw it as saying and showing about God himself. But when I have seen this, my next task is to let the book's message universalize itself in my mind as God's own teaching or *doctrina* (to use the word that Calvin loved) now addressed to humankind in general and to me in particular within the frame of reality created by the death, resurrection, and present dominion of Jesus Christ.

That last phrase is important, for it determines my way of applying Old Testament material. I see the Old Testament in its totality laying a permanent foundation for faith by its disclosure of God's moral character, sovereign rule, redemptive purpose, and covenant faithfulness and by its exhibiting of the positive dispositions of faith, praise, and obedience contrasted with the negative dispositions of mistrust and rebellion. But on this foundation it sets a temporary superstructure of cultic apparatus for mediating covenant communion with God; and this apparatus the New Testament replaces with the new and better covenant (that is, the better version of God's one gracious covenant) which is founded on better promises and maintained by the sacrifice and intercession of Jesus Christ, the better and greater high priest. This amounts to saying that I think the Old Testament should be read through the hermeneutical spectacles that Paul (Romans and Galatians), Luke (gospel and Acts), Matthew, and the writer to the Hebrews provide. The typology of the New Testament teaches me to transpose everything in the Old Testament about typical provisions and promises (i.e., cultic prescriptions, expectations of this-worldly enrichment, and imperialist eschatological visions) into the new key, which we might call the key of fulfilment, which was established by the New Testament revelation of the corresponding antitypes—spiritual redemption through Christ, the heavenly Jerusalem, and the world to come. Reading Old Testament books in the light of this principle, which was long ago expressed in the jingle 'the New is in the Old concealed, the Old is in the New revealed,' I find in their teaching about God and godliness a significance which a Jewish colleague would miss.

My way of reading Scripture involves five distinct convictions about theological method. That one's method must be a posteriori and biblically determined is for me a truth of first importance. These five convictions together fix the method to be followed when one faces problems of faith and practice and seeks to grow in the knowledge of God. This method, as will be seen, is kerygmatic in content, systematic in character, and normative in purpose. The analytical and descriptive techniques of historical, philosophical, phenomenological, political, and sociological theology have their interest and use as both sources and sieves of material for kerygmatic reflection, but only as one follows the kerygmatic method can one be said to be theologizing; any God-talk that falls short of this is no more than a contribution to the history of ideas. It is now the kerygmatic method that I describe as I detail my five convictions.

First conviction: by entering into the expressed mind of the inspired writers I do in fact apprehend God's own mind. What Scripture says, God says. In the writers' witness to God and communication about him God witnesses to himself and communicates personally with the hearer or reader. When they announce the mighty works of God in creation, providence, and grace, God is in effect setting before us fragments of his own autobiography. The identity of what the writers say about God with God's own message about himself is the truth that has historically been indicated and safeguarded by calling the biblical books *inspired.* Inspiration makes it possible to achieve a theology which, to use the old terms, is *ektypal* in relation to God's own thoughts as *archetypal;* a theology which, in other words, literally thinks God's thoughts after him. Such a theology is my goal. But such theology is essentially biblical interpretation; and biblical interpretation must begin with correct exegesis, lest by misunderstanding biblical authors I misrepresent God; and correct exegesis is exegesis that is right *historically.* So I am grateful for the deepened insight in the West over the past two hundred years as to what historical understanding involves. I appreciate the critical awareness of differences between the present and the past, with techniques for determining those differences in particular cases, that the new historical sensibility has brought, and I welcome the refining of historical exegesis in Western churches that has resulted. For understanding of God can grow only as we better understand—understand, that is, with greater historical accuracy—what the biblical writers meant by what they said about him.

Second conviction: since all sixty-six books come ultimately from the mind of our self-revealing God, they should be read not just as separate items (though obviously one must start by doing that), but also as parts of a whole. They must be appreciated not only in their particular individuality of genre and style, but also as a coherent, internally connected organism of teaching. This, after all (and here I throw down the gauntlet to some of my academic peers), is what examination shows them to be. It is fashionable these days for Scripture scholars to look for substantive differences of conviction between biblical writers, but this is in my view an inquiry as shallow and stultifying as it is unfruitful. Much more significant is the truly amazing unity of viewpoint, doctrine, and vision that this heterogeneous library of occasional writings, put together by more than forty writers over more than a millennium, displays.[3] The old way of stating the principle that the internal coherence of Scripture should be a heuristic maxim for interpreters was to require that *the analogy of Scripture* be observed.[4] This is the requirement which the twentieth Anglican Article enforces when it says that the church may not 'so expound one place of Scripture, that it be repugnant to another.' The modern way of expressing the point is to require that interpretation be *canonical,* each passage being interpreted kerygmatically and normatively as part of the whole body of God's revealed instruction. Accepting this requirement, I infer from it the way in which theology should seek to be *systematic*: not by trying to go behind or beyond what the texts affirm (the common caricature of systematic theology), but by making clear the links between items in the whole compendium of biblical thought.

Third conviction: biblical teaching, like the law of the land, must be applied to the living of our lives. So, as in legal interpretation, the interpreter has a twofold task. First, one must discern the universal truths and principles that particular texts exhibit in their particularized application to particular people in particular circumstances. Second, one must reapply those same truths and principles to us in our circumstances. Therefore one must look not only *at* but also *along* the Bible, just as one looks along a ray of light to see the things that it strikes and shows up. Biblical teaching, received as instruction from God, must be brought to bear on the world and life in general and on our own lives in particular. Interpreted Scripture must be allowed to interpret its interpreters; those who in procedural terms stand over it to find out its meaning and bearing must recognize that in spiritual terms they stand under it to be judged, corrected, led, and fed by it. Interpretation has to be *imperative, self-involving,* and thus (to use an abused word) *existential* in style. The divinely authoritative claim on our compliance which biblical teaching makes must not be muffled. My ears—and yours, too—must always be open to the Bible's summons (God's, really) to what Bultmannites call *decision,* what most Anglo-Saxons call *commitment,* and what the Bible itself calls *repentance, faith, worship, obedience,* and *endurance.*

Here the Holy Spirit's ministry is decisive. Commentaries will tell us what each writer's words *meant* as an utterance spoken into that immediate historical situation, but only the Spirit who gave them can show us, by using them to search us, what they *mean* as they bear on us today. Luther's famous observation that a theologian is made by prayer, meditation, and spiritual conflict (*oratio, meditatio, tentatio*) reflects his awareness of the way in which the Spirit does this.

Fourth conviction: The basic form of obedient theology is applicatory interpretation of Scripture in the manner described, reading the books as God's witness to his saving grace in Christ and God's call to sinners to believe and respond. Such theology is of necessity a form of preaching, just as true preaching is of necessity an exercise in the theological interpretation of Scripture. The technical disciplines taught in universities and seminaries—technical dogmatics, ethics, spirituality, apologetics, missiology, historical theology, and so forth—find their value as they lead to richer biblical interpretation. Dogmatics are for the sake of Scripture study, not vice versa, and so with all technical branches of theology. (By 'technical' I mean using terms and forms of analysis that are developed within the discipline for its own furtherance.) Academically and professionally, my job description as a theologian may be to develop and teach one of these technical disciplines, but in terms of the theologian's calling and churchly identity my main task is and always will be the interpreting of Scripture.

Fifth conviction: I must be ready to give account of my interpretative encounters with Scripture not just to my human and academic peers but to God himself, who will one day require this of every theologian and of me among them. This is to say that I must follow my method *responsibly* as one who must answer for what I do.

To sum up this section, I can schematize my use of the Bible in theologizing as follows. I make use of the Bible (1) in personal devotion, (2) in preaching and pastoral ministry, (3) in academic theological work. Use (3) underlies use (2) and is fed by use (1). I approach the Bible in all three connections as the communication of *doctrina* from God; as the instrument of Jesus Christ's personal authority over Christians (which is part of what I mean in calling it *canonical*); as the criterion of truth and error regarding God and godliness; as wisdom for the ordering of life and food for spiritual growth; and, thus, as the mystery—that is, the transcendent supernatural reality—whereby encounter and fellowship with the Father and the Son become realities of experience. I attempt theological exegesis and exposition in the way and for the ends already described, depending on and expecting light and help from the Holy Spirit. I see ethics, spirituality, catechetics, preaching, and all pastoral counsel as needing to be informed and regulated by theological interpretation of Scripture, and I do not expect to see any good practical Christianity where this discipline is neglected. If you ask me for models of my kind of Bible-based theologizing, I would name John Calvin and the Puritan, John Owen.

The mention of Calvin, that most ecumenical of writers, prompts one last question: how, in seeking a canonical interpretation of Scriptures, do I relate to church tradition? The answer is that, like Calvin, I theologize in constant dialogue with the whole Christian heritage of study, proclamation, and belief insofar as I can acquaint myself with it. Theology is a cooperative enterprise, and the fellowship of its practitioners has a historical as well as a contemporary dimension. In essence, tradition means neither *theologoumena* ecclesiastically imposed nor superstitions ecclesiastically sanctioned (the common Protestant stereotype), but the sum of attempts down through the ages to expound and apply biblical teaching on specific subjects. It should be appreciated as such and, finally, be evaluated by the Bible which it aims to echo and bring down to earth. (The old Roman Catholic idea, now generally abandoned, that tradition supplements Scripture can be safely dismissed as a freak.)

In tradition, enlightenment from God's Spirit and blindness due to sin coexist and coalesce, often strangely, so that treating tradition as infallibly right or as inevitably wrong is a mistake in either case. Dismissing tradition as representing only the worldliness of the church reflects unbelief in the Spirit's work since Pentecost as the church's teacher; embracing the dogma of faultless tradition reflects a lapse into ecclesiastical perfectionism. In seeking to profit from tradition I oppose the deifying of it no less than the devaluing of it. The worth of tradition as a help in our own interpreting of Scripture depends on its being constantly exposed to the judgement of Scripture. Its relation to us is ministerial, not magisterial, and we must keep it so.

My Method Applied: A Case Study

Nobody theologizes aimlessly; as in all one's mental life, one thinks for a purpose and to a point—though agendas are sometimes hidden! My agenda is no secret, however. My concerns, biblically directed I trust, are churchly. Like my convictions, they reflect Luther rather than Erasmus; I seek to advance learning not for its own sake but for the good of souls.[5] My goal is theology that will guide and sustain evangelism, and nurture pastoral care and spiritual renewal.[6] I draw heavily on Calvin and the English Puritans, for I find in them great theological and interpretative resources for the task. I contend for biblical authority—that is, the permanent binding force of all biblical teaching—because this much-challenged facet of Christ's Christianity is basic to the theology I build and to the Christian life to which that theology leads.[7] I contend for biblical inerrancy because acknowledgement of Scripture as totally true and trustworthy is integral to biblical authority as I understand it.[8] On these various themes I have written a good deal. In the tangle of history and polemics that has marked my treatment of them it has doubtless been easy to miss what I was after, and any who have in fact failed to see it should not be blamed too harshly. They would in any case be to some extent victims of the habitual failure to probe motivation (what the Germans call one's theological intentions), which seems to me to be a chronic weakness of English-speaking scholarship. But if there is to be genuine under-standing, the question of motivation (what's it all in aid of?) needs to be asked, and it seems to me that the motivation that has produced my published work has really been clear all along.

My goal is not adequately expressed by saying that I am to uphold an Evangel-ical conservatism of genetically Reformed or specifically Anglican or neo-Puritan or interdenominational pietist type, though I have been both applauded and booed on occasion for doing all these things, and I hope under God to continue to do them. But if I know myself I am first and foremost a theological exegete. My constant purpose was and is to adumbrate on every subject I handle a genuinely canonical interpretation of Scripture—a view that in its coherence embraces and expresses the thrust of all the biblical passages and units of thought that bear on my theme—a total, integrated view built out of biblical material in such a way that, if the writers of the various books knew what I had made of what they taught, they would nod their heads and say that I had got them right. I have been asked in the present essay to illustrate my use of the Bible, and that means showing how I work my way toward the canonical interpretations which are the goal of my theological endeavour. I shall now attempt to do this, taking as my paradigm case a theme that I have not mentioned so far, the much-debated question of what is currently called role relationships between the sexes.[9]

This is a many-sided question. It answers in connection with (1) church order (may women function as elders? sole pastors? bishops?); (2) family ethics (what kind and measure of subordination, if any, of wives to husbands is biblically re-quired?); (3) socio-political ideals for the modern world (does Scripture imply that privileges, opportunities, rights, and rewards should everywhere be equal, irrespective of sex?); and (4) pastoral nurture of men and women to fulfil their

God-given vocations in relation to each other. As secular society everywhere is split on these matters, so is the church generally and the Evangelical sector of it specifically. For Christians the basic question is whether the undisputed spiritual equality of the sexes before God and in Christ sanctions equality of function, i.e., carries God's permission to share and exchange all non-biological roles in home, church, and community; or, whether God has ordained a hierarchical pattern whereby in some or all of these spheres men are to lead and certain roles are not for women. The main biblical evidence is (1) the stories of the creation (Gen. 1:26–27 with 5:1–2; 2:18–25) and the fall (3:16–20); (2) Jesus' respect for women, whom he consistently treated as men's equals (Mark 5:22–42; Luke 8:1–3; 10:38–42; 11:27–28; 13:10–17; 21:1–4; John 4:7–38; 8:3–11; 12:1–8); (3) references to women ministering in the apostolic church by prophesying, leading in prayer, teaching, practicing Good Samaritanship both informally and as widows and deacons, and labouring in the gospel with apostles (Acts 2:17–21; 9:36–42; 18:24–26; 21:9; Rom. 16:1–15; 1 Cor. 11:2–16; Phil. 4:2–3; 1 Tim. 3:11; 5:1–16; Titus 2:3); and (4) the seemingly mixed signals of Paul's assertion of equality in Christ (Gal. 3:28) alongside both his asymmetrical teaching on the duties of husbands and wives (Eph. 5:21–33; Col. 3:18–19) and his real, if problematical, restrictions on what women may do in church as compared with men (1 Cor. 11:2–16; 14:34–36; 1 Tim. 2:11–15).

This material raises many interpretative difficulties, which makes this an excellent case study of what seeking a canonical interpretation of biblical testimony on any subject involves. I offer now, not an attempted resolution of all the problems (!) but an applied statement of relevant hermeneutical principles, which will establish limits within which, here and in all cases, canonical interpretation lies. Evangelicals have not always noted the complexity of the hermeneutical task; indeed, sometimes they have let themselves speak as if everything immediately becomes plain and obvious for believers in biblical inerrancy, to such an extent that uncertainties about interpretation never arise for them. Granted, reverent Bible readers regularly see in texts practical lessons which are really there, and which doctrinaire students miss. Nonetheless, inerrancy is a concept that demands hermeneutical qualification, for what is true and trustworthy is precisely the text's meaning, and this only correct interpretative procedures will yield. Moreover, while the central biblical message of new life through Christ is expressed so fully and clearly that one who runs may read and understand (which is what Reformation theology meant by the *clarity* and *perspicuity* of Scripture), there remain many secondary matters on which certainty of interpretation is hard if not impossible to come by. The present exercise will, I think, make that clear. Here, now, are the hermeneutical principles that I propose to illustrate from the role relationship debate.

(1) *Biblical teaching is coherent and self-consistent*, for, as I said above, with whatever variety of literary form and personal style from writer to writer and

with whatever additions and amendments as redemptive history progressed, it all proceeds from one source; namely, the mind of God the Holy Spirit. Any adequate hermeneutical hypothesis on this or any topic, therefore, will have to show the internal harmony of all relevant biblical material. No hypothesis positing either the inconsistency of one biblical teacher with another or a biblical teacher's self-contradiction (as when Paul Jewett diagnosed self-contradiction in what his apostolic namesake said about Christian women[10]) can be right.

(2) *Biblical moral instruction corresponds to human nature,* for it stands in a maker's-handbook relation to us, showing the natural, God-planned, and therefore fulfilling and satisfying way for us creatures to behave. Halfway houses, therefore, must be deemed faulty when they approve women ruling men in secular affairs (because Scripture nowhere forbids it and sometimes exemplifies it) but not in the church or home (because Scripture requires male leadership in both), or when they approve women ruling in today's church (because Paul's restriction on this seems to be culturally determined) but not in the family (because biblical teaching on this seems to be transcultural and timeless). I say this not because of any particular failures or arbitrarinesses of argument, real though these may be, but because these views overlook the fact that in his enactments about role relationship, whatever they are, God is legislating for the fulfilment of human nature as it was created in its own forms, male-masculine and female-feminine. You can hold that a woman is so made that she enters into her sexual identity and so finds a particular fulfilment by giving cooperative support to a male leader, or that she is not; you can hold that a man is so made that he enters into his sexual identity and so finds a particular fulfilment by taking responsibility for a female helper, or that he is not; and you can argue across the board for whichever view of Bible teaching on role relationships fits in with your idea. But what you cannot do is argue that *both* views are true at the same time in different spheres. Human nature is either one thing or the other, and only across-the-board arguments are in place here.

(3) *Biblical narratives must be evaluated by biblical norms,* for it is not safe to infer that because God caused an event to be recorded in Scripture he approved it and means us to approve it too. As it does not follow that Paul approved of baptism for the dead because he mentions the Corinthians' practice of it (1 Cor. 15:29), so it does not follow that every action of a believing woman that Scripture records is there as a model; we must evaluate those actions by normative teaching before we can be sure. Nor can it be argued (for instance) that God, when cursing Eve after the fall and describing to her how it was now going to be ('your husband . . . shall rule over you' [Gen. 3:16]), was thereby prescribing that thus it evermore ought to be, even in the realm of redemption. Normative teaching from elsewhere must settle whether that is so or not.

(4) *Biblical texts must be understood in their human context,* for otherwise we shall fail to read their real point out of them and instead read into them points they

are not making at all. Only through contextual study can exegesis be achieved and eisegesis be eliminated. That Scripture interprets Scripture is a profound truth, but lifting biblical statements out of context to fit them into mosaics of texts culled from elsewhere is a corner-cutting operation (beloved, alas, of a certain type of 'Bible teacher') which that profound truth cannot be invoked to justify. We must know the literary genre, historical and cultural background, immediate situation and occasion, and intended function of each passage before we can be confident that we have properly understood it. When, for instance, Paul tells Co-rinthian women to be silent in church (1 Cor. 14:34) and then, maybe eight years later, tells Timothy that he requires women not to teach but to be quiet (1 Tim. 2:11), is he making exactly the same point? Contextual study of each passage is needed to determine that.

But when we look we find that the context and intended function of Paul's restrictive statements about women is less clear. What abuses or questions prompted them? Had some particular women disgraced themselves in a way that Paul was determined to clamp down on? Or did he bring in this teaching because it was part of a universal congregational order, modelled on the synagogue, which he believed that God intended for all churches at all times in the way that the un-changing gospel was intended for all churches at all times? In 1 Timothy 2:13–14 he justifies the silence rule as appropriate because of the order of creation and the sequence of events in the fall; but was he imposing this rule to be law forever, or simply as a rule of prudence which experience had shown to be expedient *pro tempore* in the churches for which he was caring? If we knew those things, we should at once know a great deal more. We should know, for instance, whether in these passages he is talking about all women or only wives (the Greek word which he uses, *gynē* regularly means both and is the only regular Greek word for both, so that linguistically this ambiguity is unresolvable). We should also know whether in 1 Timothy 2:12 he is forbidding women to teach men or to teach anybody in the public assembly (the Greek allows both renderings) and whether he would regard the completing of the canon and its availability in print to all Christians today (so that teachers need never say 'take it from me,' but always 'take it from Scripture') as so changing the situation that his ban on women teaching no longer applies. We should know too whether the silence rule of 1 Corinthians 14:34 means that, after all, women must not lead in prayer nor prophesy publicly, as 11:4–10 seemed to allow them to do, or that women must take no part in judging prophets, which is the theme of the immediate context, 14:29–33, or simply that women must not interrupt in church. But the pieces of information which alone could give us certainty on these points are lacking, and in their absence no guess as to what is probably meant can be thought of as anything like a certainty. This leads to the next point.

(5) *Certainties must be distinguished from possibilities*, for only certainties can command universal assent and obedience. In the present field of discussion

the only points of certainty seem to be these: (a) both creation and redemption establish the equality of men and women before God, as both image bearers and children of God through Christ (Gen. 1:26–27; Gal. 3:26–29); (b) within this equality the man (or at least the husband) is irreversibly 'the head' of the woman (or at least his wife), i.e., is of higher rank in some real sense (though the exact sense is disputed—causal priority only? or leadership claim too?—see 1 Cor. 11:3; Eph. 5:23); (c) Christian partners are to model in their marriage the redeeming love-responsive love relationship of Christ and the church (Eph. 5:21–33). Beyond this, everything—all that was mentioned in the last paragraph, and just how Paul would have expounded his key words about women's roles, 'be subject,' 'respect' (Eph. 5:21–24, 33; Col. 3:18; cf. Peter's 'obey,' 1 Pet. 3:5), 'submissiveness,' 'have authority over' (1 Tim. 2:11–12)—is a matter of rival possibilities, on none of which may we forget the real uncertainty of our own opinion, whatever it is, or deny to others the right to hold a different view. It is the way of Evangelicals to expect absolute certainty from Scripture on everything and to admire firm stances on secondary and disputed matters as signs of moral courage. But in some areas such expectations are not warranted by the evidence, and such stances reveal only a mind insufficiently trained to distinguish certainties from uncertain possibilities. Among those areas this is one.

(6) *What is explicitly forbidden must be distinguished from what, though unfitting, is not forbidden,* for action that is undesirable, because unfitting, is not necessarily sin. That which is unfitting by reason of God's work should not be equated with that which is unlawful by reason of God's command: the two categories are distinct. Should it appear from Scripture that woman was not fitted by creation to fulfil leadership roles in relation to man, that would not *ipso facto* make it sin for a woman to be president or prime minister or general manager or chairman, or to have a male secretary, or even (if one does not judge Paul's silence rule to forbid this) to be a missionary church-planter or a sole pastor or a bishop. It could still be argued that these roles impose strain on womanly nature; that they are not what women are made for; that they show a certain lack of respect for God's work of creation; that in fulfilling them a woman is likely to treat men maternally, which will impose undue strain on masculine nature; and that the woman's womanly dignity and worth are to some extent at risk while she does these jobs; but it could not be maintained that she and those who gave her role have sinned by disobeying God's command. The facts of creation in this as in other matters do not of themselves constitute a command, only an indication of what is fitting; and the various forms of ethical unwisdom and indignity which do not transgress explicit commands cannot be categorized as sin.

(7) *The horizons of text and student must mesh,* for only so can God's teaching in the text deliver us from the intellectual idolatry which absolutizes the axioms of contemporary culture. The 'meshing' or 'fusing' of horizons is a picture, taken from H. G. Gadamer, of how the inspired text, which we question in order to

find its meaning and relevance, questions, criticises, challenges, and changes us in the process.[11] Some who today raise the proper question, whether there are not culturally relative elements in Paul's teaching about role relationships (all the material has to be thought through from this standpoint), seem to proceed improperly in doing so; for in effect they take current secular views about the sexes as fixed points, and work to bring Scripture into line with them—an agenda that at a stroke turns the study of sacred theology into a venture in secular ideology. We need grace both to believe, as our forebears did, that we really do not know our own nature, any more than we know God's nature, till taught by Scripture and to apply this truth to our own sexual nature in particular. The biblical word of God, which lives and abides forever, must be set free to relativize all the absolutes, avowed and presuppositional, of our post-Christian, neo-pagan culture and to lead us into truth about ourselves as our Maker has revealed it—truth which, be it said, we only fully know and perceive as truth in the process of actually obeying it.

I take the discussion of role relationships no further. Suffice it to have illustrated from this one case some, at least, of the procedural principles which I try to observe when on any subject at all I seek a canonical interpretation of Scripture—the goal at which, in my view, all theologians ought centrally to aim and to which the study of theological ideas should be viewed as a means. The greatest of the Church Fathers saw the matter so; Luther, Calvin, and Owen did the same; Karl Barth, in a slightly odd manner determined by his epistemological preoccupation and his eccentric sort of christocentricity, took essentially the same road; I follow in their train, as best I can.

There are, of course, many other principles of importance in the quest for canonical theological interpretation of Scripture—for instance, the continuity of God's work in Old and New Testament times and the biblical typology that is based on it; the trinitarian identity of the God of the Old Testament; the theomorphism of humanity which makes possible and meaningful the so-called anthropomorphism of biblical language about God; the nature of redemption as a restoring of fallen creation and so a fulfilling of God's original purpose for the world; the real overlap of the age to come (that world, heaven) with the present age (this world, earth) through the ministry of Christ prolonged by the Holy Spirit—but none of these can be discussed here. Other tasks, too, besides interpreting Scripture face theologians, tasks both intramural (dealing with the church) and extramural (dialoguing with the world)—tasks of phenomenological analysis of theologies past and present and of apologetics, philosophical, evangelistic, and defensive—but these cannot be spoken of here either. I end here by repeating my conviction that the canonical interpretation of Scripture is the theologian's main job and by adding to it my further conviction that only those who give themselves to this task first and foremost will ever be fit to interpret anything else on God's behalf.

CHAPTER 16

Let's Stop Making Women Presbyters

Is there not a better way of benefiting from women's ministry than by ordaining them?

Oxford has been called the home of lost causes, and here am I, an Oxford man, pleading for an end to something that is now standard practice in Methodist, Baptist, Lutheran, Congregational, Pentecostal, and Presbyterian denominations, along with the Anglican churches of the U.S.A., Canada, New Zealand, and Ireland. Is this a lost cause? Perhaps. Yet does not wisdom urge us to stop this practice and point us to a better way of benefiting from women's ministry than by ordaining them to the presbyterate? Here are my reasons for thinking that the answer is yes.

Let me say, before moving into my argument, that I am as emphatically for women's ministry as I am against turning women into substitute men by making presbyters of them. To confine women to domestic and menial roles when God has gifted them for ministry and leadership would be Spirit-quenching, beyond doubt. Gifts are given to be used, and when God-given gifts lie fallow, whether in men or in women, the church suffers. However, by envisaging a presbyterate of manly men, the New Testament indicates that the truest womanly ministry will be distinct from this, in ways that I will specify in a moment. But two other questions must be faced first.

Question one: Why has so much of the church in our time come to think that introducing women into the presbyterate is good, right, wise, and pleasing to God? Official Roman Catholicism (though not all Catholic theologians, nor laymen) and Orthodoxy as it seems from top to bottom, and Bible-based Evangelical communities of all denominational stripes within Protestantism, agree in opposing this trend, but it cannot be denied that the general current of Protestant opinion has flowed the other way, so that many nowadays are wired to dismiss counter-arguments as foot-dragging foolishness. The trend is modern; whence came it? From a conjunction, it seems, of five factors.

First, the feminist ideology that demands equal rights everywhere, on the grounds that anything a man can do a woman can do as well if not better, naturally requires women presbyters, and women bishops, too, such as can already be found among Methodists and Anglicans in North America.

Second, the social change since World War I whereby gradually women have been moving into what were previously men's jobs, and doing them well, has made opening the presbyterate to women appear as plain common sense.

Third, it has become clear that the present-day relevance of the New Testament passages that debar women from doing what presbyteral ministry involves (speaking in church,[1] teaching and giving directions to men[2]) is problematical. If in these passages Paul is establishing a universal church order, meant for all congregations in all places at all times, then all is clear—but is he? Or is he simply legislating for his own day? And if the latter, are we wrong to allow that in a changed cultural situation, in which women were educated as men are and could come to church with well-studied Bibles in their hands, Paul might have said something different?

At this point, there is division among those who agree that what Paul says, Christ says, just as there is among those who do not believe any such thing; and no amount of general debate on the male headship principle of 1 Corinthians 11:3 and Ephesians 5:23 (which is itself differently understood by different expositors), or on anything else said about the two genders in Scripture, does anything to diminish the divergence. Understandably, those who think that if Paul were alive in the modern West he might possibly, or would certainly, remove his restrictions have not stood against, but gone with, the pressure for women clergy.

Fourth, God has blessed the ministry of ordained women. Does that not prove the rightness of their presbyteral role? Not necessarily. God has blessed his people before through intrinsically inappropriate arrangements and may be doing so again. His mercy in practice does not settle matters of principle any more than majority votes do. The conclusion that God's use of women presbyters shows that he wants them does not follow.

Fifth, the Anglican and Presbyterian restriction of leadership at the Lord's Table (and, in Presbyterianism, of power to baptize) to presbyters has spread the sense that presbyter status is an enviable privilege, without which Christian professionals do not have a fully satisfying ministry. This feeling, however unjustified (and it seems to me unjustifiable), is widespread, and makes it seem churlish to deny to all the church's professional women the job-satisfaction that those whom Anglicans call priests are thought to get from their sacramental ministrations. Do not misunderstand me. I speak as an Anglican presbyter myself.

If the above analysis is right, the present-day pressure to make women presbyters owes more to secular, pragmatic, and social factors than to any regard for biblical authority. The active groups who push out the walls of biblical authority to make room for the practice fail to read out of Scripture any principle that directly requires such action. Future generations are likely to see their agitation as yet another attempt to baptize secular culture into Christ, as the liberal church has ever sought to do, and will, I guess, rate it as one more sign of the undiscerning worldliness of late twentieth-century Western Christianity.

On, then, to question two: What considerations cast doubt on the wisdom of making women presbyters?

I see four such considerations:

(1) The authority of Scripture.

Philip Melanchthon, Luther's right-hand man, identified the authority of Scripture as the formal (i.e., formative) principle of the Reformation. He was right, and biblical authority remains the formative principle of Evangelical theology. The Reformers elucidated the principle by explaining that Scripture is sufficient as a God-given guide to faith and life under Christ, not needing additions from any worldly or ecclesiastical source, and is also clear, not needing an external interpreter but interpreting itself from within on everything that matters. With this, too, modern Evangelicals agree.

Nor are they the only ones who nowadays urge that Scripture must ever stand in a critical, corrective, constitutive, and creative relation to the church's faith. When modern Roman Catholics and Orthodox claim, as they mostly do, that their tradition is verifiable from Scripture, they are acknowledging that the written Word of God yields its own meaning and message, and the church may not sit loose to it. There has in our time been significant movement here, and as a result, the appeal to Scripture by the opponents of women's ordination sounds the same from whichever side of the Reformation divide it is made.

What in Scripture weights the scales against the practice of making women presbyters? It is just the fact that though the New Testament celebrates in all sorts of ways Jesus' affirmation of particular women as disciples and friends, and though ministering women keep appearing in the narrative of Acts and the letters of Paul, nothing is said of women being chosen as presbyters. Educated guesses as to what Jesus might do or Paul might say, were they alive now, are only guesses; all we are sure of is that as Jesus appointed no female apostles, so Paul used his apostolic authority to keep women from leading the church in worship, and actually justified this from the story of the Creation and the Fall, which he treated as disclosing universal truth about the two sexes.[3]

This being so, it is surely as likely that, were Paul with us today, he would negate women's presbyteral leadership as that he would sanction it. Second-guessing an apostle is, of course, a risky business: but who can be blamed for thinking that negation would, in fact, be more likely, and that therefore the only safe, unitive, reverent, and God-honouring way is to give Paul the benefit of the doubt and retain his restriction on women exercising authority on Christ's behalf over men in the church?[4]

(2) The knowledge of Christ.

The essence of Christianity, according to the New Testament, is knowing and trusting Jesus Christ the Lord, the incarnate Son of God, as prophet, priest, and king; as lamb, shepherd, and life giver; and as head, husband, and cornerstone of the church that is his body, bride, and building. Knowing Christ in all these respects has a relational and affectional, as well as an intellectual, dimension: it is cognition and communion, obedience, love, and adoration all combined; it is peace and joy, salvation and eternal life, heaven on earth. On all of this the New Testament writers are at one.

A further aspect of the New Testament knowledge of Christ is that he, as thus described, is the true minister in all Christian ministry; the words and acts of his ministering servants are the medium of his personal ministry to us now, whereby he makes real and vivid to us his grace to us and his purpose for us. And this is the foundation for the second argument.

That argument is in essence as follows: Since the Son of God was incarnate as a male, it will always be easier, other things being equal, to realize and remember that Christ is ministering in person if his human agent and representative is also male. This is not to deny that Christ ministers through women, unordained and ordained (and to men, too!): My point is about the ideal form of the church. Stated structures of ministry should be designed to create and sustain with fullest force faith knowledge that Christ is the true minister. Presbyteral leadership by women, therefore, is not the best option.

That one male is best represented by another male is a matter of common sense; that Jesus' maleness is basic to his role as our incarnate Saviour is a matter of biblical revelation.

Jesus Christ was not, and is not, merely a symbol of something else, or a source of teaching, that can stand on its own without reference to the teacher. The New Testament presents him as the second man, the last Adam, our prophet, priest, and king (not prophetess, priestess, and queen), and he is all this precisely in his maleness. To minimize the maleness shows a degree of failure to grasp the space-time reality and redemptive significance of the incarnation: to argue that gender is irrelevant to ministry shows that one is forgetting the representative role of presbyteral leadership. Surely it is clear, then, that, spiritually speaking, a male presbyterate is desirable, even if one does not think it mandatory.

(3) The significance of gender.

God made humanity in two genders. Both males and females bear his image and in personal dignity are equal in every way, but God has set them in a non-reversible relation to each other. This finds expression, according to the most straightforward reading of Scripture, in the story of Eve being made from Adam's rib, to be a help to him,[5] and in Paul's assertion of male headship, not simply in marriage,[6] but in the human race as such.[7] The creation pattern, as biblically set forth, is: man to lead, woman to support; man to initiate, woman to enable; man to take responsibility for the well-being of woman, woman to take responsibility for helping man. Scripture implies, and experience surely confirms, that where these relational dynamics are disregarded, the nature of both men and women is put under strain, the full self-discovery and fulfilment that God meant men and women to find in cooperation is missed, and some of the honour due to our wise Creator perishes.

The argument here is this: presbyters are set apart for a role of authoritative pastoral leadership. But this role is for manly men rather than womanly women, according to the creation pattern that redemption restores. Paternal pastoral oversight, which is of the essence of the presbyteral role, is not a task for which women are naturally fitted by their Maker.

(4) The example of Mary.

The relevance to this discussion of what we know of Jesus' mother will be differently assessed by different people, some perhaps making too much of her and some too little. But any who recognize in Mary a supreme model of devotion and developing discipleship must also see in her final proof of the non-necessity of ordination for a woman who wishes to serve the Father and the Son, and of the significance that can attach to unordained roles and informal ministries.

What has been said highlights the reason why women seek the presbyterate (they have gifts for ministry and a sense of pastoral vocation, and no lesser role offers them the scope they desire); but it also highlights the reason why ordaining them to that office is inappropriate (Scripture presents presbyteral leadership as a man's job). In practice, ordaining women presbyters has regularly proved divisive without being particularly fruitful—a state of affairs that may be expected to continue. What wisdom is there in pushing ahead with this policy? None that I can see. Even if, unlike some of its critics, one does not find oneself able to maintain that Scripture actually forbids it, one can hardly claim that there is much sense in it. The structuring of women's professional ministry in the churches needs to be rethought.

Should there be such ministry at all? Emphatically, yes. That women are gifted for and called to service in the church is plain, and gifted persons are gifts that the churches must properly value and fully use. In fact, of course, it already happens: women pastoral assistants, ministers of music, youth directors, education ministers abound, making these roles their career. It has sometimes been suggested that they should be given presbyteral status by ordination just because their ministry is their life's work, but this loses sight of the New Testament analysis of presbyteral ministry as pastoral oversight (shepherdlike rule) through the didactic discipline of directive and corrective teaching that embraces the whole congregation—which is work for a man rather than a woman. The matter needs rethinking at the level of principle rather than pragmatics, and I close with a suggestion as to how.

Three questions, it seems, need to be asked.

First: What is the distinctive quality of womanly ministry, as distinct from the ministry proper to men? Answer: It is maternal rather than paternal in flavour and style, and this quality should permeate all the activities that make it up. The natural, proper, and desirable role difference between mother and father in the human family, as found in virtually all cultures, should be reflected in the cooperative ministry of men and women in the church. The roles are complementary, and the true enrichment comes when they are being fulfilled side by side.

Second: In what situation is it most fitting that a professional woman worker should minister? Answer: In partnership with a male leader, rather than as a sole pastor. In such a partnership, the psychological dynamics of the 'helpmeet' relationship of Genesis 2:18 will be maintained, in the sense that the woman will feel herself, and be felt, to be helping a man fulfil a calling that embraces them both. If she is on her own, this cannot be, and one element of womanly satisfaction will be lacking to her.

Third: Does such ministry call for presbyteral ordination? Answer: No, nor is it particularly appropriate. The biblical ideal would seem to be that in the woman's ministry, maternal attitudes of care for the weak and attention to the needs of individuals will be central. Pastoral visitation in homes and hospitals and the spiritual nurture of children, young people, and families seem to be the natural activities in which these attitudes would find expression.

Is it proper for a woman who ministers in this way to preach? Since authority resides in the Word of God rather than in preachers and teachers of either sex, it is my opinion that a woman's preaching and teaching gifts may be used to the full in situations where a male minister is in charge and the woman's ministry of the Word has the effect of supplementing and supporting his own preaching and teaching. (We in the West are no longer in the Bible-less situation to which 1 Tim. 2:12 was directed.)

None of this, however, requires ordination as a presbyter. A title indicative of rank—deaconess, or pastoral assistant, for instance—would be helpful; surely, though, that is all that is needed.

The fomenting by rival pressure groups of secular-minded, status-oriented squabbles about the rights and wrongs of ordaining women presbyters seems endless: the feminist and fundamentalist lobbies see to that. The observed effect of presbyteral ordination of women is regularly to preoccupy them with fulfilling a man's role and so to divert them from the sort of ministry in which they would be at their best. Effective partnership between men and women in the pastorate seems rarely to be sought or found. It is hardly a happy scene.

How long, O Lord? Shall we ever get beyond this state of things? I hope so; we need to. Phasing out the female presbyterate would, in my judgement, be part of our cure. Is my cause already lost? Am I crying for the moon? I wait to see, as Oxford men habitually do.

Appendix—What Is a Presbyter?

In this article, the author, himself an Episcopal clergyperson, chooses to use the word *presbyter* because other terms are loaded with the bitter history of controversy between denominations. The English *presbyter* stands for the Greek *presbuteros*, the standard New Testament word that designates a senior person (an *elder*) who shows wisdom and exercises authority. Elders were appointed in the first churches,[8] with shepherding the flock as their task:[9] that is, instruction and direction.[10] The authoritative leaders of Hebrews 13:17 were evidently presbyters. In the history of the church, *presbyter* came to refer to the person or persons (usually professional clergy) officially charged with the oversight of a local congregation.

Presbyter, of course, reminds us of Presbyterians, who build their polity around elders—ruling elder and teaching elders. Episcopalians (like Orthodox, Catholics, Lutherans, and Methodists) organize their polity around the office of the *episcopos* (the overseer or bishop); but they, too, have *presbyters*. While Episcopalians (Anglicans) are likely to use the word *priest* in conversation, they recognized from their sixteenth-century new start that *priest* is a contraction *of presbyter*—a fact reflected in their official ordination service.

In other traditions, *elders* may be either professional clergy or lay people, but they are, in any case, persons of experience whose spiritual authority has been recognized by the church.

PART THREE

PREACHING THE WORD

CHAPTER 17

Knowing Notions or Knowing God

How should pastoral leaders read the Bible?
An interview with James I. Packer

PR: *For a pastoral leader, what are the most common blocks to the study of Scripture?*

JP: The blocks come along two lines. One is quite simply the pressure of endless day-to-day calls on him, which cry out for his concentrated attention from morning to night. He has to be strong-minded to make room for anything else.

Studying in the early morning before anyone else is about is the simplest way to manage it. But that assumes that one can get to bed at a reasonable hour, which pastors can't always do. One who is in pastoral responsibility often has to be out late in the evening. That could mean that he's just not able to maintain a routine of getting up early to study. I have sympathy with pastors who have problems at this point.

Then there is another source of blockage, something quite different. In the modern church, particularly in the seminaries, there is often great confusion about the Scriptures so that trainees for pastoral work never learn to study them in a way that is spiritually fruitful. I think that many pastoral leaders are in difficulty because of this as well.

PR: *How much time should a pastor devote to personal study of Scripture?*

JP: I hesitate to make rules for other people because, after all, we differ a great deal. But if one thinks of an hour a day as the ordinary common-sense rule, and then says to oneself, 'Well now, if it's going to be less than that, I've got to justify that reduction of time,' one will be doing well.

I think that the priority for every pastoral leader must be his own personal time with God over the Scriptures, and anything that he does by way of preparation ought to flow out of that.

The first requirement for authoritative, perceptive communication of the word of God is that you yourself should be experiencing the power of it. The Puritan John Owen said, 'A man only preaches that sermon well which first preaches itself in his own soul.' He was profoundly right. I would verify that from my own ministry.

PR: *Are there different ways of spending personal time in Scripture?*

JP: There are two different ways of reading it which seem to me fundamental for anyone who is going to lead in spiritual things.

One I call macroscopic or panoramic reading. That means going through the Bible as one would through any book—reading straight through, over and over, start to finish. One needs this to keep oneself attuned to the overall perspective of Scripture.

With that there needs to go something quite distinct, that is microscopic or detailed study of particular passages, where one takes a few verses, sets them in context, and digs into them. In both macroscopic and microscopic reading of Scripture one needs to have some kind of scheme of questions to put to the text. If one doesn't ask questions or bring questions to the Bible, it is going to remain a closed book.

People who read the Bible without any questions may get warm cheerful feelings, but they are not likely really to understand anything. The scheme that I have found helpful over years of study is constantly to be asking this sequence of questions:

1. *What does the passage show me about God?* The wise man will always start here.

2. *What does the passage show me about living?* This question opens one's eyes to notice the right ways of living, wrong ways of living, different sorts of situations in which people find themselves, the way of faith with all its difficulties and delights, the different emotional states and temptations that overtake people, and all the realities of human life that each passage presents.

3. *What does this mean for me in my own life here and now?* At this point one begins meditating and praying as one brings to the Scripture the particular tasks or pressures that lie ahead that day. Meditating is thinking it through in the presence of God. Prayer is talking to the Lord about it. Here is the proper conclusion of Scripture study. This personal discipline is quite distinct from any further digging for insights to relay in teaching and preaching. Application to oneself must come first.

PR: *But out of the personal encounter with God in Scripture will come a homiletical use of Scripture?*

JP: Yes. This is one of the three sources from which, as it seems to me, fruitful preaching and teaching come.

Source one is being in the Bible oneself, where things come clear which one wants to share with other people. What one can see, one can say. What one is not clear about, one cannot express. Faithful homiletics must start here. If we are not ourselves living in and under the Scriptures, those who hear us speak on fellowship with God will soon realize that we do not know what we are talking about.

Another source is one's sense of the congregation. A pastoral leader carries that around with him all day long. He's constantly thinking about the members and what they need from him. It's only to be expected that from time to time as he goes through the Word of God things will strike him as just what the group he is leading needs.

A third source that is often undervalued these days, but which I seek to make much of, is the church's year. I am an Episcopalian [Anglican], and we have the church's year as the basic framework for our liturgy. I think much more could be made of the Christian year than is commonly made of it. It is good to live with the question, 'This time of year what should I be doing?'

PR: *How does a pastoral leader learn to apply Scripture to his or her life?*

JP: Martin Luther said: 'Prayer, meditation, and temptation make the theologian.' By the theologian what he meant was a person who could take Scripture and apply it. Only God can turn us into theologians in Luther's sense.

It is easy to find oneself at the end of a time of Bible study feeling that it all has to do with God and people two, three, four thousand years ago, and isn't in any way directly related to me. At this point one may pull down the commentaries. But a lot of the commentaries are the reverse of helpful when it comes to making the application.

A pastoral leader ought to be working with commentaries. Commentaries are supposed to be the cream from the biblical study by devoted men in the church over many hundred years. The good commentator will put one in touch with the best that these men came up with.

But the convention for writing commentaries these days is to concentrate on the technical side of exegesis, historically conceived. Now certainly we should start with historical exegesis. The commentaries of today major on telling you what Scripture meant, past tense, and they help us by doing that.

But what we need to know is what it means in the present tense, how it applies, how it bears on life today. This is the central question of hermeneutics: what does the Bible mean for us today? Here the commentaries are not so strong.

Luther's point is the true one. Meditation and prayer, plus temptation (the discipline of living to God against contrary pressures), will enable us to perceive the application, given the help of God. While the commentaries tell us what the passage meant historically, it is really only the Spirit of God who shows us what it is saying to ourselves and others today. That is a matter of enlightenment.

Historical study of what the text meant when it was first produced does not answer the question of application, and until that question is answered the Bible is not properly understood.

PR: *Would you say that some pastoral leaders are approaching Scripture with the wrong question?*

JP: It is very important that one approaches Scripture as the Word of God, not just a mixed bag of human religious reflections and testimonies, some of which are likely to be more right-minded, some less, so that our main job is to pick out which are which. This is very inhibiting to fruitful dealing with the Scriptures.

As I look around the churches I see a broad division between pastoral leaders whose attitude to the Bible is in general one of trust, because they take the Bible as coming from God, and those whose attitude is fundamentally one of mistrust, because they see it only as a very misled collection of human testimonies. Some of these folk have been stumbled by what they've been given in seminary, because it has been fashionable for the last hundred years in many Protestant seminaries, and for some forty or fifty years in many Catholic seminaries (particularly after Vatican II), to highlight the human aspects of Scripture and dwell on differences, real or fancied, between the viewpoint of one writer and another. The effect of this can be to leave students adrift in a sea of pluralistic relativism, with a bewildering sense that the Bible offers a lot of different points of view and who is to say which is right?

I am not questioning the value of these studies of the human side of Scripture, but I see a need to balance them in a way that not all seminaries do. I would balance them by saying to all Bible students, in and out of seminary, 'Remember, all Scripture proceeds from a single source, a single mind, the mind of God the Holy Spirit, and you have not taken its measure until you can see its divine unity in and underlying its human variety.'

It is the Word of God in the form of human words, giving God's point of view on everything. The unity of Scripture at that level is something that goes far deeper than its surface differences.

PR: *You say that your book* Knowing God *is, in comparison to the Psalms, only a footnote. How important is it for a pastoral leader to know the Psalms?*

JP: I took about twenty years to get into the Psalms. I think it is partly that I was so concerned in the early years of my Christian pilgrimage to get clear on correct notions, and the Psalms, of course, do jump around. They don't analyse notions, they're meditative, they're exclamatory. The format usually does not follow a line of expository argument the way that, say, Paul does. One doesn't when one worships. But that made it difficult for me to tune into them.

The other thing that threw me was that they are simply so exuberant. The way that we are conditioned by much of our culture, both Christian and secular, means that we are not really prepared for the kind of uninhibited expression of ourselves before God that the Psalms model for us. And as long as a person feels that the psalmists were rather uncivilized fellows, because they expressed themselves so wholeheartedly, even fiercely, he will find it hard to identify with them. That was a problem for me at that time.

I am thankful to say that as the years go by I feel much more in tune with the Psalms, and I am sure that is how it ought to be. Living in the Psalms helps to turn little souls into big ones, and that is something we all should covet for ourselves.

PR: *Is there a danger of Scripture reading replacing prayer?*

JP: It is possible to let Scripture reading replace prayer at least in one way, namely, when one spends all one's time on simply getting clear the meaning and application of the text, and one doesn't then let one's heart loose in praise and petition in the light of what one now sees. Meditation should naturally lead into praise and prayer. The habit of free, uninhibited praise and thanksgiving across the board of one's life is marvellously enriching. It needs to be a big thing in every Christian's life. The Psalms help a lot in this.

Petitions too ought to be a regular part of our devotional life. It is assumed in Scripture that we will bring personal petitions and prayer for other people as well. There is something stunted about our spiritual development if we don't, particularly if we are in a leadership role.

A good rule for a preacher is that he ought to pray for people as earnestly as he preaches to them. In the same way that one talks to folk about God, one should talk to God about those folk. A compassionate preacher ought to be a compassionate prayer.

Those who do not talk to God about men in the same way that they talk to men about God will very soon become victims of their own role and, to that extent, hypocrites. It is very easy for those of us who minister the word of God to become hypocrites in this way, and I am afraid many of us do.

PR: *Pastoral leaders can form the habit of relating to Scripture merely as their stock-in-trade. How can they break out of this approach for their devotional time?*

JP: The biggest thing that keeps us pastors and leaders from getting the full benefit of Scripture is simply that we do not feel needy enough. One of the problems of the pastoral role is that it encourages leaders to think that they are fully competent; they have got it made; they know it all. This self-sufficiency is a satanic temptation. A moment of realistic thought will remind us that we are as needy as the next man.

I find it most helpful to remind myself at the beginning of my devotional period who God is and what I am. That is to say, I remind myself that God is great, transcendent, that he loves me and he wants to speak to me right now. And I recall that I am the original sinner, the perverse and stupid oaf who misses God's way constantly. I have made any number of mistakes in my life up to this point and will make a lot more today if I don't keep in touch with God, and with Christ, my Lord and Saviour, as I should.

There is nothing like a sense of hunger to give one an appetite for a meal, and there is nothing like a sense of spiritual emptiness and need to give me an appetite for the word of God. Let that be the theme of our first minute or two of prayer as we come to our devotional times, and then we will be tuned in right. God says, 'Open your mouth wide, and I will fill it' (Ps. 81:10).

The quantity of theological notions in one's mind, even correct notions, doesn't say anything about one's relationship with God. The fact that one knows a lot of theology doesn't mean that one's relationship with God is right or is going to be right. The two things are quite distinct. As a professional theologian I find it both helpful and needful to focus this truth to myself by saying to myself over and over again, 'What a difference there is between knowing notions, even true notions, and knowing God.' My times with the Bible, like those of all pastoral leaders, indeed all Christians, are meant to be times for knowing God.

CHAPTER 18

Why Preach?

By their questions, it has been said, you shall know them. Honest questions reveal what ignorance, doubt, fears, uncertainties, prejudices, and preconceptions lie within the questioner's mind. By asking questions, even more than by answering them, we lay ourselves open to each other and thereby become (to use the cant word) vulnerable. (That is why some people never ask questions! But those who never ask anything never learn anything either, so the unquestioning attitude is not really one to commend.) I take the question 'Why preach?' on which I have been asked to write, to be an honest question, expressing honest uncertainty as to whether there is a viable rationale for pulpit work in our time. I blame no one for raising the question—indeed, I see many reasons why thoughtful people might well raise it—and I shall try to treat it as seriously, and respond to it as honestly, as I take it to be put.

Whose question is it, though? Does it come from a discouraged preacher? or from a weary listener? or from a pastoral organizer who wants more time for other things, and grudges hours earmarked for sermon preparation? or from a student of communication theory, who doubts whether pulpit monologue can ever convey as much as drama or dialogue or discussion, or an audio-visual film presentation or TV? Perhaps the question comes from all four, and perhaps it does not matter for my present purpose which it comes from; for whoever voices it is putting into words real disillusionment with the medium and real doubt about the worthwhileness of the activity. Such disillusionment is, as we all know, widespread nowadays, and I am happy to acknowledge and accept it as the starting place for a discussion that, if God helps, will have a pastoral as well as a theological thrust. Throughout this essay I shall have all four sorts of disillusioned folk particularly in mind. I propose to defend preaching. But lest you imagine that I am doing this simply to order, I begin with a personal statement. In the following pages I shall magnify and glorify the preaching ministry, not because I have been asked to (though indeed I have), nor because, as a spokesman for the Reformed heritage, I think I ought to (though I certainly do), but because preaching is of the very essence of the corporate phenomenon called Christianity as I understand it. By that I mean that Christianity, on earth as in heaven, is (I echo 1 John 1:4) fellowship with the Father and with his Son Jesus Christ, and the preaching of

God's Word in the power of God's Spirit is the activity that (I echo Isa. 64:1 and John 14:21–23) brings the Father and the Son down from heaven to dwell with men. I know this, for I have experienced it.

For several months during 1948 and 1949 I sat under the Sunday evening ministry of the late Dr. Martyn Lloyd-Jones. It seems to me in retrospect that all I have ever known about preaching was given me in those days, though I could not then have put it into words as I can now. What I received then still shows me what to look and hope and pray for in listening, and what to aim at and pray for in my own preaching. And though I have read and heard much since those days, I cannot think of anything I perceive about preaching now that did not at least begin to become clear to me at that time.

When I say, as frequently I catch myself doing, that preaching is caught more than it is taught, it is partly of my own discoveries during that period that I am thinking. I do not, of course, mean that I regard Dr. Lloyd-Jones as the only preacher I ever heard do it right; over the past generation I have been privileged to hear many other real preachers really preaching. I am only saying that it was Dr. Lloyd-Jones's ministry that under God gave me my standards in this matter. And standards are needed, for not all preaching is good preaching by any means. I suppose that over the years I have heard as much bad preaching as the next man and probably done as much myself as any clergy you would like to name.

Nonetheless, having observed how preaching is conceived in Scripture, and having experienced preaching of a very high order, I continue to believe in preaching and to maintain that there is no substitute for it, and no power or stature or sustained vision or close fellowship with God in the church without it. Also, I constantly maintain that if today's quest for renewal is not, along with its other concerns, a quest for true preaching, it will prove shallow and barren. You see, then, where I am coming from as I take up the question 'Why preach?'

How is it, I wonder, that so few seem to believe in preaching as I do? I can think of several reasons why that might be, and to list them will be a good way of opening my subject.

First, *there has been much non-preaching in our pulpits.* Not every discourse that fills the appointed twenty- or thirty-minute slot in public worship is actual preaching, however much it is called by that name. Sermons (Latin, *sermones,* 'speeches') are often composed and delivered on wrong principles. Thus, if they fail to open Scripture or they expound it without applying it, or if they are no more than lectures aimed at informing the mind or addresses seeking only to focus the present self-awareness of the listening group, or if they are delivered as statements of the preacher's opinion rather than as messages from God, or if their lines of thought do not require listeners to change in any way, they fall short of being preaching, just as they would if they were so random and confused that no one could tell what the speaker was saying. It is often said, and truly, that sermons must teach, and the current level of knowledge (ignorance, rather) in the

Christian world is such that the need for sermons that teach cannot be questioned for one moment. But preaching is essentially teaching *plus* application (invitation, direction, summons); where the *plus* is lacking, something less than preaching occurs. And many in the church have never experienced preaching in this full biblical sense of the word.

Second, *topical preaching has become a general rule, at least in North America.* Sermons explore announced themes rather than biblical passages. Why is this? Partly, I suppose, to make preaching appear interesting and important in an age that has largely lost interest in the pulpit; partly, no doubt, to make the sermon sound different from what goes on in the Bible class before public worship starts; partly, too, because many topical preachers (not all) do not trust their Bible enough to let it speak its own message through their lips.

Whatever the reason, however, the results are unhealthy. In a topical sermon the text is reduced to a peg on which the speaker hangs his line of thought; the shape and thrust of the message reflect his own best notions of what is good for people rather than being determined by the text itself. But the only authority that his sermon can then have is the human authority of a knowledgeable person speaking with emphasis and perhaps raising his voice. In my view topical discourses of this kind, no matter how biblical their component parts, cannot but fall short of being preaching in the full sense of that word, just because their biblical content is made to appear as part of the speaker's own wisdom. The authority of God revealed is thus resolved into that of religious expertise. That destroys the very idea of Christian preaching, which excludes the thought of speaking for the Bible and insists that the Bible must be allowed to speak for itself in and through the speaker's words. Granted, topical discourses may become real preaching if the speaker settles down to letting this happen, but many topical preachers never discipline themselves to become mouthpieces for messages from biblical texts at all. And many in the churches have only ever been exposed to topical preaching of the sort that I have described.

Third, *low expectations are self-fulfilling.* Most modern hearers have never been taught to expect much from sermons, and their habit is to relax at sermon time and wait to see if anything that the speaker says will interest them—'grab them,' as they might put it. Today's congregations and today's preachers seem to be mostly at one in neither asking nor expecting that God will come to meet his people in the preaching, and so it is no wonder that this does not often happen. Just as it takes two to tango, so ordinarily it takes both an expectant congregation and a preacher who knows what he is about to make an authentic preaching occasion.

A century ago and earlier, in Reformed circles in Britain (I cannot vouch for America), the common question to a person returning from a service would be, how he or she 'got on' under the momentous divine influence of the preaching of the Word; nowadays, however, on both sides of the Atlantic, the question more commonly asked is how the preacher 'got on' in what is now viewed as his stated pulpit performance. This shift of interest and perspective is a clear witness to the way in which, from being venerated as an approach by God, searching and stirring our souls, preaching has come to be viewed as a human endeavour to please, so that critical detachment now takes the place of open-hearted expectation when preaching is attempted. The direct result of our having become thus cool and blasé about preaching is that we look for little to happen through sermons, and we should not wonder that God deals with us according to our unbelief.

Fourth, *the current cult of spontaneity militates against preaching.* It is characteristic of some of the liveliest Christian groups today to treat what one can only call crudeness as a sign of sincerity, whether in folk-style songs with folk-style lyrics or in rhapsodic extempore prayer marked by earnest incoherence or in a loose and seemingly under-prepared type of preaching in which raw and clumsy rhetoric matches intellectual imprecision. Charismatic 'prophecy' (unpremeditated applicatory speech, uttered in God's name) is an extreme form of this. But where interest centres upon spontaneity rather than substance, and passion in speakers is valued above preparation, true preaching must of necessity languish. Here is a further reason why some earnest Christians have no experience, nor suspicion, of its power.

Fifth, *the current concentration on liturgy militates against preaching.* This is noticeable not only in theologically vague and pluralistic sectors of Protestantism, where it might have been expected (since nature abhors a vacuum), but among Evangelicals too. One of the striking movements of our time is the flow of Evangelicals, nurtured as they feel in a world of religious individualism and kitsch, into churches where the austere theocentrism of set liturgies, harking back to patristic models, still survives. Many of them become Episcopalians, and I, an Episcopalian by upbringing and judgement, have no complaint about that. But it saddens me to observe that this liturgical interest, which has led them to leave churches that highlighted the ministry of the Word, seems to have elbowed all concern about preaching out of their minds.

It is as if they were saying, 'We know quite enough about preaching; we have had a bellyful of it, enough to last us all our lives; now, thankfully, we turn from all that to the world of ceremony and sacrament.' But that attitude involves a false antithesis, for the genuine Reformed and Episcopal, not to say biblical, way is the way of gospel-and-liturgy, word-and-sacrament—the way that informs you in effect that you are free to hold as high a doctrine of the sacrament, the visible Word, as you like, provided that your doctrine of and expectation from the preached Word remain higher. But, generally speaking, the mind-set of these refugees from non-liturgical Christendom subordinates preaching to congregational enactment of worship (of which preaching is clearly not thought to be a major part), and thus reduces its importance and lowers expectations with regard to it. Here is yet another reason why some Christians today do not share the high view of preaching that I myself uphold.

Sixth, *the power of speech to communicate significance has become suspect.* In the modern West, cool, deadpan statements of fact are as much as is acceptable; any form of oratory, rhetoric, or dramatic emphasis to show the weight and significance of stated facts tends to alienate rather than convince. That entire dimension of public speech is nowadays felt to be murky and discreditable. This is largely due to the influence of the media, on which strong feeling both looks and sounds hysterical and artificial, and a calm and chatty intimacy is the secret of success. Part of that influence, too, is the numbing of emotional responsiveness by the constant parade of trauma and horror in news bulletins and programmes on current affairs. Our sensibilities get dulled by over-stimulus; also, in self-defence against attempts to harrow our feelings, we cultivate a sense of non-involvement; and we end up unable to believe that anything told us or shown us matters very much at all. One, two, three, and four centuries ago, a preacher could use words for forty or sixty minutes together, or longer in special cases, to set forth the greatness of God the King, of Christ the Saviour, of the soul, of eternity, and of the issues of personal destiny that were actually being settled at that moment by reactions to what was being said, and the hearers would listen empathetically and believe him. Today such a response would be thought naive, and most folk would at an early stage become inwardly aloof from, and perhaps hostile to, what the preacher was doing, out of caution lest they be 'conned' by a clever man putting on an act.

In the same sense in which Jonathan Edwards was a seventeenth-century Puritan born out of due time, Dr. Lloyd-Jones was a nineteenth-century preacher born late, and I cannot be thankful enough that I was privileged to hear him doing the old thing, despite the fact that, as he knew, some of his hearers thought of his preaching as just an entertaining performance, and others found his pulpit passion distasteful, maintaining throughout his thirty-year ministry at London's Westminster Chapel a preference for the cooler communicator who had preceded him. (I knew the congregation well enough to verify this.) But few preachers in my experience have had either the resources or (more important) the resolve to swim against the stream of suspicion and to follow the old paths at this point, and hence many in the churches never hear preachers deliberately and systematically use words to create a sense of the greatness and weight of spiritual issues. This also is a reason why my estimate of preaching is a minority view in today's Christian world, and why it is so widely held that other modes of Christian instruction are as good, if not better.

But what is preaching? My general view will have emerged already, but a full formal analysis seems desirable at this stage, before we attempt to go further.

First, then, a negative point. Preaching, I urge, should be defined functionally and theologically rather than institutionally and sociologically: that is, it should be defined in terms of what essentially is being done, and why, rather than of where and when it happens, and what corporate expectations it fulfils.

The New Testament leads us to think in these terms, using one of its two main words for preach (*euangelizomai*—literally, 'tell good news') not only of Paul addressing a synagogue congregation at Pisidian Antioch and groups gathered in the marketplace at Athens, but also of Philip sitting in a chariot speaking of Jesus to its one occupant (Acts 13:32; 17:18; 8:35). Much modern criticism of preaching arises from observations of sermonizing in churches: hence the frequent wisecracks about the pulpit as a coward's castle, and the preacher as standing six feet above contradiction, and resentful references to preaching *at* rather than *to* the hearers. Of course, most attempts at preaching do take place in church buildings, but that is not the point. What I am urging here is that preaching should be conceived as an achievement in communication. Regarding sermons, my point is that once preaching is defined in this functional and theological way, the performances that draw such comments as I cited will be seen not to be good preaching, and perhaps not to qualify as preaching at all.

Putting the matter positively, I define preaching as verbal communication of which the following things are true:

1. Its *content* is God's message to man, presented as such. For the Evangelical, this means that the source of what is said will be the Bible, and furthermore that a text will be taken (a verse, a part of a verse, or a group of verses), and the truth or truths presented will be, as the Westminster Directory for Public Worship put it, 'contained in or grounded on that text, that the hearers may discern how God teacheth it from thence.' The preacher will take care to make clear that what he offers is not his own ideas, but God's message from God's book, and will see it as his task not to talk for his text, but to let the text talk through him.

Also, as one charged, like Paul, to declare 'the whole counsel of God' (Acts 20:26–27)—that is, all that God does for mankind and all that he requires in response—the Evangelical preacher will relate the specific content of all his messages to Christ, his mediation, his cross and resurrection, and his gift of new life to those who trust him. In that sense, the preacher will imitate Paul, who when he visited Corinth (and everywhere else, for that matter, *pace* some wayward theories to the contrary), 'resolved to know nothing . . . except Jesus Christ and him crucified' (1 Cor. 2:2).

That does not mean, of course, that the Evangelical preacher will harp all the time on the bare fact of the crucifixion. It means, rather, that he will use all lines of biblical thought to illuminate the meaning of that fact; and he will never let his exposition of anything in Scripture get detached from, and so appear as unrelated to, Calvary's cross and the redemption that was wrought there; and in this way he will sustain a Christ-centred, cross-oriented preaching ministry year in and year out, with an evangelistic as well as a pastoral thrust.

2. The *purpose* of preaching is to inform, persuade, and call forth an appropriate response to the God whose message and instruction are being delivered. The response will consist of repentance, faith, obedience, love, effort, hope, fear, zeal, joy, praise, prayer, or some blend of these. The purpose of preaching is not to stir people to action while bypassing their minds, so that they never see what reason

God gives them for doing what the preacher requires of them (that is manipulation); nor is the purpose to stock people's minds with truth, no matter how vital and clear, which then lies fallow and does not become the seedbed and source of changed lives (that is academicism).

The purpose is, rather, to reproduce, under God, the state of affairs that Paul described when he wrote to the Romans, 'You wholeheartedly obeyed the form of teaching to which you were entrusted' (Rom. 6:17). The teaching is the testimony, command, and promise of God. The preacher entrusts his hearers to it by begging them to respond to it and assuring them that God will fulfil his promises to them as they do so. When they wholeheartedly obey, he gains his goal.

3. The *perspective* of preaching is always applicatory. This point is an extension of the last. As preaching is God-centred in its viewpoint and Christ-centred in its substance, so it is life-centred in its focus and life-changing in its thrust. Preaching is the practical communication of truth about God as it bears on our present existence. Neither statements of Bible doctrine nor talk about Christian experience alone is preaching, not even if the speakers get excited, emphatic, and dogmatic, and bang the table to make their points. Religious speech only becomes preaching when, first, its theme is Bible truth, or rather, the God of Scripture, in the hearers' lives—when, in other words, it is about the Father, Son, and Spirit invading, inverting, illuminating, integrating, and impelling us, and about ourselves as thereby addressed, accused, acquitted, accepted, assured, and allured—and when, second, the discourse debouches in practical biblical exhortation, summoning us to be different in some spiritually significant way and to remain different whatever pressure is put on us to give in to unspiritual ways once more (Rom. 12:1–2).

The idea of practical biblical exhortation requires some comment. The traditional view was that biblical instruction and narrative reveal and illustrate general truths about God and man, and about the kinds of attitude and conduct that God loves and rewards on the one hand, and hates and judges on the other. The interpreter's task was then to distil those general principles out of the historical and cultural specifics of each passage and to reapply them to the modern world, on the assumption that whatever else has changed, God and man, sin and godliness, have not. The method of moving from what the text meant as the writer's message to his envisaged readership to what it means for us today was by principled rational analysis—a discipline requiring historical and exegetical finesse of the kind displayed in critical commentaries, plus light from the Holy Spirit for discerning the spiritual roots of modern life and so making a contemporary application of truth that goes to the modern heart.

Startlingly, it appears that the classic account of this discipline is John Owen's *Causes, Ways, and Means, of Understanding the Mind of God, as revealed in his Word, with Assurance therein: and a Declaration of the Perspicuity of the Scriptures, with the external Means of the Interpretation of them*, a work published in 1678. Though later books have of course updated and expanded many of Owen's points, none seems to cover all his ground. But however that may be, it is a matter of demonstrable fact that this is how Reformed and Evangelical preachers have reached their practical biblical exhortations for more than four hundred years, and indeed how they still do.

But since Barth it has become common to deny that Scripture reveals or embodies general principles about God's will for and ways with his human creatures, and to affirm instead that God speaks a new word directly through the biblical text to each new situation. On this view, the interpreter's task is (putting it in our post-Barthian jargon) to 'listen to' and 'wrestle with' passages till he feels that some 'insight' triggered by them has become clear to him; then he should relay that insight as 'prophetically' as he can. But with the discipline of identifying and correlating general principles removed, as this view removes it, and the analogy of Scripture (that is, its internal consistency, as the teaching of God) disregarded or denied, as it usually is by this school of thought, imprecision, pluralism, and relativism flood in whenever the attempt is made to determine what God is saying at the present time, and there is no way to keep them out. Here is not the place to analyse or critique this phenomenon in detail; suffice it to say that it is not at all what I have in mind when I speak of applicatory biblical exhortation as an integral part of preaching.

4. *Authority* is also integral to the notion of what preaching is, namely, as is now clear, human lips uttering God's message. Preaching that does not display divine authority, both in its content and in its manner, is not the substance, but only the shadow of the real thing. The authority of preaching flows from the transparency of the preacher's relation to the Bible and to the three Persons who are the one God whose Word the Bible is. It is only as the preacher is truly under, and is seen to be under, the authority of God and the Bible that he has, and can be felt to have, authority as God's spokesman. To spell this out: he must be evidently under the authority of *Scripture,* as his source of truth and wisdom; he must be evidently under the authority of *God,* as whose emissary he comes, in whose name and under whose eye he speaks, and to whom he must one day give account for what he has said; he must be evidently under the authority of *Christ,* as a subordinate shepherd serving the chief Shepherd; and he must be evidently under the authority of *the Holy Spirit,* consciously depending on him as the sole sustainer of vision, clarity, and freedom of mind, heart, and voice in the act of delivering his message, and as the sole agent of conviction and response in the lives of his hearers.

Let Paul be our teacher here. 'Unlike so many,' he wrote, 'we do not peddle the word of God for profit. On the contrary, in Christ we speak before God with sincerity, like men sent from God' (2 Cor. 2:1–17). Here we see the transparency of a consciously right relationship to the authoritative message, the authoritative God, and the authoritative Christ. (Paul, of course, knew the authoritative message from oral instruction and personal revelation, whereas preachers today must learn it from Scripture, but this does not affect the principle of fidelity to it once one knows it.) 'My message and my preaching,' wrote Paul again, 'were not with wise and persuasive words, but with a demonstration of the Spirit's power, so that your faith might not rest on men's wisdom, but on God's power' (1 Cor. 2:4). Here we see the transparency of a consciously right relationship to the Holy Spirit as the one who authenticates, convinces, and establishes in faith. In this Paul stands as a model.

Where these relationships are out of joint, the authority of preaching—that is, its claim on the conscience, as utterance in God's name—weakens to vanishing point. Where these relationships are as they should be, however, proof will be given again and again of the truth of Robert Murray McCheyne's dictum, that 'a holy minister is an awful weapon in the hands of a holy God.' In less drastic language Paul testified to what McCheyne had in view when he wrote, 'We also thank God continually because, when you received the word of God, which you heard from us, you accepted it not as the word of men, but as it actually is, the word of God which is at work in you who believe' (1 Thess. 2:13).

5. Preaching mediates not only God's authority, but also his *presence* and his *power.* Preaching effects an encounter not simply with truth, but with God himself. There is a staggering offhand remark that illustrates this in 1 Corinthians 14, where Paul is arguing for the superiority of prophecy (speaking God's message in intelligible language) over tongues.

> If the whole church comes together and everyone speaks in tongues, and some who do not understand or some unbelievers come in, will they not say that you are out of your mind? [Expected answer: yes.]

> But if an unbeliever or someone who does not understand comes in while everybody is prophesying, he will be convinced by all that he is a sinner and will be judged by all, and the secrets of his heart will be laid bare. So he will fall down and worship God, exclaiming, 'God is really among you!' (1 Cor. 14:23–25)

Whatever else in this passage is uncertain, three things are plain.

First, prophecy as Paul speaks of it here corresponded in content to what we would call preaching the gospel—detecting sin and proclaiming God's remedy.

Second, the expected effect of such prophecy was to create a sense of being in the presence of the God who was its subject matter, and of being searched and convicted by him, and so being moved to humble oneself and worship him.

Third, in the experience of both Paul and the Corinthians, what Paul described must have occurred on occasion already, otherwise he could not have expected to be believed when he affirmed so confidently that it would happen. That which has never happened before cannot be predicted with such certainty.

There have evidently been times since the apostolic age when such things have been known to take place once more: the Puritan David Clarkson, for instance, in a sermon entitled *Public Worship to be Preferred before Private,* was presumably talking from experience when he declared,

> The most wonderful things that are now done on earth are wrought in the public ordinances. Here the dead hear the voice of the Son of God, and those that hear do live . . . Here he cures diseased souls with a word . . . Here he dispossesses Satan . . . Wonders these are, and would be so accounted, were they not the common work of the public ministry. It is true indeed, the Lord has not confined himself to work these wonderful things only in public; yet the public ministry is the only ordinary means whereby he works them.[1]

What Paul describes is rare in our time, no doubt, but that does not make it any less part of the biblical ideal of what preaching is, and what it effects. Perhaps the point should be put this way: preaching is an activity for which, and in which, the awareness of God's powerful presence must be sought, and with which neither speaker nor hearers may allow themselves to be content when this awareness is lacking.

The above analysis was needed because the ordinary concept of preaching as sermonizing (filling a stated slot of time with religious monologue) is too loose and imprecise, and the usual definitions of preaching, as was said before, are not sufficiently functional and theological for our present purposes. If the definition I have given draws criticism as being too narrow, I must endure it; but I cannot see that the New Testament will sanction any lower concept of Christian preaching, and therefore it is in terms of the view I have stated, this and nothing less than this, that I continue my argument. Now that we have seen what preaching is, we can move on to the heart of this essay. We are now in a position to address directly the question of my title: Why preach?

First, it should be noted that here we have really two questions in one. Objectively, the question is, What theological reasons are there for maintaining preaching as a necessary part of church life? Subjectively, the question is, What convictions should prompt a person to take up, sustain, and keep giving his best to the task of seeking to preach according to these awesome specifications? I take the two questions in order.

With regard to the first, I herewith offer some theological reasons for regarding preaching as a vital and essential part of Christian community life in this or any age. The suspicion is voiced nowadays, as we have seen, that pulpit monologue is an inefficient way of communicating and that books, films, TV, tapes, and group study and discussion can all be fully acceptable substitutes for it. With this I disagree, and in this section of my essay I am consciously arguing against any such views. Certainly, preaching is communication, and communication must be efficient; there are no two ways about that. But preaching is more than what is nowadays thought of as communication. God uses preaching to communicate more than current communication theory is concerned with, and more than alternative forms of Christian communication can be expected under ordinary circumstances to convey. I have nothing against books, films, tapes, and study groups in their place, but the place where God sets the preacher is not their place. The considerations that follow will, I hope, make this clear.

First, *preaching is God's revealed way of making himself and his saving covenant known to us.* This is an argument drawn from the nature of God's revelatory action, as Scripture sets it forth.

The Bible shows God the Creator to be a communicator, and the theme and substance of his communication since Eden to be a gracious, life-giving relationship with believing sinners. All the factual information and ethical direction that he currently communicates through his written Word feeds into this relationship, first to establish it through repentance and commitment to Jesus Christ, and then to deepen it through increasing knowledge of God and maturing worship. This is the covenant life of God's people, which is both initiated and sustained through God's personal communion with them.

Now the Bible makes it appear that God's standard way of securing and maintaining his person-to-person communication with us his human creatures, is through the agency of persons whom he sends to us as his messengers. By being made God's spokesmen and mouthpieces for his message, the messengers become emblems, models, and embodiments of God's personal address to each of their hearers, and by their own commitment to the message they bring, they become models also of personal response to that address. Such were the prophets and apostles, and such supremely was Jesus Christ, the incarnate Son, who has been well described as being both God for man and man for God. That is the succession in which preachers today are called to stand.

Why does the New Testament stress the need for preaching (as it does in many different ways: see Matt. 10:6–7; Mark 3:14; 13:10; Luke 24:45–49; Acts 5:42; 6:2–4; 10:42; Rom. 10:6–17; 1 Cor. 1:17–24; 9:16; Phil. 1:12–18; 2 Tim. 4:2–5; Titus 1:3; etc.)? Not just because the good news had to be spread and the only way to spread news in the ancient world was by oral announcement, though that was certainly true. But it is also, surely, because of the power of 'incarnational' communication, in which the speaker illuminates that which he proclaims by being transparently committed to it in a wholehearted and thoroughgoing way. Phillips Brooks was profoundly right when he defined preaching as 'truth through personality.'

The preacher's personality cannot be eliminated from the preaching situation, and what he appears to be is a part of what he communicates—necessarily, inescapably, willy-nilly, and for better or for worse. So the preacher must speak as one who himself stands under the authority of his message and knows the reality and power of which he speaks; otherwise the impact of his personality will reduce the credibility of his proclamation, just as a man's baldness would reduce the credibility of any sales pitch he might make as a purveyor of hair restorer. The committed personality is in this sense integral to God's message, for God uses it to communicate his own reality as his messenger speaks.

But for fullest awareness of the messenger's committedness we need to have him confront us in a 'live' preaching situation; 'canned' preaching on a tape, and 'stage' preaching on TV, and 'embalmed' preaching in the form of printed sermons are all unable to communicate this awareness to the same degree. Thus the need for preaching 'live' remains as great as it was nineteen centuries ago; it is still supremely through preaching, that is, through the impact on us of the message and the messenger together, that God meets us, and makes himself and his saving grace known to us.

How to communicate the reality of the God of Scripture across the temporal and cultural gap that separates our world from the world of the Bible has exercised many contemporary minds. It is not always noticed that God provides much of the answer to this perplexity in the person of the preacher, who is called to be a living advertisement for the relevance and power of what he proclaims. The flip side of this truth is, of course, that should a preacher's words and life fail to exhibit this relevance and power, he would be actively hindering his hearers' knowledge of God. I suspect that the widespread perplexity today as to the relevance of the New Testament gospel should be seen as God's judgement on two generations of inadequate preaching by inadequate preachers, rather than anything else.

Second, *preaching communicates the force of the Bible as no other way of handling it does.* This is an argument drawn from the nature of Scripture itself.

Holy Scripture is, in and of itself, preaching. From one standpoint, it is servants of God preaching; from another, profounder, standpoint, it is God himself preaching. Some of its sixty-six books are already, explicitly, sermons on paper (I think of the prophetic oracles of the Old Testament and the apostolic letters of the New); some are not. But all of them without exception were written to edify— that is, to teach people to know the living God, and to love and worship and serve him—and to that extent they all have the nature of preaching. To preach them is thus no more, just as it is no less, than to acknowledge them for what they are, and to let their content be to us what it already is in itself. The Bible text is the real preacher, and the role of the man in the pulpit or the counselling conversation is simply to let the passages say their piece through him.

Simply, did I say?—but it is far from simple in practice! For the preacher to reach the point where he no longer hinders and obstructs his text from speaking is harder work than is sometimes realized. However, there can be no disputing that this is the task. And by preaching the Bible one makes it possible for the thrust and force of 'God's Word written' (Anglican Article 20) to be adequately appreciated, in a way that is never possible through any type of detached study, or any kind of instruction in which a person speaks for or about the Bible as distinct from letting the Bible speak for itself. Bible courses in seminaries, for instance, do not beget an awareness of the power of Scripture in the way that preaching does.

Preaching the Bible is the affirming and exploring of the relation between God's Word written and transmitted as Scripture by the agency of the Spirit (and now written on and applied to our hearts from Scripture by the same agency) and human lives—in other words, it is the exploring of its relation to ourselves.

The activity of preaching the Bible (of which I take the public reading of Scripture to be part) unlocks the Bible to both mind and heart, and the activity of hearing Scripture preached, receiving what is said, meditating on the text as preaching has opened it up, and letting it apply itself to one's own thoughts and ways actually leads us into the Bible in terms of enabling us to comprehend and lay hold of what it, or better, God in and through it, is saying to us at this moment. Where such a personal relation to the Bible has not become part of one's life, though one may know much about its language, background, origins, and the historical significance of its contents, it remains in the deepest sense a closed book. And those who in this sense do not yet know what to make of the Bible will not know what to make of their own lives either.

One way to express this is to say that our lives are in the Bible, and we do not understand them until we find them there. But the quickest and most vivid way in which such understanding comes about is through being addressed by the Bible via someone for whom the Bible is alive and who knows and can articulate something of its life-changing power. This is a further reason why preaching is always needed in the church: whenever preaching fails, understanding of Scripture in its relation to life will inevitably fail too.

Third, *preaching focuses the identity and clarifies the calling of the church as no other activity does.* This is an argument drawn from the nature of the church, as we learn it from Scripture.

In every age the church has had an identity problem, and in some ages an identity crisis. Why? Because the world always wants to assimilate the church to itself and thereby swallow it up, and is always putting the church under pressure to that end; and to such pressure the church, at least in the West, has constantly proved very vulnerable.

The results of it can be seen today in the extremely weak sense of identity that many churches have. Their adherents think of them more as social clubs, like Shriners, Elks, Freemasons, and Rotarians, or as interest groups, like political parties and hikers' associations, than as visible outcrops of one worldwide supernatural society, and they are quite unable to give substance to the biblical thought that God's people, as the salt and light for the world, are required to be different from those around them. The problem is perennial, and there is always need to proclaim the Bible, its gospel, its Christ, and its ethics, in order to renew the church's flagging awareness of its God-given identity and vocation. Preaching is the only activity that holds out any hope of achieving this; but preaching can do it by keeping before Christian minds God's threefold requirement that his people be word-oriented, worship-oriented, and witness-oriented. A comment, now, about each of these.

The church must be *Word-oriented:* that is, God's people must always be attentive and obedient to Scripture. Scripture is God's Word of constant address to them, and woe betide them if they disregard it (see 2 Kgs. 22:8–20; 2 Chr. 36:15–16; Isa. 1:19–20; Jer. 1:23–26; Rev. 2:4–7, 15–17, etc.). God's people must learn to 'tremble at his word' (Ezra 9:4; Isa. 66:5), listening, learning, and laying to heart; believing what he tells them, behaving as he directs them, and battling for his truth in a world that denies it.

Preaching, as an activity of letting texts talk, alerts Christians to the fact that God is constantly addressing them and enforces the authority of Scripture over them. The church must live by God's Word as its necessary food and steer by that Word as its guiding star. Without preaching, however, it is not conceivable that this will be either seen or done.

The church must also be *worship-oriented:* that is, God's people must regularly celebrate what God is and has done and will do, and glorify his name for it all by their praises, prayers, and devotion. The preaching of the Bible is the mainspring of this worship, for it fuels the devotional fire, constantly confronting Christians with God's works and ways in saving them (redeeming, regenerating, forgiving, accepting, adopting, guarding, guiding, keeping, feeding), and thereby leading them into paths of obedient and adoring response. Indeed, from this standpoint biblical preaching is implicit doxology throughout; the biblical preacher will follow Scripture in giving God glory for his works, ways, and wisdom at every turn, and will urge his hearers to do the same. This is the first reason why preaching should be regarded as the climax of congregational worship.

From this flows the second reason, namely that congregations never honour God more than by reverently listening to his Word with a full purpose of praising and obeying him once they see what he has done and is doing, and what they are called to do. But it is precisely through preaching that these things are made clear and this purpose is maintained.

Should it be objected that the liturgical drama of the Lord's Supper rather than the preached Word of Holy Scripture ought to be central and climactic in our worship, the appropriate answer is that without the preached Word to interpret the Supper and establish on each occasion a community context for it, it will itself become dark in meaning to us, and eucharistic worship will then be spoiled by waywardness and somnolence in our hearts. This is why, historically, Word and sacrament have been linked together as partners in the worship of God, rather than set against each other as rivals for our attention.

Finally, the church must be *witness-oriented:* that is, God's people must always be seeking to move out into the world around them to make Christ known and disciple the lost, and to that end they must 'always be prepared to give an answer to everyone who asks [them] to give the reason for the hope that [they] have' (1 Pet. 3:15). Apart from the preaching of the Word, however, the church will never have the resources to do this; it will constantly tend to forget its identity as the people charged to go and tell, and may actually lose its grip on the contents of its own message, as it has done many times in the past.

History tells of no significant church growth and expansion that has taken place without preaching (*significant*, implying virility and staying power, is the key word there). What history points to, rather, is that all movements of revival, reformation, and missionary outreach seem to have had preaching (vigorous, though on occasion very informal) at their centre, instructing, energizing, sometimes purging and redirecting, and often spearheading the whole movement. It would seem, then, that preaching is always necessary for a proper sense of mission to be evoked and sustained anywhere in the church.

Thus preaching is able to maintain the church's sense of identity and calling as the people charged to attend to God's Word, to obey it as his children, and to spread it as his witnesses. But there seems no way in which without preaching the eroding of this awareness can be avoided.

Fourth, *preaching has some unique advantages as a mode of Christian instruction.* This is an argument drawn from the nature of the church's teaching task.

Preaching is teaching, first and foremost. It is more than teaching; it is teaching *plus* application, as was said earlier; but it is never less than teaching. It is a kind of speaking aimed at both mind and heart, and seeking unashamedly to change the way people think and live. So it is always an attempt at persuasion; yet if its basic ingredient is not honest teaching, it is fundamentally flawed and unworthy. I shall now suggest that its monologue form, which is so often criticised as a hindrance both to teaching and to learning, is actually a great advantage in regard to both. Let me explain.

I grant that, because preaching is monologue, artifice is needed (some have it naturally, others have to acquire it) to ensure that hearers stay awake and are kept interested, involved, and thinking along with the speaker as he proceeds. But that is no hindrance when the preacher has the artifice and the congregation knows that it is there to learn. And when this is the case, the monologue form helps greatly.

The preacher can use words to do what he could not do in ordinary conversation, or in discussion. He can, for instance, spend time building up a sense of the greatness of what he is dealing with: the greatness of God, or of eternity, or of divine grace. Thus he can educate his hearers' sense of the relative importance of things. Or he can pile up reasons for believing a particular truth, or behaving in a particular way, or embracing a particular concern, and so hammer his points home by cumulative impact. Thus he can deepen his hearers' sense of obligation.

He can hold a mirror up to his hearers, exploring their actual states of mind, with their various conflicting thoughts, faithful and faithless, in a way that would otherwise require a full-length novel or play. He can search consciences and challenge evasions of moral and spiritual issues with a forthrightness that would be unacceptable in ordinary conversation, or in a casual chat. Also, as one who prays for the unction of the Holy Spirit for the delivery of his message, he can allow himself a more intense, dramatic, and passionate way of speaking about the awesome realities of spiritual life and death than everyday speech would sanction; then he may look to God to honour the vision of things expressed by his honest disclosure of his feelings and reactions.

In short, he will see it as his responsibility to make his message as clear, vivid, searching, 'home-coming' (Alexander Whyte's word for applicatory), and thus memorable, as he can, and to use all the rhetorical resources and possibilities of monologue form to that end. My point is simply that these resources are considerable, and if they are wisely used, hearers who are there to learn (as all hearers of sermons should be) will gain more from the sermon than they would do from any informal conversation or discussion on the same subject.

These things are said to encourage not the Spirit-quenching artificiality of 'putting on an act,' but the spiritual alertness, realism, and sheer hard work out of which effective communication of what Whyte called 'the eternities and the immensities' is born.

Another thing that monologue makes possible is the exhibiting of individuals' problems as problems of the community, by bringing them into the pulpit for biblical analysis. By this means a wise preacher may in effect do much of his counselling from the pulpit, and in so doing equip his hearers to become counsellors themselves. This is a further great advantage of the monologue form to those who have the wit to use it.

Educationists have a tag that there is no impression without expression, and teachers are taught that a third of every lesson in the classroom should be expression work. How can this requirement be met, it is asked, in the case of pulpit monologue? And how can there be effective learning from the monologue if it is not met? Organized discussion of sermons preached, congregational deliberation on the issues raised, and pastoral inquiry as to what changes (if any!) the preaching has effected in particular hearers' lives provide together the answer to these questions. That this threefold follow-up of preaching is in practice a rare thing may be a valid criticism of pastors, but it does not in any way invalidate monologue preaching from Scripture as a primary form of communication from God.

It is thus abundantly clear that no congregation can be healthy without a diet of biblical preaching, and no pastor can justify himself in demoting preaching from the place of top priority among the tasks of his calling. From the objective point of view, therefore, the question 'Why preach?' is now answered. All that remains is to say something about the convictions that, under God, work in a person's heart to make him a preacher and to keep him preaching despite all discouragements, thus constituting his personal answer to the question 'Why preach?' Jeremiah told God that the word of the LORD has brought me insult and reproach all day long. But if I say, 'I will not mention him or speak any more in his name,' his word is in my heart like a burning fire, shut up in my bones. I am weary of holding it in; indeed, I cannot. (Jer. 20:8–9)

Does anything correspond to this in the experience of Christian preachers? The answer is yes. There is a God-given vision that produces preachers, and any man who has that vision cannot sleep easy without making preaching his life's work. The vision (that is, the awareness of what God sees and wills to do, and to have his servants do) embodies a series of related convictions, somewhat as follows.

First, *Scripture is revelation.* Heaven is not silent; God the Creator has spoken, and the Bible is his written Word. God has made himself known on the stage of history by prophecy, providence, miracle, and supremely in his Son, Jesus Christ, and Scripture witnesses to that. God has disclosed his will for the living of our lives, and the Bible proclaims his law. God undertakes, through the interpreting work of the Spirit who inspired Scripture in the first place, to teach us how this revelation bears on us; thus it is promised that his Word shall function for us as a lamp for our feet and a light to illuminate our path, as on a dark night. God's Word is described as a hammer to break stony hearts, fire to burn up rubbish, seed causing birth, milk causing growth, honey that sweetens, and gold that enriches (Ps. 119:105; Jer. 23:29; 1 Pet. 1:23–2:2; Ps. 19:10). The Bible is in truth, as the Moderator of the Church of Scotland tells the monarch in the British coronation service, the most precious thing that this world affords.

There is, then, available in this world a sure message from God, tried and true, unfailing and unchanging, and it needs to be proclaimed so that all may know it. The messenger who delivers it will have the dignity of being God's spokesman and ambassador. No self-aggrandizement or self-advertisement is involved, for the messenger neither invents his message nor asks for attention in his own name. He is a minister—that is, a servant—of God, of Christ, and of the Word. He is a steward of God's revealed mysteries, called not to be brilliant and original but diligent and faithful (1 Cor. 4:1–2).

Yet to be God's messenger—to run his errands, act as his courier, and spend one's strength making him known—is the highest honour that any human being ever enjoys. The servant's dignity derives from the dignity of his employer, and of the work he is set to do. 'Ministers are ambassadors for God and speak in Christ's stead,' wrote Charles Simeon.

> If they preach what is founded on the Scriptures, their word, as far as it is agreeable to the mind of God, is to be considered as God's. This is asserted by our Lord and his apostles. We ought therefore to receive the preacher's word as the word of God himself.[2]

There is no nobler calling than to serve God as a preacher of the divine Word.

Second, *God is glorious.* God has shown his wisdom, love, and power in creation, providence, and redemption, and all of his self-revelation calls for constant praise, since it is infinitely praiseworthy. Man's vocation, in essence and at heart, is to give his Maker glory (praise) for all the glories (powers and performances) that God shows him. The chief end of man is to glorify God, and in so doing to enjoy him, and that forever, as the first answer of the Westminster Shorter Catechism puts it. God's doings should be known and celebrated everywhere, and when his rational human creatures fail to honour him in this way, they rob him of his due, as well as robbing themselves of their own highest happiness. For human life was meant to be an infinitely enriching love affair with the Creator, an unending exploration of the delights of doxology, and nothing makes up for the absence of those joys that come from praise.

It is the preacher's privilege to declare the works of God and lead his hearers to praise God for them. 'I will bless the LORD at all times; his praise will always be on my lips. My soul will boast in the LORD; let the afflicted hear and rejoice. Glorify the LORD with me; let us exalt his name together' (Ps. 34:1–3). Some have thought that what makes men into preachers is the desire to dominate, but what really animates them is a longing to glorify God and to see others doing the same.

Third, *people are lost*. Mankind's state is tragic. Human beings, made for God, are spiritually blind and deaf, and have their backs turned to him. Whether clear-headed or not, they are bent on self-destruction through self-worship and self-indulgence. Their souls starve in a world of spiritual plenty, and they mar their angelic abilities by their brutish and beastly behaviour. Made for God's love, they bring down on themselves his wrath by defying his will. Made for glory, they are consigning themselves to hell. The preacher sees this, and compassion drives him to speak. He wants to take the arm of everyone he meets, point to Christ, and say 'Look!' He sees his ministry as a form of Good Samaritanship to ravaged souls—an expression of love to neighbour, therefore, as well as of love to God. He is a man driven by zeal to share Christ.

Fourth, *Christ is unchanging*. 'Jesus Christ is the same yesterday and today and forever' (Heb. 13:8). The Christ who is to be preached today is the Christ of whom Bernard wrote in the twelfth century.

Jesus, thou joy of loving hearts,
   Thou fount of life, thou light of men,
From the best bliss that earth imparts
   We turn unfilled to thee again;

and of whom John Newton wrote in the eighteenth century,

How sweet the name of Jesus sounds
   In a believer's ear!
It soothes his sorrows, heals his wounds,
   And drives away his fear.

Jesus, my Shepherd, Brother, Friend,
    My Prophet, Priest, and King,
My Lord, my life, my way, my end,
    Accept the praise I bring.

So the preacher knows that when he depicts the Christ of the New Testament as the living Lord and Saviour of guilty, vile, and helpless sinners today, he presents not fancy but fact, not a dream but a reality. The need of this Christ is universal; the adequacy of this Christ is inexhaustible; the power of this Christ is immeasurable. Here is a wonderfully rich message on which to expatiate, a gospel worth preaching indeed!

Furthermore, the preacher knows that Christ's way is to step out of the pages of the New Testament into the lives of saints and sinners through the speech that is uttered about him by his messengers. In Gustav Wingren's words:

> Preaching is not just talk about a Christ of the past, but is a mouth through which the Christ of the present offers us life today . . . Preaching has but one aim, that Christ may come to those who have assembled to listen.[3]

To be the human channel of Christ's approach in this way is unquestionably a huge privilege, and no preacher can be blamed for feeling it so and making much of his role accordingly.

Fifth, *persuasion is needed.* God treats us as the rational beings that he made us. Accordingly, he does not move us to Christian responses by physical means that bypass the mind, but by persuading us to obey his truth and honour his Son. The preacher, as God's mouthpiece, has the task of persuading on God's behalf, and the role is a vital one since where there is no persuasion people will perish. Preaching is the art not of browbeating, but of persuading, in a way that shows both respect for the human mind and reverence for the God who made it. Christian persuasion requires wisdom, love, patience, and holy humanness. It is a fine art as well as a useful one, and it becomes for preachers a lifetime study, concern, and challenge.

Sixth, *Satan is active.* The devil is malicious and mean, more so than any of us can imagine, and he marauds constantly with destructive intent. Though he is, as Luther said, God's devil, and is on a chain (a strong one, though admittedly a long one), he is tireless in opposing God, and sets himself to spoil and thwart all the redemptive work that God ever does in human lives. As one means to this end, he labours to ensure that preachers' messages will be either misstated or misheard, so that they will not have the liberating, invigorating, upbuilding effect that is proper to the preached Word. Preaching is thus, as all real preachers soon discover, an endless battle for truth and power, a battle that has to be fought afresh each time by watchfulness and prayer.

Preachers know themselves to be warriors in God's front line, drawing enemy fire; the experience is gruelling, but it confirms to them the importance of their task as ambassadors for Christ and heralds of God, sowers of good seed, stewards of saving truth, shepherds of God's flock, and fathers guiding their spiritual families (2 Cor. 5:20; Luke 8:4–15; 1 Cor. 4:1; Acts 20:28–32; 1 Pet. 5:2–4; 1 Cor. 4:15; Gal. 4:19). In the manner of front-line troops they frequently get scared by the opposition unleashed against them, but they do not panic, and their morale remains high. The challenge of beating back Satan by God's strength, like that of communicating effectively for Christ, is one to which they rise.

Seventh, *God's Spirit is sovereign.* Through the Spirit's agency in both preacher and hearers, the Word of God becomes invincible. If fruitfulness depended finally on human wisdom and resourcefulness, no preacher would dare to speak a word, for no preacher ever feels that in his communication he has been wise and resourceful enough. And if God's power was exerted only in helping the preacher to speak and not in causing the listeners to hear, preaching, however wise and resourceful, would always be a barren and unfruitful activity, for fallen human beings have no natural power of response to the divine Word. But in fact fruitfulness depends on the almighty work of God the Holy Spirit in the heart. So preachers, however conscious of their own limitations, may nonetheless speak expectantly, knowing that they serve a God who has said (Isa. 55:10–11) that his Word will not return to him void. With this knowledge supporting them, it is the way of real preachers to show themselves undaunted and unsinkable.

Such, in sum, are the convictions that produce *reformed* preachers. As we review them, it becomes very obvious that a 'reformed' preacher in the seventeenth-century sense of that word, which corresponded roughly to our use of 'renewed' and 'revived,' will need to be a Reformed preacher in the twentieth-century sense of that word, that is, Augustinian and Calvinistic in belief; for all the seven items I have mentioned are characteristically Reformed tenets. Nor should this discovery surprise us, for it is a matter of historical fact that the Reformed tradition has been more fertile in producing reformed preachers over the centuries than has any other viewpoint in Christendom.

I affirm with total confidence, as I conclude, that able men with these seven convictions burning in their hearts will never need to scratch their heads, in this or any age, over the question whether preaching is a worthwhile use of their time. They will know that preaching God's gospel and God's counsel from the Scriptures was, and is, and always will be, the most honourable and significant activity in the world, and accordingly they will tackle this task with joy. It cannot, surely, be doubted that it will be a most happy thing if God increases the number of such preachers in our time.

CHAPTER 19

Expository Preaching:
Charles Simeon and Ourselves

Two preliminary points:

First, we must make clear to ourselves *what we mean when we speak of expository preaching*. This is necessary because the word 'expository' is often used nowadays in a restricted sense to denote simply a sermon preached from a long text. Thus, Andrew Blackwood writes: 'An expository sermon here means one that grows out of a Bible passage longer than two or three verses . . . an expository sermon means a textual treatment of a fairly long passage.'[1] He goes on to suggest that young pastors should preach such sermons 'perhaps once a month,'[2] and to give hints on the problems of technique which they involve.

Without suggesting that Blackwood's usage is inadmissible for any purpose, I must dismiss it as too narrow for our present purpose—if only because it would exclude all but a handful of Charles Simeon's 2,536 published discourses from the category of 'expository' sermons (his texts, you see, are too short!). We shall find it better to define 'expository' preaching in terms, not of the length of the text, but of the preacher's approach to it, and to say something like this: Expository preaching is the preaching of the man who knows Holy Scripture to be the living Word of the living God, and who desires only that it should be free to speak its own message to sinful men and women; who therefore preaches from a text, and in preaching labours, as the Puritans would say, to 'open' it, or, in Simeon's phrase, to 'bring out of the text what is there'; whose whole aim in preaching is to show his hearers what the text is saying to them about God and about themselves, and to lead them into what Barth called 'the strange new world within the Bible' in order that there they may be met by him who is Lord of that world.

The practice of expository preaching thus presupposes the biblical and Evangelical account of the relation of the written words of Scripture to the speaking God with whom we have to do. Defining the concept in this way, we may say that every sermon that Simeon preached was an expository sermon; and, surely, we may add that every sermon which we ourselves preach should be an expository sermon. What other sort of sermons, we may ask, is there room for in Christ's church?

Then, second, we must make clear to ourselves *why we are so interested in expository preaching at the present time*. Professor Blackwood had in view the American scene when he wrote: 'Pastors everywhere are becoming concerned about expository preaching';[3] but it is no less true of ourselves. And we do well to stop and ask ourselves: why is this? What lies behind this concern? Why are we all thinking and writing and talking about expository preaching these days? I suspect that we are seeking something more than tips for handling long texts. It is at a deeper level that we want help.

What troubles us, I think, is a sense that the old Evangelical tradition of powerful preaching—the tradition of Whitefield and Wesley and Berridge and Simeon and Haslam and Ryle—has petered out, and we do not know how to revive it. We feel that, for all our efforts, we as preachers are failing to speak adequately to men's needs. In other words what lies behind our modern interest in expository preaching is a deep dissatisfaction with our own ministry. There is a delightful seventeenth-century tract by John Geree entitled *The Character of an Old English Puritane* (1646), in which we learn that such a man 'esteemed that preaching best wherein was most of God, least of men.'[4]

Our own constant suspicion, I think, is that our own preaching contains too much of man and not enough of God. We have an uneasy feeling that the hungry sheep who look up are not really being fed. It is not that we are not trying to break the bread of life to them; it is just that, despite ourselves, our sermons turn out dull and flat and trite and tedious and, in the event, not very nourishing. We are tempted (naturally) to soothe ourselves with the thought that the day of preaching is past, or that zealous visiting or organizing makes sufficient amends for ineffectiveness in the pulpit; but then we re-read 1 Corinthians 2,—'my speech and my preaching was . . . in demonstration of the Spirit and of power'—and we are made uneasy again, and the conclusion is forced upon us once more that something is missing in our ministry. This, surely, is the real reason why we Evangelicals today are so fascinated by the subject of expository preaching: because we want to know how we can regain the lost authority and unction which made Evangelical preaching mighty in days past to humble sinners and build up the church.

When we ask: 'what is expository preaching?' our question really means: 'how can we learn to preach God's Word in demonstration of the Spirit and of power?' What is the secret of the preaching that achieves what our own sermons are failing to achieve?

Suppose we could put the clock back a century and a half, and set our problem before Charles Simeon at one of his famous conversation parties—what would he say to us? The records suggest a number of things of which he would wish to remind us.

Being a supremely practical man, he would begin at the beginning, and say: *expository sermons are sermons,* and must therefore obey the ordinary formal rules of sermon construction. Otherwise, however good their matter, they will fail of their purpose.

'Simeon,' wrote Canon Charles Smyth, 'was almost the first man ... to appreciate that it is perfectly possible to teach men how to preach, and to discover how to do so.'[5] In his edition of Claude's *Essay on the Composition of a Sermon,* and in his weekly conversation parties, Simeon tirelessly hammered away at the basic lessons. A sermon is a single utterance; therefore it must have a single subject. Its divisions (which should be clearly marked, to help the listener follow and remember) should act like the joints of a telescope: 'each successive division ... should be as an additional lens to bring the subject of your text nearer, and make it more distinct.'[6] In the interests of effective communication, all obscure and artificial forms of expression must be avoided. Of his own 2,536 skeletons, Simeon wrote: 'The author has invariably proposed to himself three things as indispensably necessary in every discourse; UNITY in the design, PERSPICUITY in the arrangement, and SIMPLICITY in the diction.'[7] Since a sermon is meant to instruct, it must not be above the congregation's heads ('do not preach what you can tell, but what your people can receive'[8]). Nor must it be too long, or their concentration will go, and 'where weariness or exhaustion comes upon people, there is very little chance of your doing them more good on that occasion.'[9]

A sermon, Simeon would further remind us, is as long as it seems, and an unnatural and monotonous way of talking in the pulpit can make it seem very long very quickly. Again, sermons are more than lectures, and have a further aim than the mere imparting of information. 'The understanding must be informed, but in a manner ... which *affects the heart*; either to comfort the hearers, or to excite them to acts of piety, repentance, or holiness.'[10] Claude elsewhere lays it down that a sermon has a threefold aim—'to instruct, to please and to affect:'[11] the introduction being designed chiefly to please, to win the hearers' interest and goodwill; the exposition to instruct, to win their minds and judgements; and the application to affect, to win their hearts and wills. Don't cheapen your message, if you can help it, Simeon adds, either by cracking jokes in the pulpit ('a very painful style and manner'),[12] or by saying odd, fantastic things ('the pulpit is the seat of good, natural sense; and the good sense of good men').[13]

> As to the mode of delivering your sermons, speak exactly as you would if you were conversing with an aged and pious superior. This will keep you from undue formality on the one hand, and from improper familiarity on the other.[14]

And so on, down to the best method of voice-production.[15]

Neglect these rules, Simeon would say, and your sermons will deservedly fail, however good your heart and your material, for communication will not be achieved. Moreover, he would add, there is no excuse for such failure; for anyone can master the art of effective communication from the pulpit if he will only take the trouble. Daniel Wilson, in his memorial essay on Simeon, says the same. 'Nor is anyone destitute of the means of engaging the attention of others, if he will but take pains early, and be persevering in his use of the natural means of acquiring the faculty of teaching with effect. Every man can be plain, and intelligible, and interesting when his own heart is engaged on other subjects, and why not in religion?'[16] Of course, it takes time—Wilson notes in the same paragraph that 'few (of Simeon's sermons) cost him less than twelve hours of study—many twice that time.' But who are we as clergy to grudge such an outlay?

Such would be Simeon's first point to us. Then he would go on to remind us that *expository sermons should be textual in character.* The preacher's task, according to him, was not imposition, giving texts meanings they do not bear; nor was it juxtaposition, using texts merely as pegs on which to hang general reflections imported from elsewhere ('preachments of this kind are extremely disgustful');[17] it was, precisely, exposition, bringing out of the texts what God had put in them. 'I never preach,' said Simeon, 'unless I feel satisfied that I have the mind of God as regards the sense of the passage.'[18] The motive behind his almost obsessive outbursts against Calvinistic and Arminian 'system-Christians,' as he called them, was his belief that, through reading Scripture in the light of their systems, both sides would be kept from doing justice to all the texts that were there. Whether or not we agree, we must at least endorse Simeon's 'invariable rule . . . to endeavour to give to every portion of the word of God its full and proper force.'[19]

Sermon-texts should be chosen with care, for the sermon should come out of the text whole and rounded, 'like the kernel out of a hazel-nut; and not piecemeal . . . like the kernel out of a walnut.'[20] Therefore, do not take a text that is too long to manage properly, and, on the other hand 'never choose such texts as have not a complete sense: for only impertinent and foolish people will attempt to preach from one or two words, which signify nothing.'[21] The text chosen should so shape the sermon 'that no other text in the Bible will suit the discourse,'[22] and nothing foreign to the text must be allowed to intrude. For the prime secret of freedom and authority in preaching, as Simeon was well aware, is the knowledge that what you are saying is *exactly what your text says,* so that your words have a proper claim to be received as the Word of God.

The next thing, I think, that Simeon would tell us is this: *expository sermons must have a doctrinal substructure.*

Let me explain, lest this be misunderstood. I do not mean that expository sermons should take the form of doctrine lectures, nor that they should be weighed down with theological technical terms not used in the text itself—the less of that, we may say, the better. The point is rather this: Doctrines are to Scripture as the sciences are to nature. And as the scientist is to nature, so should the expositor be to Scripture.

The scientist, just because he has studied the laws which natural phenomena illustrate and embody, is able to explain these phenomena individually to the non-scientist, who observes them without understanding them. Similarly, the expositor who knows his doctrine (the truths and principles exhibited in the acts of God) is able to see the significance and implications of each particular text in a way that another man is not. And this is what he is called to do: to open up individual texts in the light of the *analogy of faith,* i.e., in terms of the broad framework of doctrinal truth which the Bible embodies.

Simeon did not have to stress this in his own lifetime, for it was everywhere taken for granted. As we saw, the characteristic error of Evangelicals then, both Calvinists and Arminians, was, to his mind, not neglect of the analogy of faith in their interpreting, but an over-rigid application of it. But he avowed the principle quite explicitly (in exposition 'I have in mind the analogy of faith,' he wrote),[23] and I think he would emphasize it strongly could he speak to us now. For his own sermons are doctrinal through and through, abounding in clear and exact (though often unobtrusive) formulations of the great foundation-truths of Scripture—God, creation, sin, the trinitarian plan of salvation, the atonement, the work of grace, the means of grace, the church—and one suspects that by comparison he would find our would-be expository sermons distinctly foggy from a doctrinal standpoint.

One suspects too that, whereas he told the Evangelicals of his day that their handling of Scripture was cramped and lopsided because of their undue preoccupation with doctrinal matters, he would tell us that ours was cramped and lopsided because of our undue neglect of them; for, he would say, we have our few favourite subjects, which we can see in every text, but we leave great expanses of biblical teaching untouched, as if we were unaware of their existence. The truth seems to be that part, at any rate, of the recipe for maintaining breadth and variety in one's regular exposition of particular texts is a thorough acquaintance with the doctrinal contents of the Bible as a whole, and no better proof of this could be given than the remarkable variety of theme and freshness and fullness of matter maintained throughout Simeon's own 2,536 printed sermons.

Next, Simeon would remind us that *expository sermons will have an evangelical content.* Always in some way they will set forth the gospel in its double aspect as a revelation and a remedy; always in some way they will throw light on the twin themes of sin and grace; for these are the things that the whole Bible is about. Always, therefore, their tendency will be threefold—'to humble the sinner; to exalt the Saviour; to promote holiness'[24]—for that is the tendency of the Bible, and of every part of the Bible. Whatever part of the counsel of God they deal with, expository sermons will relate it to 'Christ, and him crucified,' for the Christ of Calvary is, so to speak, the hub around which the whole biblical revelation revolves. It was in this sense that Simeon, following Paul, insisted that 'Christ, and him crucified' was the whole of his message. And the preacher is not handling his texts biblically, Simeon would say, unless he is seeing and setting them in their proper relation to Christ. If the expositor finds himself out of sight of Calvary, that shows that he has lost his way. Again, Simeon's own sermons provide the best illustration of his principles here.[25]

The fifth point he would wish to make to us would, I think, be that *expository sermons must have a theocentric perspective.*

The key that unlocks the biblical outlook is the perception that the real subject of Holy Scripture is not man and his religion, but God and his glory; from which it follows that God is the real subject of every text, and must therefore be the real subject of every expository sermon, as he is of Simeon's own sermons. This, again, is a point which Simeon could take for granted in his day, but on which he would need to expostulate with us; for we, to a greater extent, perhaps, than we realize, have inherited the later nineteenth-century outlook which sets man at the centre of the stage, even in religion, and our thoughts and interests in the spiritual realm have become habitually and oppressively man-centred.

What, really, do we preach about? *Man*—man and his religion, his needs, his problems and his responsibilities; for all the world as if man was the most important being in the universe, and the Father and the Son existed simply for man's sake.

This is an age of great thoughts of man and small, sentimental thoughts of God, within Evangelical Christendom hardly less than outside it. Simeon would tell us that we have things topsy-turvy; nor can we expect God to honour our preaching unless we honour him by giving him his rightful place in the centre of our message, and by reducing man to what he really is—a helpless, worthless rebel creature, saved only by a miracle of omnipotent holy love, and saved, not for his own sake, but for the praise of his Saviour. He would tell us that we can only expect great blessing on our preaching when our sole concern is to do what he himself was solely concerned to do—to magnify the great God who works all things to his own glory, and to exalt his Son as a great Saviour of great sinners.

But what about the thing that most concerns us—this question *of power* in preaching? What would Simeon say to help us there? He would tell us that ultimately this was a matter of God's sovereign gift. 'It is easy,' he once said, 'for a minister to prate in a pulpit, and even to speak much good matter; but to preach is not easy—to carry his congregation on his shoulders as it were to heaven; to weep over them, pray for them, deliver the truth with a weeping, praying heart; and if a minister has grace to do so now and then, he ought to be very thankful.'[26] Meanwhile, he would say, we should seek to put ourselves in the way of such an inducement, first, by making it a matter of conscience to observe in all our sermon preparation the five principles set out above, and then by labouring constantly to be compassionate, sincere, and earnest in heart whenever we preach—men possessed by our message, saying what we say as if we meant it. How can we do this? By taking care deeply to digest the bread of life in our own hearts before we set it in the view of others.

'Do not seek to preach what you do not feel' [Simeon advises]; 'seek to feel deeply your own sins, and then you will preach earnestly . . . preach . . . as fellow sinners.'[27]

Simeon himself is our example here. The feature of his preaching which most constantly impressed his hearers was the fact that he was, as they said, 'in earnest;' and that reflected his own overwhelming sense of sin, and of the wonder of the grace that had saved him; and that in turn bore witness to the closeness of his daily fellowship and walk with his God. As he gave time to sermon preparation, so he gave time to seeking God's face.

'The quality of his preaching' [writes a past Archbishop of Canterbury] 'was but a re-flection of the quality of the man himself. And there can be little doubt that the man himself was largely made in the early morning hours which he devoted to private prayer and the devotional study of the Scriptures. It was his custom to rise at 4 a.m., light his own fire, and then devote the first four hours of the day to communion with God. Such costly self-discipline made the preacher. That was primary. The making of the sermon was secondary and derivative.'[28]

That was primary. If our question is: where is the Lord God of Charles Simeon? we now have our answer. As so often with God's answers, it takes the form of a counter-question: where are the preachers who seek after the Lord God as Simeon did? This, surely, is the final word, if not of Simeon, at least from God through Simeon to us who would preach the gospel of Christ in the power of God's Spirit today. God help us to hear it, and to heed it.

CHAPTER 20

From the Scriptures to the Sermon

Some Perspectives on Preaching

'I urge you, Timothy, as we live in the sight of God and of Christ Jesus (whose coming in power will judge the living and the dead), to preach the Word of God. Never lose your sense of urgency, in season or out of season. Prove, correct, and encourage, using the utmost patience in your teaching.' Thus J. B. Phillips, that prince of paraphrasts, renders the first two verses of 2 Timothy 4. Note the aspects of the communicative action that Paul prescribes (they are all there in the Greek): proclamation, demonstration, correction, instruction. Note the commitment to the preaching ministry for which Paul calls: press on, he says, with utmost urgency and stick-to-it-iveness (a fine North American word that catches the force of *makrothumia* better than does the English scholar's 'patience'). And now consider whether we Evangelicals, who so often cite these words of Paul to each other and who claim to know so clearly that the preaching of the Word is the power-source of the church, can be said to succeed in rising to the demands of this insight that we inherit. I think it must be honestly admitted that often we fail here; we do not succeed in preaching the Word of God as plainly, pungently, and powerfully as we would like to do. What follows is offered in the hope that it will help us to preach better. If you do not find my thoughts useful, please remember that, like so many of our unsuccessful sermons, they were at least well meant.

I

First let me focus the concept of preaching the Word of God as I think it ought to be focused. I do not define preaching institutionally or sociologically, but theologically and functionally. An institutional definition would present preaching in terms of buildings, pulpits, and pews.[1] A sociological definition would view preaching as a special kind of monologue fulfilling specific corporate expectations on the part of the group being addressed. Both types of definition are no doubt useful in their place; but if one is, or hopes to be, a preacher oneself, and wants to know what fulfilling the ministry that Paul urged upon Timothy really involves, then a theological definition that shows what should happen when preaching takes place is what one needs. Here, then, is my attempt to formulate this concept in normative theological terms.

Christian preaching, I urge, is *the event of God bringing to an audience a Bible-based, Christ-related, life-impacting message of instruction and direction from himself through the words of a spokesperson.* Please note the following points about this definition. First, it is *theological:* it conceptualizes preaching in terms not of human performance but of divine communication. Also, it is *prophetic:* it views God as speaking his own message via a messenger whose sole aim is to receive and relay what God gives. Furthermore, it is *incarnational:* for it envisages God embodying his communication in the person of the messenger who both delivers it and, in delivering it, models response to it. Phillips Brooks's famous delineation of preaching as truth through personality points to the way in which personal attitudes to God and man come through in the course of declaring God's message, and the demeanour of preachers in their messenger-role as bearers of God's truth and wisdom to people whom God loves will always, for better or for worse, become part of their message and affect the impact that they make. Jesus himself, God's incarnate Son, is of course the paradigm case here. Finally, this normative definition of preaching has a *critical* function to fulfil; for it obliges us to test pulpit utterances, and to say of any that was not Bible-based, Christ-related, and life-impacting, in a sufficient sense, that, whatever else it was, it was not preaching in the full and proper meaning of that word.

Preaching as described is necessary for a healthy church. Without a regular diet of Bible-based, Christ-related, life-impacting messages from God the mindset of a congregation will become either institutionalist and sacramentalist, as in old-style Roman Catholicism where there was no effective preaching, or moralistic and legalistic, as in liberal Protestant congregations where the agenda is social service and God is expected to accept one for doing it. Where there is preaching of the type described, however, the Bible will be revered as the Word of God; which is as it should be.

So I do not equate preaching with what is called sermonizing or pulpiteering. Not every performance from the preacher's podium is preaching. It is notorious that some sermonizing produces only bitter wisecracks about the pulpit as a coward's castle, and preachers as standing six feet above contradiction, talking at rather than to their hearers, and as climaxing invisibility during the week with incomprehensibility on Sunday, and so on. But such sermonizing, which is certainly bad preaching, may by my definition not be preaching at all, though the institutional and sociological definitions would compel us to call it that. From my theological standpoint, what is said from the pulpit is only preaching if its content conforms to the specification stated above. Conversely, any communication that fulfils these specifications ought to be categorized as preaching, wherever and however it is done—as when Philip sat in the Ethiopian eunuch's chariot and 'told him the good news about Jesus' (Acts 8:35 NIV; KJV had 'preached unto him Jesus'; the Greek word is *euangelizomai,* one of the two main New Testament terms for declaring the gospel). For the New Testament, a Christian spokesman preaches (*kerusso*) only when some aspect of the God-given message concerning Christ (the *kerygma*) is the content of the utterance. This is not our usual modern way of looking at the matter, but it is the biblical way, and it is always best to follow the Bible because it is the Word of God, which when followed will constantly be impacting people as just that. Jesus Christ will be then known and loved, because he will constantly be projected as lover and Saviour of our souls; and Christians will grow and flourish through being fed on true spiritual food. Surely it is beyond dispute that a church made and kept healthy by authentic preaching must ever be our goal.

Today's Evangelicalism has behind it a noble heritage of preaching. The Reformation itself grew out of practical biblical preaching with Christ at the centre. The great Puritan movement (and it was great) was sustained on both sides of the Atlantic by preaching of this kind. The eighteenth-century revival in Britain and the Great Awakening in New England were profound spiritual movements with powerful evangelical preaching at their heart. In the nineteenth century men like Charles H. Spurgeon sustained magnificent ministries by preaching in this fashion, and more recently men like Donald Barnhouse and Martyn Lloyd-Jones have done the same. But the great tradition is currently tapering off. Why is this? we ask: what has happened to eclipse the grand-scale presentations of the works, ways, and will of God, through which Evangelicalism once grew lively and strong? It is not, I think, that preachers as a body have stopped caring about preaching or trying to do it properly; the problem goes deeper, and arises in the first instance from the drift of our culture. We live in days in which the credibility of faithful biblical preaching is radically doubted, not only outside but also inside the church, and misguided but insistent expectations on the part of listeners put many difficulties in the way of faithful preaching that were not there before. Five factors in particular operate in this way; we need to be aware of them, so I propose to review them now.

First, the prevalence of non-preaching in Christian pulpits has eroded awareness of what true preaching is.

Lack of good models tends always to lower standards, and unfortunately good models have been in short supply throughout this century. Far too many pulpit discourses have been put together on wrong principles. Some have failed to open up Scripture; some have expounded biblical doctrine without applying it, thus qualifying as lectures rather than preachments (for lecturing aims only to clear the head, while preaching seeks to change the life); some have been no more than addresses focusing the present self-awareness of the listeners, but not at any stage confronting them with the Word of God; some have been mere statements of the preacher's opinion, based merely on his own expertise, rather than mes-sages from God carrying divine authority. Such discourses are less than preaching, as was stated previously, but because they were announced as sermons they are treated as preaching and people's idea of preaching gets formed in terms of them, so that the true conception of preaching is forgotten.

It is often said, and truly, that sermons must teach Bible truth, and that the renewal of preaching needed today will take its rise from a fresh awareness that this is so: my slighting reference to some content-laden sermons as lectures rather than preachments may therefore have seemed perplexing. But preaching is more than teaching—not less, but more! Preaching is essentially teaching plus applica-tion (invitation, direction, summons), and where that plus is lacking something less than preaching takes place. Study of printed sermons from past generations reveals that older Evangelical preachers kept a careful balance between doctrinal content as such (biblical orthodoxy) and practical and experiential applications (biblical orthopraxy)—something like half and half in most messages. In our day, however, the balance has been largely lost, and sermons tend to be either all doc-trinal content without application, or all exhortation without doctrinal content; and to the extent to which either form of imbalance prevails, both types of utter-ance become instances of non-preaching, and very inadequate models, therefore, of what preaching ought to be. Many in our churches have never experienced preaching of the historic Evangelical sort at all.

Second, topical as distinct from textual preaching has become common in North America (less so in Britain and elsewhere).

For sermons to explore announced themes rather than biblical passages is a twentieth-century development, and hardly a happy one. Why should it have occurred? Partly, I suppose, to make preaching appear interesting and important to a generation that has largely lost interest in the pulpit; partly, no doubt, to make the sermon seem different from what goes on in the Bible class before public worship starts; partly, too, I am sure, because many topical preachers do not trust their Bible enough to let it speak for itself and utter its own message through their lips. Whatever the reasons, however, the results are unhealthy. In a topical sermon any text taken is reduced to a peg on which the speaker hangs his own line of thought. The shape and thrust of his message thus reflect no more than his own idea of what is good for people, and then the only authority that the sermon can have is the human authority of a knowledgeable person speaking with emphasis (raising his voice, perhaps, and even banging the pulpit). To my mind, topical sermons of this sort, no matter how biblical their component parts may be, cannot but fall short of being preaching in the full sense, just because in them the authority of God speaking is dissolved, more or less, into the authority of human religious expertise. Many in our churches have only ever been exposed to topical preaching of this kind: no wonder then that they do not appreciate what real preaching might be.

Third, low expectations become self-fulfilling. Where little is expected from sermons, little is received.

Many moderns have never been taught to expect sermons to matter much, and so their habit at sermon time is to relax, settle back, and wait to see if anything the preacher says will catch their interest. Most of today's congregations and preachers seem to be at one in neither asking nor anticipating that God will come to meet his people in the preaching; so it is no wonder if this fails to happen. According to your unbelief, we might say, be it unto you! Just as it takes two to tango, so ordinarily it takes an expectant, praying congregation, along with a preacher who knows what he is about, to make an authentic preaching occasion. A century ago in Reformed circles in Britain the regular question to a person coming from church was, how did he or she 'get on' under the preaching of the Word: this reflected the expectancy of which I am speaking. Nowadays, however, on both sides of the Atlantic, the commoner question is, how did the preacher 'get on' in his stated pulpit performance, and this shows how interest has shifted and the mental attitude has changed. It is now assumed that those who sit under the preaching are observers, measuring the preacher's performance, rather than participants waiting for the Word of God. Many in our congregations do not know that there is any other way of listening to sermons than this way of detached passivity, and no one should be surprised to find that those who cultivate such passivity often dismiss preaching as an uneventful bore. Those who seek little find little.

Fourth, the power of speech to communicate significance has in our Western culture become suspect, so that any form of oratory, rhetoric, or dramatic emphasis to show the weight and significance of stated facts tends to alienate rather than convince.

This development is due mainly to the media. On radio and television strong expressions of feeling sound and look hysterical; cool and chatty intimacy is required if one is to communicate successfully. This standard of communicative sincerity is now applied everywhere. Prior to this century a preacher could use words dramatically and emphatically for up to an hour to set forth the majesty of God the King, the glory of Christ the Saviour, the greatness of the soul, the momentous importance of eternity, and the significance of present reactions to the gospel message for determining personal destiny, and congregations appreciated the manner as being appropriate to the matter. Nowadays, that kind of utterance is widely felt to be false, as if passionate speech as such argues a purpose of browbeating and bludgeoning the mind, pulling the wool over the eyes, and carrying through a confidence trick. To avoid this suspicion, many preachers nowadays talk of spiritual life and death in a style better fitted to reading the sports results, and their cozy intimacy makes the theme itself seem trivial or unreal. The discrediting among us of grand-scale public speech puts preachers into what might well be felt to be a no-win situation.

It was my privilege, forty years ago, to spend a winter under the preaching ministry of the late Dr. Martyn Lloyd-Jones, and to enjoy a working relationship with him for twenty years after that so that I was able to observe from many angles his approach to the preacher's task. His gifts fitted him for grand-scale ministry, and his sense of spiritual reality told him that great things must be said in a way that projected their greatness. He could fairly be described as a nineteenth-century preacher born out of due time, and though he was fully aware that the older type of preaching had become suspect and unfashionable he continued to practice it and to encourage others to do the same. Combining the electric energy of the orator with the analytical precision of the courtroom or the clinic, and focusing his businesslike rhetoric on the inner drama of the gracious hound of heaven capturing and changing sinners' benighted hearts, he communicated an overwhelming sense of the greatness of God and the weight of spiritual issues, and left behind him a large body of hearers, myself among them, who will forever be thankful that as a modern man he deliberately swam against the stream and did the old thing. The vision of preaching that I gained from him, as from no one else, stays with me, and what I am saying now reflects, I am sure, my experience of the power of preaching through his ministry. From the vantage point that this experience gave me, I urge that the only real way forward for preachers today is to follow Dr. Lloyd-Jones in cultivating an honesty with words that earns us the right to fly in the face of our laid-back culture and to dwell passionately, urgently, dramatically, and at appropriate length, on the desperately important agenda of the relationship between God and man. In this, as in so much else, the old paths constitute the good way. But how few today, preachers or people, know it!

Fifth, spiritual issues themselves, issues of radical repentance, self-despairing faith, costly cross-bearing as central to discipleship, spending and being spent in order to do others good, putting holiness before happiness, and keeping the world out of one's head and heart, are felt to be irrelevant by many church attendees.

The problem that preachers face here is that church attendance for many has little or nothing to do with the quest for God. Why then are they in church at all? The answers are all too familiar. Because churchgoing is the mark of a respectable and trustworthy citizen; or because attending an appropriate ethnic or denominational church helps one keep alive one's cultural heritage; or because the genial and relaxed regularities of Sunday worship help to stabilize a hectic life; or because faithful churchgoing is thought to guarantee some kind of happy lot in the next world; or because one likes the people one meets at church; and so on. There are many such reasons, but none of them has anything to do with knowing and loving God and none of them, therefore, fosters any spiritual interest in preaching. So when preachers point the way to a richer relationship with God, this type of hearer feels a sense of irrelevance, and his or her heart is inclined to say: here is a religious professional talking about the things he is paid to talk about; I am not a religious professional, so none of that is really my business; however, I will sit through it patiently, as good manners require. Preachers, for their part, know that this is how many of their hearers are thinking, so they strain every nerve to speak in a way that will lead persons without spiritual interest to rate them fascinating, relevant, and smart. How we love to be rated smart! But this preoccupation makes against faithful spiritual preaching, and results in congregations not experiencing faithful spiritual preaching for long periods together.

All these factors tend to set up wrong standards and thus constitute obstacles to the kind of preaching that I seek to commend. However, difficulties are there to be overcome; so I proceed.

II

In what I have said so far I have been clearing the ground for discussion of my main concern in this presentation, which is to show what authority in preaching means and to suggest how it might be re-established in today's churches. My interest at this stage centres not on homiletics, that is, the technical procedures whereby preachers bring to us what they have to tell us about God, but rather on the theology of preaching, that is, the supernatural process whereby God through his messenger brings to us what he has to tell us about himself. Preaching as a work of God, mediating the authority of God, is my theme, and the rest of my space will be devoted to its development in a direct way.

My first step in opening up my theme must be to outline what I mean when I speak of the authority of God. Authority is a multi-faceted relationship with a moral and intellectual as well as a governmental side: the basic idea is of a claim to exercise control that is founded on having the right, power, and competence to do it. The authority that belongs to God springs from his sovereign dominion over us as his dependent creatures, linked with the moral perfection of all his dealings with us. Holy Scripture, 'God's Word written' (Anglican Article 20), is the instrument of God's authority; our Lord Jesus Christ exercises and embodies it; and the Holy Spirit induces acknowledgement of it by making us realize the reality of the Father and the Son as they address us in all their awesomeness, holiness, and graciousness. God speaks through his Word, written and preached, and our preaching of the Word should match the Spirit's strategy—that is, we should always be seeking to bring home God's reality and authority to human minds and hearts by elucidating and applying Holy Scripture. Encounter with the living, authoritative Lord brings spiritual understanding and life as we hear and respond to his call for trust and obedience, praise and worship, and the preacher's aim should ever be to occasion this edifying encounter. The discussion on which we now enter seeks to show something of what this means, and so to help us set our sights as preachers more effectively.

I ask three questions.

First: what does it mean for preaching to be marked by authority?

The answer I propose is that authority in preaching is a reality in every situation in which the following things are true.

(1) There is no doubt about the *nature* of what is happening: *the Bible is doing the talking.* The preacher is treating himself as a mouthpiece for the biblical word of God, and that word is coming through. He has resisted the temptation to stand in front of his text, as it were, speaking for it as if it could not speak for itself, and putting himself between it and the congregation: instead, he is making it his business to focus everyone's attention on the text, to stand behind it rather than in front of it, to become its servant, and to let it deliver its message through him. As the Westminster Directory for Public Worship put it, three and a half centuries ago, what the preacher presents must be 'contained in or grounded on' (his) text, *'that the hearers may discern how God teacheth it from thence.'* Preaching has authority only when the message comes as a word from God himself, and that only happens when what is said is perceived as, in the words of the Westminster Confession (I.x), 'the Holy Spirit speaking in the Scripture;' and that perception only occurs as the preacher labours to let the text talk through him about that with which, like every other text in the Bible, it is ultimately dealing—God and man in relationship, one way or another. If what is presented appears as the preacher's ideas, it can have only human authority at best. When, however, the preacher serves the written Word in a way that lets it speak for itself, its divine authority is felt.

(2) There is no doubt about the *purpose* of what is happening: *response to God is being called for.* The preacher, as spokesman for the text, is seeking not only to inform and persuade, but to evoke an appropriate answer to what God through the text is saying and showing. Man's answer will consist of repentance, faith, obedience, love, effort, hope, fear, zeal, joy, praise, prayer, or some blend of these; for such are the dispositional qualities, springing from the heart into devotional and doxological expression, that God everywhere requires. The preacher is hoping, under God, to reproduce the state of affairs that Paul looked back to when he wrote to the Romans, 'you wholeheartedly obeyed the form of teaching to which you were entrusted' (Rom. 6:17). The teaching is God's testimony, command, and promise; the preacher entrusts his hearers to it by begging them to respond to it and assuring them that God will fulfil his promises to them as they do so; and in this process the divine authority of the message is felt.

(3) There is no doubt about the *perspective* of what is happening: *the preaching is practical.* This point is an extension of the last. What is being said would not be preaching at all were it not life-centred. Communication from the text is only preaching as it is applied and brought to bear on the listeners with a life-changing thrust. Without this, as was said earlier, it would only be a lecture—that is, a discourse designed merely to clear people's heads and stock their minds, but not in any direct way to change their lives.

I must confess that I do not think that the present-day Evangelical pulpit is strong here. Reacting against the kind of preaching that too often marks the liberal pulpit, in which the speaker offers personal reflections on human and religious life, too many of us preach messages that suffer from what might be called 'doctrinal overload.' With thirty minutes in which to preach, we spend twenty-eight of them teaching general principles of divine truth from our text, and only for the last minute or two do we engage in any form of application. But there is little sense of God's authority where so much of the message is lecture and so little application is found.

A wiser way of proceeding, and one that mediated a very vivid sense of divine authority, was that followed by Dr. Martyn Lloyd-Jones in the greatest days of his preaching ministry. The introductions to his pastoral and evangelistic sermons were very cunningly conceived. Having announced his text, he would spend the first few minutes of the sermon talking about some widely-felt perplexity of modern life, pointing out in everyday language that no adequate solution or remedy seemed to be in sight. In this he was operating on the wise principle, 'scratch where it itches,' and involving his hearers in a realization that this was their problem, pressing and inescapable. When he had secured their interest at this level, he would begin to demonstrate that his text gives God's angle on the problem and his answer to it, and the demonstration would be applicatory all the way. Not everyone who experienced the authority of God in the preaching of 'the Doctor' discerned its source. Certainly, Dr. Lloyd-Jones's personal power as a speaker and his humble, insightful submission to his text had much to do with it, but much of the authority flowed from the fact that he was applying the truth in a searchingly practical way throughout to remedy the need that he had already brought his hearers to face and own. The more explicit the practical perspective, and the more overtly it involves the listeners, the more the divine authority of the preaching will be felt.

(4) There is no doubt about the *impact* of what is happening: *the presence and power of God are being experienced.* The preaching mediates an encounter not merely with truth, but with God himself. A staggering throwaway line in 1 Corinthians 14 illustrates this. Paul is showing the superior usefulness of prophecy (speaking God's message in intelligible language) over tongues, and he says: 'If the whole church comes together and everyone speaks in tongues, and some who do not understand or some unbelievers come in, will they not say that you are out of your mind?' (Expected answer: yes.) 'But if an unbeliever or someone who does not understand comes in while everybody is prophesying, he will be convinced by all that he is a sinner and will be judged by all, and the secrets of his heart will be laid bare. So he will fall down and worship God, exclaiming, "God is really among you!"' (1 Cor. 14:23–25). Whatever else in this passage is uncertain, four things at least are plain. First, prophecy as Paul speaks of it here corresponds in content to what we would call preaching the gospel: detecting sin,

and announcing God's remedy. Second, the expected effect of such prophecy was to create a sense of being in the presence of the God of whom it spoke, and of being searched and convicted by him, and so being moved to humble oneself and worship him. Third, in the experience of both Paul and the Corinthians what Paul describes must have actually occurred, otherwise he could not have expected the Corinthians to believe his assertion: for that which never happened before cannot be predicted with such certainty. Fourth, Paul is anticipating a situation in which a divine authority in and through the preaching would be felt.

To sum up, then: preaching is marked by authority when the message is a relaying of what is taught by the text, when active response to it is actively sought, when it is angled in a practical, applicatory way that involves the listeners' lives, and when God himself is encountered through it. So much for the first question.

Second: what are the hindrances to authority in our preaching? I can be brief here, since the points are so obvious.

Lack of a clearly Bible-based, applicatory message, summoning its hearers one way or another to a deeper relationship with God in Christ, precludes the possibility of authority.

Imprecision, confusion, and muddle in presentation, so that the message and its application cannot be clearly grasped, has the same effect.

Self-projection also undermines and erodes authority. If by his words and manner the preacher focuses attention on himself, thus modelling some mode of self-absorption or self-satisfaction rather than humble response to the word that he proclaims, he precludes all possibility of his channelling any sense of divine authority: what he does not feel himself he cannot mediate to others. James Denney said somewhere that you cannot convey the impression both that you are a great preacher and that Jesus Christ is a great Saviour; he might have added: or that the Lord is a great God. God-projection and Christ-projection rather than self-projection is the way to communicate and engender in one's hearers a sense of divine authority in one's preaching.

Self-reliance in the act of preaching is a further hindrance to true authority in preaching, just as self-projection is. It too has the effect of inducing the hearers to attend to the messenger rather than the message—in other words, to man rather than to God—and authentic authority is eliminated when that happens.

So to my final question.

Third: what are the conditions of authority in our preaching?

To this question I offer first a general and then a specific answer.

The general answer is that preaching has authority when both its substance and its style proclaim in a transparent way the preacher's own docile humility before the Bible itself and before the triune God whose Word the Bible is. It is as the preacher himself is truly under, and is clearly seen to be under, the authority of God and the Bible that he will have authority, and be felt to carry authority, as God's spokesman. It needs to be obvious to the hearers that he has put himself wholeheartedly under the authority of the God as whose emissary he comes; of Christ the chief shepherd, whom he serves as a subordinate shepherd, and to whom he must one day give account of his service; and of the Holy Spirit, whom he trusts each moment as he preaches actually to communicate the divine message to his hearers' hearts. A preacher who has authority will come across as one who consciously depends on the Holy Spirit to sustain in him vividness of vision, clarity of mind and words, and freedom of heart and voice as he delivers his message, just as he trusts the Holy Spirit to be the agent of conviction and response in the lives of his hearers. It is those under authority who have authority; it is those whose demeanour models submission to the Scriptures and dependence on the Lord of the Word who mediate the experience of God's authority in preaching. 'Unlike so many,' writes Paul, 'we do not sell the word of God for profit'—that is, we do not preach with mercenary motives, nor do we modify the message in order to please hearers who, if pleased, will smile on us, but if displeased, might become obnoxious to us. 'On the contrary; in Christ we speak before God with sincerity, like men sent from God' (2 Cor. 2:17). Only those preachers who could say the same, by reason of their conscious and conscientious fidelity to the written Word, are likely ever to be able to say, as Paul elsewhere said: 'we also thank God continually because when you received the word of God which you heard from us, you accepted it not as the word of men, but as it actually is, the word of God, which is at work in you who believe' (1 Thess. 2:13).

Specifically, and looking at the matter directly from our own standpoint as preachers, the conditions of authority are four in number, each of which we should now recognize as a summons and a directive to us from the Lord himself.

(1) The heart of our message on each occasion must be an application of biblical material to the heart and conscience, to lead folk to know, love, worship and serve God through Jesus Christ. Is this our constant purpose when we preach?

(2) The way we preach must display a transparent wholeheartedness of response to our own message, as well as a thoroughgoing commitment to persuade our hearers to trust, love, honour, and serve the Lord as we ourselves seek to do. Constant self-scrutiny is therefore required of preachers in particular, to make sure that our own hearts are right before we attempt to speak in the Lord's name. Do we practice this self-scrutiny?

(3) We need the unction of the Holy Spirit for the act of preaching itself.[3] Richard Baxter, the Puritan, in his classic volume *The Reformed Pastor* (which every would-be pastor-preacher will be wise to read once a year), spoke of 'a communion of souls' that takes place in preaching, whereby the hearers catch the preacher's mood.[4] This being so, it is vital that the preacher should be full of the Holy Spirit for his appointed task, so that he is clear-headed, warm-hearted, ardent, earnest, and inwardly free to concentrate on the task of instruction and persuasion that each message imposes. An anointing of the Spirit, therefore, giving *parrhasia*—uninhibited freedom to say from one's heart what one sees with

one's heart—is to be sought every time we preach. Beethoven wrote on the score of his *Missa Sollemnis* (Mass in D, op. 126): 'From the heart it comes, to the heart may it go,' and these same words should express the preacher's desire every time he ventures to speak. But it is only as we seek and receive the divine unction, sermon by sermon, that it will be so. Do we seek unction as we should?

(4) Finally, we need grace to be spontaneous when we preach: by which I mean, easy and free-flowing in appropriate expression. This, too, is a gift from God—it is in fact an aspect of the *parrhasia* that the Spirit bestows—but it does not come without hard work in preparation: preparation not just of the message but also, and even primarily, of the messenger. The appropriate formula here comes, I believe, from W. H. Griffith Thomas, and runs as follows: 'Think yourself empty; read yourself full; write yourself clear; pray yourself keen; then into the pulpit—and let yourself go!' That is the sort of preparation that produces spontaneity. Is this how we prepare to preach?

God bless us all in our preaching ministry, and empower us to preach with authority—as we ought to preach!

The Problem of Paradigms

The word *paradigm* has become something of a technical term in modern academic discussion.[5] It is used to mean what we would once have called an overall frame of reference, or a controlling point of view. A paradigm is a large-scale hypothesis about reality that is presupposed and taken for granted as a basis for interpreting data and determining values, goals, and procedures. One's paradigm determines one's mind-set, shaping one's thinking by giving it direction and establishing boundaries and limits beyond which belief may not go. Paradigms thus exert control, and usually without our realizing what is happening; who, under ordinary circumstances, reflects on how much he or she is taking for granted? So our paradigms of reality determine how we process informational data—what we make of it, to speak in everyday terms—for processing data is essentially a matter of fitting the bits into our overall frame of reference. Thus paradigms become the pathway to understanding if the paradigm is a good one, or to misunderstanding if it is not.

Paradigms are always present with us, even if they go unnoticed. The human mind abhors incoherence and demands to fit everything into a single frame of reference, so that it can see how things relate. You, I, and everyone else do in fact fit incoming data into categories of thought and judgement provided by our paradigms, which are regularly those of the groups with which we identify—our family, school, club, gang, firm, church or whatever. The paradigms thus operate in our minds like coloured spectacles, or sunglasses, which filter out glare and cause us to see objects as having a colour that the glasses themselves have imparted. There is, for instance, a Marxist paradigm for viewing reality, also a secular humanist paradigm, also a New Age paradigm, also a Jewish paradigm, also a Muslim paradigm, and alongside these and others, stands the Christian paradigm. Each paradigm yields a distinctive mind-set and colours perceptions in a distinctive way, and communication between the adherents of different paradigms is stultified if the reality and potency of the paradigms themselves is overlooked and ignored.

Our present concern is with preaching—preaching viewed as Christian communication, that is, the communication of Christianity. The point I want to develop now is that in a post-Christian culture like ours, the preacher of the gospel needs to be aware that the paradigms that currently possess people's minds rarely match the Christian paradigm that controls his own thinking. What they take for granted is not identical with what he takes for granted, nor vice versa. Once, in the Christendom era, a broadly Christian paradigm could be assumed in all Western minds, but in today's world that is no longer so. So the effective Christian communicator will be the person who can bring into consciousness and challenge, in terms of God's revelation, the secular paradigms that control modern society and the people who make it up. He needs to understand how these paradigms work, and the best way to do that is to see where they came from and how they developed. My point, in other words, is that preachers for our time need to appreciate the *paradigm shifts* that have taken place in our culture with regard to God, man, and religion, and to equip themselves for the task of reversing them.

I

Let me illustrate what I mean by a paradigm shift. Here are two examples.

The first is the paradigm of the universe, the physical order of reality to which we belong. Here there have been several shifts over the centuries. First came the shift from the earth-centred Ptolemaic world-view, which supposed that the universe consisted of spheres within spheres circling round this planet, to the Copernican heliocentric concept of planets revolving round the sun. Newton then amplified Copernicus by explaining the movements of the planets in terms of universal gravitation, and Einstein amplified Newton by his theory of relativity and curved space. In each era speculative and experimental physicists have fitted their proposed explanations of puzzling phenomena into the currently accepted paradigm.

A second example is the shift from accepting to rejecting external authority as a guide for living, which came about through the European Enlightenment. Starting in England in the seventeenth century, gathering strength on the continent of Europe in the eighteenth century, and carrying all before it in the Western world in the nineteenth and twentieth centuries, the Enlightenment was the watershed between the Christendom era and the post-Christian modern world.

To characterize it as anti-clerical, as its French exponents did at the time of the Revolution, is not to say enough; at deepest motivational level the Enlightenment was an abandoning of all forms of external authority in favour of intellectual and moral individualism. The self-directed, self-affirming individualism that is commonly traced to the Romantic movement rode in on the Enlightenment's back. The effect of this individualism was that one's own personal reason, rather than the church or the community or the cultural tradition, became one's definer of reality; it was for each thinking person to work out for him—or herself a personal solution to the riddles of life. In the nineteenth century artists and philosophers did this and the guardians of conventional values clucked their tongues, wondering how long it would be before society fell apart. In the twentieth century most people have done it, and society today holds together mainly through a shared embrace of materialist values projected by the press and media. For all except conservative Roman Catholics and adherents of some sects, the idea of having one's thought-life and conduct controlled by official church pronouncements, accepted without question because questioning the church is not right, now seems utterly strange and unconvincing. That, we feel, is certainly not the way to go! Intellectually and morally, it nowadays has to be every man for himself, for no external authority can be fully trusted. Every particular problem must now be dealt with as a matter about which one makes up one's own mind. This modern mind-set evidences a major paradigm shift from the willingness to trust authorities in matters of truth and right that was there before.

This second example of a paradigm shift brings us right up to our present task, which is to focus the post-Christian outlooks of the West in their characteristic form as they relate to the older Christian understanding of God, man, and religion. In this regard, as we shall see, it is possible to generalize about them without being unduly simplistic, even though in terms of positive commitment they fan out, and end up as far away from each other as each is from historic Christianity. But in the terms in which they distance themselves from their Christian heritage they stand pretty much together, and their stance is reinforced by the media, the schools, the world of literature, the news industry and just about every opinion-making institution in North America and Europe, apart from the church itself. And to say 'apart from the church itself' is, alas, something of an overstatement, for significant bodies of opinion within the Christian constituency have themselves accepted from the drifting culture post-Christian attitudes to Christian realities and now seek to define the faith in these terms. Ever since Schleiermacher, the liberal Protestant way has been to keep in step with secular philosophy and adjust Christian belief accordingly, so that it has operated as something of a Trojan horse, or fifth column, in the institutional churches, and many (not all of them Protestants, be it said) are treading this path today.

The result of the shift from Christian trust in external authority (church or Bible) to post-Christian mistrust of both is, so far as the United States is concerned, rather curious. Americans, as de Tocqueville noted long ago, are remarkably religious people, and most of them, it seems, still want to have a Christian veneer on their lives. But when they use Christian words to make Christian-sounding affirmations, it is apparent that many of the words have been redefined and their biblical meaning has been largely forgotten. What is said about God and Christianity in popular religious talk is not what used to be said, and what used to be said (about holiness, self-denial, and judgement, for instance) is hardly heard any more. So Christian spokespersons—preachers and teachers, I mean—in North America nowadays have to be alert to the problem created for them by the prevalence in their hearers' minds of alien paradigms, just as cross-cultural missionaries have to be. The problem is to ensure that the gospel heard verbally will be understood substantively. That requires both a return to authentic biblical definitions of Christian key words and a corrective interaction with the new paradigms to make room again in people's minds for authentic Christian thoughts. The title of one of Carl Henry's early books, *Remaking the Modern Mind,* aptly sums up the task. One may tackle it by head-on encounter, as Francis Schaeffer for instance did, or indirectly and in a sense incidentally, as Billy Graham for example does; but, one way or another, it must be tackled, or our preaching and teaching will achieve little.

We look now at three themes—God, man, and religion, or godliness—to see how at paradigm level minds have changed, and how they need to be changed back again.

II

With regard to God, I ask you to take note that we stand at the end of four centuries of God-shrinking. In the era of the Reformation the biblical faith in God as one who rules, judges and saves, the source, sustainer, and end of all things, took possession of people's minds in a vivid, clear, compelling way. But by the start of the seventeenth century Lutherans and Arminians were already denying God's total sovereignty, and were thus dethroning him at a crucial point. By the end of the seventeenth century Deism, the concept of God as the mighty mechanic who, having made the world, now sits back and watches it go without involving himself in it in any way, was well-established, and thus God was in effect being barred from his world. At the end of the eighteenth century Immanuel Kant, the most influential philosopher for the next hundred years, silenced God by denying all possibility of God communicating with us in words. Inevitably, therefore, with no word from God to check man's thoughts by, nineteenth-century thinkers equated God with their own feelings and fancies about God, thus in effect absorbing him into themselves in a way that prompted the atheist Feuerbach to comment that when men talked of God they were really talking about themselves in a loud and solemn voice. It was this God, God-in-the-mind as we may call him, whom Nietzsche pronounced dead, and whom Marxists, Darwinists, and Freudians decided in due course that they could get on better without.

With that history behind us, it is no wonder that concepts of God current today display a drastic diminishing of Reformation faith. Outside conservative Christendom, the man in the street thinks of God in one of two ways. The first concept is of a God who is personal but limited in power, so that he cannot always do what he wants to do or prevent what he would like to prevent. He is prepared to overlook the sins of people who are not in the social sense vicious; he makes no claims, is infinitely kind and tolerant and behaves like Father Christmas, seeking to show benevolence and practice beneficence toward everybody. Process theology draws the profile of this finite, well-meaning, struggling, unipersonal deity. The second concept is of God as an immanent cosmic principle rather than a sovereign person, an animating and energizing aspect of the universe rather than its Maker and its Lord. The latest expression of this concept is found in the New Age movement, in the teaching of people like Shirley MacLaine. It has much in common with the monism of Hindu philosophy, which is known to be one of the main sources of New Age thought.

Neither concept corresponds at all closely to the God of Scripture; a very different theological grid is needed for that.

The God in whom biblical Christians believe is not a product of human speculation and guesswork, but a self-announcing, self-defining deity who takes the initiative to tell mankind who and what he is. The Bible, which from one standpoint is the interpretative record of God's self-revelation in history, is from another standpoint revelation in its own right, the word of God testifying to himself in the words of men; and in the Bible God shows us four fundamental facts about himself, which we may conveniently alliterate in order to make them memorable.

First, God is *plural.* He is essentially tripersonal, one in three; he is they, a society, Father, Son, and Holy Spirit united in a oneness of being that finds expression in an eternal fellowship of love. Jesus, the incarnate Son, reveals by his words and life a relationship between himself and the Father, between the Father and the Spirit, and between the Spirit and himself, in which each seeks honour and glory for the other (see especially John 14–16): this is the true nature of love, and the ultimate, eternal truth about God's being. God, self-named as Yahweh in the Old Testament, is one in the sense of being the only creator, the only Lord, the only guide of history, the only source of hope for the future; but he is, and always was, triune, though this fact was not revealed until Jesus made it known. Fact it was, however, and it is properly read back into the Old Testament, as indeed the New Testament writers actually do.

The answer given, therefore, to the question *who and what is God?* must be trinitarian. The world's religions and philosophies are ignorant of the Trinity; it is known only to those who know about the One who made demands on his disciples that only God has a right to make, who called himself the Son and prayed to One whom he called Father, and who promised, when he left this world, to send One whom he called the Holy Spirit in order to secure a continuance of his presence with his disciples and his ministry to them. The rationalistic and relativized Protestant theology that calls itself liberal has been characteristically unipersonal in its view of God, and has often represented the Trinity as no more than a way of saying that through the God-filled man Jesus we experience God as above us, beside us, and within us; but there is more to it than that. The Father above us, the Son beside us, and the Spirit within us are not one person playing three roles (as if God were like the late Peter Sellers, who could play three roles in the same film!), but one God whose nature it is to be three persons in the fullest sense of that word.

Second, God is *powerful.* Scripture answers the question, *how does God exist?* by pointing to the reality of a self-sustaining, self-determining, infinite life that has neither beginning nor end. The mystery of God's *aseity* (derivation of life and energy from himself unendingly) is central to the biblical revelation. All created things are limited one way and another, and sooner or later run out of steam, or decay, but not God! He is like the burning bush, constantly using energy yet remaining just as energetic and potent as before.

Created things only continue to exist as he, their creator, actively upholds them in being, but we do not sustain God; God sustains himself.

So Paul, explaining basic theism to the polytheistic Athenians in Acts 17, takes pains to state that God draws life from himself and does not need anything we can give him to keep him going. He gives us life and health and everything that we have; we can give him nothing save our worship. He is not limited by time or space or any power, agency, or dimension found in the world that he made. He is omnipotent, omniscient, and omnipresent. He is Spirit (that is, personal power and energy, unrestricted). He has life in himself; he is the living God. We cannot direct him, control him, or thwart him. He is the sovereign God, the Lord who reigns, God on the throne.

Third, God is *perfect,* in the moral sense of that word. Scripture answers the question, *how does God behave?* by saying, in effect: *gloriously,* from every point of view. Observe the revelation of God's *name* (i.e., his nature and character) in Exodus (it is one of the book's main themes). At the burning bush, the first level of meaning in the name Yahweh is blocked in: it means that God is self-sustaining and self-determining, and makes sovereign covenant commitments (Exod. 3:13–15). Then, after the episode of the golden calf, when Moses, having interceded successfully for the people, says very boldly, 'Now show me your glory' (33:18), God allows Moses to see what he mysteriously calls his back and passes before him, proclaiming: 'Yahweh, Yahweh, the compassionate and gracious God, slow to anger, abounding in love and faithfulness, maintaining love to thousands, and forgiving iniquity, rebellion and sin. Yet he does not leave the guilty unpunished;

he punishes the children and their children for the sin of the fathers to the third and fourth generation' (34:6f.). Here is God declaring his moral glory, his goodness, love, mercy, grace, faithfulness and trustworthiness, patience, forbearance, and readiness to pardon the penitent, alongside his holiness and purity and righteousness, which express themselves in awesome retributive judgement on the impenitent.[6] This is moral majesty, the perfection of a God committed in covenant love, and whose 'name is Jealous' (34:14)—that is, who, like any lover, presses an exclusive claim on the affection and loyalty of the people he loves and blesses. This is the second level of meaning in the name Yahweh.

Elsewhere, Scripture rounds off its presentation of God as morally perfect by celebrating his wisdom (Rom. 11:33; 16:27; Eph. 3:10, etc.). Wisdom means choosing in each situation the best goal at which to aim and the best means for attaining it; God's wisdom means this, as well as man's. The climactic thought about God's moral perfection in the Bible is that all the qualities mentioned—goodness, wisdom, justice—find supreme expression in the redemption of the world through the cross of our Lord Jesus Christ, where heaven's love, heaven's justice, and heaven's wisdom met together for our salvation. Blood atonement by penal substitution is looked on askance in some quarters, as if it were an embarrassingly barbaric idea; but the truth is that none of God's doings displays his moral perfection as a covenant God so overwhelmingly. And this leads on to the final point.

Fourth, God is *praiseworthy*. His works of creation, providence, and grace have displayed his glory; now it is for mankind to give him glory in response to this demonstration of his glory. 'Glory' in both Testaments is systematically ambiguous, signifying both God's demonstration of his praiseworthiness and man's responsive offering of the praise that is due. Giving God glory for what we see of his glory will be the life of heaven, and we should be practicing for it here on earth. So Paul, a praising man if ever there was one, breaks out repeatedly into doxology in the course of his theological arguments and admonitions (Rom. 1:25; 9:5; 11:33–36; 16:25–27, etc.). So the book of Revelation pictures heaven as a place of praise (chs. 4; 5; 7; 19:1–10, etc.). And the book of Psalms models glory-giving as the central activity of one's life.

Some have queried the Creator's requirement of worship as if it were dishonourably self-centred. Should a human being make such a requirement, it would be dishonourable and vicious—that we grant. But the Creator is not a human being, and his requirement of us that we focus on him, honour and love him, and show our appreciation of his love for us by praise and adoration is ennobling to our nature; it is entirely appropriate in a love relationship (yes, the Christian life is meant to be a love affair); and God has so made us that glorifying him is the way of supreme fulfilment for our humanness. When we discover by experience that giving glory and worship to our lover-God brings supreme joy, delight, happiness, and inner contentment, our doubts and hesitations about the divine demand for glory-giving melt away.

Here, then, are the central truths about God that the post-Christian paradigms—the God who is Father Christmas, and the God who is Shirley MacLaine—lose sight of. Our task is to detect and dispel these degenerate and unworthy notions, challenging them wherever they are found, in the churches as well as outside them, and reintroducing those who have been embracing these ideas to the God who is plural, powerful, perfect, and praiseworthy in ways that at present they have not begun to conceive. The new paradigm needs correction by the old one; in this case, at any rate, the old is indeed better.

III

With regard, now, to *man*, what we face in the modern world is less a coherent paradigm than an incoherent pose, a grandiose self-image produced by wishful thinking that we find impossible to sustain consistently. For the past two centuries, egged on by the Enlightenment, Western man has been playing the role of Wizard of Oz. We have set up for ourselves a magnificent facade of technological competence and mastery, power and glory, and our official claim, if I may put it that way, is that man is the measure of all things and the monarch of all he surveys. Behind that facade, however, over the same two centuries Western man has increasingly found himself unable to avoid feeling that real life is desperately dreadful. Our optimistic triumphalism masks deep pessimism and anxious fear, and we oscillate constantly between the two moods.

Politicians, journalists, and media people labour to maintain in us the feeling that our society is going somewhere good and that they themselves are helping to lead us there. But writers and artists, who mirror the sensitivities of the culture around them, have long been saying, and with increasing vehemence, that man is not so much the master as the maniac, and that his madness is making for unutterable misery. Dostoevsky and Camus among writers, and Francis Bacon among painters, come to mind as exponents of this theme, who inexorably map modern nihilism and pinpoint the guilt, anxiety, loneliness, and disgust that it engenders. Publicly, we continue as optimists, talking as if Utopia is just round the corner; privately, we have become pessimists, feeling more and more with Thomas Hobbes that human life is nasty and with the early Eliot that as individuals we are bankrupt and empty. In our moments of truth we see ourselves as pathetic little persons lurking, Wizard of Oz style, behind our facade of fantastic technology, knowing that our supposed magic is a sham. There is an inward failure of hope, of vision, and of nerve. We feel lost—as in truth we are.

What must be said to correct this post-Christian, split-minded perception of ourselves, with its unattainable purpose of re-erecting the broken-down Enlightenment paradigm of man the master? Three things.

First, the human individual's true *dignity* derives from being made as God's image, steward, and partner (Gen. 1:26–28). Exegetically, the basic understanding of God's image in man is to be drawn from Genesis 1:1–25, where God appears as rational, forming and fulfilling purposes; as creative, calling into being what previously did not exist; as managerial, establishing and maintaining order in place of chaos; and as a value-producer, whose achievements are 'very good.' Add to these qualities God's capacity for personal relationships and the moral perfection of his dealings—facets of the divine life already apparent by the end of Genesis 3—and you have the fullness of the image that man was made to express. Older theology in the Thomist tradition construed the statement that God made man in his own image statically, as if the image consisted in abstract rationality and conscious selfhood as such. But the statement should in fact be understood dynamically, as telling us that God made man upright (Eccl. 7:29), so that he images God more or less according to how far he uses his natural endowments for obedience, love, and righteousness and how far he does not. It is this perspective that explains how Scripture can affirm both the continuance of the image-relationship after the fall (Gen. 9:6; 1 Cor. 11:7; Jas. 3:9) and its restoration in Christ by new creation (Eph. 4:23; Col. 3:9): our human powers as such do indeed image God to some degree, but God-like righteousness is a dimension of the image too, and here it is a matter of less in our natural fallenness and more through the moral transformation that flows from supernatural saving grace (Matt. 12:33; Eph. 2:10). The call to express God's image in our lives remains, however, the basic and universal human vocation.

A further element in human dignity is that as God is eternal and everlasting, so each human being has been created for eternity, and the choices and commitments made in this life have unending significance, since they determine what sort of experience the eternity that follows our leaving this world will be. This world is a vestibule and rehearsal-room for that which is to come, and our doings here will determine our destiny there. (See Rom. 2:6–10; 2 Cor. 5:10.) The biblical answer to the feeling that life is trivial and meaningless is that through saving knowledge and steady service of God in Christ we may lay hold of unimaginable glory, whereas failure at this point will result in unimaginable loss. The everlastingness of the individual, and the momentousness of present life as determining future life, are the twin themes to which the Puritan phrase 'the greatness of the soul' refers, and this destiny-making significance of the present is an aspect of the dignity of man that we need to hear more about from present-day pulpits than we do.

But now, second, each human individual's life has become a *tragedy*—that is, a story of goodness wasted, potential squandered, and value lost. Each of us has fallen from the image of God, and all that is natural to us now is what Scripture calls sin—egocentricity (always looking after number one), pride (always seeking to be on top, in the know and in control), sensuality, exploitation, indifference to evil, carelessness about truth, and a lifelong quest for whatever forms of self-indulgence appeal to us most. Much of this, in our post-Christian culture, is thought of as admirable and ideal, but it all appears vicious and demeaning when measured by the call and law of God and the example of Jesus. It is in fact ruinous folly, and folly of which we are quite unable by our own resources to shake free, for we are by nature slaves of sin. This, the inescapable bad news with which the gospel starts, must be affirmed against all ideas of the natural goodness and perfectibility of man (which ideas are themselves products of egocentric pride).

And now, third, restoration by grace to life in God's image is the glory and *felicity*—the only true glory, and the only lasting felicity—of sinful human beings. Granted, to the self-seeking eye of the natural man the path of faith, love, and obedience, of repentance, conversion, self-denial, and cross-bearing does not look like either glory or felicity, but the way of life is in truth to die to self in order to live to God. One loses to gain; one gives up in order to receive; one repudiates and negates the life of self-serving in order to experience new life with Christ in Christ, his resurrection life lived out in and through our own living.

This is the baptismal paradigm: dying to live. 'Remember always,' says the classic Anglican Prayer Book, 'that Baptism represents unto us our profession; which is, to follow our Saviour Christ, and to be made like unto him; that as he died and rose again for us, so should we, who are baptized, die from sin, and rise again unto righteousness, continually mortifying all evil desires, and daily increasing in all virtue and godliness of living.'

To fulfil this pattern is a life's task; laying hold of God's salvation, which in itself costs nothing, costs everything. Yet those who take this road are rich beyond all telling, for God himself is their shield and their great reward.

The pride, self-sufficiency, proclaimed independence, and lurking despair of the post-Christian paradigm of human fulfilment must be challenged antithetically by appeal to the baptismal paradigm of humility, self-denial, acknowledged dependence, and happy hope in Christ. Each view of man is a direct negation of the other, and the gospel cannot be grasped where the secular view holds sway.

IV

With regard to religion, little need be added to what has already been said. The secular assumption is that religion should be seen as a hobby; if practiced at all, it will be as a venture in self-fulfilment, a quest for a crutch of transcendent help and support. Presentations of Christianity as a recovery of self-esteem (Schuller) or a discovery of health and wealth (Hagin and Copeland) appear to endorse this. But Scripture conceives religion as the living of a life of God-esteem and self-abasement, and of faith in Jesus Christ that blossoms into a love affair of doxology and devotion, and insists that without such religion life is inescapably maimed. The secular paradigm must be repudiated; the biblical paradigm must be affirmed.

V

Ladling Tabasco sauce into a frying pan is not the way to start preparing a meal, and I do not suggest that orchestrating a paradigm clash in the pulpit is the way to start preparing a sermon. But I do suggest that if Christ's messengers fail to realize how much of the application of sermons an alien mind-set in the audience regarding God, man, and religion will filter out, they will preach much less effectively than they might do.

Further, I suggest that preachers who pander to these secular paradigms and try to fit their message into the frames that the modern mind-set provides cannot but be unfaithful to God at a deep level, and put their labour into a bag with holes. Fragments of truth and wisdom will no doubt get across, but overall the story of their ministry will be one of qualified failure due to the distortions involved in their frame of reference.

So, finally, I do suggest that in preaching and teaching each gospel truth we should regularly call attention to the difference between God's viewpoint about himself and ourselves and the contrasting mind-set of our culture on the same subject. This task can be looked at picturesquely in the manner of the late G. K. Chesterton, out of whose book Thomas Howard and I took a leaf when we titled the last chapter of *Christianity: The True Humanism*[7] 'Upside-Down Is Right Way Up.' Through his journalism, apologetics, poems, novels, and Father Brown stories, Chesterton projected a consistent vision of the human race as intellectually inverted through sin, so that mankind now naturally lives and thinks upside-down in relation to the truth that should lead and guide us. It is commonplace to say that the gospel message, and the Christ who comes to us in and through that message, turns us upside-down in relation to what we were before. What is not so common is to see with Chesterton that to turn upside-down those who are inverted already is to set them right way up, and so in a real sense restore them from craziness to sanity.[8] But that is in fact what the authentic message of Christ will do when set within the authentic paradigms of biblical faith. The pastoral and evangelistic preaching of Evangelicals, I believe, desperately needs this emphasis on the proper paradigms in these confused and confusing days, and that is why I have spoken about it so strongly and at such length.

CHAPTER 21

The Preacher as Theologian: Preaching and Systematic Theology

It is widely imagined that one can fulfil the preacher's role without being a theologian. This thought is of a piece with the idea that one can fulfil the theologian's role without being a preacher. I should like to assault both notions together, for both are perverse; but you cannot kick with two feet simultaneously, and in any case the title to which I have been asked to write limits me to countering the first. So here I aim simply to show how needful it is for a preacher to be a theologian. To this end I shall reflect first on the nature of theology, second on the nature of preaching, and third on the vital value of theological awareness and competence for the performing of the preacher's task.

Theology

At the start of each academic year at Regent College all professors are asked to strut a few minutes of their stuff for the orientation of incoming students. I regularly begin my bit of the programme by declaring myself to be a servant of the Queen—that is, of theology, the true queen of the sciences; and then I give a sort of Identikit profile of the lady who commands my allegiance. I refer to her *sight*, explaining that she has to wear glasses, since she can see nothing clearly till she looks at it through the lens of Holy Scripture. I speak of her *shape*, indicating that she has a graceful—that is, a grace-full—figure, which she works to keep by devotional and doxological habits of God-centred thinking. And I say that she is *sassy*—which is American for *saucy*, and signifies a perkiness that Americans admire (not as it was in the England of Dick Lucas's and my youth, where *sauce* meant *cheek*, and 'None of your sauce!' was an ultimate put-down). I define the sassiness of theology as an unwillingness to keep quiet when God is misrepresented and revealed truth is put in jeopardy. Then I urge that these character qualities should appear in all the Queen's servants, particularly those who plan to preach.

Pursuing the picture, we may truly say that though the Queen is not always properly clad in public, when she is, she is most impressive. Truth, wisdom, devotion, breadth, clarity, and practicality are then the leading motifs of her ensemble, and the ensemble itself consists of ten linked disciplines. The first is *exegesis*, for which the question always is: what was this or that biblical text written to convey to its readers?[1] The second is *biblical theology* for which the question is: what is the total message of the canonical books on this or that subject? The third is *historical theology*, the bonding glue of church history, exploring how Christians in the past viewed specific biblical truths. The fourth is *systematic theology*, which rethinks biblical theology with the help of historical theology in order to restate the faith, topic by topic and as a whole, in relation to current interests, assumptions, questions, hopes, fears, and uncertainties in today's church and world. The fifth is *apologetics*, which seeks to commend and defend the faith as rational and true in face of current unbelief, misbelief, and puzzlement. The sixth is *ethics*, which systematizes the standards of Christian life and conduct and applies them to particular cases. The seventh is *spiritual theology*, sometimes called devotional or ascetic theology or Christian spirituality, which studies how to understand and maintain sanctifying communion with God. The eighth is *missiology*, which aims to see how God's people should view and tackle their gospel-spreading, church-planting, and welfare-bringing tasks across cultural barriers world-wide. The ninth is *liturgy*, which asks how God is best and most truly worshipped, and how true worship may be achieved in existing churches. The tenth is *practical theology*, embracing pastoral theology, family theology, and political theology as it explores how to further God's work and glory in home, church, and society.

Full-dressed as distinct from half-dressed theology, if I may put it so, will show competence in all these disciplines. Theology is often described as a quadrilateral of biblical, historical, theological, and practical studies, but the ten-discipline analysis is more precise.[2] Theological education latches on to it, and constructs its syllabi accordingly.

The main garment of the Queen's outfit—its eye-catching focus, we may say—is systematic theology, which draws its raw material from the first three disciplines and serves the church by providing resources of digested truth for the last six. It is called *systematic* not because it works by speculative inferences about God, or by scaling him down so as to dissolve away the mystery of his being and render him manageable by our minds (both those procedures would falsify his reality), but because it takes all the truths, visions, valuations, and admonitions with which the Holy Spirit feeds the church through the Scriptures and seeks to think them together in a clear coherent and orderly way. It separates out seven main topical fields—revelation; God; man; Christ; the Holy Spirit; the church; the future[3]—and fills in all that Scripture is found to say about each. In the past this discipline was called *dogmatic theology* and given the task of analysing, crystallizing, and where necessary recasting those biblical truths that the church has committed itself to uphold and teach. The description derives not from dogmatism and rigidity as a personal style among theologians (perish the thought!)

but from *dogma,* a Greek word meaning that which has been decided. *Systematic,* however, seems to me the better label, both because integrated spelling out of revealed truth as such is the goal and because everything taught in the Bible is theology's business, whether or not the church's creeds include it.

Systematic theology moves between, and regularly blends, three styles of thought and speech, each of which needs separate appreciation for the job it does. These are the *kerygmatic,* exploring in comprehensive terms the question 'What is the Bible telling us?'; the *confessional,* exploring in contemporary terms, with all sorts of interactions, the question 'How should the church assert this so as to be heard?'; and the *philosophical,* exploring in logical terms the question 'What is the exact meaning of these biblical and churchly affirmations?' For success in the first mode, listening to the Bible is all-important; for success in the second mode, listening to the world is what matters; for success in the third mode, listening to the technicians of language and communication is what counts. Still pursuing our parable, we could describe these three styles as the three-tone colour scheme of the Queen's dress. We should note that theology's technical terms mostly belong to styles two and three, where their role is to highlight the gems displayed in essentially biblical language by style one.

The fact that systematic theology provides the raw material for disciplines five through to ten as listed above shows clearly enough that systematic theology is to the church's health as diet is to the body's health: health suffers if what is ingested is not right. All aspects of practical Christianity will be weakened if 'systematics' is neglected. Christian history has seen many movements of experience-oriented reaction against theology's supposedly barren intellectualism. These movements have thought they could get on without serious theological study, and have discouraged their adherents from engaging in it. In the short term, while living on theological capital brought in from outside by their founders, they have often channelled spiritual life in an impressive way, but with the passage of time they have again and again lapsed into old errors and forms of imbalance and stuntedness which, for lack of theological resources, they are unable effectively to correct, and which prompt the rest of the church to stand back from them. 'No-one ever tried to break logic but what logic broke him' is a dictum ascribed to A. S. Pringle-Pattison;[4] something similar has to be said about systematic theology.

The above portrayal of the Queen of the sciences is, of course, ideal. In practice systematic theologians often fall short through overlooking or disregarding biblical data, or handling it in terms of some distorting paradigm of understanding or of truth that is abroad in either the church or the world or both. There are only three methods of procedure, fundamentally speaking, in theological work; the one we have surveyed, which I call *Biblicist;* that which appeals to supposedly infallible pronouncements by the church as the ultimate standard, a method which I call *traditionalist;* and the procedure which, having reviewed the deliverances of Scripture and the history of Christian thought by the light of contemporary secular opinions, treats the dictates of the theologian's reason, conscience, or immediate religious awareness as God's truth for that time, a method which I call *subjectivist*. No one can study theology without coming to regard two of those three as radically wrong; but any of them can be adulterated by inconsistent slidings from time to time at the level of method. So, with God's help, self-assessment (in terms of our bit of whimsy, the Queen examining herself in the mirror of Holy Scripture), and self-reformation (the Queen tidying herself as the mirror shows she needs to do) are regularly required of those who, correctly, follow the Biblicist method as best they can. I say 'as best they can' because we should not expect ever in this world to reach a point where the church and the Christian have nothing more to set straight or to take in at convictional level: such perfection is for heaven, and is not given here.

But here and now we all need the best theology we can get. Every time we mention God we become theologians, and the only question is whether we are going to be good ones or bad ones. And this touches both thought and life. Older writers affirmed, and our ten-discipline analysis showed, that theology is a 'theoretico-practical' study—'the science of living blessedly for ever,' as William Perkins, the Puritan, breathtakingly defined it.[5] As a critical and analytical exploration of the evidence of revelation about reality (God, and life under God), and as a developed intellectual organism interpreting and prescribing for the human condition according to its own insight into reality, theology may well be called a science, with a life enriched by God as its end product. It moves to that end product in two stages.

First, it leads to a deeper understanding of the Bible, by giving us an ordered overview of what is demonstrably in the Bible and so telling us what to look for in the Bible. When my wife and I walk in the country, she sees far more than I do, not because her eyes work better than mine, but because she is a naturalist who recognizes birds, trees, plants, little animals, and much more when she sees them. I, by contrast, see without understanding—without observing, as Sherlock Holmes expressed it in his criticism of Dr. Watson. To be sure, the boot is on the other foot when we inspect old-fashioned steam railway locomotives: all my wife knows is that they are water-boilers on wheels, self-propelled; but I, who once hoped to be an engine-driver, know more about them than that, and consequently see more of what I am looking at than she does. The point is that prior theoretical knowledge enables you to observe more of what is there. In Bible study, the theologically unaware are likely to overlook the significance of what they read; which is why Calvin tailored the second and subsequent editions of his *Institutes* as a preparation for exploring the Scriptures themselves.[6] In this he may have shown more wisdom than do some of the theorists of what is called nowadays 'inductive Bible study,' who tell you to 'observe' without giving you any theological orientation to help you do it.

Since the Reformation the cardinal principle of biblical interpretation among Protestants has been *Sacra Scriptura sui ipsuis interpres*—the Holy Scripture is its own interpreter, interpreting itself. The assumption is that proper interpretation will bring out a rational coherence and consistency that are already there in the text, since it all comes from a single divine mind, and God the Holy Spirit can be trusted not to have contradicted himself in masterminding the writing of the sixty-six books. The assumption is valid and the method is right, but we shall still get along far faster if we have available a catechetical-level theology, that is, a crystallized and digested overview of biblical teaching as a whole, with the main emphases brought out, that will help us to see what we are looking at in each biblical passage. Especially is this so with regard to biblical statements about God, where each noun, adjective, and verb that is used of God—that is, that God, the primary author of the text, uses of himself—bears a sense that at points differs from its sense when used of humans. The appropriate adjustment for us to make in each case is to drop the associations of finitude and moral limitation that all words used of humans naturally carry, and replace them with notions of the infinite self-existence and moral glory that some texts ascribe to God explicitly. Inductive Bible study would doubtless make one aware of the need for this adjustment as one kept comparing Scripture with Scripture over the years, but to have theology make it explicit and drill one in it from the start advances one's understanding more quickly. From this standpoint, to speak of theology as the science of Bible study is both true and illuminating.

Second, theology teaches us how to apply revealed truth for the leading of our lives; thus theology guides our steps, grants us vision, and fuels our worship, while at the same time disinfecting our minds from the inadequate, distorted, and corrupt ideas of God and godliness that come naturally to our fallen intellect. These ideas, if not correct, will mislead us and hold us back, and perhaps totally derail us, in our Christian practice, and will certainly be a stumbling-block to those whom we seek to help. Before you can become a physician or a garage mechanic you need a thorough theoretical grounding, in the one case in physiology and pathology, in the other in the mechanisms and maintenance of cars, and without it you would inevitably do damage, perhaps a great deal of damage. Similarly we need a proper theoretical grounding in the life of faith and obedience before we can either live that life consistently ourselves or help anyone else to do so. Guided by theology, however, we may start to experience 'living blessedly for ever' in peace, hope, joy, and love Godward, and be able to help others into that same supernaturalized existence.

These enrichments to which theology leads are crucial for all Christians, but particularly for preachers, as we shall see.

Preaching

A theological account of theology, formally viewed, is now before us. In this section a similar account of preaching will be set beside it.

What is preaching? Sociologically and institutionally, preaching has to be defined in terms of pulpits and pews, meetings and programmes and corporate expectations fulfilled more or less by the monologue of a stated leader. Our biblical and theological approach, however, leads to a definition in terms of divine purpose rather than human performance. This definition comes out thus: preaching is incarnational communication from God, prophetic persuasive and power-ful—that is, power-full. Let me explain.

First, preaching is *communication*. God, our Maker and Redeemer, is constantly speaking his word to the human race, and within it particularly to his own believing people. That word is his message of grace to sinners, which he spoke definitively in and through the Christ-centred revelatory and redemptive process that the Bible records, and now speaks definitively in and through the biblical record itself. God makes himself known by telling us specific things about himself and about ourselves in relation to him, and thus he invites and draws us into repentance, faith, love, and new life in restored friendly fellowship with himself. The text of the Bible, which from this standpoint may properly be described as God preaching to us, is the primary form of this communication, and the messages of preachers who faithfully relay the elements of God's total message constitute its derivative form. Jesus Christ, the Son of God incarnate, crucified, risen, ascended, reigning, and returning, is the focal centre of God's communication; the new-covenant relationship between God and ourselves through Christ is its immediate announced objective; and the sanctifying of all life under Christ to the glory of God and the blessing of mankind is its ultimate goal. Preachers are only preachers, that is, messengers of God, so far as they understand these things, keep them in sight, and make them the staple substance of their own messages. Pulpiteers who deliver anything different or anything less are failing to communicate God's message, and that means they are not preachers in the theological sense of that word.

Second, preaching is *prophetic* communication. The prophets of Bible times functioned as God's spokesmen and sounding-boards. They passed on oracular and visionary messages, admonitory, hortatory, and revelatory, which God had given them; they were not sources, but channels. The Christian preacher must function in the same way. To be sure, he will do it in a didactic mode, like the apostles, who spoke as God-taught teachers, rather than in the proclamatory mode of the prophets, whose ministry of instruction was limited to faithfulness as God's messenger-boys whom he could trust to deliver his oracles word for word. But in making it his business to confront people not with his own ideas as such, but with the contents of the Word of God, the Christian preacher will show himself to stand in the prophetic succession. The words of the man who preaches must carry the word of the God who speaks.

It thus appears that all true preaching is biblical interpretation—that is, elu-cidation and application of 'God's Word written.'[7] Preaching means speaking

God's own message in his name, that is, as his representative; and this is possible for us, with our sin-twisted minds, only as we labour faithfully to echo, re-state and re-apply God's once-for-all witness to himself in Holy Scripture. Biblical interpretation means theological exegesis of the text, in relation to the rest of the organism of revealed truth, for the scripturally defined purposes of teaching, reproof, correction, and training in righteousness (cf. 2 Tim. 3:16–17). Such applicatory interpretation chimes in with the nature and purpose of all the canonical books as their human authors conceived them, and is in fact the most faithful and right-minded handling of them that can be imagined. It is worth pausing to illustrate this.

In their character as God's mouthpieces the prophets proclaimed, and then wrote down, messages that were essentially God's appeals to Israel for repentance, righteousness, fidelity, and true worship. Christians' hearts are to be searched by them, just as were the hearts of Old Testament saints and sinners, and true preachers will apply them so.

In their role as Christ's commissioned agents and ambassadors (cf. 2 Cor. 5:20), the apostles wrote letters of exhortation and direction, epistolary sermons, designed to keep Christians on track. God means them to do that job for us today, and true preachers will use them accordingly.

The Old Testament historians, whom the Jews perceptively called the former prophets, told of God's dealings with people and nations in a way that was clearly meant to evoke praise and teach lessons about faith and obedience on the one hand, and unbelief and disobedience on the other. These lessons were meant to mould and shape readers' lives for God, and true preachers today will enforce them to that end.

The Gospels prove on inspection to be not artless memoirs of Jesus (as was once thought) but four careful selections of stories about his sayings, doings, and sufferings, all so arranged and angled that 'the gospel'—the life-changing news of a divine Saviour—will leap out into the thoughtful reader's mind and heart. True preachers will bring this out, and spend their strength to make it happen.

The wisdom books (of which it was well said[8] that the Psalms teach us how to praise, the Proverbs how to live, the Song of Solomon how to love, Job how to endure, and Ecclesiastes how to enjoy) are didactic preaching in substance, and should be expounded accordingly.

So we might go on. When Paul said that 'everything that was written in the past was written to teach us, so that through . . . the encouragement of the Scriptures we might have hope' (Rom. 15:4), his thought was that God meant all the Old Testament books to function in due course as his own preaching to Christians. So the Bible itself must preach, and must be seen and felt to preach, in all our preaching. The Westminster Directory for Public Worship was right to require preachers, when raising a point from a text, to labour to let their hearers see 'how God teaches it from thence'[9]—in other words, to show that it is being read out of the sacred text, not read into it. This is the true prophetic dimension of preaching.[10]

Third, preaching is *persuasive* communication. Persuasion in a good cause expresses both respect for others as rational beings and concern for their welfare, as persons not yet fully abreast of the way of truth and wisdom. Persuasion was how Paul defined his evangelistic ministry ('we try to persuade . . . we implore . . . we urge'; 2 Cor. 5:11, 20; 6:1), and persuasion was how Luke described it (Acts 18:4; 19:8; 28:23). Though the Bible is clear that hearts are changed, and faith and faithfulness generated, only by the new-creating power of God, it is equally clear that persuasion is the means we are meant to use if changed lives are what we want to see. Christian persuasion is a matter of giving reasons, factual and prudential, for embracing the belief and behaviour that constitute discipleship to Jesus Christ, and then of pressing God's commands, promises, warnings, and assurances, with a view to winning one's hearer or hearers (or, if it is being done by writing, one's readers) to a positive response. Preaching is not bludgeoning and browbeating, but persuading. This is its only proper style, the path of patent and patient love.

Fourth, preaching is *power-full* communication. The reference here is not to loud shouting, pulpit-beating for emphasis, or any other display of animal energy but to the way God is pleased to link the ministry of the Holy Spirit with the ministry of the Word, so that the preached message pierces hearers' hearts. Paul speaks of this when he says that at Corinth, where people expected him as a travelling pundit to show off his learning, and where he had resolved to stick to 'the testimony about God . . . Jesus Christ and him crucified,' 'my message and my preaching were not with wise and persuasive words [he is being ironic and means "frivolously captivating"; he is not contradicting 2 Corinthians 5:11!], but with a demonstration of the Spirit's power, so that your faith might not rest on men's wisdom, but on God's power' (1 Cor. 2:1–5). The assumption reflected here is that, other things being equal, the Holy Spirit will give the preacher a gift of understanding and utterance that will cause the word spoken to make a spiritual impact and bring forth spiritual fruits. In experience, other things are not always equal. The preacher's message, heart, life, and approach to the particular preaching situation may be insufficiently Christ-centred and bad in a number of ways. He may fail to be clear or to commend himself credibly as a serious and humble servant of Jesus Christ. He may have grown proudly self-reliant, and neglected to pray for his preaching. If he comes across as a mechanical formalist whose heart is not in his communicating, or as a self-absorbed, manipulative, and untrustworthy person, or as a play-actor indulging in unreality with his pulpit dramatics and rhetoric, no spiritual impact is likely. Factors in the hearers as well as in the speaker may also quench the Spirit. But where the Spirit is unquenched the power of God will be present to work with and through the Word, and an impact will be made for God.

Fifth, preaching is *incarnational* communication. Phillips Brooks indicated this when he declared that preaching is truth through personality, though 'personhood,' I think, would express his thought more precisely. The point is that the preacher is inescapably part of the message. He must model by his demeanour both the authority of the truths he is communicating and the response to them that he seeks to evoke. There is no substitute for this: spiritual reality in the sense defined is a 'must.' Preachers should seek it, but only their hearers will know if they have found it. Without it, however, preaching in the theological sense does not occur, and so the speaker's post-sermon question 'Did I *preach?*' becomes a necessary inquiry.

Preacher and Theologian

Having seen, at least in formal theological outline, what theology and preaching essentially are, we can now develop the point toward which we have been driving from the start, namely that a preacher needs to be a theologian of some competence in order to do his job.

I make here a number of assumptions. The first is that the preacher is a congregational leader, recognized as such, to whom people look as an embodiment of true Christianity, and whose preaching is heard as setting standards for himself and his hearers alike. The second is that his role makes him the principal agent in the theological and spiritual formation of those to whom he regularly preaches, and that he is answerable to God for the strategy of teaching and application that he pursues as a means to that end. The third is that teaching with application—preaching, that is—in a worship context is the main means of a congregation's spiritual formation, whatever other occasions and modes of instruction may be programmed into its life. The fourth is that the anti-intellectual thrust of pietisms in the church and relativisms in the world has left late-twentieth-century congregations, and the Christians who make them up, much less concerned about doctrinal truth than they need to be, so that a conscience about and an appetite for learning the Word of God has to be created. The fifth is that all members of all modern Western congregations are constantly confronted by deviant opinions and value systems, such as the anti-Christianity of Jehovah's Witnesses, Mormons, and the New Age, the out-of-shape Christianity of Roman Catholicism, the watered-down, indeed washed-out Christianity of Protestant liberalism, and the post-Christian hedonism, materialism, and cynicism projected by the media, the movies, and the books, plays, newspapers, magazines, schools, universities, and politicians that combine to become opinion-makers for tomorrow; and Christians have to be taught how to resist the brainwashing impact of these aberrations. The present-day preacher faces a formidable task of adult Christian education, and must plan his pulpit strategy in a way that will teach discrimination in face of deviation and fortitude in holding fast to truth. It will not suffice, in an age like ours, for sermons to be isolated utterances, however noble each might be; they need to form a syllabus, covering the whole water front of challenges to revealed truth as well as the full landscape of the truth itself. Whether the sermons are announced in syllabus terms is not important; what matters is that the preacher should be facing up to his instructional and formational responsibility, and preaching according to his own thought-out strategy for discharging it.

My submission is that he cannot hope to meet this requirement completely unless he knows his way around in the fields of systematic theology, apologetics, ethics, and spiritual life. He needs to be well versed in the implications of a God-centred view of this created world and life within it. He needs to be deeply knowledgeable about the damage done to mankind's thought-life and moral nature by sin, the anti-God allergy in our fallen make-up that controls our pre-regenerate existence. He needs a thorough understanding of God's plan of salvation through Jesus Christ the mediator and of the regenerating work of the Holy Spirit in its intellectual, volitional, emotional, and transformational aspects. He needs to be especially clear on what is involved in the authentic Christian life of faith, repentance, hope, love, self-denial, humility, dependence, and pleasing and worshipping and glorifying God; the life of faithful perseverance under pressure and of sustained spiritual warfare against the world, the flesh, and the devil; the life of prayer to, and fellowship with, the Father and the Son; the life of sanctification and service, adoration and assurance, through the inward ministry of the Holy Spirit. He must know, and be able to show, what is involved, not only at the centre but also at the edges, in maintaining biblical standards, attitudes, and lifestyle distinctives in a world of competing religions and ideologies on the one hand and rampant irreligion and demoralization on the other. Amid all the cross-currents of our tempest-tossed culture he must be able to communicate in and through his expositions—that is, to let the Bible communicate through him—a sustained vision of consistent, triumphant, God-fearing, and God-honouring Christian life. I venture to affirm that if he is not something of a theologian, permanently apprenticed to the ten disciplines listed earlier because he sees them as fundamental to the pastoral life, the task will prove to be far beyond him.

For, in the first place, only theology as described will secure for our preaching *adequacy of coverage*. All we who preach have our favourite themes on which we like to harp, and our areas of chronic neglect where, because our interest is less, we are tempted to leave the necessary thinking and teaching to somebody else. But the pastoral preacher's mandate, like Paul's, is 'to proclaim . . . the whole will [counsel, plan, purpose, intention, requirement] of God' (Acts 20:27). The substance and thrust of our sermons must come not only from personal vision and excitement about an old warhorse theme or a recent enthusiasm, plus our general sense of what might do some people some good, but from our focused knowledge of the range of revealed truth as well. We must know what are the fundamentals, the trunk and main branches of the Christian tree—the sovereignty of God in creation, providence, and grace; the trinitarian specifics of the Apostles' Creed; justification by faith alone through Christ's substitutionary atonement; salvation by grace alone through the regenerating work of the Holy Spirit; the centrality of the church in the Father's purposes; the coming return of Christ in judgement, and the certainty that heaven's glory or hell's misery will be everyone's final destiny. These fundamentals must be faithfully and thoroughly taught, just as the basic principles of our spiritual life at home, in the church, and in the world must be. Countering mistaken notions as one goes along, and showing that Christianity is a faith that has reason on its side, are further elements in the preacher's task; how much of this is done on each occasion will depend on the text and the preacher's judgement of what the congregation needs, but though incidental it is very much part of the agenda. I should state explicitly that in saying these things I have in view not topical theological lectures in the pulpit—that, to my mind, could never be right—but rather biblical expository sermons, appropriately angled. Unless our preparation for regular preaching includes regular theological study, however, the above specifications are unlikely to be met. We who preach might well examine ourselves on this point before going further with the argument.

In the second place, only theology as described will secure *accuracy of exposition*. The story of the unskilled preacher who took the text, 'How shall we escape if we neglect such a great salvation?' (Heb. 2:3), and announced that his headings would be (1) the greatness of the salvation and (2) hints for escaping if we neglect it, has a warning for us here.

Exposition must be accurate. Because the preacher shows what the text means for us today, and does not stop short at what it meant for its first readers, he rather than the academic commentator is the true interpreter of the Bible. But we reach the present-day meaning via the historical meaning, and while inductive exegesis of the text in its context is the finally authoritative method for achieving this, systematic theology, which is a digest of the findings of generations of Bible students, will constantly point us in the right direction. Donald Macleod thus comments on the description of Jesus Christ, God's Son, only as 'the first-born of all creation' (Col. 1:15 NRSV): 'All that the church learned in the Arian controversy forbids us to tolerate any exegesis that compromises either the pre-existence or the deity (creator-hood) of the Saviour,'[11] and he is right. To be sure, the references in the letter itself to all the fullness of God being in Christ (1:19; 2:9) confirm the wrongness of the Arian exegesis, which made the Son the first and noblest of the creatures, called 'Son' only as an honorific courtesy title; but guidance in this matter from seventeen centuries of text-tested theology is not to be sneezed at.

Macleod gives a further example:

... the notorious crux, Hebrews 6:4ff.: 'For it is impossible for those who were once enlightened and have tasted the heavenly gift and been made partakers of the Holy Spirit and have tasted the good word of God and the powers of the age to come, if they fall away, to renew them to repentance.' *Prima facie* this passage suggests that true believers can commit apostasy. Dogmatics alerts us, however, to the fact that such an interpretation is untenable, and closer examination of the passage itself confirms that it is pointing in the direction of another doctrine altogether—the doctrine of temporary faith.[12]

So we might go on, if there was need. As a guide in, and a check on, exegesis, theology can be invaluable.

There are areas of revealed truth that confront us starkly with the incomprehensible mystery of God's being and ways. In these areas the basic biblical conceptions are not always easy to hold on to, and it is easy to mishandle texts that embody them. If, for instance, we lack a biblical understanding of the Trinity, one that avoids tritheism on the one hand and Sabellianism (God is one person playing three parts in one story, like the late Peter Sellers) on the other, we are not likely to be accurate in our handling of texts that speak of God's plan of salvation, the team job in which Father, Son, and Holy Spirit work together to bring sinners to glory; nor are we likely to deal accurately with texts on the transactional reality of the atonement, the Son offering himself to the Father through the Spirit to bear the penalty due to us for our sins.

Or if we lack a biblical understanding of God's upholding of us as free and responsible decision-makers while overruling all our thoughts and actions according to his own will as to what shall be, we are not likely to deal accurately with texts about our life in Christ, where self-reliant activism is ruled out and God-dependent activity is to be the pattern, where the faith we exercise is the gift of God, where the indwelling Spirit energizes moral effort, and where we live and obey in awe and reverence, knowing that it is God who works in us to make us will and act as he wants us to do.

These are sample spheres of reality in which we need the help of theology to achieve exposition that is accurate and precise.

In the third place, only theology as described will secure *adequacy of application* when we preach. Theology offers a ready-made grid for making applications, and this is help that we need, for the theory of application is not on the whole well understood. The rhetoric, style, and technique of application will of course vary from preacher to preacher, but the activity of application as such has an unvarying logic, which we can state thus: if this principle is truth from God, what difference should it make to our thinking, our resolves, our emotional attitudes, our motivation, and our view of our own spiritual state at this moment? More fully: if this principle is truth that God teaches and guarantees, then the following questions arise:

1. What particular judgements, and ways of thinking, does it require of us, and what habits of mind and particular opinions does it forbid us to entertain,

and charge us to change if they are part of our life at present? (This is application to the mind.)

2. What particular actions, and what types of virtuous behaviour, does it require of us, and what vicious acts and habits does it forbid, and tell us to renounce herewith? (This is application to the will.)

3. What does it teach us to love, desire, hope for, insist on, and rejoice in, and what does it direct us to hate, abhor, fear, shrink from, and be sad at? (This is application to those emotionally freighted dispositional attitudes that the Puritans called 'affections.')[13]

4. What encouragements are there here to embrace righteousness, or a particular aspect of righteousness, and persevere in it, and what discouragements are there here to dissuade us from lapsing into sinful habits and actions? (This is application at the level of motivation.)

5. How do we measure up to the requirements of this truth at this moment? And what are we going to do about our present shortcomings here, as self-scrutiny reveals them? And what conformity to the truth's requirements do we find in ourselves, for which we ought to thank God? And how do we propose to maintain and increase that conformity? (This is application for self-knowledge and self-assessment, as a step toward salutary adjustments of our life.)[14]

Clearly, not all the possible applications of each truth to all the different sorts of people one thinks one is preaching to (formalists, seekers, the self-righteous, the self-despairing, young Christians, veteran Christians, struggling Christians, and so on) can be made in every sermon, or it would never end! But the Puritans, the all-time specialists in application, gave something like half their preaching time to this task, and when one is preparing an expository sermon that is a good rule of thumb.

Comparison with the Puritans, the pioneer Evangelicals, and expositors like J. C. Ryle and Arthur Pink will soon convince us that the applicatory aspect of pastoral preaching today is underdeveloped. One reason for this is that in an age like ours, in which the Scriptures are not well known or well respected, we are preoccupied with communicating biblical content and vindicating its divine authority, so that searching applications get crowded out. But a deeper reason is that, lacking a full-scale biblical and theological understanding of the Christian life—a systematic spirituality as we might call it—we simply do not see what applications need to be made. Yet application is crucially important, partly because without it the preached Word will not humble and change people, and partly because it is in the process of application, as the Word is brought home to search the heart, that the sense of its divine authority becomes strongest, and the habit of submitting to it is most thoroughly formed. So the Westminster Directory was right to declare that the preacher

> is not to rest in general doctrine . . . but to bring it home to special use, by application to his hearers: which albeit it prove a work of great difficulty to himself, requiring much prudence, zeal, and meditation, and to the natural and corrupt man will be

very unpleasant; yet he is to endeavour to perform it in such a manner, that his auditors may feel the word of God to be quick and powerful, and a discerner of the thoughts and intents of the heart.[15]

And we who preach today will do well to follow the Puritan lead at this point.

Conclusion

The thrust of this essay can be summed up thus: theology helps the preacher as the coach helps the tennis player, grooming and extending his performance by introducing him to the range of strokes that can be made and drilling him in the art of making them correctly. As the coach is the embodiment of decades of experience in playing tennis, so theology is the embodiment of centuries of study, debate, and interpretative interaction as the church has sought to understand the Scriptures. One can play tennis after a fashion without ever having been coached, and one can preach from the Bible after a fashion without ever having encountered serious theology in a serious way. But, just as one is likely to play better with coaching, so one is likely to preach better—more perceptively, more searchingly, more fruitfully—when helped by theology; and so the preacher who is theologically competent will, other things being equal, be more use to the church. That, in a nutshell, is what I had to say.

CHAPTER 22

Preaching as Biblical Interpretation

This essay seeks to explore the thesis that, the Bible being what it is, all true interpretation of it must take the form of preaching. With this goes an equally important converse: that, preaching being what it is, all true preaching must take the form of biblical interpretation. The basis for the former thesis is that Scripture is the God-given record, explanation, and application of God's once-for-all redemptive words and deeds on the stage of space-time history, and that its intended function is to 'instruct . . . for salvation through faith in Christ Jesus.'[1] To give this instruction is precisely, in the biblical sense of the word, to preach. The basis for the latter thesis is that preaching means speaking God's own message in his name, that is, as his representative, and this is possible for fallen men, with their sin-twisted minds, only as they labour faithfully to echo, restate, and reapply God's once-for-all witness to himself, which, as we said, is the sum and substance of Holy Scripture.

Current debate about the veracity of particular biblical statements tends to lose sight of the fact that God in his providence gave us the Bible not to be a sort of encyclopedia catering to curiosity (*Enquire Within Upon Everything*[2]), nor to be a means of increasing historical knowledge for its own sake, but to introduce us to the living, speaking God who made us, and to the crucified, risen, reigning, and returning Christ, man's Redeemer, and in so doing to show us all what we should believe and do and hope for as we travel home to God through this present world. It is because this is so that preaching must be seen as the paradigmatic way of handling the Bible; and no method of studying it, however erudite and formally orthodox, can be approved further than it embodies the preacher's kerygmatic perspective and purpose.

The maxim that exegesis and biblical interpretation are for the sake of an adequate systematic theology is true, yet if one stops there one has told only half the story. The other half, the complementary truth which alone can ward off the baleful misunderstanding that a particular rational orthodoxy is all that matters, is that the main reason for seeking an adequate systematic theology is for the sake of better and more profound biblical interpretation. Calvin's *Institutio* is a classic of systematic theology, yet in the Preface to the second and later editions he described it as a propaedeutic for biblical interpretation;[3] and interpretation means theological exegesis of the text, in relation to the rest of the organism of revealed truth, plus reapplication of what it yields for our illumination and reformation—in other words, for the scripturally-defined purposes of teaching, reproof, correction, and training in righteousness.[4] But this is, precisely, preaching. In always identifying himself as, by calling, a preacher of the Word, Calvin showed that he understood his own logic very well. Those who, like myself, are called to teach systematic theology need often to ponder the same point.

Preaching and the Bible

The basic reason why biblical interpretation must take the form of preaching is that the Bible itself is preaching. What is preaching? Teaching, and more; not just shovelling information into the head, but appealing to the heart, to the whole man; as one declares truths in God's name, he calls on God's behalf for a response of faith, obedience, and worship. Here is the essential difference between sermons, which are acts of preaching, and mere lectures.

The main New Testament words for preaching are *kerusso, kerux* meaning to make a public announcement as a herald (*keru*) does, and *euangelizomai*, meaning to impart the good news, the gospel (*euangelion*). The scope of preaching as an activity is shown in 2 Corinthians 5:20–6:1:

> We are ambassadors for Christ, God making his appeal through us. We beseech you on behalf of Christ, be reconciled to God . . . Working together with him . . . we entreat you not to accept the grace of God [i.e., the message about it] in vain. (RSV)

Such poignant appeal for response, expressing not only the messenger's personal concern for the welfare of his fellow men but also the compassion of the God whose ambassador he is, has always been integral to true preaching.[5]

Preaching appears in the Bible as a relaying of what God has said about himself and his doings, and about men in relation to him, plus a pressing of his commands, promises, warnings, and assurances, with a view to winning the hearer or hearers (or, if it is being done by writing, the readers) to a positive response. So it is a mistake to define preaching institutionally, in terms of buildings, pulpits, pews, and stated services, however true it is that preaching has been institutionalized among us in these terms. But preaching should in the first instance be defined functionally, as an activity of communication, whether by monologue or in dialogue, whether to a group or to one person only (as when Philip 'preached . . . Jesus' to the Ethiopian eunuch,[6] or when Jesus preached to the woman at the well[7]), which has in view the evoking of a positive response to some aspect of God's call to humankind.

If, now, we apply this definition to the Bible itself, we soon perceive that all sixty-six books are, directly or indirectly, preaching. When Paul says that 'whatever was written in former days was written for our instruction, that . . . by the encouragement of the scriptures we might have hope,'[8] his thought is that God's intention in causing the Old Testament books to be set down included their functioning in due course as his own preaching to Christians. So these books are not human preaching only, but God's preaching too. The New Testament writers evidently thought of what they put on paper in the same way. They wrote, not to express their own opinions, but to testify to God and to deliver his message. Indeed, there is no truer or happier way to describe the Scriptures of both Testaments, in their once-for-all God-givenness and present dynamism, than as *God preaching*. Their inspiration, in the sense of divine origin and authenticity as expressions of God's mind, and their instrumentality as God's means of addressing mankind today, are both comprehended in this phrase.

Two things follow. First, since divine-human preaching is its nature, it is only as divine-human preaching that Scripture can be understood, and that is tantamount to saying that it will be understood only through actual preaching of it. It is the special merit of Gustaf Wingren's book, *The Living Word*,[9] to follow Luther in emphasizing this. Only as we hear the biblical message preached and applied to us, and as we preach and apply it ourselves in our private meditations, and as (to adopt a phrase from John Owen) it 'preaches itself in our own souls,'[10] do we come to appreciate what its real burden is. Apart from this, the most we can have is correct notions about the message, but correct notions do not constitute spiritual understanding. It is the work of the Holy Spirit in and through preaching to cause that which is God's Word in itself to be understood and received as God's message to ourselves, and its contents to be apprehended as direct communication to us from heaven. Where there is no such preaching there will be no such understanding, no matter how carefully Scripture is studied and explored from a historical standpoint.

This explains how it is possible for highly motivated students, even in Evangelical seminaries, to find that the effect of their technically disciplined biblical studies is to make Scripture seem more remote and less alive than before; if they are not constantly exposed to applicatory preaching, preaching which constantly discloses to them the character of Scripture as both the content and the means of God's communication with us here and now, this can very easily happen. If it does, however, the fault is not, as obscurantist reaction sometimes urges, in technical Bible study, but in the lack of true preaching within the student's personal milieu.

Second, the Bible must itself preach in our preaching. It is not for us to speak on the Bible's behalf, but to let the Bible speak for itself through us. 'Preach the word,' said Paul;[11] he did not say, preach about the Word. The Westminster Directory for Public Worship rightly required preachers, when raising a point from a text, to labour to let their hearers see 'how God teacheth it from thence'[12]— in other words, to demonstrate that the point is being read out of the text, not read into it. This is the true prophetic element in preaching: as biblical prophets mediated God by relaying his Word as they found it in their hearts, so Christian preachers are to mediate God by relaying his Word as it meets them in their texts.

The Puritans, like many since, spoke of preaching, in echo of Luke 24:32, as 'opening' or 'opening up' the Scriptures, as one opens up a previously locked house or garden. The image is suggestive: through the opened entry you see in and can be led in, and the owner may come out to meet you himself. So with Scripture: as it is 'opened' in preaching, you see glories that are new, and find yourself in fellowship with God. But this can happen only where the preacher's purpose and strategy are to serve the text and let Scripture itself speak.

Preaching the Bible

The preacher's task, as we have said, is biblical interpretation—which means not just historical exegesis, but application too. The Bible is an ancient library; it consists of sixty-six books, written at different times from just under two to rather more than three millennia ago. biblical interpretation is the art of so reading and explaining these old books that they become—or rather, are seen to be, for in themselves they always were—relevant to the modern reader. That is a formal definition; its material counterpart would be, the act of so elucidating these books that God's personally directed message is discerned in them and his presence as he speaks to us is thereby realized.

Schleiermacher and his followers, seeing Scripture as essentially a transcript of religious feeling by the use of appropriate conceptual imagery (a view strikingly parallel to Wordsworth's definition of poetry as emotion recollected in tranquillity), understood the interpretative process empathetically, in terms of readers' 'tuning in' to the feelings expressed. The neo-orthodox, seeing Scripture as essentially a human word of witness which by grace becomes God's means of addressing us, understood the interpretative process dynamically and dialogically, in terms of identifying with and directing to our own situation the outlook of biblical people who, under God's promise and command, humbly listened for his word of judgement and mercy. An adequate view of biblical interpretation will start by asserting what both liberals and neo-orthodox deny, namely, that the sixty-six books are inspired in the sense that God is their ultimate author, so that all their affirmations must be received as God-taught truth; but beyond this it will embrace the positive thrusts of both positions. The profile of such a view may be sketched in as follows:

1. Models

The neo-orthodox insistence that biblical interpretation is first and foremost a matter of learning to listen to the living God, and letting him interpret us through the text, is right. There are two models or analogies whereby we may picture the process.

The first model is the *tutorial*. In a British university, a tutor may meet with a group of students for an hour's instruction in a subject on which one of the group has written an essay. The tutor may ask him to read his essay and then, as an alternative to inviting class discussion, criticise it directly, while the rest of the group listen and learn from the exchange. If the tutor does his job well, they will soon see what he would think of the ideas they might bring to the class, and where those ideas would in fact need amplifying and amending.

Similarly, interpreters of Scripture go to school, as it were, with men of Bible times: Noah, Abraham, David, Peter, the Jews at various periods in their history, the Christians at Corinth, at Thessalonica, at Laodicea, and so on. We overhear God dealing with these people, encouraging, correcting, instructing; thus we learn his thoughts about our thoughts, and his purposes for and ways with our lives. Now God has appointed preaching as a means to enable his church to learn of him in this way.

The second, complementary model is *coaching*. If you have ever been coached in any sport, you know how the coach breaks up the even tenor of playing habits that have come to seem natural, and insists that in order to do it right (a golf swing, or a tennis shot, or whatever) you must learn to do it differently, in a way which at first you find unnatural and difficult. Similarly, as interpreters of Scripture we find ourselves confronted with God the coach, who insists on teaching us how to live, forcing us to break bad habits which seem natural and to learn new ones which at first seem hard. Often the discipline is felt to be irksome, but the profit of accepting it is untold. God has appointed preaching as a means of drawing his people into acceptance of his discipline for their lives.

Current reflection on the interpreting of Scripture stresses the need to take account of cultural differences between the various eras from which the biblical books come, and rightly insists that these differences run very deep. When exponents of the so-called new hermeneutic dwell on the traumatic effect of having biblical 'horizons,' or perspectives, intersect with and challenge our own, those horizons which belong to us as cultural and religious children of our own time, they do well. We are all of us more limited and provincial, culturally speaking, than we ever succeed in realizing, and on this account are in constant danger of mishearing, misconstruing, or simply disregarding biblical instruction; therefore, the insistence of the new hermeneutic that we must self-consciously 'distance' the horizons of our contemporary outlook(s) from those of the biblical outlook(s) before we attempt to 'fuse' them, should be heeded.

We may not domesticate the Bible by slotting it directly into our world and forgetting how far a cry it is from the late twentieth-century West to the biblical period in the Near East; we shall miss a great deal of the Bible's meaning and challenge if we do. Yet, granted all that, there is need to balance this emphasis on the relativities of culture by stressing that some things do not change, even when cultures mutate.

The triune God, to start with, remains the same; so, at bottom, does fallen human nature; so do the law and the gospel; so do repentance, faith, joy, praise, love to God and neighbour, and all the other qualities which make up godliness; so do the demonic dynamics that animate godless society; so do God's covenant relation with his people, and his saving grace in Christ. Our two models assume these and related continuities. The assumption seems a safe one, and we shall not apologise for making it, nor for insisting that preaching which is authentically biblical will certainly embody it.

2. Materials

What is the Bible, this composite of sixty-six books that we are to interpret, really all about? All ventures in interpretation imply some answer to this question, and interpretations vary according to the answer that is assumed. All interpretation reflects our personal interest, or preoccupation, or blinkers (for which Americans say, blinders: put it as you wish). Thus, if ancient history or the history of religions is our interest, our biblical interpretation will focus on that; if our concern is with theological truth, or religious experience, or the ways of the living God, our interpretation will reflect that too. Similarly, if our approach to Christianity is shaped by an uncriticised individualism, we are likely to overlook the Bible's corporate and churchly perspective; if it is shaped by anti-intellectualism in any form, we shall probably miss the Bible's challenge to our minds.

Every theology has its built-in hermeneutic, and every hermeneutic is implicitly a total theology. Theology in the tradition of Luther sees Scripture as essentially law and gospel; theology in the tradition of Calvin reads the Bible as essentially God's declaration of his covenant; theology in the tradition of Schleiermacher views what is written as the verbalizing of a felt affinity with God; theology in the tradition of Barth construes the Bible as witness to the God-man Jesus Christ, who (so Barth held) is the sum and substance of all our knowledge both of God and of ourselves; and so on. Wise interpreters will accept enrichment from all these hermeneutical approaches, and more besides, but their final goal will be to let the Bible, as God's own preaching, speak for itself and shape their interest to itself. And, doing that, they will find that it is *both* a complex proclamation and celebration of God's saving plan and action in Christ *and* a book of life, exhibiting in a multitude of particular cases what human relationships with the living God really involve.

It is *both* a declaring of redemptive revelation *and* a demonstration of believing response to it; *both* an interpretative history of those unique events whereby God has created a people for himself through Jesus Christ *and* a spelling out of the universal relevance of these events for every man in every age; *both* an announcement that the living God has come to us in Christ, *and* a consequent summons to mankind to come through Christ to God, with promises and commands showing how, individually and in our various communal relationships, he is to be served. Thus attentive interpreters will understand the Bible, and thus they will preach it.

3. *Method*

A full-scale discussion of how Scripture can be successfully interpreted would require, on the one hand, a good deal of paradigmatic analysis of what the sixty-six books contain and, on the other, some sustained reflection on the conditions of theological and spiritual understanding—a field in which Luther's dictum that prayer, meditation, and temptation (*oratio, meditatio, tentatio*) make the theologian remains the best starting point.[13] Here, however, we can attempt neither of these things, and must limit ourselves to laying down three procedural principles which are basic conditions of success, in the sense that any violation of them is of itself, immediately and inescapably, a failure in the interpretative task.

(1) Hold to the Literal Meaning.

'Literal' here is defined as the meaning which the human writer, inspired as he was, has actually expressed in the words that he has chosen to use. To call this method 'literal' is to follow sixteenth-century usage, and to echo the Reformers' antithesis against 'allegorical' interpretation, which reads into biblical passages meanings that cannot be read out of them because they were not demonstrably in the author's mind. The 'literal' sense is thus the 'natural,' 'historical' sense, the sense that each author, as a responsible communicator, was concerned to convey, and that the persons to whom each book was first addressed should have gathered from the words he had written. The 'literal' method is thus the 'grammatico-historical' method of Reformation and post-Reformation exegesis, in which linguistic usage, historical background, cultural presuppositions, and conventions of communication in each writer's own day are allowed to be decisive for determining what each document means.

There is, to be sure, a sense in which Old Testament writers constantly express and communicate to Christian readers more than they themselves knew, for Christians read the Old Testament in the light of New Testament knowledge of the fulfilling of types and prophecies, and of the further unfolding of God's plan for world history, through our Lord Jesus Christ; thus realities which were opaque to the prophets[14] are clear to Christians, and Old Testament foreshadowings of them are correspondingly more meaningful to Christians than they could be to their original authors. But such enhanced meanings simply extrapolate from the expressed meaning, in the light of God's unfolded plan, and do not in any way involve the element of arbitrariness and flight from the literal sense which was the vice of medieval allegory.

There is also a sense in which every New Testament writer communicates to Christians today more than he knew he was communicating, simply because Christians can now read his work as part of the completed New Testament canon. Each book by each writer gains new significance in this larger context, where comparisons and cross-references can be made; and each book is constantly found both to supplement, and to be supplemented by, others. But in each case it is, precisely, the literal sense that gains significance, not any other sense. Indeed, there is no other!— for the whole point of the doctrine of inspiration is that thereby man's word and God's Word have become one, so that the human literal sense is in truth God's message, and the way into God's mind is via the human author's expressed meaning.

(2) Hold to the Principle of Harmony.

Inspiration, as was said, is God's work of so determining men's testimony to him that their witness becomes identical with his own instruction to us. The basic theological significance of calling Scripture 'inerrant' is as an avowal of this identity, for if all that the human authors affirm is also affirmed by God, it must follow that whatever they have affirmed is true. It is a pity that the association of 'inerrant' in some minds, and indeed in some circles, with unnatural and invalid exegesis of Scripture discourages some from using the word to make this point, for the point needs making and 'inerrant' makes it neatly. Only assertions of inspiration which entail inerrancy are assertions of that inspiration, that total identity of human and divine witness, of which Scripture speaks.

But if all that the biblical writers affirm should be taken as true, it can never be right to posit a real and substantial contradiction between one biblical statement and another, nor to suppose that where biblical statement and secular information appear to conflict, the Bible may be wrong. We may of course have misunderstood the biblical passages in question (when discrepancies appear, we should check our exegesis and see), but as a matter of intellectual method we should hold fast to the certainty that their genuine meaning, if we can determine it, is true, because they are inspired.

So in all our biblical interpretation we should use the concept of inerrancy as a control, and seek to exhibit the harmony of Scripture both with itself and with secular information whenever questions of consistency arise. We should not be so mesmerized by these questions that we think of nothing else, but equally we should not evade them when they come up. And should it happen that for the present we can find no harmonistic hypothesis that seems sufficiently cogent, we should choose to wait for one to appear, and be willing temporarily not to know the answer, rather than be stampeded into joining those who in one way or another accuse particular biblical passages of theological or empirical falsehood.

(3) Follow Round the Interpretative Spirals.

By 'interpretative spirals,' I mean three particular mental procedures whereby understanding of particular elements in the biblical revelation may be constantly refined and deepened. I speak of 'spirals' because in each case we return to the point from which we set out, but higher up, so to speak, because now we see more of what we are looking at. Anyone who has travelled round the successive loops of an ascending spiral on a railroad (in Switzerland, for instance, or India or New Zealand) will take my meaning. It appears to me that in any preaching ministry in which the Bible is regularly being interpreted to the same congregation, constant travelling upward round these interpretative spirals is of very great importance.

The first upward spiral concerns *the exploration of the Bible from within*.

If you want to take the measure of the mind of a versatile and prolific teacher, such as Karl Barth, or C. S. Lewis, or to get a proper understanding of some period of history, or some major philosophical debate, you will have to read a series of books—books by the teacher, books about the period, books bearing on the problem. These books will often comprise more than one literary form. The more you read, the more deeply you will understand each new item, for your overall acquaintance with the field is becoming more adequate, and both your discernment and your judgement are ripening. But in due course you will need to go back and reread the items you read first, and link them up with your more mature understanding, for at first reading you were only a beginner and so could not help missing much of their significance.

So with our progressive grasp of the contents of Scripture. The Bible is an organism of revealed truth, to which all sixty-six books contribute in various ways. Within this organism are internal links of several kinds—for example, thematic links (e.g., such themes as God, godliness, church, covenant, atonement, salvation, God's kingdom, the Messiah, judgement, prayer); links of parallel subject matter (e.g., Kings and Chronicles, the four Gospels, Ephesians and Colossians); links of typology (e.g., Leviticus and Hebrews) and fulfilled prophecy (e.g., Isaiah and the Gospels); and links of common authorship (e.g., the works of Paul, Luke, Peter, John, and, if one dare say it, Moses). Preaching must constantly explore these links, elucidating the relation of the different ingredients in the Bible to each other, so that our sight of the total biblical landscape may, so to speak, spiral up, becoming progressively more adequate and full.

The second upward spiral concerns *the intersecting of biblical horizons with our own*.

I say 'horizons' rather than 'perspectives' or 'viewpoints' because that word suggests the *limits* of a field of vision, and it is a point about limits that I wish to make. The spiritual horizons of professed Christian people are always more limited than they should be, sometimes scandalously so, and our sense of reality is always more or less defective as a result. Unconsciously we are man-centred, self-centred, self-sufficient, self-confident; we think about our living in ways which magnify man and diminish God; we appear as individualists not concerned enough about community, or as ministers with a social conscience not concerned enough about individuals, or as pietists so heavenly minded as to be of no earthly use, or as pragmatists so materially and managerially minded that our hearts are entirely earthbound. Also, as children of our age (which we all are, however much we wish we weren't and perhaps claim not to be), we have our horizons narrowed by any number of conventional prejudices, assumptions, and insensitivities.

The Bible's point of view must constantly be brought to challenge and correct these limited horizons of our own present vision. Thus, for instance, we shall need again and again to be faced with the double reality of our creation in God's image (which shows us our true dignity and destiny) and our constant moral perversity at the motivational level (which shows us our real wretchedness and disgrace apart from Jesus Christ).

We shall need from time to time to relearn the doctrine of justification by faith, not only as a counter to the paralysis of past guilt but also as God's support for living with the knowledge of present failure. We may need too to learn and relearn its Christ-centred, God-honouring thrust, and to be weaned away by it from the bondage of pious self-observation. Or we may need to be corrected and challenged ethically regarding areas of liberty where we have not behaved responsibly and areas of responsibility where we have hitherto behaved frivolously.

These random examples illustrate the kind of encounter between God's Word and our ways which preaching must constantly aim to bring about. Through such encounters our horizons may be enlarged and refocused, and under such judgements from the Word our understanding will be increased. This is edification. And because the channels in our hearts along which spiritual awareness and conviction flow tend constantly to silt up, the same lessons will need to be preached to us over and over again. Thus our insight under God may grow, as through preaching basic challenges recur, spiralling up in repetitions of the old lessons with ever more searching and far-reaching applications.

The third upward spiral concerns *the growth of self-knowledge through knowledge of God.*

Just about all our wisdom, said Calvin in the famous opening sentence of his *Institutio*, consists in knowing God and knowing ourselves; and the process begins with knowing God.[15] It was when Isaiah in the temple 'saw the Lord' and heard the angels celebrate his holiness that he came to know himself as unclean in God's sight, and to experience God's pardon existentially. The shape of the spiral here is that the more clearly we see God's transcendent power, holiness, and glory, the more clearly we shall be made aware of our weakness, sinfulness, and utter need; our helplessness will drive us back to God in that self-distrust which is basic to faith in him and thereby we shall come to appreciate his glory the more as his mercy touches our needs. It is the task of preaching to ensure that our sense of God's glory should spiral up constantly as the realities of his judgement and mercy touch us in ever deeper and more probing ways.

The Bible Preaching

Preachers whose beliefs about biblical inspiration and inerrancy vacillate can hardly avoid trying from time to time to guard against supposedly unworthy thoughts which the Bible, if believed as it stands, might engender. This presumptuous procedure, at once comic and pathetic, will not, however, mark the preacher who receives the Bible as God's teaching and testimony. His aim, rather, will be to stand under Scripture, not over it, and to allow it, so to speak, to talk through him, delivering what is not so much his message as its. In our preaching, this is what should always be happening.

In his obituary of the great German conductor, Otto Klemperer, Neville Cardus spoke of the way in which Klemperer 'set the music in motion,' maintaining throughout a deliberately anonymous, self-effacing style in order that the musical notes might articulate themselves in their own integrity through him. So it must be in preaching; Scripture itself must do all the talking, and the preacher's task is simply to 'set the Bible in motion.' Happy are those hearers to whom the Bible—that is, God in and through the Bible—talks in this way, through the lips of preachers who honour the Bible as God's true Word and whose purpose is simply and solely to be its servant.

CHAPTER 23

Speaking for God

Defining the Sermon

Before we can think about preparing sermons, we must know what a sermon is; so I shall start by offering a definition. Not all will endorse it: a theological liberal couldn't, and my guess is that many Evangelicals, who could, don't and won't. (If my guess is wrong, no one will be happier than I am—nor, I think, more surprised!) I will state the definition, however, as plainly as I can, and my readers shall judge for themselves what acceptance it merits.

First, let me focus the definition. An institutional definition of a sermon would describe it as a hortatory monologue delivered from a pulpit to people in pews as part of a liturgical programme. A sociological definition would highlight the expectations that sermons seek to fulfil and the responsibilities that they are thought to impose. A homiletical definition would view the sermon as didactic communication, put over by means of a special rhetorical technique. Such definitions certainly have their place, but at this moment I am on a different track. The definition I offer—the definition with which I live, which commands my conscience, and guides me in preparing specific messages—is theological (that is, trinitarian and theocentric) and functional (that is, centring on intention and effect).

This definition, or concept, was given me in embryo during the winter of 1948–49, when I was privileged on Sunday evenings to sit under the preaching of the late D. Martyn Lloyd-Jones at Westminster Chapel in London, England. Yehudi Menuhin has written of how overwhelmed he was the first time he played Beethoven's Violin Concerto under Furtwängler, by reason of the power with which the great conductor recreated Beethoven's music all around him. Well, that was how I felt that winter as I heard Dr. Lloyd-Jones preach the gospel of Christ from the gospel of Matthew, opening up Matthew 11 with magisterial weight and passion in some twenty discourses.

Since then I have lived, worshipped, and preached under an ineffaceable sense of the authority of what Dr. Lloyd-Jones was doing. It is only in recent years, however, that I have been able to verbalize it to myself and others in a way that seems to me anything like adequate to the reality. And even so, my definition may not communicate all that from my standpoint it expresses, for preaching is ordinarily caught by contact rather than taught by rote. If my readers, preachers though they themselves may be, have never experienced such preaching as I encountered forty years ago, they may well miss much of the meaning of my words. Nonetheless, I hope that my definition will in fact strike some sparks.

A sermon is an applicatory declaration, spoken in God's name and for his praise, in which some part of the written Word of God delivers through the preacher some part of its message about God and godliness in relation to those whom the preacher addresses. This definition grounds a particular view of the preacher's task on a particular view of the nature of Scripture. Fuller explanation is needed on both these points, and it is convenient to take them in reverse.

The Nature of Scripture

Holy Scripture, the inspired Word (message) of the living God, may truly be described as God preaching—preaching, that is, in the sense of instructing, rebuking, correcting, and directing every reader and hearer for the furthering of faith, praise, holiness, and spiritual growth. God preaches thus in and through all the various stories, sermons, soliloquies, schedules, statistics, songs, and supplications that make up the individual books of the canon. All that Bible writers tell us about God and man, God himself tells us; for the sacred text is not just man's witness to God, but is also, and indeed primarily, God's own witness to himself, given us in this human form. Everything in Scripture teaches something of the Father's plan, something of the ministry and majesty of the Son as fulfiller of it, and something too about the gift and glory of eternal life, and the way to set forth God's praise. Furthermore, it teaches it as from God himself. The approach to Scripture followed by preachers in the older Reformational-Puritan-Pietist-Evangelical tradition, from Luther to Lloyd-Jones, was determined by the clarity with which they grasped this truth, and it is our own urgent need to get back on this wavelength. Only as God himself is perceived to be preaching in our sermons can they have genuine spiritual significance, and God will be perceived to speak through us only as we are enabled to make plain the fact that it is really the Bible that is doing the talking.

The Role of the Preacher

Since the triune God—the Father and the Son, through the Spirit—already preaches to us in every part of the Bible, the human preacher's task resolves into becoming a mouthpiece and sounding board for the divine message that meets him in his text. It is not for the preacher to stand, as it were, in front of and above the Bible, setting himself between it and the people and speaking for it, as if it could not speak for itself. Rather, his role is to stand behind and below it, letting it deliver its own message through him, and putting himself explicitly and transparently under the authority of that message, so that his very style of relaying it models response to it. From this standpoint preaching is, indeed, in Phillips Brooks's phrase, 'truth through personality' and the preacher is, indeed, half of his sermon. Only as he manifests both the mentality of a messenger and the disposition of a disciple will the preacher communicate any sense of God speaking in what he says. Insofar as he fulfils these two roles his preaching will be genuinely prophetic: he will speak from God in his character as a servant of God. The Holy Spirit who enables him to do this will lead God's people to recognize God's authority in what he is saying. The form of authority that is acknowledged in Scripture as authentically moral and spiritual is the authority of God and so preachers can only claim authority to the extent that they can make good their claim. That is how it is here. The authentic authority of the pulpit is the authority, not of the preacher's eloquence, experience, or expertise, but of God speaking in Scripture through what he says as he explains and applies his text.

So the preacher, rather than the critical commentator or the academic theologian, is the true interpreter of Scripture; for the preacher is the person whose privilege it is to bridge the apparent gap between the Bible and the modern world by demonstrating the relevance of what Scripture says to the lives of those whom he addresses.

Interpretation means, among other things, bringing literary and artistic legacies to life and showing their significance for those who stand at a distance, temporal or cultural or both, from the producers of these materials. Biblical interpretation involves both grammatical-historical exposition of what the text meant as instruction for the writer's envisaged readership, and contemporary application of it at the level of principle to show what it means for us today and what response it (or, rather, God in it) is calling for. Commentaries and theologies are resources for this task, but only preachers can fully perform it; and they perform it fully only as they apply their text in a rational and realistic way. To pass on biblical content, unapplied, is only to teach, not to preach. A lecture, as such, is not a sermon. Preaching is teaching plus—plus, that is, application of truth to life. One's adequacy as a preacher, interpreting God's Word to God's people, is finally determined not by the erudition of one's exegesis but by the depth and power of one's application. This is the next matter that my definition of a sermon requires me to discuss.

The Theory of Application

A largely forgotten part of the Evangelical heritage with regard to preaching is the procedure sometimes called 'discriminating application,' which Puritan writers were the first to formulate. I offer now a functional analysis of application, formally and schematically viewed, which is essentially a restatement in modern terms of what this procedure requires. Three guidelines are involved.

Application should constantly focus on the unchanging realities of each person's relationship to God.

The most important question that anybody ever faces is the issue of one's relationship with God. Both exposition and application in preaching must centre here. Within the Bible story, cultures and circumstances changed and the externals of worship and devotion took different forms at different times. The New Testament era saw the coming of God incarnate, the establishing of Christ's kingdom, the eschatological gift of the Spirit, the superseding of type by antitype and of ethnic Jewishness by a global outlook, and the new reality of life in Christ. But the basic elements in relating rightly to our holy, gracious Creator remained in essence the same from Genesis to Revelation, and are so still. These elements include faith, love, hope, obedience, humility, repentance, forgiveness, fidelity, thankful praise and trustful prayer, stewarding gifts, sanctifying one's activities, serving others, and resisting evil both in one's own heart and in the world outside. These are the unchanging realities that the preacher's elucidations of Scripture, whatever else they deal with, must regularly highlight and illustrate, and that his applications, one way and another, must regularly cover. The Bible is given us to teach us godliness. All our preaching ought to further that purpose.

Application should constantly focus on the person, place, and power of Jesus Christ.

The Bible in its entirety is witness to Christ and to the Father's plans involving him. By setting these before us it makes us 'wise for salvation' through faith in him (2 Tim. 3:15). Central to application in preaching, therefore, is the task of systematically relating God's love in Christ to the whole wide range of needs and perplexities to which, as we say (with truth), 'Christ is the answer.' This requires us both to dwell on his mediatorial office as our prophet, priest, and king, and also to present his person as set forth in the Gospels, so that he will be known and trusted as the individual that he was and is, and will never be reduced to an unknown 'x' in soteriological equations. Yet, just as it would not be enough to require faith in the office and work of Christ without delineating his personal profile in this way, so too it is not enough to exhibit Jesus the man as our example and ignore the work of his saving lordship—which is a continuing defect, unhappily, of the North American liberal tradition. In application, both the compassionate wisdom of this man from Galilee dealing with various kinds of sinners, and the saving power of 'Jesus! my Shepherd, Husband, Friend, / My Prophet and King, / My Lord, my Life, my Way, my End,' must be brought to bear together.

Application should constantly search the consciences of the hearers.

It is the preacher's responsibility to plan the applicatory part of his sermon to this end, so that the message is 'homecoming' (Alexander Whyte's word) in a specific way to as many of his congregation as possible. In every congregation there are likely to be people in each of the following categories (which, as will be seen, are not entirely exclusive):

1. Unconverted and self-satisfied, needing to be awakened and humbled.

2. Concerned and inquiring, wanting to be told what being a Christian today involves.

3. Convicted and seeking, needing to be guided directly to Christ.

4. Young Christians who need to be built up and led on.

5. Mature Christians, aging both physically and spiritually, who need to be constantly encouraged, lest they flag.

6. People in trouble; through moral lapses, circumstantial trauma, 'losses and crosses' (a Puritan phrase), disappointment, depression, and other such afflictions.

It has also been wisely observed that in every congregation there will be at least one broken heart. Just as homemakers who prepare meals try to ensure that there will be enough kinds of food to satisfy all who are there, so too we who prepare sermons must try to see that, over a period of time if not in each single message, applications are made that will be home-coming and health-giving, through God's blessing, to each of these classes of people.

There are basically four types of application, each of which can be developed from any Bible truth about God and man, and each of which may and should be made from time to time to all six sorts of people. (Not that all twenty-four specific applications could actually be developed in one sermon! My point is that they are there to be developed, as wisdom directs.) There is, first, application to our mind, where the logical form is: the truth presented shows us that we ought not to think thus-and-so (and if we have thought it up to now, we must stop thinking it); instead, we should think such-and-such. Second, there is application to our will, where the logical form is: the truth presented shows us that we ought not to behave thus-and-so (and if we have started, we must stop at once); instead, we ought to do such-and-such. Third, there is application to our motivating drives, where the logical form is: the truth presented shows us that if we are living as we should, we have very good reason to carry on, and if we are not living so, we have very good reason to change our ways. Fourth, there is application to our condition, where the logical form is: How do we stand in relation to the truth presented? Have we faced it, taken it to heart, measured and judged ourselves by it? How do we stand in relation to the God who speaks it to us? It is through these four types of application, whether made to us from the pulpit or by us to ourselves in private meditation, that Scripture fulfils to us its appointed function of correcting, rebuking, and training in righteousness (2 Tim. 3:16).

How the preacher will express and angle each type of application on each occasion is something that he must of necessity decide for himself in light of what truth he is applying, what he knows about those he is addressing, what was said to them in previous sermons, and a host of other factors. A good rule of thumb for pastoral sermons, however, is that half the message should be in essence instruction in biblical truth about God and man, and half should be in essence specific application of that truth. Observing these proportions, it seems to me, one cannot go far wrong.

Preparing the Sermon

How do I prepare my own sermons? The short answer is that I try to produce messages that conform to the specifications already set out. Being an academic without a stated pastoral charge, I often find myself preaching to congregations about which I know very little, but I sieve my material as best I can through my applicatory grid in hope of ensuring that I shall say something relevant and timely to as many as possible of the six types of people who I expect will be there.

Where do sermon messages come from? For most preachers, I think, and certainly for me, there are two main sources: First, the known needs of congregations, which suggest particular themes and passages on which to preach, and maybe even series of sermons; second, our own experience of being taught and disciplined by God, which leaves us with insights and wisdom that we find ourselves wanting to pass on. Sometimes a lectionary or prior church decision prescribes the passage on which one must preach. In that case, one will search it and meditate and pray over it, seeking in it an important truth with an application that one has the skill to handle. Sometimes the occasion (Christmas, Easter, a national crisis, or some other event) dictates one's theme; then one will seek a passage to expound and apply appropriately. I would add here that a rounded theological understanding of the will and ways of God, and of the nature, demands, and resources of the Christian life is a great help in enabling one to see what truth one is looking at in particular Bible passages. Calvin's *Institutes,* covering these themes in classical fashion, is one theological guide that has suggested to me many messages over the years.

What routines and resources do I use in preparing sermons? My method (which I share simply because I have been asked to, and without wishing to make rules for anyone else) is, so to speak, first to walk round my text, or whatever I suspect will be my text (for at first, I am not always sure about that), looking at it in its larger context (i.e., as part of the book from which it comes, and of the Bible as a whole), and scribbling possible schemes of points to teach, angles of interaction with life and its problems to pursue, and personal applications to develop. I find that I need to start this process several days before the message has to be produced, for getting an outline that seems right—that is, one that expresses my heart and that I see how to use in searching the hearts of others—often takes me some time.

Only when I think I have such an outline do I turn to the church's expository legacy of commentaries and homiletical materials, exploring it and drawing on it to fill out the scheme I already have. Ordinarily, reading others' work before my own outline is clear makes it harder, rather than easier, to settle in my mind what my message from the text is supposed to be. For the record (though I do not suppose I am typical in this), modern expositions do not help me half as much as does Matthew Henry, the Puritan, and modern printed sermons do not suggest to me half as much as do those of C. H. Spurgeon and the sermonic writings of J. C. Ryle. As for illustrations, whenever I can, I use Bible stories to illustrate Bible doctrine. Beyond this, I find that there are usually illustrations enough in everyday events. For me, at least, exotic illustrations turn preaching into a performance remote from life, so that sermon time ceases to be an encounter with God and becomes an entertainment break, and accordingly I expend no effort in hunting for them.

How much preparatory writing do I do? As much as is necessary to ensure that I know my message and have words at my command to make all my points, both expository and applicatory, in a clear, pointed, weighty way that gives no offence other than the inescapable offence of the gospel itself. How much writing is needed to get to this point varies, I find, from preacher to preacher.

How much written material do I take with me into the pulpit? As much as I need to be exact, as well as free and spontaneous, in the way that I speak. This, for me, means a half-sheet of paper, with skeletal notes in abbreviations of my own devising, for each half-hour of talk. Some preachers need less; some need more. Some need to have a complete script with them, not to read word for word, but to give them confidence as they speak, knowing that should words suddenly fail to come spontaneously they can drop their eyes to the script and find there what they need to start the flow again.

Furtwängler, whom I mentioned earlier, was always thorough in his orchestral rehearsals, describing them as his preparation for improvising at the performance. In the same way, thorough preparation equips the preacher to be spontaneous in the pulpit. Fumbling spontaneity, which indicates insufficient preparation, is always a depressant, but controlled creativity, carrying the sense that the person knows what he is doing even though he is doing some of it on the spur of the moment, generates a sort of communicative electricity that keeps people on the edge of their seats. So it was when Furtwängler played Beethoven, Brahms, and Bruckner. So it was when Dr. Lloyd-Jones preached, as I can testify. So I pray, over and over, that it will be each time I preach. I hope that you who read this do the same.

This goal, no doubt, was what W. H. Griffith Thomas had in view when he offered young preachers his formula for sermon preparation: 'Think yourself empty; read yourself full; write yourself clear; pray yourself keen; then into the pulpit, and let yourself go!' But Thomas's sprightly words are not to be heard as sanctioning the frivolity of exhibitionist exuberance. Preaching is too serious a business for that, since the glory of God and the issues of eternity are bound up with it; and the act of preaching is spiritually demanding. 'It is easy,' said Charles Simeon, nearly two centuries ago, 'for a minister to prate in the pulpit, and even to speak much good matter; but to preach is not easy—to carry his congregation on his shoulders as it were to heaven; to weep over them, pray for them, deliver the truth with a weeping, praying heart; and if a minister has grace to do so now and then, he ought to be very thankful.' One can only agree; and I wish to make Simeon's words my own exit line.

Notes

Notes to Chapter 1

ENCOUNTERING PRESENT-DAY VIEWS OF SCRIPTURE was originally published in *The Foundation of Biblical Authority,* ed. James M. Boice (Grand Rapids: Zondervan, 1978), pp. 61–84. Reprinted by permission.

1. Ian Breward, ed., *William Perkins* (Appleford: Sutton Courtenay, 1970), p. 177.

2. Francis Turretin, *Institutio Theologiae Elencticae* (Utrecht and Amsterdam, 1701), Locus I, Question VII, 6,15. See also Gisbert Voetius: "'Practical theology" may mean, in the broad sense, all theology that follows Scripture or is based upon it . . . because all theology among pilgrims on earth is in its nature practical, and no portion of it can be correctly and completely discussed unless it is developed practically; that is, applied to the practice of repentance, faith, hope, and love, or to consolation or exhortation' (*Reformed Dogmatics,* ed. John W. Beardslee III [New York: Oxford University Press, 1965], p. 265).

3. E. L. Mascall II, *Theology and the Gospel of Christ: An Essay in Reorientation* (London: SPCK, 1977), p. 60. Mascall alludes to a remark that he quoted from Bernard Lonergan: 'The real menace to unity of faith does not lie either in the many brands of common sense or the many differentiations of human consciousness. It lies in the absence of intellectual or moral or religious conversion' (pp. 54–55).

4. Clark Pinnock, 'Three Views of the Bible in Contemporary Theology,' in *Biblical Authority,* ed. Jack Rogers (Waco: Word, 1977), pp. 49–73.

5. This was the point of Calvin's famous image of the spectacles: 'Just as, when you put before old or bleary-eyed and weak-sighted men even the most beautiful book, though they may recognize that there is something written they can hardly make out two words, yet with the aid of spectacles they will begin to read distinctly; so Scripture, gathering up the otherwise confused knowledge of God in our minds, having dispelled our dullness, clearly shows us the true God' (*Institutio Christianae Religionis,* I. vi. 1).

6. See J. I. Packer, '"Sola Scriptura" in History and Today,' in *God's Inerrant Word,* ed. John Warwick Montgomery (Minneapolis: Bethany Fellowship, 1974). [Included in *Honoring the People of God: Collected Shorter Writings of J. I. Packer,* chap. 9.]

7. For the text of the Lausanne Covenant, together with the Congress papers and addresses that lay behind it, see *Let the World Hear His Voice,* ed. J. D. Douglas (Minneapolis: World Wide Publications, 1975).

8. Pinnock, 'Three Views of the Bible,' p. 53.

9. Ibid., p. 51.

10. John Hick, ed., *The Myth of God Incarnate* (London: SCM, 1977; Philadelphia: Westminster, 1978). The contributors are John Hick, Michael Goulder, and Frances Young (Birmingham University); Maurice Wiles, Dennis Nineham, and Leslie Houlden (Oxford University); and Don Cupitt (Cambridge University). The thesis the essays seek to establish is that 'Jesus was (as he is presented in Acts 2:21) "a man approved by God" for a special role within the divine purpose, and that the later conception of him as God incarnate, the second person of the Trinity living a human life, is a mythological or poetic way of expressing his significance for us' (p. ix).

11. Pinnock, 'Three Views of the Bible,' p. 54.

12. Colin Brown, *Karl Barth and the Christian Message* (London and Chicago: Tyndale Press, 1967), p. 140.

13. For a bird's-eye view of this, see Brown, *Karl Barth,* chap. 4, 'Barth's Christ-centred Approach to God, Creation and Reconciliation,' pp. 99–139.

14. The best study of the knots into which Brunner's dialectic ties him is that by Paul King Jewett, *Emil Brunner's Concept of Revelation* (London: James Clarke, 1954).

15. Reasons for doubting Barth's success at this point are given by C. Van Til in *Christianity and Barthianism* (Philadelphia: Presbyterian and Reformed, 1962).

16. See Brown, *Karl Barth,* pp. 35–67, 143–47; Gordon H. Clark, *Karl Barth's Theological Method* (Philadelphia: Presbyterian and Reformed, 1963), pp. 185–225; Klaas Runia, *Karl Barth's Doctrine of Holy Scripture* (Grand Rapids: Eerdmans, 1962); and, from a distinctively Barthian standpoint, J. K. S. Reid, *The Authority of Scripture* (London: Methuen; New York: Harper, 1957), pp. 194–221. Barth's own discussions are in *Church Dogmatics,* I. 1, chap. 1, pp. 51–335 and I. 2, chaps. 3 and 4, pp. 457–884 (Edinburgh: T. & T. Clark, 1936, 1956).

17. 'The prophets and apostles as such even in their office . . . were . . . actually guilty of error in their spoken and written word' (*Church Dogmatics,* I. 2, pp. 528–29). Scripture's 'capacity for error . . . extends to its religious or theological content.' Yet 'we must be careful not to be betrayed into . . . playing off the one biblical man against the other, into pronouncing that this one or that has "erred." From what standpoint can we make any such pronouncement?' (p. 509).

18. Pinnock, 'Three Views of the Bible,' p. 57.

19. Brown, *Karl Barth,* pp. 62, 146.

20. Pinnock, 'Three Views of the Bible,' pp. 69–70, referring to Dewey M. Beegle, *Scripture, Tradition, and Infallibility* (Grand Rapids: Eerdmans, 1973), and Paul King Jewett, *Man as Male and Female* (Grand Rapids: Eerdmans, 1975).

21. Reid, *Authority of Scripture,* p. 103, *Providentissimus Deus,* xxiii, echoing the statements of the Council of Trent (Session IV) in 1546 that Holy Scripture was 'dictated either orally by Christ or by the Holy Ghost,' and of the First Vatican Council in 1870 that the Scriptures 'contain revelation, with no admixture of error,' and that 'having been written by the inspiration of the Holy Ghost, they have God for their author' (*Constitution on Revelation,* chap. 2). For ways in which Roman Catholic theologians have worked out these formulae, see J. T. Burtchaell, *Catholic Theories of Biblical Inspiration since 1810* (Cambridge and New York: Cambridge University Press, 1969).

22. Cited from David F. Wells, *Revolution in Rome* (Chicago: InterVarsity; London: Tyndale Press, 1973), p. 29.

23. Reid, *Authority of Scripture*, p. 155.

24. *Constitution on Revelation*, p. 11.

25. Butler, *The Theology of Vatican II* (London: Darton, Longman and Todd, 1967), p. 56. See also John Warwick Montgomery, 'The Approach of New Shape Roman Catholicism to Scriptural Inerrancy: A Case Study for Evangelicals,' in *Ecumenicity, Evangelicals and Rome* (Grand Rapids: Zondervan, 1969), pp. 73–93.

26. See *Infallible? An Inquiry* (Garden City, N.Y.: Doubleday, 1971).

27. Pinnock, 'Three Views of the Bible,' p. 68.

28. Clark Pinnock, 'The Inerrancy Debate among the Evangelicals,' in *Theology, News and Notes* (Fuller Theological Seminary: special issue, 1976), p. 11.

29. Ibid., p. 12. He goes on to say that when inerrancy is qualified, as it should be, by reference to the author's purpose in writing, one can 'fairly say that the Bible *contains* errors but *teaches* none, [and] that inerrancy refers to the *subjects* rather than all the terms of Scripture [and] to the *teaching* rather than to all the *components* utilized in its formulation.'

30. Pinnock, 'Three Views of the Bible,' pp. 62–70.

31. James I. Packer, *'Fundamentalism' and the Word of God* (London: Inter-Varsity Press; Grand Rapids: Eerdmans, 1958), p. 99. It must be a private mental extrapolation from this phrase that led Pinnock to suppose that I should not agree with Francis Schaeffer's insistence in *No Final Conflict* (Downers Grove: InterVarsity Press, 1975), pp. 33–34, that the special creation of Adam, and of Eve from Adam, is part of what Genesis 2 teaches (see Pinnock, 'Inerrancy Debate,' p. 13, note 8). But a glance at the paragraph from which this phrase comes will show that Pinnock's inference was unwarranted and that his supposition is in fact quite false. His whole footnote is most unfortunate.

32. See G. C. Berkouwer, *Holy Scripture* (Grand Rapids: Eerdmans, 1975), p. 265.

33. The Fuller Seminary Statement of Faith declares: 'All the books of the Old and New Testaments, given by divine inspiration, are the written word of God, the only infallible rule of faith and practice. They are to be interpreted according to their context and purpose and in reverent obedience to the Lord who speaks through them in living power' (III). David Hubbard, president of the Seminary, formulates the questions currently in debate as follows: '1) Is inerrancy the best word to use to describe the Bible's infallibility and truthfulness? 2) If inerrancy is to be used, how do we define it in a way that accords with the teaching and the data of Scripture?' ('The Current Tensions: Is There a Way Out?' *Biblical Authority*, p. 178).

Notes to Chapter 2

THE ADEQUACY OF HUMAN LANGUAGE was originally published in *Inerrancy*, ed. Norman Geisler (Grand Rapids: Zondervan, 1980), pp. 197–226. Reprinted by permission.

1. See Acts 28:25; Heb. 3:7; 10:15.

2. See John 7:16ff.; 8:26–28, 38–47; 12:48–50.

3. See Matt. 7:28ff.; 24:35.

4. Karl Barth, *Church Dogmatics*, part 1: 'The Doctrine of the Word of God,' 2 vols. (Edinburgh: T. & T. Clark, 1956), 1:504. Barth glosses *theopneustos* as meaning 'given and filled and ruled by the Spirit of God, and actively outbreathing and spreading abroad

and making known the Spirit of God.' This combination of passive and active meanings may be expressing truth, but the word *theopneustos* signifies only the former, not the latter.

5. B. B. Warfield, 'God-inspired Scripture,' in *The Inspiration and Authority of the Bible* (Philadelphia: Presbyterian and Reformed, 1948), pp. 245ff.

6. If, as grammatically possible, though somewhat more harsh linguistically and less appropriate contextually, the first words of the verse are rendered, 'All Scripture inspired by God is also profitable,' the point remains unaffected. It is inspiration (= inspiredness) as such that constitutes the ground of canonicity. On the translation, see the judicious remarks of Donald Guthrie, *The Pastoral Epistles* (London: Tyndale Press; and Grand Rapids: Eerdmans, 1957), pp. 163ff.

7. On prophecy and the passion, see Matt. 26:52–54; Mark 8:31–33; 9:31; 10:33; 12:10ff.; 14:21; Luke 9:31; 18:31–33; 22:37; etc.

8. See Rom. 16:25ff.; 1 Cor. 2:1–36; 14:37 (cf. 7:30, where 'I think' expresses not doubt but ironical challenge—'I, too think I have God's Spirit—don't you agree that I have?'); 1 Thess. 1:5; 2:13; 4:1ff., 15; 2 Thess. 3:4, 6, 10–14; 1 John 1:1–5; 4:1–6, et al.

9. It is fashionable today to stress the linguistic diversity of New Testament documents rather than the substantial oneness of their teaching (see, e.g., James D. G. Dunn, *Unity and Diversity in the New Testament* [London: SCM, 1977]); however, their oneness has often been established (see, e.g., A. M. Hunter, *The Unity of the New Testament* [London: SCM, 1944]).

10. Ludwig Wittgenstein, *Tractatus Logico-Philosophicus,* trans. C. K. Ogden (London: Kegan Paul, 1922), pp. 27, 186–89. A current counterpart of Wittgenstein's philosophically based denial that life-problems are expressible and thus communicable is Dennis Nineham's denial, based on his personal and amateur reading of the sociology of knowledge, that we can ever get into the minds of persons shaped by bygone cultures so as to grasp with certainty the thoughts behind their words when they spoke of ultimate realities. See Nineham, *The Use and Abuse of the Bible* (London: Macmillan, 1976); and for criticism, Ronald H. Preston, 'Need Dr. Nineham Be So Negative?' *Expository Times* (June 1970), pp. 275ff.

11. John Macquarrie, *God-Talk* (London: SCM; and New York: Harper and Row, 1967), pp. 23ff.

12. For more on this, see A. C. Thiselton, 'Understanding God's Word Today,' in *Obeying Christ in a Changing World,* I: *The Lord Christ,* ed. John Stott (London: Collins, 1977), pp. 90–122; idem, 'Semantics and New Testament Interpretation,' in *New Testament Interpretation,* ed. I. Howard Marshall (Exeter: Paternoster; and Grand Rapids: Eerdmans, 1977), pp. 75–104; James Barr, *The Semantics of Biblical Language* (London: Oxford University Press, 1961).

13. Ian T. Ramsey, *Religious Language* (London: SCM, 1957); *Models and Mystery* (London: Oxford University Press, 1964); *Christian Discourse* (London: Oxford University Press, 1965).

14. Macquarrie, *God-Talk.*

15. Austin Farrer, *The Glass of Vision* (London: Dacre, 1948).

16. Eric L. Mascall, *Existence and Analogy* (London: Longmans, 1949); idem, *Words and Images* (London: Longmans, 1957).

17. See their contributions to *Faith and Logic,* ed. Basil Mitchell (London: Allen and Unwin, 1957).

18. Frederick Ferré, *Language and God* (London: Collins, 1970), pp. 231ff.

19. John Frame, 'God and Biblical Language,' in *God's Inerrant Word*, ed. J. W. Montgomery (Minneapolis: Bethany Fellowship, 1973), pp. 173f. It is worth underlining the point implicit in Frame's equation of transcendence with lordship. Lordship, comprising the relation of upholding, directing, and controlling all created things in both their motion and their rest, is the only concept of transcendence that Scripture yields; the Kantian-Barthian ideas of metaphysical remoteness from us, obscurity to us, and evasion of all the categories of human (though God-given!) language are simply not there.

20. C. S. Lewis, 'Introduction' to J. B. Phillips, *Letters to Young Churches* (London: Bles, 1947).

21. Calvin, *Institutes* I.viii.1, referring to the New Testament preaching of the kingdom.

22. Calvin, *Commentary on John*, on John 3:12.

23. See R. B. Braithwaite, *An Empiricist's View of the Nature of Religious Belief* (Cambridge: Cambridge University Press, 1955) Cambridge:, reprinted in *The Philosophy of Religion*, ed. Basil Mitchell (Cambridge: Cambridge University Press, 1971), pp. 72ff. 'A religious assertion, for me, is the assertion of an intention to carry out a certain behaviour policy, subsumable under a sufficiently general principle to be a moral one, together with the implicit or explicit statement, but not the assertion, of certain stories,' p. 89.

24. For expositions of this line of thought, see A. J. Ayer, *Language, Truth and Logic*, 2nd ed. (London: Gollancz, 1946); A. Flew, in 'Theology and Falsification,' *The Philosophy of Religion*, pp. 13ff.; Kai Nielsen, *Contemporary Critiques of Religion* (London: Macmillan, 1971).

25. The critique is well developed by Ferré, *Language, Logic and God*, chap. 6; see also E. J. Carnell, *An Introduction to Christian Apologetics*, 4th ed. (Grand Rapids: Eerdmans, 1952), pp. 140–51.

26. Mitchell, *The Justification of Religious Belief* (London: Macmillan, 1973), p. 19.

27. See on this C. F. H. Henry, *God, Revelation and Authority*, vol. 1 (Waco: Word, 1976), chap. 5.

Notes to Chapter 3

THE BIBLE AND THE AUTHORITY OF REASON was originally published in *Churchman* 75. 4, December 1961. Reprinted by permission.

Notes to Chapter 4

CONTEMPORARY VIEWS OF REVELATION was originally published in *Revelation and the Bible*, ed. Carl. F. H. Henry (Grand Rapids: Baker, 1959). Reprinted by permission.

1. London: Oxford University Press, and New York: Columbia University Press, 1956.

2. *The Authority of Scripture* (London: Methuen, and New York: Harper, 1957), pp. 162f.

3. *Nature, Man and God* (London: Macmillan, 1934), Lectures XII, XIII; essay in *Revelation*, ed. D. M. Baillie and H. Martin (London: Faber, 1937).

4. Ibid., p. 353.

5. 'Dictation' in old Protestant thought was a theological metaphor declaring the relation of the written words of Scripture to the divine intention, with no psychological implications whatever.

6. *Nature, Man and God,* p. 317.

7. See Williams, *Interpreting Theology 1918–1952* (London: SCM, 1953), *passim.* The passage quoted comes from his *What Present-day Theologians Are Thinking* (New York: Harper, 1952), pp. 64f., drawing on Temple, op. cit., pp. 316ff.

8. Cf. Dodd, *History and the Gospel* (London: Nisbet, 1938); and Robinson, *Inspiration and Revelation in the Old Testament* (London: Oxford University Press, 1946).

9. Cf. Barth, *Church Dogmatics,* I: *The Doctrine of the Word of God* (Edinburgh: T. & T. Clark, 2 vols., 1936, 1956; Brunner, *The Divine-Human Encounter* (London: SCM, 1944); *Revelation and Reason* (London: SCM, 1947); H. Richard Niebuhr, *The Meaning of Revelation* (New York: Macmillan, 1941); Reinhold Niebuhr, *The Nature and Destiny of Man,* I (London: Nisbet, 1941); *Faith and History* (London: Nisbet, 1949); Tillich, *Systematic Theology,* I (London: Nisbet, 1953); Bultmann, 'New Testament and Mythology,' in *Kerygma and Myth,* ed. H. W. Bartsch (London: SPCK, 1953).

10. Cf. Temple, loc. cit.; Richardson, *Christian Apologetics* (London: SCM, 1947); Baillie, *Our Knowledge of God* (London: Oxford University Press, 1939).

11. I.e., *Revelation and the Bible.*

Notes to Chapter 5

AN EVANGELICAL VIEW OF PROGRESSIVE REVELATION was originally published in *Evangelical Roots,* ed. Kenneth Kantzer (Nashville: Thomas Nelson, 1978), pp. 143–58. Reprinted by permission.

1. *The Bible in the Modern World* (London: SCM, 1973), p. 144.

2. *The Authority of the Bible* (London: Fontana, 1960), p. 248.

3. Dodd, *Authority of the Bible,* p. 263.

4. Ibid., p. 228. 'The evidence does not suggest anything like a smooth and uniform evolution,' p. 229.

5. Ibid., p. 255.

6. *The Principles of Theology* (London: Church Book Room, 1930), p. xix.

7. *Special Revelation and the Word of God* (Grand Rapids: Eerdmans, 1961), pp. 91, 103ff.

8. Ibid., p. 104.

Notes to Chapter 6

THE NECESSITY OF THE REVEALED WORD was originally published in *The Bible: The Living Word of Revelation,* ed. Merrill C. Tenney (Grand Rapids: Zondervan, 1968), pp. 31–49. Reprinted by permission.

1. See William Temple, *Nature, Man and God* (London: Macmillan, 1934), Lecture XII, and his essay in *Revelation,* ed. D. M. Baillie and H. Martin (London: Faber, 1937).

For a critique, see J. I. Packer, *God Speaks to Man* (Philadelphia: Westminster Press, 1966), pp. 52ff. and pp. 71–73 above.

2. Matt. 11:25; 16:17; 1 Cor. 2:10; Eph. 3:3; cf. 2 Cor. 4:1–6; 1 John 5:20.

3. John 1:1–14; cf. 1 John 1:1.

4. *'Fundamentalism' and the Word of God* (London: Inter-Varsity Press, and Grand Rapids: Eerdmans, 1958); *God Speaks to Man* (Philadelphia: Westminster Press, 1966; published in London as *God Has Spoken,* 1964).

5. See for Reformed theology, H. Heppe, *Reformed Dogmatics* (London: Allen and Unwin, 1950), pp. 31f.; for Lutheran theology, R. Preuss, *The Inspiration of Scripture* (Edinburgh: Oliver and Boyd, 1955), pp. 23ff.

6. *The Inspiration and Authority of Holy Scripture* (Philadelphia: Westminster Press, 1948), pp. 219f; from an article written in 1893. The last sentence is cited from an address of Warfield's own, published in 1880.

7. Op. cit., p. 212.

8. L. Köhler, *Old Testament Theology* (Philadelphia: Westminster Press, 1957), p. 106.

Notes to Chapter 7

OUR LORD'S UNDERSTANDING OF THE LAW OF GOD was originally presented at Westminster Chapel, London, as the G. Campbell Morgan Memorial Bible Lecture, 14 June, 1962, and published at Glasgow, by Pickering & Inglis. Reprinted by permission.

1. See D. M. Lloyd-Jones, *The Sermon on the Mount* (London: Inter-Varsity Fellowship, 2 vols., 1959, 1960).

2. C.J. Cadoux, *The Historic Mission of Jesus* (London: Lutterworth, 1941), p. 138.

Notes to Chapter 8

A LAMP IN A DARK PLACE was originally preached at the first summit Conference held by the International Council on Biblical Inerrancy, and published in *Can We Trust the Bible? Leading Theologians Speak Out on Biblical Inerrancy,* ed. Earl D. Radmacher (Wheaton: Tyndale House Publishers, 1979), pp. 15–32. Reprinted by permission. The extempore homiletic style remains as it was. The statement on biblical inerrancy that came from the Summit Conference is printed as Appendix 1 in J. I. Packer, *God Has Spoken* (London: Hodder & Stoughton; Grand Rapids: Baker) from the second (1979) edition onward.

Notes to Chapter 9

UPHOLDING THE UNITY OF SCRIPTURE TODAY was originally published in the *Journal of the Evangelical Theological Society* (San Diego: Bethel Theological Seminary) 25.4, December 1982, pp. 409–14. Reprinted by permission.

Notes to Chapter 10

UNDERSTANDING THE BIBLE: EVANGELICAL HERMENEUTICS was originally published in *Restoring the Vision: Anglican Evangelicals Speak Out,* ed. Melvin Tinker (Eastbourne, East Sussex: Monarch Publishing, 1990), pp. 39–58. Reprinted by permission.

1. See James Barr, *Fundamentalism* (London: SCM Press, 1977, second edition 1980), and *Escaping from Fundamentalism* (London: SCM Press, 1984), *passim.* Barr's critique follows in the footsteps of Gabriel Hebert, *Fundamentalism and the Church of God* (London: SCM Press, 1957).

2. This does not mean that no Evangelicals have engaged in the academic discussion of these matters. Among Anglicans, Anthony C. Thiselton, for one, has contributed masterfully and at length in *The Two Horizons: New Testament Hermeneutics and Philosophical Description* (Exeter: Paternoster Press, 1980) and in many other places.

Notes to Chapter 11

INERRANCY AND THE DIVINITY AND THE HUMANITY OF THE BIBLE is an address that was originally published in *The Proceedings of the Conference on Biblical Inerrancy, 1988* (Nashville: Broadman, 1988). Reprinted by permission.

Notes to Chapter 12

THE CHALLENGE OF BIBLICAL INTERPRETATION: CREATION is a transcribed and edited address that was originally published in *The Proceedings of the Conference on Biblical Inerrancy, 1988* (Nashville: Broadman, 1988). Reprinted by permission.

1. See chapter 11 above.

Notes to Chapter 13

THE CHALLENGE OF BIBLICAL INTERPRETATION: WOMEN is a transcribed and edited address that was originally published in *The Proceedings of the Conference on Biblical Inerrancy, 1988* (Nashville: Broadman, 1988). Reprinted by permission.

Notes to Chapter 14

THE CHALLENGE OF BIBLICAL INTERPRETATION: ESCHATOLOGY is a transcribed and edited address that was originally published in *The Proceedings of the Conference on Biblical Inerrancy, 1988* (Nashville: Broadman, 1988). Reprinted by permission.

Notes to Chapter 15

IN QUEST OF CANONICAL INTERPRETATION was originally published in *The Use of the Bible in Theology: Evangelical Options,* ed. Robert K. Johnston (Atlanta: John Knox Press, 1985), pp. 35–55. Reprinted by permission.

1. Jesus' acceptance of the truth and authority of his Bible (our Old Testament) has often been demonstrated. See, for instance, John W. Wenham, *Christ and the Bible* (London: Tyndale Press, 1972), pp. 11–37, and 'Christ's View of Scripture,' in *Inerrancy,* ed. Norman L. Geisler (Grand Rapids: Zondervan, 1980), pp. 3–37; J. I. Packer, *'Fundamentalism' and the Word of God* (London: Inter-Varsity Fellowship; Grand Rapids: Eerdmans, 1958), pp. 54–62.

2. Calvin, *Institutes,* I.viii.5: 'Enlightened by him (the Spirit), no longer do we believe that Scripture is from God on the basis of either our own judgement or that of others; but, in a way that surpasses human judgement, we are made absolutely certain, just as if we beheld there the majesty (*numen*) of God himself, that it has come to us by the ministry of men from God's very mouth . . . I speak of nothing but what every believer experiences personally (*apud se*), only my words fall far short of an adequate (*justam*) account of the reality' (author's translation).

3. The Westminster Confession speaks of 'the consent of all the parts' as one argument whereby the Bible 'doth abundantly evidence itself to be the Word of God' (I.v). Demonstrations of the Bible's thematic coherence were made by various writers of the British Biblical Theology school: e.g., A. M. Hunter, *The Message of The New Testament* (Philadelphia: Westminster Press, 1944); A. G. Hebert, *The Bible from Within* (London: Oxford University Press, 1950); H. H. Rowley, *The Unity of the Bible* (Philadelphia: Westminster Press, 1955).

4. The phrase 'analogy of Scripture' or 'of (the) faith' goes back to Calvin, who took Romans 12:6 to mean that what is preached must accord with revealed truth, and spoke of 'the analogy of faith, to which Paul requires all interpretation of Scripture to conform' (*Institutes,* IV.xvii.32). The principle covered interpreting what is peripheral by what is central, what is obscure by what is clear, and what is ambiguous by what is orthodox in the sense of being firmly established by thorough exegetical and theological testing.

5. See Martin Luther, *The Bondage of the Will,* tr. J. I. Packer and O. R. Johnston (London: James Clarke; Old Tappan: Fleming H. Revell, 1957), *passim.*

6. Examples are *Knowing God* (London: Hodder & Stoughton; Downers Grove, Ill.: InterVarsity Press, 1973); *Knowing Man* (Westchester: Cornerstone, 1979); *God's Words* (Leicester: Inter-Varsity Press; Downers Grove, Ill.: InterVarsity Press, 1981); *Evangelism and the Sovereignty of God* (London: Inter-Varsity Fellowship; Downers Grove, Ill.: Inter-Varsity Press, 1961); *Keep in Step with the Spirit* (Old Tappan: Fleming H. Revell; Leicester: Inter-Varsity Press, 1984); *I Want to Be a Christian* (Wheaton, Ill.: Tyndale House, 1977); now *Growing in Christ* (Wheaton, Ill.: Crossway, 1994); a contribution to catechetics: 'Steps to the Renewal of the Christian People' and 'An Agenda for Theology,' in *Summons to Faith and Renewal,* ed. Peter S. Williamson and Kevin Perrotta (Ann Arbor: Servant, 1983), pp. 107–27, 151–55; reprinted in *Collected Shorter Writings of J. I. Packer* (Carlisle: Paternoster, 1998), vol. 2, pp. 69–85, vol. 1, pp. 199–202.

7. Cf. *'Fundamentalism' and the Word of God*; *God Has Spoken*, 2nd ed. (London: Hodder & Stoughton: Downers Grove, Ill.: InterVarsity Press, 1979); *Freedom and Authority* (Oakland: International Council on Biblical Inerrancy, 1981); *Freedom, Authority and Scripture* (Leicester: Inter-Varsity Press, 1981).

8. Cf. *Beyond the Battle for the Bible* (Westchester: Cornerstone, 1980), esp. chap. 2, 'Inerrancy in Current Debate'; *God Has Spoken*, 3rd ed. (London: Hodder & Stoughton, 1993), pp. 134–70 (the Chicago Statements on Biblical Inerrancy and Biblical Hermeneutics).

9. My own tentative thoughts on this subject are in 'Thoughts on the Role and Function of Women in the Church,' in *Evangelicals and the Ordination of Women*, ed. Colin Craston (Bramcote: Grove Books, 1973), pp. 22–26; 'Postscript: I Believe in Women's Ministry,' in *Why Not?*, 2nd ed., ed. Michael Bruce and G. E. Duffield (Appleford: Marcham Manor Press, 1976), pp. 160–74; and chapter 13 above. Among advocates of relational subordination of women, with more or less fixed roles, see esp. Stephen B. Clark, *Man and Woman in Christ* (Ann Arbor: Servant, 1980); James B. Hurley, *Man and Woman in Biblical Perspective* (Leicester: Inter-Varsity Press; Grand Rapids: Zondervan, 1981); George W. Knight III, *The New Testament Teaching on the Role Relationship of Men and Women* (Grand Rapids: Baker Book House, 1977); Fritz Zerbst, *The Office of Woman in the Church* (St. Louis: Concordia, 1955); Karl Barth, *Church Dogmatics* (Edinburgh: T. & T. Clark), III.1.288–329, section 41 (1958); III.2.295–316, section 45 (1960); III.4.116–240, section 54 (1961). Among advocates of relational egalitarianism, free from role restriction upon women, see esp. Paul King Jewett, *Man as Male and Female* and *The Ordination of Women* (Grand Rapids: Eerdmans, 1975, 1980); Don Williams, *The Apostle Paul and Women in the Church* (Van Nuys: BIM, 1977); Letha Scanzoni and Nancy Hardesty, *All We're Meant to Be: A Biblical Approach to Women's Liberation* (Waco: Word, 1977); Virginia Ramey Mollenkott, *Women, Men and the Bible* (Nashville: Abingdon, 1977). For analyses of the biblical interpretation on both sides, see Willard M. Swartley, *Slavery, Sabbath, War, and Women: Case Issues in Biblical Interpretation* (Scottdale, Pa: Herald Press, 1983), pp. 152–91; Robert K. Johnston, *Evangelicals at an Impasse: Biblical Authority in Practice* (Atlanta: John Knox Press, 1979), pp. 48–76.

10. Jewett, *Man as Male and Female*, pp. 119, 134, 138.

11. I use this image as Anthony C. Thiselton does in 'Understanding God's Word Today,' in *Obeying Christ in a Changing World* I, ed. John R. W. Stott (London: Collins, 1977), pp. 90–122, esp. pp. 101–5, and in his book *The Two Horizons: New Testament Hermeneutics and Philosophical Description* (Grand Rapids: Eerdmans, 1980), esp. pp. 15–17, 307–10. I do not suggest that Gadamer views Scripture as the Word of God in the way that I do.

Notes to Chapter 16

LET'S STOP MAKING WOMEN PRESBYTERS was originally published in *Christianity Today*, February 11, 1991. Reprinted by permission.

1. 1 Cor. 14:34f.
2. 1 Tim. 2:11–14.

3. 1 Tim. 2:12–14.
4. 1 Tim. 2:11.
5. Gen. 2:2–23.
6. Eph. 5:23.
7. 1 Cor. 11:3, 11f.
8. Acts 14:23; 15:2; 20:17; 21:18.
9. Acts 20:28; 1 Pet. 5:2–4.
10. 1 Tim. 5:17.

Notes to Chapter 17

KNOWING NOTIONS OR KNOWING GOD was originally published in *Pastoral Renewal* 6.9, March 1982, pp. 65–68. Reprinted by permission.

Notes to Chapter 18

WHY PREACH? was originally published as the introduction to *The Preacher and Preaching*, ed. Samuel T. Logan (Phillipsburg, N.J.: Presbyterian and Reformed, 1986), pp. 1–29. Reprinted by permission.
1. David Clarkson, *Works* (Edinburgh: James Nichol, 1865), III. 193–94.
2. Charles Simeon, *Let Wisdom Judge*, ed. Arthur Pollard (London: Inter-Varsity Press, 1959), pp. 188–89.
3. Gustav Wingren, *The Living Word* (London: SCM, 1960), pp. 108, 208.

Notes to Chapter 19

EXPOSITORY PREACHING: CHARLES SIMEON AND OURSELVES was an address to clergy originally published in *Churchman*, LXXIV, 1960, pp. 94–100. Reprinted by permission.
1. *The Preparation of Sermons* (Nashville: Abingdon, 1948) p. 69.
2. Ibid., p. 70.
3. Ibid., p. 69.
4. Op. cit., p. 2.
5. *The Art of Preaching*, p. 175.
6. A. W. Brown, *Recollections of the Conversation Parties of the Rev. Chas. Simeon* (London, 1863), p. 177.
7. *Horae Homileticae*, (21 vols. 1832–3), I.vi (Preface).
8. Brown, p. 183.
9. Ibid., p. 189.
10. Claude's, *Essay on the Composition of a Sermon with notes and illustrations* ... (1866), p. 5.

11. Ibid., p. 114.

12. Brown, p. 376.

13. Claude, p. 5.

14. W. Carus, *Memoirs of . . . the Rev. Charles Simeon:* 3rd ed. (1848) p. 483f.

15. Ibid., pp. 481ff.

16. Ibid., p. 595.

17. Claude, p. 4.

18. Brown, p. 177.

19. *Horae Homileticae,* I.xxiii.

20. Brown, p. 183.

21. Claude, p. 1.

22. Carus, p. 505.

23. Ibid., p. 376.

24. *Horae Homileticae,* I.xxi.

25. See by all means the seventeen discourses by Simeon reproduced in *Let Wisdom Judge*, ed. Arthur Pollard (London: Inter-Varsity Fellowship, 1959).

26. Brown, p. 105f.

27. Ibid., p. 332.

28. F. D. Coggan, *Stewards of Grace* (London: Hodder and Stoughton, 1958), p. 32.

Notes to Chapter 20

FROM THE SCRIPTURES TO THE SERMON was based on two addresses to the students of Ashland Theological Seminary, and was originally published in the *Ashland Theological Journal,* 1990, pp. 42–64. Reprinted by permission.

1. Most books on preaching assume an institutional definition. Typical is this, from D. Martyn Lloyd-Jones: 'What then is preaching? What do I mean by preaching? Let us look at it like this. There is a man standing in a pulpit and speaking, and there are people sitting in pews or seats and listening. What is happening? Why is this? Why does that man stand in that pulpit? What is his object? Why does the Church put him there to do this? Why do these other people come to listen? What is this man meant to be doing? What is he trying to do? What ought he to be doing? These it seems to me are the great questions . . .' (*Preaching and Preachers* [Grand Rapids: Zondervan, and London: Hodder & Stoughton, 1972], p. 53).

2. 'Preaching is the bringing of truth through personality' (Phillips Brooks, *Lectures on Preaching* [London: H. R. Allenson 1877], p. 5).

3. See Lloyd-Jones, op. cit., pp. 304–25.

4. *The Reformed Pastor* (London: Banner of Truth, 1974), p. 149.

5. Thomas Kuhn, *The Structure of Scientific Revolutions,* 2nd ed. (Chicago: University of Chicago Press, 1970) has done more than anyone to give the word technical status, and to focus the idea of a *paradigm shift* (the replacement of one frame of reference by another, due to some kind of pressure). I make free use of this idea in the present discussion.

6. Punishment for parental sin to the third and fourth generation does not imply the injustice of penalizing innocent parties. There is a back reference to Exodus 20:5, '. . .

punishing the children for the sin of the fathers to the third and fourth generation *of those who hate me.*' The assumption is that children will follow in their parents' footsteps, and the divine form of words is intended to alert parents to the damage they may do to their families, and to children yet unborn, by sinning, over and above the damage they will do to themselves by provoking their God to be angry with them. It remains a stubborn fact that children will do what they see their parents doing.

7. J. I. Packer and Thomas Howard, *Christianity: The True Humanism* (Waco: Word, 1985, and Vancouver: Regent College, 1996), pp. 231ff.

8. The title of Alzina Stone Dale's study of Chesterton, *The Outline of Sanity* (Grand Rapids: Eerdmans, 1982) catches this idea, though there is more to it than Dale brings out.

Notes to Chapter 21

THE PREACHER AS THEOLOGIAN was originally published in *When God's Voice Is Heard: Essays on Preaching Presented to Dick Lucas* (Leicester: Inter-Varsity Press, 1995), pp. 79–95. Reprinted by permission.

1. 'The exegete who is doing his work properly is forever asking the question: But what is the point? What is the author driving at? That is, he is always raising the question of the author's intent. At the same time, it is to be hoped that he is also asking questions about the content, questions of lexicography, syntax, background, and so forth. And, also, he is wary of over-exegeting, for example, finding something that would stagger the author were he informed someone had found it in his writing, or building a theology upon the use of prepositions, or discovering meaning in what was *not* said.' So wrote my wise colleague Gordon Fee, 'Hermeneutics and Common Sense,' in Roger R. Nicole and J. Ramsey Michaels (eds.), *Inerrancy and Common Sense* (Grand Rapids: Baker, 1980), pp. 178f.

2. For the quadrilateral analysis, cf. the discussion by Edward Farley, *Theologia: The Fragmentation and Unity of Theological Education* (Philadelphia: Fortress, 1983).

3. Most textbooks of systematic theology follow this seven-part order; see, for instance, Millard J. Erickson, *Christian Theology,* 3 vols. (Grand Rapids: Baker, 1983–85); Bruce Milne, *Know the Truth* (Leicester: IVP, 1982); Thomas C. Oden, *Systematic Theology,* 3 vols. (San Francisco: Harper and Row, 1986–92); James Montgomery Boice, *Foundations of the Christian Faith* (Downers Grove, Ill.: IVP, 1986).

4. I met it quoted without a reference in Paul King Jewett, *Emil Brunner's Concept of Revelation* (London: James Clarke, 1954).

5. Ian Breward (ed.), *William Perkins* (Appleford: Sutton Courtenay Press, 1970), p. 177.

6. This is how Calvin explains the role of his *Institutes,* from the second edition onward: 'It has been my purpose . . . to . . . instruct candidates in sacred theology for the reading of the divine Word . . . For I believe I have so embraced the sum of religion in all its parts, and have arranged it in such an order, that if anyone rightly grasps it, it will not be difficult for him to determine what he ought especially to seek in Scripture, and to what end he ought to relate its contents' (*Institutes of the Christian Religion,* trans. Ford Lewis Battles [Philadelphia: Westminster, 1967], I.4).

7. Article 20 of the Church of England's Thirty-nine Articles.

8. By Oswald Chambers, I believe, though I cannot track down the reference.

9. 'The Directory for the Public Worship of God,' in *The Confession of Faith* (Edinburgh: Banner of Truth, 1985), p. 380.

10. In the 1570s the preaching meetings that Queen Elizabeth I told Archbishop Grindal to suppress were called prophesyings; and the first Reformational textbook on preaching in England was *The Arte of Prophesying*, by William Perkins (*The Workes of that Famous Minister of Christ in the Universitie of Cambridge, Mr. William Perkins*, 1617, II, 646–73; brief extract in Ian Breward ed.), *William Perkins*, pp. 325–49.

11. Donald Macleod, 'Preaching and Systematic Theology,' in Samuel T. Logan (ed.), *The Preacher and Preaching* (Phillipsburg, N.J.: Presbyterian and Reformed, 1986), p. 250.

12. Ibid.

13. The Puritan concept is precisely stated by Jonathan Edwards: '*Affection is* a word that, in its ordinary signification, seems to be something more extensive than *passion*, being used for all vigorous lively actings of the will or inclination . . . As all the exercises of inclination and will are concerned either in approving and liking, or disapproving and rejecting; so the affections are of two sorts, they are those by which the soul is carried out to what is in view, cleaving *to* it, or *seeking* it; or those by which it is averse from it, and *exposes* it. Of the former sort are *love, desire, hope, joy, gratitude, complacence*. Of the latter kind are *hatred, fear, anger, grief*, and such like . . .

'And there are some affections wherein there is a *composition* of each of the aforementioned kinds of actings of the will; as in the affection of *pity*, there is something of the *former kind*, towards the person suffering, and something of the *latter*, towards what he suffers. And so in *zeal*, there is in it high *approbation* of some person or thing, together with vigorous *opposition to* what is conceived to be contrary to it. (*A Treatise concerning Religious Affections*, in vol. I of *The Works of Jonathan Edwards*, ed. H. Hickman [Edinburgh: Banner of Truth, 1974], p. 237).

14. For more discussion of application, see the relevant pages in 'Speaking for God,' in Richard Allen Bodey (ed.), *Inside the Sermon* (Grand Rapids: Baker, 1990), pp. 188–90.

15. *The Confession of Faith*, p. 380.

Notes to Chapter 22

PREACHING AS BIBLICAL INTERPRETATION was originally published in *Inerrancy and Common Sense*, ed. R. Nicole and J. R. Michaels (Grand Rapids: Baker Book House, 1980), pp. 187–203. Reprinted by permission.

1. 2 Tim. 3:15.

2. Ed. *Enquire Within Upon Everything* is a Victorian-era how-to book on domestic life in England.

3. *Institutes of the Christian Religion*, trans. F. L. Battles (Philadelphia: Westminster, 1967), vol. I, p. 7.

4. Cf. 2 Tim. 3:16.

5. Cf. Deut. 30:15–20; Ezek. 33:7–11.

6. Acts 8:35 KJV

7. John 4.

8. Rom. 15:4 RSV.

9. Gustaf Wingren, *The Living Word* (Philadelphia: Muhlenberg, 1960).

10. John Owen, *The True Nature of a Gospel Church* in *Works,* ed. W. H. Goold (Edinburgh: T. & T. Clark, 1862; reprinted London: Banner of Truth, 1967), vol. 16, p. 76.

11. 2 Tim. 4:2.

12. *The Directory for the Public Worship of God* states: 'In raising doctrines from the text, [the preacher's] care ought to be, *First,* That the matter be the truth of God. *Secondly,* That it be a truth contained in or grounded on that text, that the hearers may discern how God teacheth it from thence' (*The Confession of Faith . . . ,* Edinburgh: Banner of Truth, 1985, p. 379).

13. Preface to the Wittenberg Edition of Luther's German Writings, 1539, in *Luther's Works,* American edition (Philadelphia: Muhlenberg, 1960), vol. 34, 285. Cf. Weimarer Ausgabe, 50. 659.

14. Cf. 1 Pet. 1:10–12.

15. John Calvin, *Institutes of the Christian Religion*, I.i.1.

Notes to Chapter 23

SPEAKING FOR GOD was originally published in *Inside the Sermon: Thirteen Preachers Discuss Their Methods of Preparing Messages,* Richard A. Bodey, ed. (Grand Rapids: Baker Book House, 1990), pp. 185–93.